D1290968

# Linux Sendmail Administration

Craig Hunt

San Francisco  Paris  Düsseldorf  Soest  London

SYBEX

Associate Publisher: Dick Staron
Contracts and Licensing Manager: Kristine O'Callaghan
Acquisitions and Developmental Editors: Maureen Adams, Tom Cirtin
Editor: Suzanne Goraj
Production Editor: Liz Burke
Technical Editors: Randolph Russell, James Eric Gunnett
Book Designer: Bill Gibson
Electronic Publishing Specialist: Nila Nichols
Proofreaders: Jennifer Campbell, Nelson Kim, Yariv Rabinovitch, Nanette Duffy, Nancy Riddiough, Laurie O'Connell, Andrea Fox
Indexer: Nancy Guenther
Cover Designer: Ingalls & Associates
Cover Illustrator: Ingalls & Associates

Library of Congress Card Number: 2001087202

ISBN: 0-7821-2737-1

Manufactured in the United States of America

10 9 8 7 6 5 4 3 2

*To Sara, David, and Rebecca, who make me proud every day.*

# Foreword

You may already be familiar with the Craig Hunt Linux Library. If you are, you know it is a library of books for professional system administrators that focuses directly on Linux. The reason for creating such a high quality library is simple: Linux and the professionals who administer Linux systems deserve it. The goal of the library is to provide highly technical books that are clear, accurate, and complete.

Creating comprehensive, concise books that focus on only Linux and that have a consistent structure has had a serendipitous side effect. These books tell the story of the underlying technology, whether it is DNS, Samba, or Sendmail, in a clear and organized manner. This turns out to be particularly important for Sendmail. Sendmail is an essential component of every Linux distribution. Yet a fog of confusion has surrounded Sendmail and particularly Sendmail configuration. Books about Sendmail have done little to alleviate this situation. Some books become so enmeshed in the minutiae of Sendmail configuration syntax that they become little more than giant reference books that are about as useful as reading a dictionary. Others are too superficial; they lack details needed to help the professional system administrator. What is needed is a balance between enough detail and too much detail.

*Linux Sendmail Administration* cuts through the fog by presenting the story of Sendmail in a clear, organized manner. Reference material is where it should be, in an appendix. The content of the book respects the reader's technical skills, providing all of the information you need in a form that you can use. At last! A true Sendmail tutorial.

Craig Hunt
December 2000

# Acknowledgments

I have now written my third book for Sybex, which, frankly, I never thought would happen. I thought writing *Linux Network Servers 24seven*, my first book for Sybex, would be a one-shot deal. But then came the opportunity to write a series of books all focused on Linux. As much as I love writing, I love writing about Linux even more. To add to the joy of this project, the people at Sybex have been wonderful. Like the other books, this one has been written with the support of some excellent people.

I have been surprised by the consistent quality of the people I work with because the cast of characters has changed. It is perfectly normal for different books to have different editors, but fate has been a bigger player in these changes than management. Guy Hart-Davis, the Associate Publisher who first listened to my proposals for this library, inherited a large home in England and went off to be "Lord of the Manor." (Like everyone else at Sybex, I'm dying to go to England to visit him.) By great good luck, Neil Edde took over as Associate Publisher for the Linux Library. Neil is the person who introduced me to Sybex. He was the first person to hear my ideas about the Linux Library and to encourage me to propose them to Sybex. I couldn't have a better publisher than Neil.

Maureen Adams, who started as the Acquisition Editor for this series, has been promoted to Mom. She left the project to give birth to Emma. Now instead of baby-sitting me, she is sitting with a real baby. I'd call that a major promotion!

Tom Critin, who took over as Acquisition Editor, is a career publishing professional. Tom's no-nonsense style helps him deal with me and the other authors in the Craig Hunt Linux Library. Tom deserves special thanks for understanding that the technical quality and not the production schedule was the most important factor in creating this library.

The Production Editor for this book was Liz Burke—my thanks to Liz for her flexibility in working around my schedule. Suzanne Goraj was the Editor. I want to thank her for respecting my writing style while still doing a great job of improving my grammar. Randy Russell and Eric Gunnett were the Technical Editors. Their suggestions were very helpful in creating a more accurate book. Randy has a particularly fine eye for technical details.

I would like to thank all of the production people and artists for their hard work: Nila Nichols, Jennifer Campbell, Nancy Guenther, Nelson Kim, Yariv Rabinovitch, Nanette Duffy, Nancy Riddiough, Laurie O'Connell, and Andrea Fox.

I'd also like to thank Karen Ruckman of KJR Design in Washington, D.C. Karen is a professional photographer and designer. I can attest to the fact that she is one of the best. Only the best of photographers could make my mug look presentable enough for the cover of a book.

Twelve-hour days. No vacations. Not even weekends off. When the schedule gets tight and deadlines loom, I'm not the easiest person to live with. Kathy, thanks for living with me.

# Contents at a Glance

# Contents

## Appendices

# Introduction

Electronic mail is one of the most fundamental services your network can provide. It is the essential link between people, and person-to-person communication is still the foundation upon which organizations are built. Because of this, the reliability of e-mail must be very high. Lose or delay someone's mail, fail to provide them with instant access to their mailbox, and you'll hear about it! Linux is a perfect platform for a reliable e-mail service.

First, of course, is the incredible reliability of Linux itself. Everyone involved with Linux has heard the stories of servers that run for years without a single crash or reboot. Equally important is the reliability of the software tools used to build an Internet mail server on Linux. Unlike some server operating systems where support for Internet mail protocols is a grudging concession to users added after the vendor failed to sell users a proprietary mail system, Linux was designed from the start to use the most thoroughly tested and widely used mail software in the Internet. The Simple Mail Transport Protocol (SMTP) is provided by the Sendmail software, the Post Office Protocol is provided by the POP daemon, and the Internet Message Access Protocol is provided by the IMAP daemon. These packages have been in use on millions of computers in the Internet for longer than many server operating systems have been in existence.

Unfortunately, the name "Sendmail" strikes fear in the hearts of many system administrators. Sendmail has a reputation for being unnecessarily complex and arcane. The thousand-page books written about Sendmail do little to alleviate this fear. I hope that this book will. Much of the complexity in Sendmail is historical in nature. Sendmail has been around for almost 20 years. It includes support for mailers and mail systems that are long gone from most organizations. This book simplifies Sendmail by concentrating on what is important. We focus on the configuration options you will actually use to create a real mail server for today's Internet. And we focus on doing this on a Linux platform. There are no examples from other operating systems to clutter the text and confuse the reader. Unused mail systems are ignored or relegated to an appendix. The result is a book that focuses on what you actually need to know to master Sendmail and illustrates that Sendmail, while not simple, is less complex than you might imagine.

# Who Should Buy This Book

This book is for anyone who is building a network mail server using Linux and Sendmail. The book doesn't assume that you know much about Sendmail. But it does assume that you have a good understanding of computers and IP networks, and of Linux system administration. If you feel that you need to brush up on these topics, start with *Linux System Administration* by Vicki Stanfield and Roderick W. Smith (Sybex, 2001) and *Linux*

*Network Servers 24seven* by Craig Hunt (Sybex, 1999). Those books will provide you with all the background you need.

Linux system administrators will find this book invaluable as their primary resource for Sendmail information. It provides detailed instruction about how a Sendmail server is built on a Linux platform. Examples of compiling, installing, and configuring Sendmail to run with Linux are provided. Security features specific to Linux are covered. Information about Linux that is overlooked by other Sendmail books is provided here.

Even administrators of Unix systems will find this book a useful companion text. This book provides a detailed description of the underlying Internet mail protocols and ties that discussion to the values used to configure Sendmail. It provides this information in a clear and organized manner. The insights into how e-mail works and why certain configuration values are used will be helpful to anyone running Sendmail—even if they don't use Linux.

This book is not simply a reference to all of the Sendmail configuration options. Instead, it provides insight into how real servers are actually configured. This book helps you understand how things really work so that you can make intelligent configuration decisions that relate to your environment. No book, no matter how well thought out or how long, can provide accurate examples for every possible situation. This book strives to provide you with the information you need to develop the correct solution for your situation on your own.

# How This Book Is Organized

This book is divided into five parts: "How Things Work," "Essential Configuration," "Advanced Configurations," "Maintaining a Healthy Server," and Appendices. The five parts are composed of twelve chapters and three appendixes.

A reader who understands the fundamentals of the mail protocols and architecture can jump to the Essential Configuration section. An experienced administrator who understands all of basic Sendmail configuration can jump to the Advanced Configuration part of the book. However, the book was designed as a unit and was meant to be read as a whole, and many chapters reference material covered in other chapters. The book starts with foundation material that explains the underlying system, moves through essential configuration skills that every system administrator needs, and then concludes with specialized configurations that are needed for special situations. Most system administrators will benefit from reading the entire text.

While this book is intended to be read as a whole, I understand that many system administrators simply do not have the time to read an entire text. They must go to the topic in question and get a reasonably complete picture of the "why" as well as the "how" of that topic. To facilitate that understanding, necessary background material is summarized where the topic is discussed and accompanied by pointers to the part of the text where the background material is more thoroughly discussed.

**Part 1: How Things Work**    Part 1 provides the information you need to understand how mail is moved across a network. Chapter 1 describes the protocols used to move the mail and Chapter 2 describes the architectural components that handle mail as it moves from its source to its destination. Chapter 3 describes installing and running the Sendmail program.

**Chapter 1: Internet Mail Protocols**    Network protocols are needed to reliably move mail from the sender to the recipient. This chapter explains the function and purpose of Simple Mail Transfer Protocol (SMTP), Multipurpose Internet Mail Extensions (MIME), Post Office Protocol (POP), and Internet Mail Access Protocol (IMAP).

**Chapter 2: Understanding E-Mail Architecture**    Domain Name Servers, mail servers, mailbox servers, and mail readers all play a role in delivering the mail. This chapter describes these components and how to use them to build your own e-mail architecture. The tasks performed by Sendmail in delivering the mail and the roles of POP and IMAP are explained.

**Chapter 3: Running Sendmail**    The sendmail command and when and how it is invoked are covered, as are downloading, compiling, and installing Sendmail.

**Part 2: Essential Configuration**    Part 2 covers the basic configuration skills needed by every Sendmail administrator. It is composed of three chapters: Chapter 4, "Creating a Basic Sendmail Configuration," Chapter 5, "Understanding a Vendor's Configuration," and Chapter 6, "Using Sendmail Databases."

**Chapter 4: Creating a Basic Sendmail Configuration**    Sendmail requires a configuration that is compatible with the version of Sendmail that is installed. The configuration is built from the m4 library delivered with the Sendmail source code distribution. This chapter explains how to build your own simple configuration with m4. A sample configuration is built step by step.

**Chapter 5: Understanding a Vendor's Configuration**    Most Linux systems come with a default Sendmail configuration. This chapter explains that configuration, what it does, and what you have to do to provide the services you need with the default configuration. The generic Linux configuration delivered with the Sendmail source code and the Red Hat configuration are covered.

**Chapter 6: Using Sendmail Databases**    A number of databases are used to customize Sendmail. Frequently, the key to getting Sendmail to do what you want is in one of these databases and not in the Sendmail configuration file. The chapter covers the purpose, structure, and syntax of every Sendmail database.

**Part 3: Advanced Configuration**    Part 3 examines the sendmail.cf file, explains address rewriting, and describes optional Sendmail configurations that are used to handle special circumstances. Chapter 7 describes the structure and syntax of the sendmail.cf file. Chapter 8 explains the purpose and syntax of Sendmail rewrite rules. Chapter 9 describes many advanced m4 features.

**Chapter 7: The *sendmail.cf* File**    The m4 macros create the sendmail.cf file that contains the actual Sendmail configuration. This chapter explains the structure of that file and the syntax of the commands it contains. An example of directly editing and testing the sendmail.cf file is provided and explained.

**Chapter 8: Understanding Rewrite Rules**    The bulk of the sendmail.cf file is composed of address rewrite rules. These rules rewrite the e-mail addresses received from user mail programs into the format necessary to deliver the mail. Associated rules are grouped together into "rulesets." This chapter explains the execution flow of the rulesets and the syntax of the individual rules.

**Chapter 9: Special *m4* Configurations**    There are literally hundreds of m4 configuration options. Some are very useful while others can be ignored. This chapter points out the useful features and provides sample configurations showing how these features are used to solve specific problems.

**Part 4: Maintaining a Healthy Server**    Part 4 focuses on tasks that are essential to maintaining a secure and reliable server. This part contains Chapter 10, "Testing Sendmail," Chapter 11, "Stopping Spam," and Chapter 12, "Sendmail Security."

**Chapter 10: Testing Sendmail**    Sendmail is a large and complex system. Fortunately, it comes with a rich set of test tools. This chapter covers these built-in test features and the proper techniques for applying them to solve your server configuration problems.

**Chapter 11: Stopping Spam**    Unwanted junk mail, called spam e-mail, is a widespread problem. Properly configured mail servers and mail readers are an essential part of controlling this problem. This chapter explains the anti-spam features available in Sendmail. Mail filtering using procmail is also covered.

**Chapter 12: Sendmail Security**    A recent survey of security exploit scripts shows that the Sendmail program was the number one target of security crackers and that IMAP was number two. Clearly, e-mail is a service that network intruders seek to exploit. This chapter provides detailed advice on what you can do to minimize the security risk.

**Appendixes**   The book concludes with a series of appendixes.

**Appendix A: *m4* Macro Command Reference**   This appendix provides a summary of the m4 macros that are available to build a custom Sendmail configuration.

**Appendix B: The *sendmail* Command**   This appendix is a reference for the large number of command line options available for the sendmail command.

**Appendix C: Sendmail Variables, Options, and Flags**   Sendmail stores configuration values in specific macro variables and class variables. It defines optional environment settings with options. It controls mailer processing with flags. This appendix explains which values are stored in which variables, options, and flags.

# Conventions

This book uses certain typographic styles in order to help you quickly identify important information, and to avoid confusion over the meaning of words. This introduction shows an example of this in the use of Sendmail to refer to the Sendmail program in general and the use of sendmail when referring specifically to the sendmail command. The following conventions are used throughout this book:

- *Italicized text* indicates technical terms that are introduced for the first time in a chapter. (Italics are also used for emphasis.)

- A monospaced font is used for listings and examples and to identify the Linux commands, filenames, and domain names that occur within the body of the text.

- *Italicized monospaced text* is used in command syntax to indicate a variable for which you must provide the value. For example, a command syntax written as Help-File=*path* means that the variable name *path* must not be typed as shown, and that you must provide your own value for *path*.

- **Bold monospaced text** is used to indicate something that must be typed as shown. This might be user input in a listing, a recommended command-line or fixed values within the syntax of a command. For example, a command syntax written as **Help-File=***path* means that the value **HelpFile=** must be typed exactly as shown.

- The square brackets in a command's syntax enclose an item that is optional. For example, ls [-l] means that -l is an optional part of the ls command.

- A vertical bar in a command's syntax means that you should chose one keyword or the other. For example, **true|false** means chose true or false.

In addition to these text conventions, which can apply to individual words or entire paragraphs, a few conventions are used to highlight segments of text:

---

**NOTE**   A Note indicates information that's useful or interesting, but that's somewhat peripheral to the main discussion. A Note might be relevant to a small number of networks, for instance, or refer to an outdated feature.

---

**TIP**   A Tip provides information that can save you time or frustration, and that may not be entirely obvious. A Tip might describe how to get around a limitation, or how to use a feature to perform an unusual task.

---

**WARNING**   Warnings describe potential pitfalls or dangers. If you fail to heed a Warning, you may end up spending a lot of time recovering from a bug, or even restoring your entire system from scratch.

---

**Sidebars**

A Sidebar is like a Note, but is longer. Typically, a Note is one paragraph in length; Sidebars are longer than this. The information in a Sidebar is useful, but doesn't fit into the main flow of the discussion.

# Help Us Help You

Things change. In the world of computers, things change rapidly. Facts described in this book will become invalid over time. When they do, we need your help locating and correcting them. Additionally, a 400-page book is bound to have typographical errors. Let us know when you spot one. Send your improvements, fixes, and other corrections to support@sybex.com. To contact the author for information about upcoming books and talks on Linux, go to www.wrotethebook.com.

# Part 1

# How Things Work

**Featuring:**

- The commands that constitute the command portion of the SMTP command/response protocol

- The SMTP response codes and what they mean

- The structure of a basic mail message

- The ESMTP and MIME extensions for multi-media mail

- The POP and IMAP mailbox protocols

- The meaning of MUA, MSA and MTA and the role these things play in mail delivery

- The role that Sendmail plays in you mail architecture

- The interaction between Sendmail and DNS

- How Sendmail is run to collect inbound mail

- How to control Sendmail at startup and how to control it with signals

- How to install the Sendmail binaries with RPM

- How to compile Sendmail for a Linux system

# 1

# Internet Mail Protocols

The complexity of Sendmail configuration is legendary. Tales of administrators becoming entrapped in the maze of terse commands that make up the Sendmail configuration file are part of the folklore of Linux system administration. Surprisingly, the network protocols that underlie Sendmail are very simple.

A *network protocol* is the set of rules that computer systems must follow in order to exchange information over a network. Network protocols that operate over the Internet are part of the Internet Protocol suite. Unlike most Internet protocols that need to be explained at the network packet level, the e-mail protocols are simple command/response protocols that you can easily understand and manipulate. This chapter will both explain the e-mail protocols and show examples of how they can be easily observed and manipulated by the average user.

Understanding the e-mail protocols can help you understand what Sendmail does, which in turn can help you understand when and why certain configuration options are necessary. The ability to directly manipulate e-mail protocols from the Linux console is also a useful troubleshooting tool. And beyond these practical applications lies an equally important reason: True mastery of any subject requires that you really understand how the thing works.

# The Internet Protocol Suite

The Internet is built with the Internet Protocol suite. The Internet Protocol (IP) is the foundation of the protocol suite, and the Simple Mail Transport Protocol (SMTP) is the mail delivery protocol in that suite.

IP defines the network addressing, thus the term *IP address*, and it defines the basic unit of information that moves though the network. This unit of information is a block of data, called a *datagram*, that contains addressing and administrative information as well as application-specific data. Because the datagram carries its own addressing information with it, it can move through the network independent of any other datagram. The benefits of this independence are robustness and efficiency. Robustness comes from the fact that each datagram can choose its own path through the network. If part of the network fails, the datagram can move around it on any available path. Efficiency comes from the minimal overhead involved in this scheme. Because each packet is independent, there is no need to keep track of other packets in the flow, which simplifies processing. The weakness of this independence is that sometimes the application data must span multiple datagrams. The IP protocol does not provide a way to sequence the data across datagrams.

The Transmission Control Protocol (TCP) offers applications a way to address the weaknesses of IP. When an application needs to send a stream of related data, TCP provides the features necessary for the data to arrive at the remote location reliably and in sequence. It maintains the sequence by embedding sequence numbers in the stream of transmitted data and ensures reliability by requiring acknowledgements from the remote end. SMTP creates a connection between the source and the destination of the e-mail. It uses TCP to create and manage this connection, and to guarantee that the information sent to the destination arrives in sequence and without errors. SMTP systems communicate over TCP port 25. The stream of data sent over the connection contains the commands of the SMTP protocol as well as the e-mail message.

# A Simple Mail Transport Protocol

The SMTP protocol is defined in RFC 821 ("A Simple Mail Transport Protocol"). It is a cleartext command/response protocol. The e-mail source sends a command to the destination and waits for a response to the command. Table 1.1 lists the SMTP commands defined in RFC 821.

**Table 1.1**    Basic SMTP Commands

| Command | Syntax | Purpose |
|---------|--------|---------|
| Hello | **HELO** *<sending-host>* | Opens the SMTP session and identifies the source host. |
| From | **MAIL FROM:***<from-address>* | Specifies the sender's mail address. |
| Recipient | **RCPT TO:***<to-address>* | Specifies the mail address of the recipient. |
| Data | **DATA** | Signals the start of the mail message. The mail ends when a line containing only a dot (.) is sent. |
| Reset | **RSET** | Aborts a message. |
| Verify | **VRFY** *<address>* | Verifies an e-mail address. |
| Expand | **EXPN** *<list-name>* | Displays the e-mail addresses contained in the specified mailing list. |
| Help | **HELP** [*<command>*] | Displays a summary of all supported commands or, optionally, information about a specific command. |
| No Op | **NOOP** | Asks the destination host to do nothing except send an "OK" response. |
| Quit | **QUIT** | Ends the SMTP session. |

RFC 821 defined some other commands that were not widely implemented. These obsolete commands are:

SEND   Sends the mail message to a terminal.

SOML   Sends the mail message to a terminal or delivers it to a mailbox.

How Things Work

PART 1

SAML    Sends the mail message to a terminal and delivers it to a mailbox.

TURN    Turns the connection around so that the mail source is now the destination and the mail destination is now the source.

RFC 821 was written way back in 1982 when central computers with user terminals were in widespread use. SEND, SOML, and SAML assumed that there would be times when the source system would want to display a message on the recipient's terminal in a manner similar to the Linux write command. In reality, SMTP turned into a pure mail system that sends e-mail to a mailbox and does not send messages to a terminal.

The TURN command reverses the role between the sending and receiving mail systems. In a normal connection, the system that initiates the connection is the system that has mail to send. With the TURN command, the system that initiates the connection does not necessarily have mail to send. The initiating system is hoping to receive mail. It creates the connection to find out if the remote system has any mail to send to it. In a global Internet it is, of course, impossible to know what systems have mail to send you. So the TURN command was really intended as a way to move mail from a mailbox server to a client that has limited network service. Mailbox protocols like POP and IMAP, covered later in this chapter, reduced the demand for TURN, as did the wide deployment of full-time Internet access. Security concerns about the TURN command killed it.

For these reasons, SEND, SOML, SAML, and TURN were never widely implemented and you can safely ignore them when you see them in RFC 821. The 10 commands listed in Table 1.1 are the basic SMTP commands implemented on most systems.

As you'll see in the following sections, SMTP is such a simple protocol that it is possible to watch the protocol in action and to understand what is happening when you do. This is both a useful way to learn how the protocol functions and to detect when it is malfunctioning.

## Using SMTP through *telnet*

The SMTP protocol is simple enough for you to "do it yourself." Use telnet to connect to port 25 on a destination host and manually type in a few SMTP commands. The example in Listing 1.1 was created on a Red Hat system running Sendmail 8.11.0.

**Listing 1.1**  Telnetting to the SMTP Port

```
[craig]$ telnet wren.foobirds.org 25
Trying 127.0.0.1...
Connected to wren.foobirds.org.
Escape character is '^]'.
220 wren.foobirds.org ESMTP Sendmail 8.11.0/8.11.0; Mon, 23 Oct 2000
     11:23:14 -0400
```

```
helo robin
250 wren.foobirds.org Hello robin [172.16.5.2], pleased to meet you
help
214-2.0.0 This is Sendmail version 8.9.3
214-2.0.0 Topics:
214-2.0.0      HELO    EHLO    MAIL    RCPT    DATA
214-2.0.0      RSET    NOOP    QUIT    HELP    VRFY
214-2.0.0      EXPN    VERB    ETRN    DSN     AUTH
214-2.0.0      STARTTLS
214-2.0.0 For more info use "HELP <topic>".
214-2.0.0 To report bugs in the implementation send email to
214-2.0.0      sendmail-bugs@sendmail.org.
214-2.0.0 For local information send email to Postmaster at your site.
214 2.0.0 End of HELP info
vrfy <norm>
250 2.1.5 <norm@24seven.wrotethebook.com>
vrfy <frank>
550 5.1.1 <frank>... User unknown
expn <staff>
250 2.1.5 <becky@ani>
250 2.1.5 <sara@hawk>
250 2.1.5 <david@ani>
250 2.1.5 Craig Hunt <craig@24seven.wrotethebook.com>
250 2.1.5 <kathy@robin>
quit
221 wren.foobirds.org closing connection
Connection closed by foreign host.
```

In Listing 1.1, a sample user sitting at the computer robin uses telnet to connect to the SMTP port on wren. The first three messages displayed (Trying, Connected, and Escape) are telnet messages that have nothing to do with SMTP or Sendmail. The first SMTP message begins with the code 220. This message comes from the remote server wren, and is issued in response to the TCP connection created by telnet. This message lets the local system know that the remote system will accept SMTP commands. This first message provides several pieces of information. The message

- identifies the remote host as wren.foobirds.org
- states that the remote system is running ESMTP, which is extended SMTP, a topic covered later in this chapter
- says that wren is running Sendmail version 8.11.0
- displays the time the connection is made

The first command entered by the user is HELO, which identifies the local system as robin and starts the SMTP session. The remote server responds with a message that begins with code 250, and indicates that the session has begun. In Listing 1.1, the user then types in the HELP command. In response to that, the remote system displays 10 lines, all of which start with the code 214. The most interesting part of this response are the commands listed under the heading Topics. These are the SMTP commands supported by wren.

> **NOTE**    There are more commands listed in response to the HELP command in Listing 1.1 than are listed as part of RFC 821 in Table 1.1. That is because three of the commands in Listing 1.1 are extended SMTP commands that we have not yet discussed, two are new security protocol keywords (AUTH and STARTTLS), and one (VERB) is a non-standard command supported by Sendmail that is also discussed later.

The next two commands entered by the user are VRFY commands, which verify whether or not an e-mail address is valid. Listing 1.1 shows two different responses. One tells us that norm is a valid e-mail address and the other tells us that frank is not. If the address entered in a VRFY command does not contain a domain name or contains the domain name of the local computer, it is checked against both the user accounts and the aliases available on the system. If the address contains the domain name of a remote host, the address is only checked to see that it is syntactically valid. The system assumes that an address on a remote host will be forwarded to that host and that it is the responsibility of the remote host to determine whether or not the address is valid and the mail can be delivered.

The EXPN command is used to expand a mailing list. In Listing 1.1, the name of the mailing list is staff. The system responds to the query by listing all of the e-mail addresses contained in that mailing list.

The strangest thing about the HELP, VRFY, and EXPN commands is that they are designed more for interactive use than for communications between e-mail programs. The HELP command is clearly designed for interactive users. Program-to-program communications do not use the EXPN command because the responsibility for expanding a mailing list and delivering to the members of that list falls to the destination program. Therefore, the source program does not need to check the contents of the list. Even the VRFY command, which on the surface appears to have some utility in program-to-program communications, is not needed because the e-mail addresses are verified by default at the start of the delivery process, as shown below:

```
mail from: <craig@24seven>
250 <craig@24seven>... Sender ok
```

```
rcpt to: <frank>
550 <frank>... User unknown
```

The user closes the SMTP session in Listing 1.1 with the QUIT command. The remote system responds with a message that starts with the code 221. The last line in Listing 1.1 is not part of the SMTP session. The line that starts with "Connection closed" is a message from telnet.

## SMTP Response Codes

Listing 1.1 shows that all of the response messages from the remote SMTP server begin with a numeric code. Table 1.2 lists the response codes defined in the RFCs.

**Table 1.2**    SMTP Server Response Codes

| Response Code | Meaning |
| --- | --- |
| 211 | This is a system status message. |
| 214 | This is a help message. |
| 220 *hostname* | The SMTP service is ready. |
| 221 *hostname* | The SMTP connection is closing. |
| 250 | The requested action was completed successfully. |
| 251 | The recipient address is not local, and the mail will be forwarded. |
| 252 | The address cannot be verified, but it will be accepted for forwarding. |
| 354 | The destination server is ready to accept the mail data. |
| 421 *hostname* | The requested service is not available, and the connection is closing. |
| 450 | The requested action was not performed. |
| 451 | The requested action aborted because of an error. |
| 452 | The requested action failed because of insufficient disk space. |
| 500 | The command was not recognized. |

**Table 1.2** SMTP Server Response Codes *(continued)*

| Response Code | Meaning |
| --- | --- |
| 501 | The command had a syntax error in its parameters or arguments. |
| 502 | The command is not implemented on this server. |
| 503 | The sequence of commands is incorrect. |
| 504 | A parameter included with the command is not implemented on this server. |
| 550 | The requested action was not performed. |
| 551 | The recipient address is not local, and the mail must be manually forwarded. |
| 552 | The requested action was aborted because of insufficient disk space. |
| 553 | The mailbox name was invalid. |
| 554 | The transaction failed. |

Every SMTP command elicits a response. A command is sent and a response comes back. From the explanations of the response codes in Table 1.2, it is easy to tell that response codes in the 200s and 300s indicate a successful transaction, while codes in the 400s and the 500s indicate failure, as shown by the few lines below:

```
RCPT TO: <craig>
503 Need MAIL before RCPT
```

The response code is only returned to the user who sent the message when the code indicates a failure. Most of the time, of course, you don't see these codes. Cooperating Sendmail programs on the local system and the remote system go about their business silently exchanging SMTP commands and responses. To watch Sendmail interact with the remote system, run the sendmail command in verbose mode.

## Observing SMTP with Verbose Mode

Using telnet to connect to the SMTP port is a useful way to get a feel for the SMTP protocol, and it can be a useful test technique when you want to completely bypass your local copy of Sendmail to test the responses of a remote Sendmail server. But it is by its nature artificial. A user typing in SMTP commands *approximates* the exchange of protocol information based on a best guess of how the two systems will interact. In most cases, it is much better to sit back and observe the systems actually interacting. The -v (verbose) option of the sendmail command lets you do exactly that. Listing 1.2 shows a piece of mail being sent with verbose mode enabled.

**Listing 1.2**   The Protocol as Displayed by Verbose Mode

```
[craig]$ sendmail -v -t
To: craig@wren
From: craig@ani
Subject: Test
Please ignore this test.
^D
craig@wren... Connecting to wren.foobirds.org. via esmtp...
220 wren.foobirds.org ESMTP Sendmail 8.11.0/8.11.0; Mon, 23 Oct 2000
    11:42:34 -0400
>>> EHLO ani.foobirds.org
250-wren.foobirds.org Hello root@ani.foobirds.org [172.16.12.1],
    pleased to meet you
250-ENHANCEDSTATUSCODES
250-EXPN
250-VERB
250-8BITMIME
250-SIZE
250-DSN
250-ONEX
250-ETRN
250-XUSR
250-AUTH DIGEST-MD5
250 HELP

>>> MAIL From:<craig@ani.foobirds.org> SIZE=73
250 <craig@ani.foobirds.org>... Sender ok
>>> RCPT To:<craig@wren.foobirds.org>
250 <craig@wren.foobirds.org>... Recipient ok
>>> DATA
```

```
354 Enter mail, end with "." on a line by itself
>>> .
250 NAA01047 Message accepted for delivery
craig@wren... Sent (NAA01047 Message accepted for delivery)
Closing connection to wren.foobirds.org.
>>> QUIT
221 wren.foobirds.org closing connection
```

In addition to the verbose option, the `sendmail` command in Listing 1.2 is invoked with the `-t` option that accepts the mail message directly from the keyboard. In Listing 1.2, the user types in the To: address, the From: address, a Subject: line, and a one-line message. The user input is terminated by a Ctrl+D. Everything else in Listing 1.2 is output displayed by Sendmail.

Three of the lines displayed are informational messages directly from Sendmail. The first line displays the delivery triple: the delivery address `craig@wren`, the remote server name `wren.foobirds.org`, and the internal mailer name `esmtp`. You'll hear much more about the delivery triple later on. The other two lines created by Sendmail appear near the bottom of Listing 1.2. The first of these two lines displays the message identifier used to send the message, which is NAA01047 in the example. The second line informs us that Sendmail is ready to close the connection.

Most of the output displayed by `sendmail` is the SMTP protocol interaction. Every line that begins with >>> is a command sent from the local system to the remote system. Every line that begins with a response code is a response from the remote system. Only six commands are used to send the message:

**EHLO**   This is the hello command. It is different from the one shown in Table 1.1 because this is the extended hello used by Extended SMTP, which is covered later in this chapter.

**MAIL From:**   This is the From: address. Addresses used in the SMTP protocol exchange are called envelope addresses and are distinct from the header addresses sent as part of the message data, although header addresses and envelope addresses usually contain the same values. You'll hear more about these different address types when we discuss address rewriting and testing in Chapter 8, "Understanding Rewrite Rules."

**RCPT To:**   This is the To: address. It is also an envelope address.

**DATA**   The DATA command marks the beginning of the message.

**.**   The dot (.) is used to mark the end of the message.

**QUIT**   The QUIT command closes the session.

The SMTP protocol exchange is simple and straightforward and can easily be observed using the `sendmail -v` option. Observing an SMTP session shows you if the mail is leaving your system and whether or not it is accepted by the remote system. This can be valuable information when you suspect a problem.

The one thing that is not shown in Listing 1.2 is the mail message that Sendmail sends between the DATA command and the closing dot (.). The exchange of protocol commands and responses is only a small part of the information that flows over an SMTP connection. The real purpose of SMTP is to carry data in the form of mail messages.

# A Basic Mail Message

The format of the basic e-mail message is defined in RFC 822 ("Standard for the Format of ARPA Internet Text Messages"). According to RFC 822, an e-mail message consists of two parts: headers and a message body. As the name implies, the headers come at the head of the message before the message body. The message body is separated from the headers by a blank line—a line that contains nothing but a carriage return/line feed (CRLF) character. The message body is composed of lines, each of which contains fewer than 1000 bytes of seven-bit ASCII text.

## Message Headers

Headers are individual lines of text that begin with a header name (also called a *field name* in RFC 822) separated by a colon from the variable data related to that header (this data is also called the *field body* in the RFC). Headers provide a record of the information used to deliver the mail. Headers tell you whom a message is bound for, whom it came from, when it was sent, and what computers handled the message as it moved through the network.

Message headers are distinct from the envelope headers we saw in the SMTP protocol exchanges. Envelope headers are limited to the From: and To: addresses. There are From: and To: headers in the message, but there are also a large number of other possible headers, which provide more information about how a message was handled than observing the SMTP interaction does. Listing 1.3 shows the headers that were created for the message sent in Listing 1.2.

**Listing 1.3**   A Complete Mail Message

```
From craig@ani.foobirds.org  Mon Oct 23 11:42:34 2000
Return-Path: <craig@ani.foobirds.org>
Received: from ani.foobirds.org (root@ani.foobirds.org [172.16.12.1])
    by wren.foobirds.org (8.9.3/8.9.3) with ESMTP id NAA01047
    for <craig@wren.foobirds.org>; Mon, 23 Oct 11:42:33 -0400
From: craig@ani.foobirds.org
```

```
Received: (from craig@localhost)
        by ani.foobirds.org (8.11.0/8.11.0) id JAA01401;
        Mon, 23 Oct 2000 09:47:44 -0400
Date: Mon, 23 Oct 2000 09:47:44 -0400
Message-Id: <200007291347.JAA01401@ani.foobirds.org>
To: craig@wren.foobirds.org
Subject: Test

Please ignore this test.
```

Listing 1.3 is the e-mail sent in Listing 1.2 as it was stored in /var/spool/mail/craig on wren, which is a Red Hat Linux system. /var/spool/mail is the directory that holds user mail. Each user is given a mailbox that is identified by the user's name. In this example, the mail was sent to the user craig, so the mail was written to the mailbox /var/spool/mail/craig.

The first line in Listing 1.3 is not a real message header. It is a special line, inserted by Sendmail to mark the beginning of each message in a mailbox. The line is sometimes called the *Unix header* or the *Unix From line*. The second line is the first message header. This message has a total of eight message headers:

**Return-Path:** This header contains the sender address from the envelope, which can be different than the sender address shown by the From: header. The address in the Return-Path: header is used only to notify the source of a message if a delivery error occurred.

**Received:** A Received: header is created by each site that handles a piece of mail. There are as many Received: headers as there are sites that processed the mail. In Listing 1.3, there are two Received: headers—one from ani, which was the site that originated the message, and one from wren, which was the site that accepted the message. The fact that there are only two Received: headers shows that the mail went directly from ani to wren. The first Received: header tells us that a message, which ani identified with message ID NAA01047, was received from ani by wren for the user craig.

**From:** This header identifies whom the mail is from.

**Received:** This second Received: header records the fact that the local host also handled the mail. The local host, wren, assigned a message ID of JAA01401 to the message.

**Date:** This header specifies the date and time the message was received.

**Message-Id:** This header provides a unique identifier for the message, composed of the time the message was received, the local message ID, and the domain name of the local computer.

**To:**   This header identifies who is to receive the mail.

**Subject:**   This header contains the subject line entered by the originator of the message.

Even though Listing 1.3 contains eight header lines, there are only seven different header types because Received: is repeated. These seven different header types are the set found on most pieces of mail. There are, however, many other headers besides these. Sendmail supports more than 30 different types of headers, and not all of the headers in a mail message are inserted by Sendmail. Some come directly from the user, as did the To:, From:, and Subject: headers in Listing 1.3. Others come from the user's mailer when it formats the mail. Sendmail ensures that all of the headers are correctly formatted and that all of the necessary headers are provided.

A blank line immediately follows the headers. This line separates the headers from the message body. In Listing 1.3, the message body is composed of only a single line of text. RFC 822 defines a protocol that can carry only text messages. Modern e-mail systems need to carry a much wider variety of data, so the e-mail protocols have been extended to do just that.

# Multipurpose Internet Mail Extensions

RFC 822 defines a mail message that is composed completely of lines of seven-bit ASCII text. No provisions are made in that RFC to carry any other type of data. This is a major limitation for a modern network because it does not provide support for languages with a larger character set than U.S. English, and it does not support binary data. Imagine the complaints you would receive if your mail server could not handle the binary data produced by your users' favorite applications! RFC 822 also does not provide support for complex message bodies. In fact, it says almost nothing about the content and structure of the message body. The focus of RFC 822 is almost entirely on defining message headers.

The Multipurpose Internet Mail Extensions (MIME) were defined to address these weaknesses. MIME defines encoding techniques to carry a wide variety of data, and it defines a structure for complex message types. RFC 2045 ("Multipurpose Internet Mail Extensions (MIME) Part One: Format of Internet Message Bodies") defines two new headers that are used to give the mail message structure, to identify the type of data the message is carrying, and to identify the encoding techniques used for that data.

## The Content-Type Header

The Content-Type: header identifies the type of data that the message is carrying. The general format of this header is:

**Content-Type:** *type***/subtype** [*attribute***=value;** ...]

The *type* field of the header defines the major type of data, and the *subtype* field defines the specific type of data. An example of this is application/msword, which defines the message as application data for Microsoft Word. The optional *attribute=value* pairs are used with some data types to provide additional information about the data carried in the message. An example of this is text/plain; charset=us-ascii, which states that the message is plain text composed of U.S. ASCII characters. RFC 2046 ("Multipurpose Internet Mail Extensions (MIME) Part Two: Media Types") defines seven fundamental media types:

**text**   Basic text data. Examples of subtypes that go with the text type are plain, enriched, and html.

**image**   Still graphic images. Some common subtypes for image data are jpeg, gif, and tiff.

**audio**   Audio data. The subtype described in RFC 2046 is basic, which is the name for Pulse Code Modulation (PCM) data.

**video**   Moving graphic images. Subtype examples of video are mpeg and quicktime.

**application**   Binary data or data that must be processed by a specific program. Subtype examples include octet-stream, which is eight-bit binary data, and msword, which is data that is to be processed by a specific word processor.

**multipart**   A message composed of several independent parts, each of which can contain its own type of data. The RFC defines four subtypes for this:

- mixed, in which each part is completely independent
- alternative, in which each part contains the same data in different formats
- parallel, in which each part should be viewed simultaneously
- digest, in which each part of the message is an encapsulated message

**message**   The data is an encapsulated mail message, which can in turn contain any valid message type.

In addition to the seven data types, a few subtypes are mentioned in RFC 2046. But that is just the tip of the iceberg. There are literally hundreds of data subtypes. Vendors register the subtype of their data following the instructions in RFC 2048 ("Multipurpose Internet Mail (MIME) Part Four: Registration Procedures"). The large number of data subtypes that have been registered indicates the number of applications that want to move data via e-mail. To see the latest listing of registered data types, download the file media-types from the in-notes/iana/assignments directory at ftp.isi.edu.

Because of the fact that MIME adds structure to a mail message, headers are no longer limited to the beginning of a message. Content-Type: headers can occur multiple times in a message. Listing 1.4 shows a mail message from a Caldera Linux system that uses MIME to encapsulate a message within the message.

**Listing 1.4**   A Message with MIME Headers

```
Received: from localhost (localhost)
        by ani.foobirds.org (8.9.3/8.9.3) with internal id IAB01301;
        Sat, 29 Jul 2000 08:13:52 -0400
Date: Sat, 29 Jul 2000 08:13:52 -0400
From: Mail Delivery Subsystem <MAILER-DAEMON@ani.foobirds.org>
Message-Id: <200007291213.IAB01301@ani.foobirds.org>
To: craig@ani.foobirds.org
MIME-Version: 1.0
Content-Type: multipart/report; report-type=delivery-status;
        boundary="IAB01301.964872832/ani.foobirds.org"
Subject: Returned mail: User unknown
Auto-Submitted: auto-generated (failure)
Status:

This is a MIME-encapsulated message

--IAB01301.964872832/ani.foobirds.org

The original message was received at Sat, 29 Jul 2000 08:13:12 -0400
from root@localhost

    ----- The following addresses had permanent fatal errors -----
frank@wren

    ----- Transcript of session follows -----
.... while talking to wren.foobirds.org.:
>>> RCPT To:<frank@wren.foobirds.org>
<<< 550 <frank@wren.foobirds.org>... Relaying denied
550 frank@wren... User unknown
```

```
--IAB01301.964872832/ani.foobirds.org
Content-Type: message/delivery-status

Reporting-MTA: dns; ani.foobirds.org
Arrival-Date: Sat, 29 Jul 2000 08:13:12 -0400

Final-Recipient: RFC822; frank@wren.foobirds.org
Action: failed
Status: 5.1.1
Remote-MTA: DNS; wren.foobirds.org
Diagnostic-Code: SMTP; 550 <frank@wren.foobirds.org>... Relaying denied
Last-Attempt-Date: Sat, 29 Jul 2000 08:13:52 -0400

--IAB01301.964872832/ani.foobirds.org
Content-Type: message/rfc822

Return-Path: <craig>
Received: (from root@localhost)
        by ani.foobirds.org (8.9.3/8.9.3) id IAA01301;
        Sat, 29 Jul 2000 08:13:12 -0400
Date: Sat, 29 Jul 2000 08:13:12 -0400
Message-Id: <200007291213.IAA01301@ani.foobirds.org>
To: frank@wren.foobirds.org
From: craig@ani.foobirds.org
Subject: Test

Please ignore this test.

--IAB01301.964872832/ani.foobirds.org--
```

The message in Listing 1.4 contains three different Content-Type: headers, each of which I marked in bold to make them easier to find. The first one identifies this as a message of type multipart. It is in fact a message composed of three distinct parts. The subtype of this multipart message is report. (The subtype report was not defined in RFC 2046; it was added later.) Two parameters are also defined on the first Content-Type: header. The report-type argument tells us this is a delivery-status report. The boundary argument defines the line that is used to separate each part in this multipart message. The boundary lines are also in bold to make them easier to find in the listing.

The second Content-Type: header declares that the second message in the multipart message is also a delivery status message. The third and final Content-Type: header states that the last message in the multipart message is an RFC 822 message. This is a copy of the original message that generated the error.

MIME allows for complex message bodies, as Listing 1.4 illustrates. However, everything in Listing 1.4 is basic ASCII text. MIME permits a wider range of data types.

## The Content-Transfer-Encoding Header

The large number of data types supported by MIME means that not everything can be sent as seven-bit ASCII data. The Content-Transfer-Encoding: header identifies the type of encoding used for the data in a MIME message. RFC 2045 defines five types of encoding:

**7bit**   This is the standard seven-bit U.S. ASCII that e-mail has always supported. The data in this message is composed of lines of U.S. ASCII characters. Each line is less than 1000 characters long. This type identifies the encoding inherent in the data. No additional encoding is done.

**8bit**   This is eight-bit binary data formatted into lines that are less than 1000 octets long. This type identifies the encoding inherent in the data. No additional encoding has been done.

**binary**   This is eight-bit binary data that is not formatted into lines less than 1000 octets long. There is no difference between the eight-bit encoding type and the binary encoding type except for the fact that binary data is not restricted to a maximum line length. This type identifies the encoding inherent in the data. No additional encoding is done.

**quoted-printable**   This is encoded text data. The bulk of the data in a quoted printable message is printable ASCII text, which is sent unencoded. Bytes of data that are not normally printable—those with a hexadecimal value less than 33 or greater than 127—are encoded as a string made up of the equal sign and characters representing the hexadecimal value of the desired byte. Thus, a byte containing the ASCII form feed, which has a hexadecimal value of 0C, would be sent as the three-byte string =0C. The equal sign itself is sent as =3D.

**base64**   This is encoded binary data. Three octets (24 bits) of binary data are sliced into four six-bit pieces. Two zero bits are prepended to each six-bit chunk to create four eight-bit characters. All of the characters created in this manner are a subset of U.S. ASCII that can be handled by any mail system. This allows encoded binary data to pass through any mail server. The disadvantages of base64 encoding are that it increases the size of a binary file by at least 33 percent and it has a maximum line length of 76 bytes that can further increase the size of the file by adding newline characters to meet this line-length requirement.

Of the five encoding techniques specified in RFC 2045, two are techniques for encoding the data in a message and three are used to identify the encoding already there. The quoted-printable and base64 techniques make it possible to send data through any e-mail system. 7bit encoding is compatible with any system, because it is the original e-mail encoding system. The other two techniques, 8bit and binary, require a new mail system that can handle these new data formats without additional encoding. SMTP was extended to handle these new formats and the requirements of MIME mail.

# Extended SMTP

SMTP was not designed to handle multiple data types; thus, it needed enhancements to handle MIME data. RFC 1869 ("SMTP Service Extensions") defines an extensible version of SMTP, not by defining specific service extensions, but by specifying a technique that systems can use to negotiate which SMTP extensions they support. RFC 1869 defines a new version of the SMTP HELO command named EHLO.

A system that runs ESMTP sends EHLO as the hello greeting to start the session. If the receiving system does not run ESMTP, it rejects EHLO as an error. The sending system can then initiate the session with the old HELO command or terminate the session. If the receiving system runs ESMTP, it responds to the EHLO command by sending a listing of the extended SMTP features it supports. Each feature is identified by a standard keyword. Thus the sending system knows the capabilities of the receiving system and can use any of the features that the remote system advertises.

Listing 1.2 shows a full ESMTP session. It opens with an EHLO command and the list of keywords sent in response to those commands. That EHLO command and response are excerpted in Listing 1.5.

**Listing 1.5**   The EHLO Command and Response

```
>>> EHLO ani.foobirds.org
250-wren.foobirds.org Hello root@ani.foobirds.org [172.16.12.1],
    pleased to meet you
250-ENHANCEDSTATUSCODES
250-EXPN
250-VERB
250-8BITMIME
250-SIZE
250-DSN
250-ONEX
250-ETRN
250-XUSR
250-AUTH DIGEST-MD5
250 HELP
```

The format of the EHLO command is simple—just the keyword EHLO followed by the domain name of the sending system. The response from the receiving system is the standard hello acknowledgement followed by a list of keywords. The keywords shown in Listing 1.5 are from a Red Hat Linux system running Sendmail version 8.11.0. By its very nature, the EHLO command evokes different responses from different systems.

## Extended Service Keywords

Two of the advertised services are basic SMTP commands defined in RFC 821. HELP provides access to the online help system, and EXPN displays the addresses in a mailing list. This system advertises these services in the keyword list because many sites do not implement these basic commands.

Some of the keywords in the list indicate service extensions that are defined in various RFCs.

**ENHANCEDSTATUSCODES**   This server uses the enhanced status codes that go with Delivery Status Notifications (DSNs). The enhanced status codes are defined in RFC 1893, "Enhanced Mail System Status Codes."

**8BITMIME**   This keyword indicates that the server can accept eight-bit binary data, which means that 8bit and binary data types can be sent to this system without any additional encoding. This extension was defined in RFC 1652 ("SMTP Service Extension for 8bit-MIMEtransport").

**SIZE**   This server supports the SIZE extension, which was defined in RFC 1870 ("SMTP Service Extension for Message Size Declaration"). The sending system uses SIZE to tell the receiving system how large the message is in bytes. The receiving system uses the information to decide whether or not it can accept the e-mail. The MAIL From: line in Listing 1.2 is an example of the SIZE extension in action:

```
>>> MAIL From:<craig@ani.foobirds.org> SIZE=73
```

In this example, the SIZE keyword tells the receiving system that the message contains 73 bytes.

**DSN**   This server can provide delivery status notification. For example, the remote user can request a return receipt notification when the message is read. This extension is defined in RFC 1891 ("SMTP Service Extension for Delivery Status Notifications").

**ETRN**   This server allows remote sites to retrieve messages from the server's queue that are bound for the remote site . ETRN is an updated version of the TURN command that fixes the security problems that existed in TURN. This extension is defined in RFC 1985 ("SMTP Service Extension for Remote Message Queue Starting").

**AUTH DIGEST-MD5**   The AUTH keyword advertises the type of authentication supported by this server. In this case, the server supports Message Digest 5 (MD5) for authentication. The AUTH extension is defined in RFC 2554 ("SMTP Service Extension for Authentication").

There are also a few keywords in this list that are not standard services. VERB sets the remote mail server in verbose mode. ONEX limits the SMTP session to the transfer of a single message. XUSR is used when a user mail agent sends mail directly to a remote server instead of passing it through a mail transfer agent, such as Sendmail. (I don't know of any user mail agents designed to work this way.) VERB, ONEX, and XUSR are specific to Sendmail version 8; they are not defined in an RFC.

# Mailbox Protocols

SMTP moves mail between e-mail servers, and MIME allows that mail to contain anything the user wants to send. SMTP is the protocol implemented by Sendmail, but it is not the only protocol used in delivering the mail to the end user. As we saw in Listing 1.3, Sendmail stores the mail it receives in a mailbox on the Linux server. Any user that can log in to the server can read their mail there. Many users, however, cannot or don't want to read their mail on the server. Those users want to move the mail from the server mailbox to a mail reader located on their desktop systems. There are two popular protocols designed to move mail from the mailbox server to the desktop client: Post Office Protocol (POP), which is the traditional mailbox protocol, and Internet Message Access Protocol (IMAP), which has recently become more popular.

A Sendmail server turns into a mailbox server when it runs either the POP or the IMAP daemon. All Linux systems can run both. Both POP and IMAP can be installed during the initial installation or later using a package manager like RPM. The POP and IMAP protocols are simple command/response protocols very similar to SMTP.

## Post Office Protocol

The POP protocol verifies the user's login name and password, and moves the user's mail from the server to the user's local mail reader. There are two versions of POP: POP2 and POP3. Both protocols perform the same basic functions, and they both create connections using TCP to ensure reliability and data sequencing. But the two protocols are incompatible. POP2 uses TCP port 109 and POP3 uses TCP port 110. Linux systems come with both versions of POP, but most clients use POP3. For that reason, this section describes only the POP3 protocol.

POP3 is defined in RFC 1939 ("Post Office Protocol —Version 3"). It is a simple request/ response protocol like SMTP. The client sends a command to the server and the server responds to the command. Table 1.3 shows the set of POP3 commands defined in RFC 1939.

**Table 1.3**    POP3 Commands

| Command | Function |
| --- | --- |
| USER *username* | The username required for the login. |
| PASS *password* | The user's password required for the login. |
| STAT | Requests the number of unread messages/bytes. |
| RETR *msg* | Retrieves message number *msg*. |
| DELE *msg* | Deletes message number *msg*. |
| LAST | Requests the number of the last message accessed. |
| LIST [*msg*] | Requests the size of message *msg* or of all messages. |
| RSET | Undeletes all messages and resets the message number to 1. |
| TOP *msg  n* | Prints the headers and the first *n* lines of message number *msg*. |
| NOOP | Does nothing except request an OK response from the remote server. |
| APOP *mailbox string* | Identifies a mailbox and provides an MD5 digest string for authentication. Used as an alternative to USER/PASS. |
| UIDL [*msg*] | Requests the unique ID for the specified message number, or a listing of unique IDs for all messages. |
| QUIT | Ends the POP3 session. |

Like SMTP, the POP3 protocol is simple enough to be done by hand over a `telnet` connection. Listing 1.6 shows a sample POP3 session that demonstrates the function of several of the protocol commands.

**Listing 1.6**   Using the POP Protocol with `telnet`

```
[craig]$ telnet localhost 110
Trying 127.0.0.1...
Connected to ani.foobirds.org.
Escape character is '^]'.
+OK POP3 ani.foobirds.org v7.64 server ready
USER craig
+OK User name accepted, password please
PASS Wats?Watt?
+OK Mailbox open, 4 messages
STAT
+OK 4 8184
LIST
+OK Mailbox scan listing follows
1 1951
2 1999
3 2100
4 2134
.
RETR 1
+OK 1951 octets
... an e-mail message 1951 bytes long ...
.
DELE 1
+OK Message deleted
QUIT
+OK Sayonara
Connection closed by foreign host.
```

The first three lines after the `telnet` command (Trying, Connected, and Escape) are output from the `telnet` command, as is the very last line (Connection closed). All of the other lines in Listing 1.6 are POP3 commands and responses. Positive responses start with the string +OK, which indicates that the command executed successfully. When a command fails, the response begins with the string -ERR. The first +OK response in Listing 1.6 is in reply to the connection request from `telnet`. The response indicates that the POP server is ready.

The user then logs in with the USER and PASS commands. The username and password provided here must match a valid username and password found in the /etc/passwd file. Notice that the password is sent as clear text. POP3 provides a more secure MD5 login mechanism that is discussed in Chapter 12, "Sendmail Security."

The STAT command and the LIST command are used to inquire about the messages stored in the mailbox. STAT shows that there are four messages with a combined length of 8184 bytes. The LIST command shows the size of each individual message in the mailbox. When it comes to mail, size matters because the system downloading the mail needs to know it has sufficient disk space to store the mail. In Listing 1.6, all of the mail messages are small so storage is not an issue.

The first message from the mailbox is downloaded with the RETR 1 command. It is then removed from the server mailbox with the DELE 1 command. Normally, messages are retrieved in order and are deleted after they are retrieved, but they don't have to be. When using telnet to input the POP commands, you're in complete control. You can download messages out of order, you don't need to delete the messages you download, and you don't need to download messages you delete. Deleting messages instead of downloading them is often very useful. On occasion a corrupted or overly large message stored on the server causes download problems for the desktop client. From the client the user can log on via telnet and delete the offending message to get everything running normally again.

Of course, a POP connection is not normally run manually over a telnet connection. This is only done here to illustrate the function of the protocol. You will only telnet to the POP port for testing. Using your knowledge of the protocol and the configuration, you can telnet to the POP port and test whether your server responds. The telnet test proves that the daemon is available, installed, and ready to run.

## Internet Mail Access Protocol

IMAP is an alternative to POP. It provides the same basic service as POP and adds features to support mailbox synchronization. Mailbox synchronization is the ability to read individual mail messages on a client or directly on the server while keeping the mailboxes on both systems completely up-to-date. On an average POP server, all contents of the mailbox are moved to the client and either deleted from the server or retained as if never read. Deletion of individual messages on the client is not reflected on the server because all of the messages are treated as a single unit that is either deleted or retained after the initial transfer of data to the client. IMAP provides the ability to manipulate individual messages on the client or the server and to have those changes reflected in the mailboxes of both systems.

IMAP uses TCP for reliable, sequenced data delivery. The IMAP port is TCP port 143. Like the POP protocol, IMAP is also a request/response protocol with a small set of commands. Table 1.4 lists the basic set of IMAP commands from version 4 of the IMAP protocol as defined in RFC 2060 ("Internet Message Access Protocol—Version 4rev1").

---

**NOTE** The /etc/services file lists two different ports for IMAP: 143 and 220. Port 220 is used by IMAP3. However, the current IMAP, which is IMAP4, was derived from IMAP2, which used port number 143. Confused? Don't be. Just remember that the correct port is 143.

---

**Table 1.4** IMAP4 Commands

| Command | Use |
| --- | --- |
| CAPABILITY | Lists the features supported by the server. |
| NOOP | Literally "No Operation," but sometimes used as a way to poll for new messages or message status updates. |
| LOGOUT | Closes the connection. |
| AUTHENTICATE | Requests an alternative authentication method. |
| LOGIN | Opens the connection and provides the username and password for plain text authentication. |
| SELECT | Opens a mailbox. |
| EXAMINE | Opens a mailbox as read-only. |
| CREATE | Creates a new mailbox. |
| DELETE | Removes a mailbox. |
| RENAME | Changes the name of a mailbox. |
| SUBSCRIBE | Adds a mailbox to the list of active mailboxes. |
| UNSUBSCRIBE | Deletes a mailbox name from the list of active mailboxes. |
| LIST | Displays the requested mailbox names from the complete set of all available mailbox names. |

**Table 1.4** IMAP4 Commands *(continued)*

| Command | Use |
| --- | --- |
| LSUB | Displays the requested mailbox names from the set of active mailboxes. |
| STATUS | Requests the status of a mailbox. |
| APPEND | Adds a message to the end of the specified mailbox. |
| CHECK | Forces a checkpoint of the current mailbox. |
| CLOSE | Closes the mailbox and removes all messages marked for deletion. |
| EXPUNGE | Removes from the current mailbox all messages that are marked for deletion. |
| SEARCH | Displays all messages in the mailbox that match the specified search criterion. |
| FETCH | Retrieves a message from the mailbox. |
| STORE | Modifies a message in the mailbox. |
| COPY | Copies the specified messages to the end of the specified mailbox. |
| UID | Searches for or fetches messages based on the message's unique identifier. |

This command set is more complex than the one used by POP because IMAP does more. These commands clearly illustrate the "mailbox" orientation of IMAP. The protocol is designed to remotely maintain mailboxes that are stored on the server. The protocol commands show that. Despite the increased complexity of the protocol, it is still possible to run a simple test of your IMAP server using telnet and a small number of the IMAP commands. Listing 1.7 shows just such a test.

**Listing 1.7** Telnetting to the IMAP Port

```
[craig]$ telnet localhost 143
Trying 127.0.0.1...
Connected to ani.foobirds.org.
Escape character is '^]'.
```

```
* OK ani.foobirds.org IMAP4rev1 v12.252 server ready
a0001 login craig Wats?Watt?
a0001 OK LOGIN completed
a0002 select inbox
* 3 EXISTS
* 0 RECENT
* OK [UIDVALIDITY 965125671] UID validity status
* OK [UIDNEXT 5] Predicted next UID
* FLAGS (\Answered \Flagged \Deleted \Draft \Seen)
* OK [PERMANENTFLAGS (\* \Answered \Flagged \Deleted \Draft \Seen)]
* OK [UNSEEN 1] first unseen message in /var/spool/mail/craig
a0002 OK [READ-WRITE] SELECT completed
a0003 fetch 1 body[text]
* 1 FETCH (BODY[TEXT] {1440}
... an e-mail message that is 1440 bytes long ...
* 1 FETCH (FLAGS (\Seen))
a0003 OK FETCH completed
a0004 store 1 +flags \deleted
* 1 FETCH (FLAGS (\Seen \Deleted))
a0004 OK STORE completed
a0005 close
a0005 OK CLOSE completed
a0006 logout
* BYE ani.foobirds.org IMAP4rev1 server terminating connection
a0006 OK LOGOUT completed
Connection closed by foreign host.
```

Again, the first three lines and the last line come from telnet; all other messages come from IMAP. The first IMAP command entered by the user is LOGIN, which provides the username and password from /etc/passwd used to authenticate this user. Notice that the command is preceded by the string A0001. This is a "tag," which is a unique identifier generated by the client for each command. Every command must start with a tag. When you manually type in commands for a test, you are the source of the tags.

IMAP is a mailbox-oriented protocol. The SELECT command is used to select the mailbox that will be used. In Listing 1.7, the user selects a mailbox named "inbox." The IMAP server displays the status of the mailbox, which contains three messages. Associated with each message are a number of flags. The flags are used to manage the messages in the mailbox by marking them as Seen, Unseen, Deleted, etc.

The FETCH command is used to download a message from the mailbox. In Listing 1.7, the user downloads the text of the message, which is what you normally see when reading a message. It is possible, however, to download only the headers or flags.

After the message is downloaded, it is deleted. This is done by writing the Deleted flag with the STORE command. The DELETE command is not used to delete messages; it deletes entire mailboxes. Individual messages are marked for deletion by setting the Deleted flag. Messages with the Deleted flag set are not deleted until either the EXPUNGE command is issued or the mailbox is explicitly closed with the CLOSE command, as is done in Listing 1.7. The session in Listing 1.7 is then terminated with the LOGOUT command.

Clearly, the IMAP protocol is much more complex than SMTP or POP. It is just about at the limits of what can reasonably be typed in manually. Of course, you don't really enter these commands manually. The desktop system and the server exchange them automatically. They are only shown here to give you a sense of the IMAP protocol. About the only IMAP test you would ever do manually is to test if imapd is up and running. To do that, you don't even need to log in. If the server answers the telnet, you know it is up and running. All you then need to do is send the LOGOUT command to gracefully close the connection.

IMAP and POP are not part of Sendmail. Sendmail provides SMTP but other daemons are needed for POP and IMAP. Those protocols are covered here, however, because they are an important part of building a complete e-mail architecture for your enterprise. In the next chapter, we discuss the selection and placement of servers for your e-mail architecture. Mailbox servers running IMAP or POP will be an important part of that discussion.

# In Sum

The simplicity of the protocols that underlie Sendmail stand in stark contrast to the complexity of Sendmail itself, particularly to the complexity of Sendmail configuration. The number of configuration options and the difficult concepts embodied in some of the configuration choices are the enemies of understanding Sendmail as a whole. The details of Sendmail can easily overwhelm the important concepts. It is the proverbial problem of not being able to see the forest because of all the trees. To attack this problem, the summary of each chapter will include a "complexity summary" to show the relative importance of the details covered, to reinforce the key concepts covered, and to provide some hints about how you can filter out the unneeded complexity. This chapter, however, does not need a "complexity filter" because the protocols used by Sendmail have a surprising lack of complexity.

The protocols that are the basis of the global e-mail system are simple command/response protocols that are so easy to understand that a system administrator can manually interact with a mail server over a `telnet` connection. Internet mail is carried by the Simple Mail Transport Protocol. SMTP, which is implemented by the Sendmail program, moves mail from server to server. The MIME extensions and ESMTP permit the mail system to move any kind of data. IMAP and POP move the mail from the mailbox located on the server to the mail reader located on the user's desktop. These protocols make it possible to move any type of data through the mail from any user to any other user in the world. Planning a complete enterprise e-mail architecture constructed from these protocols is the subject of our next chapter.

# 2

# Understanding E-Mail Architecture

The capabilities of the network protocols described in Chapter 1, "Internet Mail Protocols," define the technical boundaries of the Internet mail architecture. The global scope of Internet mail makes it obvious that these protocols can create a flexible architecture supporting an enormous amount of e-mail traffic.

SMTP provides direct end-to-end mail delivery. This is one of its great strengths. In Chapter 1, `telnet` was used to simulate an SMTP connection for the purpose of examining the protocol interactions. Another thing the `telnet` test showed is that SMTP runs over the reliable, connection-oriented TCP transport. Using TCP means that end-to-end mail delivery is guaranteed. The person at the remote end might not read your mail, you may accidentally address it to the wrong person, or the server may redirect your mail, but you can rely on the fact that your mail message arrives intact.

Because of the direct delivery model, SMTP systems like Sendmail can provide immediate feedback about delivery. Everyone, at one time or another, has sent a message and gotten an immediate response saying that user so-and-so does not have an account on the remote host to which the mail was directed. This immediate feedback is available because the local system directly connects to the remote host, delivers the mail to that host, and accepts responses back from that host. If the response is an error, the error message can be immediately returned to the sender.

Some other mail systems use store-and-forward protocols like UUCP and X.400 that move mail toward its destination one hop at a time, storing the complete message at each hop and then forwarding it on to the next system. The message proceeds in this manner, one hop at a time, until final delivery is made. With a system like UUCP, your server will communicate directly only with hosts that are directly attached to your server. UUCP is a particularly good example of the store-and-forward model because the traditional UUCP bang address format clearly shows the path that the mail takes to its destination. In the UUCP bang address format, each host in the forwarding sequence is explicitly named and the last value in the address is the name of the user to whom the mail is addressed. Figure 2.1 uses UUCP and SMTP to illustrate both store-and-forward and direct delivery mail systems.

**Figure 2.1**    Direct delivery versus store-and-forward

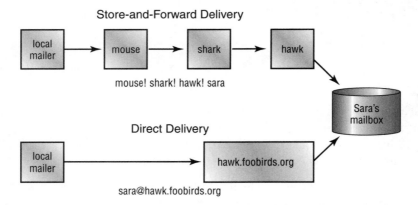

Direct delivery allows SMTP to deliver mail without relying on intermediate hosts. If the delivery fails, the local system knows it right away. It can inform the user that sent the mail or queue the mail for later delivery without reliance on remote systems. The disadvantage of direct delivery is that it requires both systems to be fully capable of handling mail. Sometimes that's not the case, particularly with small systems such as PCs or mobile systems such as laptops. These systems are usually shut down at the end of the day and are frequently offline. Mail directed from a remote host fails with a "cannot connect" error when the local system is turned off or is offline. To handle these cases, SMTP can simulate the store-and-forward model by delivering the message to a mail server instead of delivering it to the end system. The remote mail server is then responsible for moving the mail to the end system.

The Domain Name System (DNS) tells the SMTP server when mail needs to be routed to another server instead of the end system.

# The Role of DNS

All Internet connections depend on IP addresses. DNS is a distributed database system that maps hostnames to IP addresses. However, DNS can do much more than just map addresses. Address (A) database records are only part of the story. DNS running on Linux supports about 40 different database record types.

---

**NOTE**  Some knowledge of DNS is needed to fully understand e-mail architecture. However, this is not a book about DNS. If you need to run a DNS server, see *Linux DNS Server Administration* by Craig Hunt (Sybex, 2000), part of the Craig Hunt Linux Library.

---

DNS database records all have the same basic format. For the purposes of this book, the format of DNS database records can be simplified to three basic fields:

- The *name* field contains the name of the object to which the record applies. Generally, this is a domain name or hostname.
- The *type* field contains the database record type. For example, an address record has a type field that contains the letter A.
- The *data* field contains the data specific to the type of record. For example, an address record contains an IP address in the data field.

Of the forty possible record types, only a handful are used to build real DNS databases. Of this handful of records, one of the most important is the Mail Exchange (MX) record. MX records tell Sendmail where to deliver mail. The *name* field of an MX record contains the hostname that appears in the e-mail address, and the *data* field contains the hostname of the server to which the mail should be delivered. Two MX records that define the mail servers for the foobirds.org domain might contain the following:

```
foobirds.org.     MX      10 wren.foobirds.org.
foobirds.org.     MX      20 parrot.foobirds.org.
```

The *name* field contains the domain name foobirds.org., meaning that these records pertain to the entire domain. If mail is addressed to *user*@foobirds.org, the mail is directed to the mail exchangers defined by these records. This is a popular configuration, particularly when combined with the ability of the mail server to masquerade the hostname in outbound mail. Masquerading makes it look as if the mail sent by the local user came from *user@domain*, which creates a balanced addressing scheme for both inbound and outbound mail.

---

**NOTE** See Chapter 9, "Special m4 Configurations," for detailed information about masquerading hostnames.

---

The first sample MX record says that wren is the mail server for the foobirds.org domain with a preference of 10. The second MX record identifies parrot as a mail server for foobirds.org with a preference of 20. The lower the preference number, the more preferred the server is. The record with the preference of 10 is used before the record with the preference of 20, meaning wren is the preferred mail server for the foobirds.org domain and parrot is the backup server.

A backup mail exchange server is used only when the preferred server is down or offline. The backup server holds the mail and periodically attempts to send it on to the preferred server. When the preferred server comes back online, the backup server sends the mail to the preferred server. At that point, the backup server's job is done. A backup mail exchange server never deals directly with the mail recipient. Its only job is to get the mail to the preferred server.

The sample MX records redirect mail addressed to the domain foobirds.org, but they do not redirect mail addressed to an individual host. Therefore, if mail is addressed to jay@hawk.foobirds.org, it is delivered directly to hawk; it is not sent to a mail server. This is a very flexible configuration that permits people to use e-mail addresses of the form *user@domain* when they like, or to use direct delivery to an individual host when they want that.

Some systems are not capable of handling direct-delivery e-mail. An example is a Microsoft Windows system that doesn't run an SMTP mailer daemon. Mail addressed to such a system would not be successfully delivered, and worse, would probably be reported to you as a network error! To prevent this, MX records are generally assigned to these individual hosts to redirect mail addressed to the hosts to a valid mail server. Here are two examples:

```
puffin.foobirds.org.    MX      5 wren.foobirds.org.
robin.foobirds.org.     MX      5 wren.foobirds.org.
```

These MX records redirect mail addressed to puffin or robin to wren. In both cases, only one mail server is named for each host. With these records, mail addressed to daniel@puffin.foobirds.org is delivered to daniel@wren.foobirds.org. Sendmail does not need to select a server. All of the mail goes to wren. The next section examines how Sendmail uses the DNS responses.

## Processing *MX* Records

When Sendmail has mail to deliver, it queries DNS for the MX records for the hostname in the e-mail address. It then sorts those MX records by preference number. Thus, the lower the preference number, the earlier in the list a server appears, which makes servers with low preference numbers preferable to servers with high preference numbers.

Sendmail then tries to deliver the mail to each mail server in order. It stops processing the list if it finds a server that will accept the mail or if it finds its own hostname in the mail exchange server list. If it cannot deliver the mail to any of the servers, it will use the address of the host and attempt to deliver directly to that host.

> **NOTE**  The process of first querying for MX records and then querying for address records is an idealized process described in RFC 974 ("Mail Routing and the Domain System"). In reality, Sendmail uses the DNS ANY query to get any and all records about a host. That one query retrieves the MX records and the A records.

A backup mail exchange server determines how to deliver mail just like any other server by querying DNS for a list of MX records. However, it cannot just send the mail to each server in turn in the MX list because, in the hands of an MX server, MX records have the potential to create mail-routing loops.

Assume that we have three MX servers in this order of preference: wren, parrot, and jay. wren is down so the mail is delivered to parrot. parrot fetches the MX records and attempts to deliver the mail to wren. wren is still down. parrot would queue the mail and not attempt to deliver it to any other server on the MX list. This is to avoid loops. If parrot tries to deliver the mail to itself, a tight loop will ensue. If parrot tries delivering the mail to jay, a bigger loop ensues because jay would then start sending the mail back to parrot, who would send it back to jay, and so on. To avoid these loops, a mail server stops attempting to deliver the mail when it finds itself in the MX list and queues the mail for later delivery. In effect, a backup server only attempts to deliver mail to MX servers that are more preferred than it is. Thus, in this list of three servers, parrot will try to deliver mail only to wren.

Using the same three servers, wren, parrot, and jay, assume that both wren and parrot are down:

1. The mail comes to jay.
2. jay discovers that the more preferred servers are down.
3. jay queues the mail for later delivery.
4. Later, jay processes its queue. wren is still down but parrot is back in operation.

5. This time, jay delivers the mail to parrot and it becomes parrot's responsibility to deliver the mail.

6. parrot keeps the mail in its queue until wren finally comes back online.

By sending mail only to more-preferred servers, mailers avoid mail-routing loops and gradually move mail closer to its final destination.

The MX record is only the first step in creating a mail server. The MX record is necessary to tell the remote computer where it should send the mail, but for the mail server to successfully deliver the mail to the intended user, it must be properly configured. How wren handles the mail as the preferred mail exchange server is a function of how Sendmail is configured on wren. DNS identifies servers and Sendmail is configured to create different types of servers. These servers are the components of mail architecture.

# The Components of Mail Architecture

Conceptually, mail delivery is a simple thing—you want to get a message from point A to point B. All of the components of the mail system focus on doing this one task. They vary in how they do it and when they are needed to do it. A terminology has grown up to describe the different roles of the pieces of the mail architecture. Some of the terms are formally defined and others are loosely used. Understanding the terminology used to describe mail architecture and the role of the various components is a necessary part of understanding the mail system.

## Formal Definitions

Most mail starts and ends its life in a message user agent (MUA). The MUA is the mail interface with which the user interacts. It is the application program that the user uses to read and write mail. pine, elm, and Netscape Messenger are some examples. Sendmail itself can be used as an MUA by running the sendmail command from the shell prompt, although this is generally only done for testing. MUA is the formal term used to describe the programs with which users create and read mail. Sometimes an MUA will be loosely called a mail "client," but as with most generalized terminology, calling an MUA a client is not very accurate because even a server can be a client in the right circumstances.

> **NOTE**   The word "message" is sometimes replaced by the word "mail" in these acronyms. Message user agent (MUA), message transfer agent (MTA), and message submission agent (MSA) are also commonly called mail user agent, mail transfer agent, and mail submission agent, respectively.

Message transfer agents (MTAs) move mail through the network. In the case of the Internet, an MTA is a program that uses SMTP to move complete mail messages over the network. Sendmail is the most widely used MTA for Linux systems. The Sendmail daemon runs a listener that attaches to TCP port 25, the SMTP port, to collect inbound mail coming from remote MTAs. MTA is a formal definition. An MTA is sometimes loosely referred to as a mail relay or a mail hub; however, relays and hubs do much more than just transfer mail.

As formally defined, an MTA is supposed to receive and send complete mail messages. Because the messages are complete, the MTA limits any modifications it makes to the message to just those mail headers that should be updated by every agent that handles the mail, such as the Received: header. When Sendmail receives mail from a remote server, it is clearly acting as an MTA. But when it receives mail directly from an MUA, Sendmail does more than modify a few headers—it may add headers and correct addresses. In this latter case, Sendmail is acting as a message submission agent (MSA). An MSA is the first MTA after the MUA, and it is permitted to make modifications to the message before transferring the mail. An MSA is sometimes loosely called a mail server; however, the term "server" encompasses many meanings.

TCP port 587 is used by MSAs. During start-up, the Sendmail daemon attaches a listener to port 587 to accept mail from MUAs that speak SMTP. On Linux systems, most MUAs do not speak SMTP to the Sendmail daemon through port 587. Instead, individual instantiations of Sendmail are launched by the MUAs to act as MSAs for outbound mail. They move the message to Sendmail using some form of interprocess communication—e.g., a pipe. The MUAs then rely on Sendmail to properly format the mail and handle the SMTP communication with the remote server.

---

**NOTE**  At one time, an MUA that spoke SMTP could use it to communicate with Sendmail by invoking the sendmail command with the -bs option. Now, the MUA can send the SMTP traffic to port 587 without invoking a separate instantiation of Sendmail.

---

Formal language is needed by protocol developers to accurately define the functions of the various components of the system. But just reading a paragraph full of MUA, MSA, and MTA is enough to make your head ache. People simply don't talk that way. Most of the time, the components of the e-mail architecture are described with more general terms.

### Commonly Used Terminology

Most people do not use the terms MUA, MSA, and MTA when speaking about e-mail architecture. The more commonly used terms are described below.

**Client**   A mail client is generally the end system on which mail is read or written. This could be an MUA, or a POP or IMAP client. However, the term "client" can also be applied to a remote system that is acting as a client during a protocol exchange. For example, later in this book you will see a variable named `client_addr` that holds the client's IP address. In that case, however, the "client" is not an end system at all; it is the remote MTA that initiated an SMTP connection. Look at the context in which the term "client" is used to discern the proper meaning.

**Server**   A mail server is any system that handles either MSA or MTA functions. Any Linux system running Sendmail can be called a server. "Server" is the most general term. There are several different types of servers.

**Hub**   A mail hub is a server that acts as a central collection point for all of its clients' mail. The mail hub may handle all of the mail processing for its clients. An extreme example of dependence on a hub is the Sendmail `nullclient` configuration. In a `nullclient` configuration, all mail, even messages between two users of the client system, is sent to the hub for processing and is stored on the hub. Generally, the term is used to refer to any server that is a collection point for mail.

**Mailbox server**   A mailbox server is a server that holds mail until its clients are ready to read the mail. It is similar to a hub server except that "mailbox server" is generally used only when the clients are POP or IMAP clients. The terms "hub server" and "mailbox server" are often used interchangeably.

**Relay**   A relay server acts as an MTA for its clients. It accepts mail from clients and sends that mail on to the destination address. Proper relay configuration is an important part of setting up Sendmail, particularly in the fight against spam e-mail. Chapter 11, "Stopping Spam," covers relay configuration extensively.

A mail server may handle more than one of these functions. A server may be called a relay when referring to its role in handling outbound mail. That same server may be called a hub or a mailbox server when referring to its role in storing inbound mail for its clients. And when it is referred to in general terms, it may just be called a mail server.

Client configuration acknowledges the dual role of mail servers. The configuration of a Windows client shown in Figure 2.2 identifies a Linux server to act as a POP3 mailbox server for inbound mail and a separate Linux server to act as a relay for outbound mail.

Of course, these could be the same Linux system, and they often are. In the example, two different systems are used to emphasize the two major server roles.

**Figure 2.2**    A PC client configuration

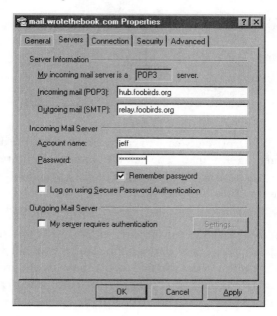

Often the simple view of the configuration seen from a Windows client does not reflect the true e-mail architecture of a network. In the next section, we examine two sample networks to put the components of e-mail architecture into context.

## Sample Mail Architectures

The first sample architecture can be seen in Figure 2.3. It shows an engineering department in which every user has a Linux desktop. The cloud represents the outside world. The directional arrows indicate the flow of mail into and out of each system. As this figure illustrates, each Linux system is acting as its own server. It collects inbound mail and sends outbound mail for its own users. It does not, however, act as a relay or hub for any client systems or for any users on other systems.

**Figure 2.3** A sample engineering department

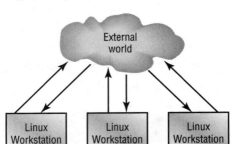

This configuration is surprisingly easy to create because it is the default configuration of a Linux system running Sendmail. The default Linux configuration runs the Sendmail daemon, which provides an SMTP listener on port 25 to collect inbound mail, and all of the MUAs running on Linux know about Sendmail and use it to send outbound mail. Further, the default Sendmail configuration blocks relaying from outside systems.

The configuration for the engineering department is simple, but maintenance is complex. Every system needs to be kept up to date with the latest Sendmail patches. In a department with just a few systems this is not too bad, but if the network grows very large, keeping all of the systems updated could be a big headache. To cope with a configuration like this you need sophisticated users who can help with the maintenance, which is why we showed this as a configuration for a small engineering department. Less sophisticated users require a more complex architecture.

Figure 2.4 shows a sales department. Pre- and post-sales technical support personnel and top sales people get Linux desktops. Sales trainees and clerical personnel get Windows desktops. The dashed arrows indicate that the Windows clients periodically retrieve mail from the server using POP or IMAP; the solid arrows to the Linux clients indicate that mail is immediately forwarded to those clients via SMTP.

The server is configured as both a relay and a mailbox server. The relay configuration is carefully created so that all systems within the local network can relay through the server but no remote systems can relay mail though the server. The server is also configured to forward all of the mail it receives for its Linux clients on to those clients. The Linux clients are configured to send all outbound mail through the server. (In Sendmail configuration, all mail can be sent through a single server by defining a SMART_HOST value in the configuration of the client.)

**Figure 2.4**    A sample sales department

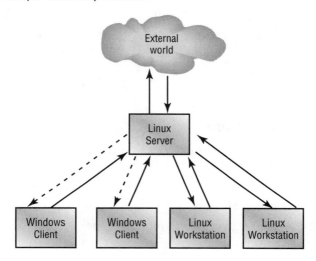

The fact that all mail flows through one server simplifies maintenance. Patches can be applied to a single system and yet benefit the entire network. Mail can be filtered at a single point. If a firewall is put in place, it only needs to allow mail through to a single system. The biggest problem with this configuration is that it creates a potential single point of failure.

In these two simple sample networks, Sendmail systems are used as both clients and servers. Sendmail performs multiple tasks that are essential for efficient mail delivery, and Sendmail systems take on multiple roles in the e-mail architecture.

# Sendmail's Roles

MSA, MTA, relay, and server are all terms used to describe the functions of components within the e-mail architecture. These words will appear again and again throughout this book. Understanding them is essential. Sendmail also has its own language to describe the functions it performs. Mailers, rulesets, rewrite rules, and aliasing are all words used to describe the work that Sendmail does. To read this book and understand the role of Sendmail, you need to know what each of these terms means. This section introduces "Sendmail speak" and links this new terminology to the roles that Sendmail plays in the e-mail architecture.

The tasks that a Sendmail server performs can be divided into two basic functional groups: the roles that Sendmail performs as a message submission agent and as a message transport agent. The distinctions between these roles can be subtle, and the roles sometimes overlap. But these two basic roles incorporate all of the tasks performed by a Sendmail server and help explain what various configuration values do and why they need to be defined. Much of the Sendmail configuration is used to specify how Sendmail should handle its duties as a message submission agent.

## A Message Submission Agent

The functions of Sendmail described in this section might not meet the RFC definition of an MSA, but they come mighty close. An MTA that accepts a message directly from an MUA and takes an active role in formatting a complete mail message is an MSA. Sendmail

- accepts mail from an MUA
- determines the mail delivery program for the mail
- reformats the mail addresses for the selected mailer
- adds the headers required by the mailer
- sends the message to the mailer for delivery

In this book I'm using "message submission agent" to describe the role that Sendmail fills as the interface between the user's e-mail program (the MUA) and the mail delivery program (the MTA). Even when Sendmail is the MTA, things must be done to the mail received from the MUA to prepare it for delivery, and, of course, Sendmail is not the only MTA that can run on a Linux system. A user can create a wide variety of mail with an e-mail program. The mail entered by the user could be local mail bound for another local user; it could be Internet mail bound for a remote user; it could be data bound for a Linux program; it could even be mail bound for any one of a large number of obsolete mail systems. (See Appendix A, "m4 Macro Command Reference," for a full list of the mailers supported by Sendmail.) All that a user mail program running on a Linux system needs to do is pass the mail message on to Sendmail. Sendmail is equipped to select the appropriate delivery agent and to properly prepare the mail for that delivery agent.

### Sendmail Mailers

The mail delivery programs are called *mailers* in Sendmail terminology. The mailers available to Sendmail are defined inside the Sendmail configuration file. A mailer definition assigns an internal mailer name to a mail delivery program. These names are arbitrary, but most Linux systems use the standard mailers defined by the default Sendmail configuration. Chapter 5, "Understanding a Vendor's Configuration," describes each of the default mailers.

A mailer definition also provides Sendmail with the full pathname of the mail delivery program and the command-line arguments Sendmail should use when it launches that mailer. If the mail delivery program is Sendmail itself, as it is for all of the SMTP mailers, a symbolic name, either IPC, which stands for Inter-Process Communication, or TCP, which stands for Transmission Control Protocol, is used instead of a pathname.

Mailer definitions take up a substantial portion of the Sendmail configuration file. Each mailer definition provides the instructions that Sendmail needs to properly prepare a message for a given mailer. This includes the commands that are used to process sender addresses and recipient addresses for the mailer. There are also flags associated with each mailer. The flags define optional processing required by the mailer and identify the message headers needed for the mailer. The number and type of headers vary from mailer to mailer.

The Sendmail configuration contains several mailers. Sendmail must select the correct mailer to deliver a piece of mail.

## Determining the Delivery Triple

When Sendmail receives a piece of mail from an MUA, it determines what mailer will deliver the mail. Sendmail determines this from the delivery address included in the mail. It does this by literally converting the delivery address into a *delivery triple*. A delivery triple contains up to three values:

- the recipient's e-mail address
- the name of the mail server to which the mail will be sent
- the internal name of the mailer that will deliver the mail to the server

You can see the delivery triple that is produced for any given address by running the sendmail command with the -bv option and the address you want processed. Listing 2.1 shows the output of sendmail -bv for two different delivery addresses.

**Listing 2.1**   Examining the Delivery Triple

```
[craig]$ sendmail -bv ed@xy.com
ed@xy.com... deliverable: mailer esmtp, host xy.com, user ed@xy.com
[craig]$ sendmail -bv craig
craig... deliverable: mailer local, user craig
```

The first line in Listing 2.1 is a command that asks Sendmail to evaluate the delivery address ed@xy.com. Sendmail responds that the address is deliverable—which in this case means only that it is properly formatted, because the copy of Sendmail running on your server does not have any direct knowledge of whether or not the remote host can actually deliver mail to this address. The delivery triple for the address is also displayed. The name of the internal mailer that Sendmail will use to transport mail to this address is esmtp, which is the default name used for the extended SMTP mailer. The host to which Sendmail will transfer the mail is named xy.com, and the e-mail address that the mail will be delivered to is ed@xy.com.

The second command in Listing 2.1 is slightly different. It evaluates the delivery address craig. Because the address has no hostname part—i.e., no at-sign (@) followed by a host or domain name—the address is assumed to be the name of a user on the local system. Sendmail checks that the username is deliverable on the local host. The host value is not provided as part of the delivery triple for local mail delivery because no remote host is involved. The internal mailer name for local mail delivery is local, and in Listing 2.1 the user value that would be passed to the local mailer is craig.

### Formatting E-Mail Addresses

Once Sendmail selects a mailer, it must properly format the mail for that mailer. Sendmail uses commands called *rewrite rules* to transform the e-mail address received from the MUA into the format required by the MTA. The bulk of the Sendmail configuration file is composed of rewrite rules. These are individual lines that define a pattern match and a transformation. If the input address matches the pattern defined in a rule, it is rewritten using the transformation defined in that rule.

Rules are grouped together into rulesets, which are internally identified by a name or a number. Rulesets can be called like functions from individual rewrite rules to process complex addresses. Certain rulesets are assigned special roles by Sendmail and are used to process different types of addresses. For example, delivery addresses are processed by the canonify ruleset (also known as ruleset 3), which processes all addresses to put them into the format expected by Sendmail, and then by the parse ruleset (also known as ruleset 0), which creates the delivery triple.

You can watch the rulesets in action by running the sendmail command with the -bt option. -bt places Sendmail in test mode. Once it is running in test mode, it will accept a list of rulesets and an address to process through those rulesets. In Listing 2.2, the sendmail command is run with the -bt argument and asked to process ed@xy.com through rulesets canonify and parse.

**Listing 2.2** Watching Rewrite Rules in Action

```
[craig]$ sendmail -bt
ADDRESS TEST MODE (ruleset 3 NOT automatically invoked)
Enter <ruleset> <address>
> canonify,parse ed@xyz.com
canonify          input: ed @ xyz . com
Canonify2         input: ed < @ xyz . com >
Canonify2       returns: ed < @ xyz . com >
canonify        returns: ed < @ xyz . com >
parse             input: ed < @ xyz . com >
Parse0            input: ed < @ xyz . com >
```

```
Parse0          returns: ed < @ xyz . com >
ParseLocal        input: ed < @ xyz . com >
ParseLocal      returns: ed < @ xyz . com >
Parse1            input: ed < @ xyz . com >
Mailertable       input: < xyz . com > ed < @ xyz . com >
Mailertable       input: xyz . < com > ed < @ xyz . com >
Mailertable     returns: ed < @ xyz . com >
Mailertable     returns: ed < @ xyz . com >
MailerToTriple    input: < > ed < @ xyz . com >
MailerToTriple  returns: ed < @ xyz . com >
Parse1          returns: $# esmtp $@ xyz . com $: ed < @ xyz . com >
parse           returns: $# esmtp $@ xyz . com $: ed < @ xyz . com >
> ^D
```

The `sendmail -bt` command shows much more detail than -bv did. Listing 2.2 shows that before the `canonify` ruleset returns a value the `Canonify2` ruleset is run, and before the `parse` ruleset returns five other rulesets are run. This shows that rulesets can be called by a rule from within other rulesets. That's what's happening in Listing 2.2. In all, eight rulesets process this delivery address. The result is the delivery triple. Notice here, however, that the label `mailer` is replaced by the symbol `$#`, the label `host` is replaced by `$@`, and the label `user` is replaced by `$:` in the triple. As you'll see in Chapter 8, symbols are heavily used in Sendmail rewrite rules.

The delivery address is only one type of address handled by Sendmail. Sendmail also processes the sender address and the recipient address. The sender address is the name of the user or process that initiated the mail. The recipient addresses are the list of recipients provided with the mail. The recipients are distinct from the delivery address in that only one address at a time from the list of recipients is used as the delivery address but the entire list of recipients is processed and included in each outbound mail message.

All addresses are processed through rewrite rules to convert the input addresses into a format that is acceptable for the mailer that will be transporting the mail. Because the rewriting is dependent on which mailer will be handling the mail, the delivery address is processed first to determine which mailer will be used. Once the mailer is selected, the other addresses can be processed through the standard rulesets and those that are specific to the mailer.

Processing and rewriting e-mail addresses is a central part of what Sendmail does. It is a large and complex topic. Chapter 8 covers the topic in detail.

### Formatting Headers

In addition to modifying the mail addresses to make them correct for the mail delivery program, Sendmail ensures that all of the headers required by the mail delivery program are provided and are properly formatted. As noted above, the flags in a mailer definition identify the headers required for that mailer.

The Sendmail configuration file contains header templates that define the proper format for the various message headers. Each template has an associated flag. If a matching flag is found in the mailer definition, Sendmail knows that the mailer requires that particular header and adds it if it is not already contained in the mail message. The mail headers contained in the message that Sendmail receives from the MUA are maintained and forwarded to the mail delivery program. The flags and the header templates ensure that all of the required headers are provided even if the MUA fails to provide them.

The role of a message submission agent is central to what Sendmail is. Sendmail receives mail from the user's mail program, selects the correct mail delivery program for that mail, and properly formats the message headers and e-mail addresses for the selected mailer. The MSA function is very complex and it is the focus of most Sendmail configurations. Despite its complexity, serving as a message submission agent is not the only Sendmail function.

## A Message Transfer Agent

Sendmail acts as an MTA when it receives mail from an external system because it is not the first-hop MTA and it doesn't modify the mail message. Therefore, Sendmail isn't acting as an MSA. The mail may be inbound mail destined for someone on the local system or mail being relayed through the local system to a remote server.

Sendmail is designed to deliver mail to the correct recipient. Outbound mail is handled by formatting it and passing it to the correct mailer for delivery. Inbound mail is handled by passing it to the correct user or system.

In certain circumstances, inbound mail needs to be forwarded before final delivery can be made. The To: address on the mail may be an alias for the real recipient. The recipient may define private forwarding for their mail. It is even possible that the hostname in the To: address is not the name of the local host and that the mail needs to be forwarded to a remote host for delivery. Three Sendmail features, *aliasing*, *forwarding*, and *relaying*, handle these three types of delivery.

## Sendmail Aliases

Sendmail aliases perform important functions that are an essential part of creating a mail server. Mail aliases do the following:

**Specify nicknames for individual users.** Nicknames can be used to direct mail addressed to special names, such as postmaster or root, to the real users who do those jobs. When used in conjunction with the domain MX records covered earlier, aliases can be used to create a standard e-mail address structure for a domain.

**Forward mail to other hosts.** Sendmail aliases automatically forward mail to the host address included as part of the recipient address.

**Define mailing lists.** An alias with multiple recipients is a mailing list.

Mail aliases are defined in the `aliases` file, which is the database Sendmail uses to determine where to deliver inbound mail. Processing an address through the `aliases` database is called *aliasing*. It is a multi-step process.

1.  First, Sendmail determines whether or not the address is a local address. Only mail addressed to the local system is processed through the `aliases` database. Mail is considered to be addressed to the local system when the recipient address has no host part—i.e., no @*hostname*—or the *hostname* in the host part of the address is either the name of the server itself or one of the names it recognizes as a *local host alias*. Local host aliases are not the same thing as aliases. Aliases are usernames defined in the `aliases` database. Local host aliases are hostnames defined in the `local-hostnames` file. If Sendmail decides the mail is addressed to the local system, aliasing continues. Otherwise, the mail is processed for relaying. (Relaying is described in the next section.)

2.  Next, the username from the recipient address is used as the key for an `aliases` database lookup. If the database does not return a value for the lookup, the mail is delivered to the user defined in the recipient address.

3.  If the `aliases` database returns a value for the lookup, the value becomes the new database key.

4.  Another lookup is done using the new key. If no value is returned for the lookup, the mail is delivered to the address that was used as the last key. If a value is returned, Sendmail goes back to step 3. Sendmail can loop through steps 3 and 4 up to ten times, because aliases can point to other aliases and can be nested up to ten levels deep.

5.  If Sendmail loops through steps 3 and 4 the maximum number of times without resolving the aliases, it returns an error and does not deliver the mail.

Another level of aliasing occurs after the recipient is processed through the `aliases` database. The `aliases` database defines mail forwarding for the entire system. The `.forward` file, which can be created in any user's home directory, defines mail forwarding for an individual user. Once Sendmail identifies the user to which the mail will be delivered, it looks for a `.forward` file in the user's home directory. If the `.forward` file is found, the mail is forwarded to the e-mail address contained in that file. If the file is not found or is empty, the mail is delivered directly to the user's account.

---

**NOTE** The `aliases` database, the `local-host-names` file, and the `.forward` file are all described in Chapter 6, "Using Sendmail Databases."

---

The Sendmail terms "forwarding" and "relaying" are often used interchangeably, but there is a slight difference. Forwarding refers to the act of transferring to another host mail that was originally addressed to the local host. For example, if mail addressed to `norm` on the local host is sent to `normane@hawk.foobirds.org` as a result of aliasing, you would say the mail has been forwarded to `hawk.foobirds.org`. Relaying, which is the next topic, is subtly different.

### Mail Relaying

Relaying occurs when mail is transferred on toward its destination and neither the source nor the destination address of the mail is the address of the local system. For example: If a server named `wren.foobirds.org` receives mail from `ibis.foobirds.org` that is addressed to `craig@wrotethebook.com` and re-sends that mail to the host `wrotethebook.com`, `wren` is acting as a mail relay.

At one time mail relaying was the default configuration for Sendmail systems, but no more. Spammers used unsuspecting mail servers to relay their spam in order to hide the true origin of the nuisance mail. Now the default configuration is to relay no mail at all. In Figure 2.1, the sample systems use this default configuration. Each system sends its own e-mail. None of the systems accepts mail for relaying from any other system. It is up to you to loosen those restrictions if you need to provide mail relaying for some of your clients. (Proper relay configuration is described in Chapter 11.) In Figure 2.2, the server system is configured as a relay for the systems on the local area network.

By default, Sendmail does not relay mail. A server accepts mail addressed to the server itself or any of its local hostname aliases. It rejects all other mail. To enable relaying, the specific names of the hosts or domains that should be allowed to relay mail must be provided to Sendmail. The hostnames of relay clients can be provided in the `relay-domains` file or through the `access` database. Both of these files are covered in Chapter 6.

## A Client

One possible role for a Linux system running Sendmail that is frequently overlooked is the role of a client. By default, every Linux system is a Sendmail server. It is a limited server, because it is set up to handle only mail from users who are directly logged in to the system, but it is a server nonetheless. Turning a Linux system into a true client takes some configuration effort, and it is rarely worth the effort. While the `nullclient` configuration is touched upon in Chapter 9, the true focus of this book is to properly configure the Sendmail server functions for every Linux system from a laptop to an enterprise server.

# In Sum

The SMTP protocol runs on top of the TCP protocol. TCP is a reliable, connection-oriented protocol. It ensures that mail is always delivered, and it means that SMTP directly delivers mail to the remote system without dependence on intervening systems. This is a great mail-delivery model because it provides immediate feedback from the remote server about whether or not the mail was successfully delivered. However, this system demands a remote system that is fully capable of accepting SMTP mail. Unfortunately, that is not always the case. Sendmail queries DNS and uses the MX records it provides to route mail to a fully capable SMTP server for those systems that cannot handle their own SMTP mail.

The fact that both direct delivery to end systems and delivery to intervening mail servers are available to Sendmail creates the possibility of a variety of e-mail architectures. There are clients and servers, and the servers can be described in several different ways. Servers that collect inbound mail are described as hubs or mailbox servers. Servers that handle outbound mail are called relays or simply servers. To clarify the vagueness of this language, Internet standards documents define the functions of message user agents (MUAs), message submission agents (MSAs), and message transfer agents (MTAs).

Even with the narrowly defined terms MUA, MSA, and MTA, there can be confusion because most functions do not match any definition exactly. Various functions overlap across systems and things are not easily tied up in neat packages. The easiest way to avoid making the language of e-mail architecture overly complex is simply to use a little judgment. Don't be too rigid in interpreting the meaning of a term. Always look at things in context. Sendmail frequently uses the same word to describe two different things. Context is the clue to understanding.

Sendmail is the software that turns a Linux system into an e-mail server. It acts as an MSA and an MTA and can even be used as an MUA. Chapter 3, "Running Sendmail," looks at how Sendmail is installed on a Linux system and how it is run once it is installed.

# 3

# Running Sendmail

**C**hapter 2, "Understanding E-Mail Architecture," illustrates the importance of Sendmail for a Linux system. Sendmail implements the SMTP protocol for Linux systems. It sends and receives SMTP mail for the system, and it acts as an interface between the user's mail program and the Internet. These vital tasks make Sendmail a basic component of most Linux systems.

Sendmail is such an essential part of a Linux system that it is usually installed by default and run at start-up. If it is not installed on your system, you need to know how to install it. Additionally, you need to know how to compile the Sendmail program for those times when you want to install the latest source code distribution of Sendmail on an existing Linux system. This chapter covers both of those topics. It also examines how and why the Sendmail process runs at start-up, and you'll look at the tools used to control whether or not starting the Sendmail daemon is part of the Linux boot process on your system.

## Running Sendmail at Start-Up

Sendmail runs in two distinct modes: *real-time mode* for outbound mail delivery and *daemon mode* for collecting inbound mail and queue processing. When a *mail user agent (MUA)* has mail to send, it creates an instantiation of the Sendmail program to deliver that piece of mail. The instantiation of Sendmail lives long enough to deliver that one piece of mail. If it cannot successfully deliver the mail, it writes the mail to the mail queue and terminates. Most Sendmail processes have a very short life. The Sendmail daemon, on the other hand, runs the entire time the system is running, constantly listening for inbound mail and periodically processing the queue to deliver undelivered mail. The Sendmail daemon, like most other daemons, is started at boot time.

The ps command reveals whether or not Sendmail is running on your system:

```
[root]# ps -C sendmail
  PID TTY          TIME CMD
  542 ?        00:00:36 sendmail
```

The low process ID (PID) shows that this process was started during the boot. Running this ps command on most Linux systems will show that Sendmail is running because, generally, Sendmail becomes part of the boot process when you first install Linux.

Many systems are running the Sendmail daemon unnecessarily. It is not necessary to run Sendmail as a daemon in order to send mail. Running the sendmail command with the -bd option is required only if your system directly receives SMTP mail. A Linux mail client can collect inbound mail from the mailbox server using POP or IMAP and can relay outbound mail through the mail relay server without running the Sendmail daemon. Deciding which systems should run the Sendmail daemon is part of the process of planning your e-mail architecture. Unneeded daemons consume system resources and provide holes through which network intruders can slither. Take care when selecting which systems really need any daemon, including Sendmail.

It is possible to enable or disable Sendmail after the system is installed, and there are several tools to do this. These tools vary depending on the type of start-up procedures used. Some Linux systems use BSD-style start-up procedures, while others use System V–style procedures.

On Linux distributions that use System V–style boot procedures, the script that starts Sendmail is usually found in the /etc/rc.d/init.d directory, where it is stored under a name such as sendmail, mail, or mta. On distributions that use BSD-style boot procedures, the commands that start Sendmail are stored in one of the rc scripts. For example, on Slackware 4.0, the commands to start Sendmail are found in the rc.M script located in the /etc/rc.d directory. Regardless of the name of the script used for this purpose, some start-up script is used to start Sendmail at boot time.

---

***TIP*** To locate the Sendmail start-up script on your Linux system, go to the directory that holds start-up scripts and run the command **grep sendmail** * to search every file for references to Sendmail. Not sure where the start-up scripts are stored? Go to /etc and look for files or directories that begin with the string rc. Those are start-up files and directories.

## On a BSD-Style Linux System

Linux systems such as Slackware that use BSD-style boot procedures start Sendmail by executing the `sendmail` command directly from one of the main start-up files. The code that runs the Sendmail daemon in the Slackware Linux `/etc/rc.d/rc.M` start-up script is very straightforward, as shown in Listing 3.1.

**Listing 3.1**    Starting Sendmail from a Slackware Boot Script

```
# Start the sendmail daemon:
if [ -x /usr/sbin/sendmail ]; then
  echo "Starting sendmail daemon"
  /usr/sbin/sendmail -bd -q 15m
fi
```

Listing 3.1 shows a Slackware system ready to run Sendmail. The first line is a comment, as indicated by the fact that it starts with a pound sign (#). The next lines are an `if` statement that checks whether or not the `sendmail` command is available. If the command is found, a message is displayed on the console indicating that Sendmail is starting and then the `sendmail` command is run.

The code in Listing 3.1 runs the `sendmail` command with the -bd and the -q options. In addition to listening for inbound mail, the Sendmail daemon periodically checks to see whether there is mail waiting to be delivered. It's possible that a Sendmail process that was started to send a message was not able to successfully deliver the mail. In that case, the process writes the message to the mail queue and counts on the daemon to deliver it at a later time. The -q option tells the Sendmail daemon how often to check the undelivered mail queue. In the Slackware example, the queue is processed every 15 minutes (-q15m).

To prevent Slackware from starting Sendmail at boot time, comment the lines shown in Listing 3.1 out of the `rc.M` script by placing a pound sign at the beginning of each line. To restore Sendmail to the boot process, remove the pound signs. These techniques are easy and they work, but they are far from elegant.

Directly editing a start-up script is easy, but dangerous. Most system administrators worry that an editing error will have a major negative impact on the next boot. I have never really had a major boot problem cause by an editing error, but I understand the fear. Distributions that use System V–style start-up procedures alleviate this fear by making it unnecessary to directly edit the start-up file.

## On a System V–Style Linux System

Most Linux distributions use a System V–style boot process that allows the system to be initialized in different ways depending on the runlevel. All of the service initialization scripts are located in a single directory, usually called /etc/rc.d/init.d on Linux systems that use this style of start-up. The initialization scripts are indirectly invoked by links contained in directories assigned to each runlevel. Caldera and Red Hat are good examples of System V–style Linux systems.

> **NOTE**   A detailed description of the Linux boot process is beyond the scope of this book. To learn more about the boot process, runlevels, and start-up scripts, see *Linux Network Servers 24seven* by Craig Hunt (Sybex, 1999).

The code that Caldera and Red Hat use to start the Sendmail daemon is found in the /etc/rc.d/init.d/sendmail script. It is more complex than the code used by Slackware, because Red Hat and Caldera use script variables read from an external file to set the command-line options. The file they read is /etc/sysconfig/sendmail, which normally contains these two lines:

```
DAEMON=yes
QUEUE=1h
```

Changing the values in the /etc/sysconfig/sendmail file controls the daemon configuration. The QUEUE variable sets the time value of the -q option. In this case, it is one hour (1h), which is a value that I like even more than the 15 minutes used in Slackware configuration. Don't set this time too low. Processing the queue too often can cause problems if the queue grows very large due to a delivery problem such as a network outage.

If the variable DAEMON is equal to "yes," the sendmail command is run with the -bd option. If you are configuring a mail client and don't want to run Sendmail as a daemon, you could directly edit the /etc/sysconfig/sendmail file to set DAEMON=no.

> **TIP**   While changing the DAEMON value is one way to do this, it is generally a better idea to remove the sendmail script from the start-up as described below than it is to edit the contents of a script.

With System V–style start-up, you don't have to directly edit start-up files. One of the advantages of the System V–style boot procedure is that major services have their own start-up scripts and those scripts are indirectly invoked, which makes it possible to control whether or not a service is started at boot time by controlling whether or not the script is invoked. The sendmail script is invoked indirectly from the runlevel directories by the S80sendmail script (see Listing 3.2). An examination of that script shows that it is just a symbolic link to the real sendmail script.

**Listing 3.2**  The Sendmail Link for Runlevel 3

```
[craig]$ cd /etc/rc.d/rc3.d
[craig]$ ls -l S80sendmail
lrwxrwxrwx 1 root root 18 Dec 26 1999 S80sendmail -> ../init.d/sendmail
```

To enable or disable the sendmail start-up script for a specific runlevel, simply add or remove the symbolic link in that runlevel's directory. In and of itself this would be simple enough, but Linux systems make it even easier by providing tools to manage the runlevel directories.

### Enabling Sendmail with *tksysv*

tksysv is an X Windows tool provided for the purpose of controlling scripts started at each runlevel. Figure 3.1 shows the main tksysv screen.

**Figure 3.1**  Enabling Sendmail with **tksysv**

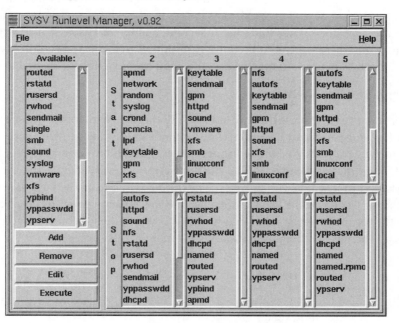

All of the scripts that can be controlled by `tksysv` are listed on the left-hand side of the screen. On the right are the services that are started and stopped for runlevels 2, 3, 4, and 5. To disable a service for a specific runlevel, simply highlight the service in the Start list for that runlevel and click the Remove button. For example, to remove Sendmail from runlevel 5, which is traditionally used as the runlevel for dedicated X Windows workstations, click `sendmail` in the Start list under runlevel 5 and then click Remove. After that, Sendmail will no longer start when the system boots under runlevel 5.

To add Sendmail to a runlevel, highlight `sendmail` in the Available list and click Add. You'll be asked to select a runlevel. An example might be runlevel 3, which is traditionally the default runlevel for multiuser servers. Select the runlevel and click Done. You're then asked to select a script number. Use the default, which is 80 for the `sendmail` script. Click Add and the script is added to the start-up. The next time the system reboots under runlevel 3, Sendmail will be started.

---

***TIP*** Of course you don't want to reboot your system just to run the `sendmail` start-up script. Use the Execute button to run the `sendmail` script immediately.

---

`tksysv` has a couple of nice features. First, it comes bundled with different versions of Linux. It runs just as well on Caldera as it does on Red Hat, and it runs just as well under Red Hat 6 as it does under Red Hat 7. Second, a clone of `tksysv` called `ntsysv` runs in text mode and therefore doesn't require X Windows. A dedicated e-mail server might not be running X Windows. In that case, you want a tool like `ntsysv` that runs in text mode.

### Enabling Sendmail with *ntsysv*

`ntsysv` is even easier to use because it doesn't bother you with lots of questions about runlevels. It assumes the current runlevel as a default unless it is run with the `--level` argument. `ntsysv` presents you with a list of services that can be automatically started at boot time. One of these is Sendmail. The start-up script for every item in the list that has an asterisk next to it will be run during the next boot. Use the arrow keys to scroll down to the `sendmail` entry in the list and then use the space bar to select or deselect `sendmail`. When the settings are just what you want, tab over to the OK button and press Enter. That's all there is to it. Figure 3.2 shows the main `ntsysv` screen.

**Figure 3.2**     Enabling Sendmail with `ntsysv`

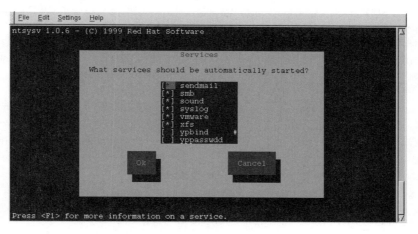

### Enabling Sendmail with *linuxconf*

Another tool that is popular on Red Hat systems is `linuxconf`. `linuxconf` is a general-purpose system administration tool. One of the features it provides is a way to manage the start-up scripts. Figure 3.3 shows the `linuxconf` screen.

**Figure 3.3**     Enabling Sendmail with `linuxconf`

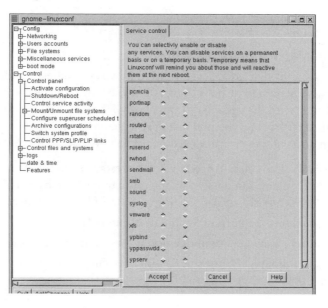

From the menu on the left-hand side of the linuxconf window, select Control ➢ Control Panel ➢ Control Service Activity. A list of services appears on the right-hand side of the window; it is the same list of services displayed by ntsysv. Again, as with ntsysv, you don't have to worry about runlevels. Simply enable or disable the sendmail script by selecting the appropriate button next to the sendmail entry.

### Enabling Sendmail with *chkconfig*

One final tool that can be used to control the scripts that are run at boot time is chkconfig. This is a command-line tool based on the chkconfig program from the Silicon Graphics IRIX version of Unix. The Linux version has some enhancements, such as the ability to control which runlevels the scripts run under. The --list option of the chkconfig command displays the current settings:

```
[craig]$ chkconfig --list sendmail
sendmail 0:off 1:off 2:on 3:on 4:on 5:on 6:off
```

To enable or disable a script for a specific runlevel, specify the runlevel with the --level option, followed by the name of the script you wish to control and the action you wish to take, either on to enable the script or off to disable it. For example, to disable sendmail for runlevel 2, enter the command shown in Listing 3.3.

**Listing 3.3**  Controlling Sendmail with chkconfig

```
[root]# chkconfig --level 2 sendmail off
[root]# chkconfig --list sendmail
sendmail 0:off 1:off 2:off 3:on 4:on 5:on 6:off
```

### Manually Running the Start-Up Script

The previous sections discussed several different ways to do essentially the same thing— enable or disable Sendmail at boot time. All of these approaches work. Choose the one that is compatible with the version of Linux you're running and that suits your tastes. But remember, most of the time you will install and enable Sendmail during the initial system configuration and will never again need to fiddle with the boot files.

It is far more likely that you will need to stop or restart a Sendmail process that is already running on your system. On most systems, this can be done by manually invoking the boot scripts. The sendmail start-up script on a Red Hat system accepts five arguments:

**stop**  terminates the current Sendmail daemon process.

**start**  starts a new Sendmail daemon if one is not currently running.

**restart**  terminates the current Sendmail daemon and starts a new one. An alternate name for the same command is reload.

**condrestart**    checks first to see if Sendmail is running. If one is running, it terminates the current Sendmail daemon and starts a new one. If Sendmail is not currently running, it starts Sendmail.

**status**    displays the process ID of the current Sendmail daemon.

Listing 3.4 is an example of restarting the Sendmail daemon on a Red Hat system.

**Listing 3.4**    Restarting Sendmail with the Start-Up Script

```
[root]# /etc/rc.d/init.d/sendmail restart
Shutting down sendmail:                              [  OK  ]
Starting sendmail:                                   [  OK  ]
```

---

**NOTE**    If you're running Red Hat 6.0 or higher, an alternative to specifying the full path name of the sendmail start-up script is to enter **service sendmail restart**. On other versions of Red Hat, use the full pathname.

---

The primary limitation of the start-up scripts is that they all start the Sendmail daemon with only the -bd and the -q options. This is correct more than 99 percent of the time. But there are a few occasions when additional command-line arguments are needed. If the occasion is a test, it is simple enough to run Sendmail from the command line. If you need additional command-line arguments for every boot, the only option is to edit the start-up scripts or create your own start-up script to include the arguments you need. See Appendix B, "The sendmail Command," for a complete listing and description of the many command-line arguments that are available for the sendmail command.

## Controlling Sendmail with Signals

Not every Linux system has a script that can be used to start, stop, and restart Sendmail. But on all systems, Sendmail can be controlled through signals. The Sendmail process handles three different signals. Well, four, if you count the fact that SIGTERM aborts Sendmail just as it does most other processes—but there are three signals that have a special meaning to Sendmail. These three signals are:

**SIGHUP**    The SIGHUP signal causes the Sendmail daemon to restart and reread its configuration file. The most common use of SIGHUP is to force Sendmail to reload its configuration after the configuration file has been updated. SIGHUP can even be used to terminate the current copy of Sendmail and run a new one after the Sendmail program has been updated because SIGHUP causes a true restart, not just a reread of the configuration file.

**SIGINT**   The SIGINT signal causes Sendmail to do a graceful shutdown. When Sendmail receives SIGINT, it removes the lock files if it is currently processing the queue, it switches back to the user ID that it started under to create a clean log entry, and then it exits without errors. Like most processes, Sendmail can be terminated by the kill signal, SIGTERM. However, SIGINT is a cleaner way to shut down Sendmail because, unlike SIGTERM, SIGINT will not leave unresolved log entries or unused lock files lying around.

**SIGUSR1**   Use the SIGUSR1 signal to cause Sendmail to write out its current status via `syslogd`. Details of Sendmail logging are covered in Chapter 12, "Testing Sendmail Security." For now, it is sufficient to understand that SIGUSR1 causes Sendmail to display information about the open file descriptors, information about its host connection cache, and output from the `debug_dumpstate` ruleset, if one is defined in your configuration. None of this output is of particular interest to a system administrator.

Listing 3.5 shows an example of passing a signal to Sendmail. In the example, the signal is SIGHUP but the same technique can be used to send any of the signals to Sendmail.

**Listing 3.5**   Restarting Sendmail with SIGHUP

```
[root]# ps -ax | grep sendmail
 542 ?        S       0:00 sendmail: accepting connections
[root]# kill -HUP 542
[root]# ps -ax | grep sendmail
 773 ?        S       0:00 sendmail: accepting connections
```

Listing 3.5 illustrates the effect of the SIGHUP signal by showing that the process ID of Sendmail changes after Sendmail is sent the signal. Clearly, a process must be terminated and restarted to change process IDs. The `kill` command used in this example is explained in the next section.

## The *kill* Command

The `kill` command is used to send a signal to a running process. As the name implies, by default it sends the kill signal (SIGTERM). To use it to send a different signal, specify the signal on the command line. For example, specify `-INT` to send the SIGINT signal. The PID is usually provided on the `kill` command line to ensure that the signal is sent to the correct process.

As usual, there is more than one way to do something on a Linux system. You can learn the PID of Sendmail using the `ps` command:

```
[root]# ps -ax | grep sendmail
 542 ?        S       0:00 sendmail: accepting connections
```

You can also learn the PID by displaying the `sendmail.pid` file:

```
[root]# head -1 /var/run/sendmail.pid
542
```

Combining the last command with `kill`, you can send a signal directly to Sendmail. For example, to restart Sendmail you could enter the following command:

```
kill -HUP 'head -1 /var/run/sendmail.pid'
```

The `head -1 /var/run/sendmail.pid` command that is enclosed in single quotes is processed by the shell first. On our sample Linux system, the first line of the `sendmail.pid` file contains the PID 542. That is combined with the shell's `kill` command and then is processed as `kill -HUP 542`.

Signals, boot scripts, and everything else in this section has assumed that you have Sendmail already installed in your system. In the next section, we look at how to install Sendmail if you don't already have it or if you want to upgrade to the latest release.

# Installing Sendmail

Sendmail is delivered with every major Linux distribution, and it is normally installed as part of the initial Linux installation. If it is not installed at that time, it can easily be added later using one of the package-management systems available for Linux.

To simplify the task of adding and deleting software on a running server, most Linux vendors have developed package-management systems. Slackware installs software from traditional tar files, but Debian and Red Hat have developed full-blown package-management systems. Debian and systems such as Corel that are based on Debian use the dpkg system. Most other Linux distributions use the Red Hat Package Manager (RPM). RPM is the most widely used package manager and the one this book covers in greatest detail. But before getting into RPM, let's take a quick look at the Debian package manager.

## Installing Sendmail with *dpkg*

Locating a binary package in the correct format is the first step in installing a new software package with any package manager. Debian packages are found at `www.debian.org/distrib/packages`. These packages are intended for installation on the current Debian distribution but will usually work on any Debian-based release, such as Corel Linux.

After locating the upgrade package, use the dpkg command to remove the old software. Remove the currently installed Sendmail package with the following command:

```
[root]# dpkg -r sendmail
```

Next, use the dpkg command to install the new Debian package. For example, to install Sendmail 8.9.3 you would enter the following:

```
[root]# dpkg -i sendmail-wide_8.9.3+3.2W-20.deb
```

---

**NOTE**   As of this writing, 8.9.3 is the most recent version of Sendmail available as a Debian package.

---

These dpkg examples are simple and clean. As we'll see in the discussion of RPM, package installations are not always this simple.

## Locating RPM Software

To install Sendmail with RPM, you need to locate an updated Sendmail RPM package. If you failed to install Sendmail during the initial Linux installation and you just want to correct that oversight, you'll find the Sendmail RPM on the Linux CD-ROM. If you want to upgrade an existing installation, you need to search for the latest RPM packages.

www.sendmail.org provides the source code distribution of Sendmail, but RPM packages are not available from www.sendmail.org. To find RPM packages, go to your Linux vendor and to www.rpmfind.net.

### Searching a Vendor Web Site

Because e-mail service is so important, all of the major Linux vendors make an effort to update their version of Sendmail when a critical bug is fixed or a major new feature is added. So a good place to start looking for updates is at your vendor's Web site.

Figure 3.4 shows the Red Hat Web site. Just like the Debian site, it contains a search page that lets you search for a binary package. In Figure 3.4, we ask Red Hat to list all of the available Sendmail RPM packages.

The search produces several matches. At this writing, the latest version of Sendmail available as an RPM is 8.11.0, which is the version of Sendmail used in the rest of this chapter. The packages returned by a search can be downloaded simply by clicking the name of the package and selecting an appropriate mirror server.

Searching the vendor site will probably provide the RPM package you need. However, I prefer a wider search that checks all of the sources of RPM packages to ensure that I don't miss the newest updates.

**Figure 3.4**    The Red Hat RPM search engine

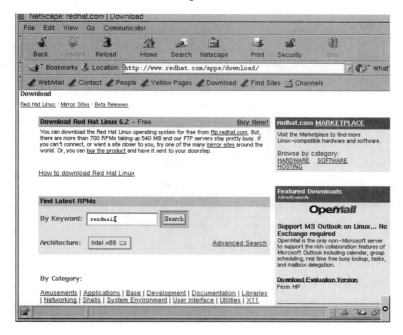

## Using *rpmfind.net* to Locate Sendmail Software

Vendors are not the only ones who make RPM packages available on the Net. To search a wide variety of RPM sources, go to `www.rpmfind.net`. Figure 3.5 shows the `www.rpmfind.net` Web site, which lists several Sendmail RPM packages.

The Web page in Figure 3.5 is the RPM repository database indexed alphabetically by name. The database is also indexed by distribution, by vendor, and by time of creation, if those things are helpful for your particular search. In this case, we are looking for Sendmail, so we just jump to "s" in the alphabetic listing.

Our sample Linux system is running Sendmail 8.9.3. Figure 3.5 shows that there are several newer Sendmail RPM packages available, with the newest being Sendmail 8.11.0-1. This particular Sendmail update contains three RPM packages:

- `sendmail-cf-8.11.0-1` contains the Sendmail configuration files, including the `cf` directory used extensively in this text.
- `sendmail-doc-8.11.0-1` contains the Sendmail documentation.
- `sendmail-8.11.0-1` is the heart of the system, including the Sendmail program.

**Figure 3.5**   The rpmfind Web site

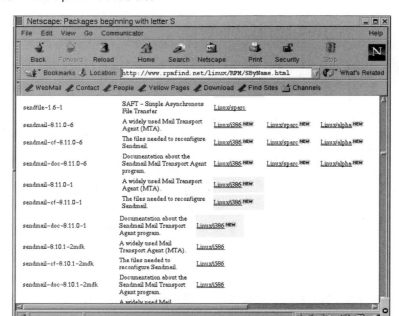

Following the links from the page shown in Figure 3.5 will lead you to detailed information about each package and a link from which the package can be downloaded. All three of the packages should be downloaded. These are the RPM packages that you'll install later in this chapter.

---

**WARNING**   Installing an RPM from an unknown source could compromise your system's security. Only use RPMs from sources you trust, such as the Linux vendor.

### Using Anonymous FTP to Download an RPM

RPM packages are also available via anonymous FTP. I prefer the Web because I can search through many packages stored at a wide variety of locations, but if you know where the package you want is located, FTP can be faster. The same packages shown in Figure 3.5 can be retrieved via anonymous FTP using the procedure shown in Listing 3.6.

**Listing 3.6**   Downloading the Sendmail RPM File

```
[craig]$ ftp rpmfind.net
Connected to rpmfind.net.
220 rpmfind.net FTP server ready.
User (rpmfind.net:(craig)): anonymous
331 Anonymous login ok, use your complete e-mail address as password.
Password:
230 Anonymous access granted, restrictions apply.
ftp> cd linux/contrib/libc6/i386
250 CWD command successful.
ftp> bin
200 Type set to I.
ftp> mget sendmail*8.11.0-1*
200 Type set to I.
mget sendmail-8.11.0-1.i386.rpm? y
200 PORT command successful.
150 Opening BINARY connection for sendmail-8.11.0-1.i386.rpm (259698 bytes)
226 Transfer complete.
ftp: 259698 bytes received in 2.63Seconds 98.74Kbytes/sec.
mget sendmail-cf-8.11.0-1.i386.rpm? y
200 PORT command successful.
150 Opening BINARY connection for sendmail-cf-8.11.0-1.i386.rpm
   (221066 bytes)
226 Transfer complete.
ftp: 221066 bytes received in 1.76Seconds 125.61Kbytes/sec.
mget sendmail-doc-8.11.0-1.i386.rpm? y
200 PORT command successful.
150 Opening BINARY connection for sendmail-doc-8.11.0-1.i386.rpm
   (482213 bytes)
226 Transfer complete.
ftp: 482213 bytes received in 4.56Seconds 105.75Kbytes/sec.
ftp> quit
221 Goodbye.
```

In this example, user input is shown in bold. The example has been edited to better fit on a book page, but is essentially what you would see if you performed this download.

In Listing 3.6 we log on to rpmfind.net with FTP. In this particular case, the files we want are in the linux/contrib/libc6/i386 directory. The FTP mget command is used to retrieve all three files relating to Sendmail 8.11. Quick and easy—but only if you know where the files are located and exactly what RPM files you're looking for.

## Installing Sendmail with RPM

Once the package is located, it can be installed using the `rpm` command. The `rpm` command is similar to the Debian `dpkg` command. It allows you to check the status of installed packages, remove outdated packages, and install updates.

Use the `rpm` command with the -q option or the --query option to check what packages are already installed in the system.

```
[craig]$ rpm --query sendmail
sendmail-8.9.3-10
```

This example queries `rpm` for the string `sendmail`. The response shows that Sendmail version 8.9.3 is installed on our sample system. At the time of this writing, the latest RPM version of Sendmail available from `www.rpmfind.net` and `www.redhat.com` is 8.11, so we decide to upgrade the sample system.

Before installing a new version of an RPM package, you can remove the old one by running `rpm` with the --erase option. (See the section "Cleaning Up After RPM" later in this chapter for an example of this.) Removing the old Sendmail RPM package is probably a good idea if you plan to compile and install the Sendmail program from the source code distribution. But if you plan to install a new RPM version of Sendmail, removing the old package is unnecessary. Use the -U option with the `rpm` command, as shown in Listing 3.7, to update an existing RPM installation with a newer package.

**Listing 3.7**   Updating Sendmail with RPM

```
[root]# rpm -U sendmail-doc-8.11.0-1.i386.rpm
[root]# rpm -U sendmail-cf-8.11.0-1.i386.rpm
[root]# rpm -U sendmail-8.11.0-1.i386.rpm
error: failed dependencies:
        openssl is needed by sendmail-8.11.0-1
        libsfio is needed by sendmail-8.11.0-1
        libcrypto.so.0 is needed by sendmail-8.11.0-1
        libsasl.so.7 is needed by sendmail-8.11.0-1
        libsfio.so is needed by sendmail-8.11.0-1
        libssl.so.0 is needed by sendmail-8.11.0-1
```

The Sendmail 8.11 package is composed of three components: the documents, the configuration files, and Sendmail itself. In Listing 3.7 the documents and configuration file components install without a hitch. The third component, however, fails to install. RPM informs us that several pieces of software required by Sendmail 8.11 are not available on this sample system. RPM calls required software *dependencies*. Sometimes other software depends on the package you're installing or removing, and sometimes the software you're installing depends on other software.

This is the worst-case scenario. We had hoped everything would be easy sailing. Now we need to track down all of the packages needed by Sendmail 8.11, install those packages, and then attempt to install sendmail-8.11.0-1.i386.rpm all over again. This bit of unpleasantness is a blessing in disguise. If we installed Sendmail 8.11 from source code and did not know that openssl and libsfio are required, some of the features of Sendmail would not work as advertised. It could take a long time tracking down the underlying problem. RPM makes sure that we know about the problem right from the start. We could force RPM to install sendmail-8.11.0-1.i386.rpm without the dependencies by adding the --nodeps argument to the rpm command line. But that's just asking for trouble. The best thing to do is track down and install the required packages.

A search of www.rpmfind.net informs us that we need three different RPM packages to fix the six dependencies: openssl-0.9.5a-1.i386.rpm, libsfio-1999-1.i386.rpm, and cyrus-sasl-1.5.11-2.i386.rpm. The first two packages, openssl and libsfio, are pretty obvious because RPM lists them as the first two dependencies needed by sendmail-8.11.0-1.i386.rpm. An examination of the list of files provided by each package shows that they provide every dependency except libsasl.so.7. A search for libsasl.so.7 tells us that it is found in cyrus-sasl-1.5.11-2.i386.rpm. We download the three packages and install them as shown in Listing 3.8.

**Listing 3.8**   Fixing Dependency Problems for Sendmail 8.11

```
[root]# rpm -i openssl-0.9.5a-1.i386.rpm
error: file /usr/man/man1/passwd.1 from install of openssl-0.9.5a-1
       conflicts with file from package passwd-0.58-1
[root]# rpm -i --replacefiles openssl-0.9.5a-1.i386.rpm
[root]# rpm -i libsfio-1999-1.i386.rpm
[root]# rpm -i cyrus-sasl-1.5.11-2.i386.rpm
[root]# rpm -U sendmail-8.11.0-1.i386.rpm
[root]# rpm -q sendmail
sendmail-8.11.0-1
```

Even this installation didn't go completely perfectly. The openssl-0.9.5a-1.i386.rpm package creates a new passwd man page. The problem is, it doesn't own the old page. That page was put on the system by the passwd-0.58-1.i386.rpm package. RPM won't let a new package change a file that belongs to another package unless you tell it to. In this case, we want the new passwd documentation so we use the --replacefiles argument with the rpm command to replace the old passwd documentation with the new documentation.

All of the other installations run smoothly. Once the dependencies are resolved, sendmail-8.11.0-1.i386.rpm installs without complaint. A quick query to RPM shows that the new package is in place.

Next, restart Sendmail to make sure that the newly installed daemon is running, and run a quick test to make sure the new daemon is alive and servicing the SMTP port. Listing 3.9 shows these two commands.

**Listing 3.9**   Restarting and Testing Sendmail

```
[root]# /etc/rc.d/init.d/sendmail restart
Shutting down sendmail:                                    [  OK  ]
Starting sendmail:                                         [  OK  ]
[root]# telnet localhost 25
Trying 127.0.0.1...
Connected to localhost.
Escape character is '^]'.
220 wren.foobirds.org ESMTP Sendmail 8.11.0/8.11.0;
    Sun, 13 Aug 2000 18:00:03 -0400
quit
221 2.0.0 wren.foobirds.org closing connection
Connection closed by foreign host.
```

As Listing 3.9 shows, Sendmail 8.11 is installed and running. Despite all of the problems encountered in this installation, Sendmail is upgraded and running after fewer than a dozen commands. Linux package managers have done much to simplify upgrades.

---

**NOTE**   I have never had a problem with dependencies upgrading Sendmail before version 8.11. This just turned out to be a lucky break. Normally, things go so smoothly when preparing examples for Linux books that problems have to be described without actual examples. This time we were lucky enough to have a real problem. You might never see dependency problems when installing Sendmail yourself, but it is good to know how they are resolved.

---

## X Tools for Installing Sendmail

In the previous section, we used the command-line version of rpm. It is easy to use, easy to explain, and it runs on most Linux systems—even those that don't have X Windows running. But if you are using X Windows, there are some graphical tools for running the Red Hat Package Manager. Several systems use a tool named glint. Systems with the KDE desktop environment use a tool named kpackage, and systems with the GNOME desktop environment use a tool called gnorpm. Figure 3.6 shows gnorpm running on a Red Hat 6 system.

**Figure 3.6**    Installing Sendmail with gnorpm

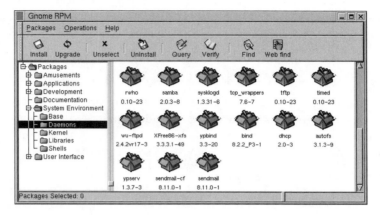

Understanding gnorpm is easy once you understand the rpm command. The icons near the top of the window clearly parallel the -U (upgrade), -q (query), -V (verify), and -e (uninstall) command-line options. Simply highlight the package you're interested in and select the action you want to take. Figure 3.6 shows the test system after Sendmail was upgraded.

Even without GUI tools, it is simpler to upgrade an existing RPM package with a new one than it is to delete the package and replace it with software you compile yourself, for a couple of reasons:

- First, using the rpm command is easier than compiling software.
- Second, the features of rpm, such as pointing out dependencies and verifying the integrity of the software, are unavailable if you don't use rpm.

But the latest software is not always available as a binary package. The Debian example in this chapter illustrates that. Sometimes you must compile your own version of Sendmail from the source code to get the latest release. Compiling Sendmail is the next topic of this chapter.

## Cleaning Up After RPM

We need to digress for a moment from the basics of upgrading with RPM. If you have RPM and your current Sendmail was installed via RPM, you should upgrade with RPM.

Take advantage of the tools your Linux system offers. However, if you are forced to upgrade with source code a system that was originally installed via RPM, you should clean out the RPM installation before upgrading.

The next section describes downloading and compiling the latest Sendmail source code. Before installing a new version of Sendmail that you have downloaded and compiled, remove the old RPM version with the `--erase` option, as in this example:

```
[root]# rpm --erase --nodeps sendmail-cf-8.9.3-1
[root]# rpm --erase --nodeps sendmail-8.9.3-1
```

The `--nodeps` option is added to this command line to force `rpm` to erase the Sendmail software, even though other packages are dependent on it. Attempting to erase Sendmail without using the `--nodeps` option displays an error message stating that other software depends on Sendmail, and it is not removed, as shown below.

```
[root]# rpm --erase sendmail
removing these packages would break dependencies:
        sendmail is needed by sendmail-cf-8.9.3-1
```

Failing to remove the Sendmail RPM package before installing a non-RPM version, such as a version that you compile yourself, means that the system will still think the old RPM version is installed. An `rpm --query` will continue to report the old Sendmail version number. If the -V option is used to verify the Sendmail RPM package, it may report false and misleading errors. Here is an example of what can happen when the components of Sendmail are changed or upgraded without using RPM and then are verified by the `rpm` command:

```
[craig]$ rpm -V sendmail
S.5....Tc   /etc/aliases
missing     /etc/rc.d/rc2.d/S80sendmail
S.5....T    /var/log/sendmail.st
```

The -V option prints out a line for each file in the package that fails verification. Values are printed at the beginning of the line to indicate which tests were failed. Each letter or number indicates a failure and each dot indicates a test that was passed. The possible values are as follows:

S   indicates that the file has the wrong file size.

M   indicates that the file is assigned the wrong file permissions or file type.

5   indicates that the file has an incorrect MD5 checksum.

D   indicates that the file is located on the wrong device.

L   indicates that the file is improperly a symbolic link.

U   indicates that the file has the wrong user ID (UID) assigned.

G   indicates that the file has the wrong group ID (GID) assigned.

T   indicates that the file has the wrong file creation time.

C   indicates that the file is a configuration file that is expected to change.

In the previous example, two files have the wrong checksum and the wrong creation date, and they are the wrong size. These are all things you would expect because these are not the original files. They are files that were installed over the original files. The file that is missing is the S80sendmail script we deleted in Listing 3.3. All of the other files associated with the Sendmail RPM check out fine. But even these three errors might set off alarm bells with the system's computer security officer. For this reason, clean out the RPM installation before installing Sendmail from source code as described in the following section.

# Downloading and Compiling Sendmail

Even if your Linux system comes with its own version of Sendmail, obtaining the latest Sendmail source code distribution provides useful documentation, tools, and sample configuration files. Additionally, there are times when you need a security fix or update and the latest version of Sendmail has not yet been posted as an RPM or other binary distribution.

The latest Sendmail distribution is available via anonymous FTP from ftp.sendmail.org, where it is stored in the pub/sendmail directory. When you change to that directory, an informational message is displayed that tells you about the latest version of Sendmail. New releases are constantly being created. The following examples are based on Sendmail V8.11.0.

> **NOTE**  Remember that things will change for future releases, so always review the readme files and installation documents that come with new software before beginning an installation.

To compile the Sendmail program, download the compressed tar file as a binary file and then uncompress and extract it with the tar command, as shown in Listing 3.10.

**Listing 3.10**  Downloading the Sendmail Source Code

```
[craig]$ ftp ftp.sendmail.org
Connected to ftp.sendmail.org.
```

```
220 pub2.pa.vix.com FTP server ready.
Name (ftp.sendmail.org:craig): anonymous
331 Guest login ok, send your e-mail address as password.
Password:
230 Guest login ok, access restrictions apply.
Remote system type is UNIX.
Using binary mode to transfer files.
ftp> cd pub/sendmail
ftp> get sendmail.8.11.0.tar.gz
local: sendmail.8.11.0.tar.gz remote: sendmail.8.11.0.tar.gz
200 PORT command successful.
150 Opening BINARY mode data connection for sendmail.8.11.0.tar.gz
    (1307858 bytes).
226 Transfer complete.
1307858 bytes received in 26 secs (50 Kbytes/sec)
ftp> quit
221-You have transferred 1307858 bytes in 1 files.
221-Thank you for using the FTP service on pub2.pa.vix.com.
221 Goodbye.
[craig]$ cd /usr/local/src
[craig]$ tar -zxvf /home/craig/sendmail.8.11.0.tar.gz
```

Next, change to the sendmail-8.11.0 directory created by the tar file, and use the Build script to compile the new Sendmail program, as shown in Listing 3.11.

**Listing 3.11**    Compiling Sendmail with the Build Command

```
[craig]$ cd sendmail-8.11.0
[craig]$ ./Build
Making all in:
/usr/local/src/sendmail-8.11.0/libsmutil
Configuration: pfx=, os=Linux, rel=2.2.10, rbase=2, rroot=2.2,
    arch=i586, sfx=, variant=optimized
Using M4=/usr/bin/m4
Creating ../obj.Linux.2.2.10.i586/libsmutil using ../devtools/OS/Linux
Making dependencies in ../obj.Linux.2.2.10.i586/libsmutil
make[1]: Entering directory
    `/usr/local/src/sendmail-8.11.0/obj.Linux.2.2.10.i586/libsmutil'
cc -M -I. -I../../sendmail -I../../include -DNEWDB
    -DNOT_SENDMAIL debug.c
errstring.c lockfile.c safefile.c snprintf.c strl.c    >> Makefile
make[1]: Leaving directory
    `/usr/local/src/sendmail-8.11.0/obj.Linux.2.2.10.i586/libsmutil'
```

```
Making in ../obj.Linux.2.2.10.i586/libsmutil
make[1]: Entering directory
      `/usr/local/src/sendmail-8.11.0/obj.Linux.2.2.10.i586/libsmutil'
cc -O -I. -I../../sendmail -I../../include -DNEWDB
      -DNOT_SENDMAIL -c debug.c -o debug.o
cc -O -I. -I../../sendmail -I../../include -DNEWDB
      -DNOT_SENDMAIL -c errstring.c -o errstring.o
... Many, many, many lines deleted...
cc -O -I. -I../../sendmail -I../../include -DNEWDB
      -DNOT_SENDMAIL -c vacation.c -o vacation.o
cc -o vacation    vacation.o ../libsmdb/libsmdb.a
      ../libsmutil/libsmutil.a -ldb -lresolv -lcrypt -lnsl -ldl
groff -Tascii -man vacation.1 > vacation.0 ||
      cp vacation.0.dist vacation.0
make[1]: Leaving directory
      `/usr/local/src/sendmail-8.11.0/obj.Linux.2.2.10.i586/vacation'
```

Build detects the architecture of the system and builds the correct Makefile for your system. It then compiles Sendmail using the newly created Makefile.

According to the documentation, running Build is all you need to do on most systems to compile Sendmail. It certainly works on Caldera Linux systems, as this example illustrates. However, the installation notes warn of several possible problems that can occur with some Linux systems, which are described in the next section, "Known Problems."

Once Sendmail compiles, it is installed by using the Build command with the install option (see Listing 3.12).

**Listing 3.12**   Installing the New Sendmail Binaries

```
# ./Build install
Making all in:
/usr/local/src/sendmail-8.11.0/libsmutil
Configuration: pfx=, os=Linux, rel=2.2.10, rbase=2, rroot=2.2,
      arch=i586, sfx=, variant=optimized
Making in ../obj.Linux.2.2.10.i586/libsmutil
make[1]: Entering directory
      `/usr/local/src/sendmail-8.11.0/obj.Linux.2.2.10.i586/libsmutil'
... Many, many, many lines deleted...
Making in ../obj.Linux.2.2.10.i586/vacation
make[1]: Entering directory
      `/usr/local/src/sendmail-8.11.0/obj.Linux.2.2.10.i586/vacation'
install -c -o bin -g bin -m 555 vacation /usr/bin
```

```
install -c -o bin -g bin -m 444 vacation.0 /usr/man/man1/vacation.1
make[1]: Leaving directory
        `/usr/local/src/sendmail-8.11.0/obj.Linux.2.2.10.i586/vacation'
```

The Build command installs the man pages in the /usr/man directory and the executables in /usr/sbin and /usr/bin. It installs the help file (sendmail.hf) and the status file (sendmail.st) in /etc/mail.

## Known Problems

The Sendmail documentation lists some problems that are known to affect compilation on Linux systems. The problems fall into several categories ranging from compiler problems to kernel problems.

Two problems relate to GNU tools that are commonly used on Linux systems. One is an incompatibility detected between GDBM and Sendmail 8.8. Later versions of Sendmail improved the heuristic to detect GDBM so that the Sendmail code can adapt to GDBM. The Sendmail release notes suggest using Berkeley DB instead of GDBM.

The other GNU problem is with the gcc compiler. Old versions of gcc, versions 2.4 and 2.5, cannot be used to compile Sendmail with the compiler optimization (-O) option set. This was fixed when version 2.6 was released. The Caldera system used to generate the example in Listing 3.10 uses the Experimental GNU Compiler Suite version 2.91, which is a follow-on to gcc.

Several problems are described that existed with very old kernels (pre–version 1.0), very old versions of libc (pre–version 4.7), and a very old version of the BIND domain name software (version 4.9.3). No one should currently be running any of this old software.

The Sendmail documentation also reports problems that relate to having previously compiled BIND on your system. The symptoms of this problem are unresolved references during the link phase of the Sendmail compile. If you have compiled BIND from source code on your system and BIND wrote header files in /usr/local/lib and /usr/local/include, these files may cause problems when Sendmail is compiled. The documentation suggests adding -lresolv to LIBS in the Sendmail Makefile to avoid this problem.

Finally, the documentation mentions problems with Linux kernel 2.2.0. This is the most worrisome of the problems reported because the documentation does not provide a workaround for this problem. I have never personally seen this problem, but if I did, I would upgrade the Linux kernel to the highest patch.

Frankly, none of the problems described in the Sendmail installation notes has ever struck any Linux system that I have worked with. A far more common occurrence is for something to change in the new distribution that makes your old configuration obsolete. We look at that challenge next.

## Configuration Compatibility

New versions of Sendmail can change things that make the old configuration incompatible with the new Sendmail program. Watch for these changes and adjust the configuration when they arise.

The /etc/mail directory is a new default location used by Sendmail version 8.11. The Build install command placed the help file and the status file in this new directory, but the help file and the status file locations are also defined in the Sendmail configuration file. If the files are not in the locations your mail server configuration expects, you can do one of two things:

- Simply move the files to the locations that you desire.

- Change the Sendmail configuration to point to /etc/mail for these files. This is the default location expected by Sendmail 8.11, so using these locations actually means removing the define macros that point to the "non-standard" locations for these files. Using the default locations means that you will have a simpler configuration file. See Chapter 5, "Understanding a Vendor's Configuration," for more information about the define macros used to specify file locations.

Regardless of what you do, the physical location of the files and the location of the files defined in the configuration must agree.

Sendmail 8.11 has also changed the location of the Sendmail configuration file (sendmail.cf). Traditionally, the file was located in the /etc directory, and that is where it is found on most Linux systems. Sendmail 8.11 uses the new /etc/mail directory for the sendmail.cf file. Attempting to run the newly compiled Sendmail binary on the sample system will fail, because Caldera keeps the sendmail.cf file in the /etc directory and Sendmail 8.11 is looking for it in the /etc/mail directory. A simple test shows this:

```
[root]# sendmail -v -t
/etc/mail/sendmail.cf: line 0: cannot open: No such file or directory
```

This needs to be fixed, and again you can either move the file or change the configuration. To change the configuration, provide the sendmail command with the correct path to the configuration file by using the -C command-line option—for example, sendmail -C/etc/sendmail.cf. The Sendmail start-up script must also be edited to insert this command-line option so that the correct configuration file is used every time the system reboots. Frankly, this is more trouble than it is worth. Just move the sendmail.cf file to /etc/mail. It is simpler and better because other newly installed mail tools might be looking for the sendmail.cf file at the new default location.

One other thing that should be checked before declaring the installation complete is the `sendmail.cf` file. New versions of Sendmail may add new configuration syntax that makes the older configuration files incompatible with the new release. The Sendmail program checks the version (V) command inside the `sendmail.cf` file to indicate the level of the configuration syntax. The easiest way to check compatibility is to use the `sendmail` command to send a piece of test mail:

```
[root]# sendmail -v -t -C/etc/sendmail.cf
Warning: .cf file is out of date: sendmail 8.11.0 supports
        version 9, .cf file is version 8
^D
No recipient addresses found in header
```

Running `sendmail` with the -v option tells the program to provide verbose messages, which is just what you want when you're testing. The -t option tells Sendmail that the mail will be typed in at the console. In this case, I immediately terminate the session with a Ctrl+D (which is what the ^D illustrates), because I don't want to send mail, I just want to see the warning message. The new Sendmail program complains about the version level of the configuration file. In this particular case, mail would not be delivered successfully because too much has changed between Sendmail 8.9 and 8.11. This is not always the case. Sometimes you can force mail through an old configuration. But you shouldn't.

This example shows that this configuration is not compatible with the new release. To solve this incompatibility, you need to rebuild your configuration. Understanding basic Sendmail configuration and building your own custom configuration is the topic of Part 2 of this book.

# In Sum

Sendmail runs in two different modes to handle outbound and inbound mail. Sendmail is started in real time to handle individual pieces of outbound mail, but runs as a daemon to collect inbound mail. There are several tools that help you control which systems run the Sendmail daemon as part of their start-up.

Before the Sendmail program can be run, it must be properly installed. Sendmail can be installed using a Linux package manager or compiled from source. Despite the complexity of Sendmail, it is installed in the same manner as all other Linux packages, and the same tools are used to control the Sendmail start-up process as are used with any other Linux start-up process. Installing and running Sendmail are two tasks that don't have any special complexity. If you know how to install and run Linux processes, you know how to install and run Sendmail on a Linux system.

Once installed, Sendmail must be configured. Configuring Sendmail is the topic of Part 2, which starts with Chapter 4, "Creating a Basic Sendmail Configuration."

# Part 2

# Essential Configuration

**Featuring:**

- Where the Sendmail m4 directories and files are located and what they do
- Understanding the basic m4 macro language
- How to build `sendmail.cf` with m4
- What the `generic-linux.mc` file contains and what it does
- Understanding the Linux OSTYPE file
- Understanding the generic DOMAIN file and how to modify it
- Analyzing and improving the Red Hat configuration
- How to add database support to your Sendmail program and its configuration
- The role of the `local-host-names` file and the `relay-domains` file
- Uses for the `aliases` database, the user database, and the `genericstable`
- The syntax and structure of the `access` database
- Uses for the `virtusertable` and the `mailertable`

# 4

# Creating a Basic Sendmail Configuration

**A**t the conclusion of the last chapter, we compiled Sendmail 8.11 from the source code distribution. Much to our dismay, we discovered that the new Sendmail program would not run even after the sendmail.cf configuration file was moved to the /etc/mail directory where the new Sendmail expected to find it. Sendmail 8.11 complained that the sendmail.cf file provided with the Linux distribution was an older version that was not compatible with the new software release. The solution to this problem is to build a new sendmail.cf file that is compatible with the new software, and in this chapter that is just what we do.

Building a new Sendmail configuration, even a very basic one, is a multi-step process. The sendmail.cf configuration file is built from m4 macros. To build your own configuration, you must

- Locate the correct m4 macro libraries and files
- Have a basic understanding of the m4 macro language
- Select an appropriate macro configuration file
- Modify the file as necessary
- Process your newly created macro configuration file through the m4 macro processor

This chapter covers all of these steps while building a very basic configuration file that solves the incompatibility problem encountered when we upgraded to Sendmail 8.11 using the source code distribution. Remember that in Chapter 3, "Running Sendmail," we installed Sendmail under Linux in two different ways. Before we compiled and installed Sendmail from source code, we installed it using RPM. A few problems emerged during the RPM installation, but once the installation completed successfully everything was ready to run. There was no compatibility problem, and thus no reason to build a simple configuration to solve a compatibility problem.

However, even if you use RPM to install Sendmail, the topics covered in this chapter will be useful to you. Building this simple configuration provides an introduction to m4 and provides the basis for understanding more complex configurations. We build on this simple configuration in later chapters to create a more robust, customized configuration suitable for a production e-mail server. This foundation is useful for all Sendmail administrators, whether or not you use RPM. Let's begin by locating the m4 macro language source files provided with the Sendmail distribution.

# The *cf* Directory Structure

m4 is a general-purpose macro processor. It has a wide variety of uses and is not specifically intended for Sendmail configuration. m4 macro definitions have been built by the people who maintain Sendmail in order to allow us to create a Sendmail configuration with m4.

The Sendmail distribution contains the m4 source files needed to build the sendmail.cf file. These source files are found in the cf directory located under the top directory created by the Sendmail distribution tar file. The top directory created by the tar file always has a name based on the Sendmail distribution's version number. The format of this directory name is sendmail-*version*, where *version* is the version number. Thus the tar file for Sendmail 8.11.0 creates a top directory named sendmail-8.11.0, and the configuration files for that release are found in sendmail-8.11.0/cf. All this, of course, is relative to the directory in which you restore the tar file. In Chapter 3, we restored the tar file in /usr/local/src, so the complete path to the configuration files on our sample system is /usr/local/src/sendmail-8.11.0/cf. A listing of that directory shows 10 entries.

```
[craig]$ ls /usr/local/src/sendmail-8.11.0/cf
README  cf  domain  feature  hack  m4  mailer  ostype  sh  siteconfig
```

The cf directory contains a README file and nine subdirectories. The README file provides useful documentation on the m4 language and how that language is used to build a sendmail.cf file. Always check this file for the latest changes and the newest features.

As you'll see later, the names of most of the subdirectories (domain, feature, hack, mailer, ostype, and siteconfig) are clearly identifiable as the names of m4 macro commands used to build a Sendmail configuration. Only the cf, m4, and sh directories do not share names with m4 macros. All of the directories, however, are worth exploring.

---

**The *sendmail-cf* RPM Files**

In this chapter, the cf directory and its subdirectories are described as part of the Sendmail source code distribution. These same files, however, are available as part of an RPM installation. In Chapter 3, we installed the RPM version of the cf directory. It was the RPM package identified as sendmail-cf-8.11.0-1.i386.rpm. It contains all of the files that are described in this chapter. The only difference is the location of the files. To find out where the files are stored, run an rpm query and ask for a file listing as follows:

```
[craig]$ rpm -q -l sendmail-cf
```

On our sample Red Hat system, this command shows that the cf directory is named /usr/lib/sendmail-cf. A listing of /usr/lib/sendmail-cf shows the following:

```
[craig]$ ls /usr/lib/sendmail-cf
```

```
README  cf  domain  feature  hack  m4  mailer  ostype  sh
siteconfig
```

Thus, if you're using an RPM installation, /usr/lib/sendmail-cf is equivalent to cf in these discussions. The same README file and the same nine subdirectories appear in /usr/lib/sendmail-cf on an RPM installation as appear in cf on a source code installation. Everything covered in this chapter applies regardless of how you installed Sendmail 8.11.

---

## Little-Used Directories

Three of the directories (hack, sh, and siteconfig) in the cf directory have very little use for most configurations. For two of these directories, this lack of use directly relates to the lack of utility of the macro commands that they represent.

The cf/hack directory holds m4 source files built by the local system administrator to solve temporary Sendmail configuration problems. Temporary code fixes are called *hacks*, thus the name for this directory and the command that uses it. The HACK command is almost never used, and thus the `hack` directory is almost never used. An `ls` of the `hack` directory shows that it contains just one file.

```
[craig]$ ls hack
cssubdomain.m4
```

The one file contained in the `hack` directory is an old fix that was used for a few months at Berkeley to handle a domain name transition. The file is there only as an example. It could not be used by anyone but Berkeley and it is no longer of any use to them. Even the domain name transition handled by this hack could now be handled more easily with the database features built into the current Sendmail. The `hack` directory and `HACK` command are still there, but there is simply no good reason to use them.

The `cf/siteconfig` directory contains files that define the UUCP connectivity for the mail server. The files list the locally connected UUCP sites using a specific `sendmail` m4 syntax. The `siteconfig` directory contains four sample files.

```
[craig]$ ls siteconfig
uucp.cogsci.m4   uucp.old.arpa.m4   uucp.ucbarpa.m4   uucp.ucbvax.m4
```

The `siteconfig` directory and the `SITECONFIG` command are still maintained for backward compatibility. However, this directory is obsolete and should no longer be used to define the UUCP connectivity for a UUCP mail server. Use the Sendmail databases described in Chapter 6, "Using Sendmail Databases," if you need to define UUCP connectivity.

The last little-used directory does not even map to an `m4` macro command. It is the `cf/sh` directory and it contains only one file.

```
[craig]$ ls -l sh
total 2
-rw-r--r--   1 craig   users     1128 Feb  7 1999 makeinfo.sh
```

Even the name of this file is different. All of the files we have seen so far are `m4` macro source files. As such, they all end with the `.m4` extension. This file, however, ends with the `.sh` extension, indicating that it is a shell script. The permission bits show that, even though it is a shell script, it is not executable. So it is probably not being used. Still, I'm curious. So I changed the permissions and ran the script.

```
[root]# chmod 744 makeinfo.sh
[root]# ./makeinfo.sh
```

```
##### built by root@ibis.foobirds.org on Thu Aug 17 09:36:03 EDT 2000
##### in /usr/local/src/sendmail-8.11.0/cf/sh
##### using as configuration include directory
define(`__HOST__', ibis.foobirds.org)dnl
```

The script produces three lines of comments that could be used to identify who built the sendmail.cf file, when they built it, and in what directory. The third line includes the name of the configuration directory when this is actually run by m4. The last line of output assigns a value to a variable. Of course, you don't really run this script. As I said, I was just curious. The script is used by the m4 process when it builds the sendmail.cf file. You never use this script directly, and you never use this directory to store any of your own configuration files.

## The *domain* Directory

The cf/domain directory is one of the directories where you are most likely to store your own configuration files. The purpose of the domain directory is to hold m4 source files that define configuration values that are specific to your domain or network. The configuration file you create for your environment is then used in the macro configuration file via the DOMAIN command. Because the intent is for you to create your own file, the six files shown when you ls the domain directory are all just examples.

```
[craig]$ ls domain
Berkeley.EDU.m4       EECS.Berkeley.EDU.m4   berkeley-only.m4
CS.Berkeley.EDU.m4    S2K.Berkeley.EDU.m4    generic.m4
```

When you create your own domain configuration file, start by copying the sample file generic.m4 to a name that is meaningful for your domain or network. For example, if your domain is foobirds.org you might copy generic.m4 to foobirds.m4. Then edit the new file to set the values needed for your environment.

Creating your own domain file is an advanced configuration topic covered in later chapters. Basic configurations do not require a custom domain file.

## The *cf* Subdirectory

Most of the work creating a basic configuration takes place in the cf/cf directory. This is the working directory of Sendmail configuration. It contains all of the macro configuration files, and it is where you will put your own macro configuration file when you build a custom configuration. Listing 4.1 shows that the cf/cf directory contains more than 40 files.

Essential Configuration

PART 2

**Listing 4.1**  Contents of the cf/cf Subdirectory

```
[craig]$ cd /usr/local/src/sendmail-8.11.0/cf
[craig]$ ls cf
Build                              generic-solaris2.cf
Makefile                           generic-solaris2.mc
chez.cs.mc                         generic-sunos4.1.cf
clientproto.mc                     generic-sunos4.1.mc
cs-hpux10.mc                       generic-ultrix4.cf
cs-hpux9.mc                        generic-ultrix4.mc
cs-osf1.mc                         huginn.cs.mc
cs-solaris2.mc                     knecht.mc
cs-sunos4.1.mc                     mail.cs.mc
cs-ultrix4.mc                      mail.eecs.mc
cyrusproto.mc                      mailspool.cs.mc
generic-bsd4.4.cf                  python.cs.mc
generic-bsd4.4.mc                  s2k-osf1.mc
generic-hpux10.cf                  s2k-ultrix4.mc
generic-hpux10.mc                  tcpproto.mc
generic-hpux9.cf                   test.cf
generic-hpux9.mc                   test.mc
generic-linux.cf                   ucbarpa.mc
generic-linux.mc                   ucbvax.mc
generic-nextstep3.3.mc             uucpproto.mc
generic-osf1.cf                    vangogh.cs.mc
generic-osf1.mc
```

Most of these files—more than 30 of them—are sample macro control files. You can identify a macro control file by the .mc extension. Some are examples meant as educational tools. But most are prototypes or generic files meant to be used as the basis of your own configuration. Particularly interesting are the generic files designed for use with different operating systems. Generic files for Solaris, HPUX, BSD, Linux, and several other operating systems are included. For a Linux system administrator, the generic-linux.mc file is the one that garners the most attention.

Several of the files are identified by the .cf extension. These files are the result of processing macro configuration files through m4 and are already in the proper format to be used as the sendmail.cf file. It is unlikely, however, that you will use one of these files directly. Unless the generic macro configuration file is exactly to your liking, the Sendmail configuration file produced from that .mc file will not be what you want. For example, the problem we want to solve is the fact that the /etc/sendmail.cf file on our sample system is not compatible with Sendmail 8.11. Using the generic-linux.cf file as the sendmail.cf file might solve this problem, but as the test in Listing 4.2 shows, it doesn't work for our sample system.

**Listing 4.2**    Testing the generic-linux.cf File

```
[root]# sendmail -v -t -C /etc/sendmail.cf
Warning: .cf file is out of date: sendmail 8.11.0 supports version 9,
      .cf file is version 8
No recipient addresses found in header
^D
[root]# sendmail -v -t -C ./generic-linux.cf
./generic-linux.cf: line 66: fileclass: cannot open
      '/etc/mail/local-host-names'
: No such file or directory
```

The first sendmail test illustrates the problem we have with the old sendmail.cf file. It is version 8, and Sendmail 8.11 wants a version 9 configuration file. The second test uses the -C command-line argument to specify the generic-linux.cf file as the Sendmail configuration file. That test also fails. This time, the configuration is looking for a file named /etc/mail/local-host-names, which does not exist. We can fix the problem by creating the desired file or by simplifying the configuration so that it doesn't need that file. In this chapter we use the latter approach. (We don't cover the local-host-names file until the next chapter.)

### The *cf/cf Build* Script

New Sendmail configurations are generally built inside the cf/cf directory. Two of the files in this directory are there to aid the build process. These are the Build shell script and the Makefile it uses. Listing 4.3 shows a Sendmail configuration file being constructed with the Build script.

**Listing 4.3**    Using the cf/cf/Build Script

```
[root]# ./Build test.cf
Using M4=/usr/bin/m4
rm -f test.cf
/usr/bin/m4 ../m4/cf.m4 test.mc > test.cf ||
    ( rm -f test.cf && exit 1 )
chmod 444 test.cf
```

The Build script is easy to use. Provide the name of the output file you want to create as an argument on the Build command line. The script replaces the .cf extension of the output file with the extension .mc and uses the macro configuration file with that name to create the output file. Thus, putting `test.cf` on the `Build` command line means that `test.mc` will be used to create `test.cf`.

Despite the simplicity of the `Build` command, I never use it to build a Sendmail configuration and you probably won't either. The reason I don't use it is that the `m4` command line used to build a Sendmail configuration is also very simple. For the average Sendmail administrator, the `Build` script doesn't offer any significant advantages. The real reason the script exists in this directory is to make it simple for the people who maintain Sendmail to build several `.cf` files with one command. This helps the source code maintainers because, as we have seen, the Sendmail configuration files need to be rebuilt every time Sendmail is upgraded to keep the version number of the configuration file compatible with the version number expected by the new Sendmail system. `Build` has four special keyword arguments that construct multiple configuration files with one command:

**generic**   The `generic` keyword builds the `.cf` files for the eight generic macro configuration files. These are the only `.cf` files that normally come with the Sendmail distribution.

**berkeley**   The `berkeley` keyword builds the 16 different configuration files that were used at Berkeley. Because the Berkeley configurations are just used as examples, the `.cf` files for these configurations are not normally built.

**other**   The `other` keyword builds any configurations listed in the `$OTHER` variable of the `Makefile`. In Sendmail 8.11, there is only one configuration listed in this variable and it is not delivered as a `.cf` file.

**all**   The `all` keyword builds all of the configurations defined in the `$GENERIC`, `$BERKELEY`, and `$OTHER` variables in the `Makefile`.

If you need to build multiple configurations, it is possible to edit the `Makefile`, changing the `$OTHER` variable so that it contains the names of all of your configurations, and to then use `Build other` to create all of your configurations at one time. It's possible, but unlikely. Most Sendmail administrators do not have enough different configurations to bother with this. We won't mention `Build` again. In the rest of the book, the `m4` command is used directly to build the Sendmail configuration file.

The `cf/cf` directory and possibly the `cf/domain` directory are the only two directories to which you are likely to add configuration files. The four remaining directories are all used to build a configuration, but you use the files that are already there. It is unlikely you will add or change files in those directories.

## The *ostype* Directory

Every macro configuration file must contain an `OSTYPE` command to process a macro source file from the `cf/ostype` directory. The files in this directory define operating system–specific characteristics for the Sendmail configuration. Listing 4.4 shows the contents of the `ostype` directory.

**Listing 4.4**   The cf/ostype Directory

```
[craig]$ ls ostype
aix2.m4         bsdi2.0.m4      irix5.m4        ptx2.m4         sunos4.1.m4
aix3.m4         darwin.m4       irix6.m4        qnx.m4          svr4.m4
aix4.m4         dgux.m4         isc4.1.m4       riscos4.5.m4    ultrix4.m4
altos.m4        domainos.m4     linux.m4        sco-uw-2.1.m4   unixware7.m4
amdahl-uts.m4   dynix3.2.m4     maxion.m4       sco3.2.m4       unknown.m4
aux.m4          gnu.m4          mklinux.m4      sinix.m4        uxpds.m4
bsd4.3.m4       hpux10.m4       nextstep.m4     solaris2.m4
bsd4.4.m4       hpux11.m4       openbsd.m4      solaris2.ml.m4
bsdi.m4         hpux9.m4        osf1.m4         solaris2.pre5.m4
bsdi1.0.m4      irix4.m4        powerux.m4      sunos3.5.m4
```

The directory contains configuration files for more than 40 different operating systems. Solaris, BSD, Linux—they are all here and easily identified by name. In fact, there are many more operating system definitions in the `ostype` directory than there are generic macro configuration files in the `/cf/cf` directory. One thing that I find slightly surprising is that there is no `redhat.6.2.m4` or `slackware.7.0.m4` file. Different Linux distributions are at least as different as AIX 3 is from AIX 4, yet different Linux vendors don't create OSTYPE files. But it doesn't matter. You can start with the standard Linux OSTYPE and do all of your customization in the macro configuration file you build in the `cf/cf` directory.

## The *mailer* Directory

In addition to an OSTYPE command, every useable server configuration must have at least one MAILER command. MAILER commands process source files from the `cf/mailer` directory. Each file in the `mailer` directory contains the definition of a set of mailers. Listing 4.5 shows the mailer definition files delivered with Sendmail 8.11.

**Listing 4.5**   The Contents of the cf/mailer Directory

```
[craig]$ ls mailer
cyrus.m4    local.m4    phquery.m4  procmail.m4  smtp.m4    uucp.m4
fax.m4      mail11.m4   pop.m4      qpage.m4     usenet.m4
```

The directory contains definitions for 11 different sets of mailers, all of which are described in this text. In this chapter, we use only the two most basic sets of mailers: `local.m4` for local mail delivery and `smtp.m4` for SMTP mail delivery.

Essential Configuration

PART 2

## The *feature* Directory

The feature directory contains the m4 source code files that implement various Sendmail features. Listing 4.6 shows that there are more than 40 features available.

**Listing 4.6**   The feature Directory

```
[craig]$ ls feature
accept_unqualified_senders.m4      no_default_msa.m4
accept_unresolvable_domains.m4     nocanonify.m4
access_db.m4                       nodns.m4
allmasquerade.m4                   notsticky.m4
always_add_domain.m4               nouucp.m4
bestmx_is_local.m4                 nullclient.m4
bitdomain.m4                       promiscuous_relay.m4
blacklist_recipients.m4            rbl.m4
delay_checks.m4                    redirect.m4
dnsbl.m4                           relay_based_on_MX.m4
domaintable.m4                     relay_entire_domain.m4
generics_entire_domain.m4          relay_hosts_only.m4
genericstable.m4                   relay_local_from.m4
ldap_routing.m4                    relay_mail_from.m4
limited_masquerade.m4              smrsh.m4
local_lmtp.m4                      stickyhost.m4
local_procmail.m4                  use_ct_file.m4
loose_relay_check.m4               use_cw_file.m4
mailertable.m4                     uucpdomain.m4
masquerade_entire_domain.m4        virtuser_entire_domain.m4
masquerade_envelope.m4             virtusertable.m4
```

Describing these features and how they are used is one of the major tasks of this book.

## The *m4* Directory

The last subdirectory in the cf directory is the m4 directory. This is the directory that contains the m4 macro definitions and the sendmail.cf skeleton code needed to build a sendmail.cf configuration file. Remember that m4 is not a language designed to build Sendmail configurations. It is a general-purpose macro language. The commands you use to build a Sendmail configuration are macros defined by the Sendmail developers. This is the directory that contains the definitions of those macro commands. The cf/m4 directory contains only four files.

```
[craig]$ ls m4
cf.m4  cfhead.m4  proto.m4  version.m4
```

Two of these files are very small. The `version.m4` file just defines one `sendmail.cf` variable—the Z variable. The Z variable is assigned the Sendmail version number, which in our examples is 8.11.0. Because this value changes with each Sendmail release, it is defined in a separate file for easy maintenance.

---

**NOTE**  The Sendmail version number is not the same thing as the `sendmail.cf` version number. In these examples the Sendmail version number is 8.11.0, but the `sendmail.cf` version number is 9. The fact that both the release number and the configuration file number are called version numbers can be confusing. Furthermore, neither one of these has anything to do with the VERSIONID macro, which is just used to store configuration control information to help you to track the changes you make to your m4 macro configuration file. No wonder system administrators find Sendmail confusing!

---

The other very small file is `cf.m4`. This is an important file because it is the file specified on the m4 command line to incorporate the library of Sendmail m4 macro commands into the m4 process. The `cf.m4` file does not contain the macro definitions. Instead it includes by reference the file that does contain those macro definitions.

The m4 macros used to configure Sendmail are defined in the file `cfhead.m4`. This file includes lots of stuff, but the most important is the definition of many of the commands used to build a configuration.

The last file, `proto.m4`, is the largest. It contains raw `sendmail.cf` data exactly as it appears in the `sendmail.cf` file. The `proto.m4` file is the source of most of the content found in the `sendmail.cf` file.

The commands defined in the `cf/m4` directory and how they are used to build a configuration are the topics of the remainder of this chapter. Let's take a look at the m4 macro language used for Sendmail configuration.

# The *m4* Macro Language

The Sendmail program reads its configuration from the `sendmail.cf` file. The `sendmail.cf` file is a few hundred lines long, and every line is written in a terse syntax that is easy for Sendmail to parse but difficult for a human to read and write. As the system administrator, your job is to create the `sendmail.cf` file. Luckily, you do that not with hundreds of lines of arcane code but with a few lines of macro code.

The `sendmail.cf` file is created from a macro configuration (`.mc`) file that usually contains fewer than 20 lines of m4 commands. The m4 commands that you will use to build a basic Sendmail configuration are listed in Table 4.1.

**Table 4.1**    Common m4 Commands

| Command | Usage |
| --- | --- |
| define | Defines a value for a configuration variable. |
| divert | Directs the output of the m4 process. |
| dnl | Deletes all characters up to, and including, the next newline character. |
| DOMAIN | Selects a file containing attributes for your specific domain. |
| FEATURE | Identifies an optional Sendmail feature to be included in the configuration. |
| MAILER | Identifies a set of mailers to be included in the `sendmail.cf` file. |
| OSTYPE | Selects a file containing operating system–specific attributes. |
| undefine | Clears the value set for a configuration variable. |
| VERSIONID | Defines version control information for the configuration. |

The commands shown in Table 4.1 are the most commonly used m4 macro commands. All of the commands shown in uppercase are macro commands defined in the `cfhead.m4` file. The commands shown in lowercase are built-in m4 commands. The subset of commands shown in Table 4.1 is all you need to build a basic configuration. As such, they all deserve a more thorough explanation.

## Controlling *m4* Output

The m4 program is a stream-oriented macro processor. It views the data it handles as a stream of text characters. It collects input data from various files, expands macros embedded in those files, and directs the output stream of characters to another file. Two of the commands in Table 4.1 are used to control the stream of output characters: `divert` and `dnl`.

The `divert` command directs the output stream to different targets. As of Sendmail 8.11, there are 11 different targets for the data stream. The 11 possible divert values are listed in Table 4.2.

**Table 4.2**    Possible Values for the `divert` Command

| Value | Meaning |
|-------|---------|
| -1 | Discard this output. |
| 0 | Send this data through normal processing. |
| 1 | Use this data for hostname resolution. |
| 2 | Add this data to ruleset 3. |
| 3 | Add this data to ruleset 0. |
| 4 | Add this data to the UUCP-specific sections of ruleset 0. |
| 5 | Use this data to define domain names this server will relay. |
| 6 | Add this data to the Local Info section of the `sendmail.cf` file. |
| 7 | Save this data as a mailer definition. |
| 8 | Use this data to define a spammers blacklist. |
| 9 | Add this data to ruleset 1 or 2. |

Most of the values that can be specified with `divert` are used only by the Sendmail developers. They are used, in essence, as buffers to hold data for specific parts of the `sendmail.cf` file. The data is collected in these buffers and then moved to the `sendmail.cf` file in the final stage of processing. It is possible to use any of these values in a configuration, but unlikely and unnecessary because commands exist to send data to the correct buffers without resorting to `divert` commands. For any reasonable configuration, the `divert` command is used with only two different settings:

- `divert` is set to -1 to discard the output. Thus `divert(-1)` is found at the start of a block of text that is not to be written to the `sendmail.cf` file. While the block of text could be anything that's not intended for the output file, it is usually the copyright statement that is found at the beginning of many of the sample configuration files. The `divert(-1)` command at the start of the copyright means that the copyright is treated as a large comment.

Essential Configuration

PART 2

- `divert` is set to 0 to direct the stream to the output file—e.g., `sendmail.cf`. If the `divert(-1)` command is used at the start of a large comment, `divert(0)` is used at the end of the comment to redirect the stream to the output file.

The `dnl` command is also used to control the output stream. The `dnl` command accepts no arguments. Its two basic functions are determined by its position on the command line:

- If the `dnl` command occurs at the end of a line, after another `m4` command, it is used to clean up unwanted blank lines from the output file. For example, `dnl` on the line `OSTYPE(linux)dnl` ensures that any extraneous output generated after the `linux` OSTYPE macro is expanded doesn't get written to the `sendmail.cf` file.

- If the `dnl` command occurs at the beginning of the line, the line is treated as a comment. For example, the line `dnlNext define the domain name` is a comment. If the sample line did not begin with `dnl`, `m4` would interpret "define" and "domain" as `m4` commands. Messy! Always start each comment line with `dnl`, unless it is a large comment bracketed by `divert` commands.

The `divert` and `dnl` commands direct `m4` output but they do not define or generate the output data. The other `m4` commands are used to generate the actual configuration file.

## The Basic Commands

In broad terms, there are two types of files used to build an `m4` configuration. One of these is the macro configuration file, which is traditionally identified by the `.mc` file extension. The macro configuration file is the input file for the `m4` command, and its name appears on the `m4` command line. The other files are `m4` source files that are referenced by the macro configuration file. Traditionally, `m4` source files are given the file extension `.m4`. Almost all `m4` macro commands from Table 4.1 can appear in either type of file, although three of the commands are generally found only in the macro configuration file:

**OSTYPE**   The OSTYPE macro is required, and it is always found in the macro configuration file. The OSTYPE macro command loads an `m4` source file that defines operating system–specific information. File and directory paths, mailer pathnames, and system-specific mailer arguments are the kind of information generally found in an OSTYPE file. The Sendmail source distribution provides more than 40 predefined operating system macro files, and you can create your own for a specific Linux distribution if you like. (We discuss this option when we evaluate the vendor-supplied macro configuration files in the next chapter.) The only argument passed to the OSTYPE command is the name of the `m4` source file that contains the operating system–specific information. Here is the command that processes the `linux.m4` OSTYPE source file:

    OSTYPE(linux)

**DOMAIN**    The DOMAIN macro loads a file that contains information specific to your domain or network. The DOMAIN source file is a perfect place for commands that affect hostnames and domain names, and that define values, such as mail relay names, that are specific to your network. Because the information is specific to your domain, you must create your own DOMAIN source file. The Sendmail source code distribution provides a sample DOMAIN source file, named generic.m4, that you can use as a starting point for creating your own configuration. Assume you created a DOMAIN source file that you called foobirds.m4. The following command, placed in the macro control file, uses foobirds.m4 to help in building the sendmail.cf file:

    DOMAIN(foobirds)

The DOMAIN command is optional. When it is used, it normally appears only in the macro configuration file.

**MAILER**    The MAILER macros identify the various sets of mailer definitions that should be included in the sendmail.cf file. A useable configuration must have at least one MAILER command; almost every Linux configuration has the following two:

**MAILER(local)**    The MAILER(local) macro command adds the local mailer and the prog mailer to the configuration. The local and prog mailers are essential, so any useable configuration will have at least this MAILER command.

**MAILER(smtp)**    The MAILER(smtp) macro adds mailers for SMTP, Extended SMTP, eight-bit SMTP, directed delivery SMTP, and relayed mail. Every Linux system that sends SMTP mail, whether directly or through a mail server, has this MAILER command.

In addition to these two important sets of mailers, there are nine other sets of mailers available with the MAILER command. Most of them are of very little interest to the average system administrator, but for the sake of completeness they are all covered in Appendix A, "m4 Macro Command Reference."

OSTYPE, DOMAIN, and MAILER are generally found only in the macro configuration file. The other four commands in Table 4.1 are found in both macro configuration and macro source files:

**VERSIONID**    The VERSIONID macro defines version control information. This macro is optional, but is found in most m4 files. The command has no required format for the argument. Use any version control information you desire. The basic format of the VERSIONID macro is:

    VERSIONID(`*version-control-data*')

Essential
Configuration

PART 2

---

**WARNING** A quoted string in the argument field of any m4 macro must begin with ` and end with '. This is important. If other quotes marks are used, you will have errors in your configuration.

**FEATURE** The FEATURE macro identifies an optional Sendmail feature for inclusion in the sendmail.cf file. A single m4 file can contain several FEATURE commands. The format of the FEATURE macro is:

FEATURE(`*feature-name*'[, `*parameter*'[, `*parameter*']...])

The *feature-name* identifies the requested feature. There are more than 40 Sendmail features available, all of which are listed in Appendix A. Some of these features can be configured with optional parameters. Many features, and the optional parameters used to configure those features, are used in examples in this book. Next to the define command, the FEATURE command is the most heavily used command in the m4 configuration.

**define** The define command is used to set the value of a configuration variable for the sendmail.cf file. As you'll see in Chapter 7, "The sendmail.cf File," this file contains hundreds of variables called macros, classes, and options. The define command identifies the variable by name and sets the value for the variable using this format:

**define**(`*variable-name*', `*value*'*)*

There are hundreds of variable names, most of which you will never use. The important ones are covered in examples in the text. A full list is provided in Appendix A.

**undefine** The undefine command is the opposite of the define command. It returns the value of a variable to the system default. Thus, the only argument provided to the undefine command is the variable name:

**undefine**(`*variable-name*'*)*

At first glance, the undefine command may seem odd. Why would you define a variable value only to undefine it? The answer is, you didn't define it in the first place—someone else did. Configurations are built by bringing together several m4 source files that already exist. An existing file may have several values you want for your configuration, and a few you don't want. The undefine command lets you use what you want from the m4 source file while resetting the values you don't want.

The basic configuration commands appear in an m4 configuration file in the following order:

- VERSIONID, when used, is the first macro in the file.
- OSTYPE is defined before the other essential macros.

- DOMAIN, when used, comes next.
- define commands that affect a FEATURE macro that will be specified in the macro configuration file must come before that FEATURE macro.
- FEATURE macros come next.
- define commands that specify variable settings for the configuration, other than those that affect a previously identified FEATURE, come after the FEATURE macros.
- MAILER macros are the last basic commands in the file.

As you'll see later, there are several more commands that can be used in the m4 configuration files. These commands add complexity to the structure, but the basic structure is as described above.

The nine commands covered so far are used to build most configurations. The syntax and the purpose of the commands have been described, but until you see the commands in the context of a configuration file, it is difficult to imagine exactly how they are used.

## A Sample Macro Configuration File

The Sendmail distribution comes with a large number of sample macro configuration files. One that is sure to draw the attention of a Linux system administrator is the file generic-linux.mc. Listing 4.7 shows the contents of this file:

**Listing 4.7**   The generic-linux.mc File

```
divert(-1)
#
# Copyright (c) 1998, 1999 Sendmail, Inc. and its suppliers.
#       All rights reserved.
# Copyright (c) 1983 Eric P. Allman.  All rights reserved.
# Copyright (c) 1988, 1993
#       The Regents of the University of California.  All rights reserved.
#
# By using this file, you agree to the terms and conditions set
# forth in the LICENSE file which can be found at the top level of
# the sendmail distribution.
#
#


#
#   This is a generic configuration file for Linux.
#   It has support for local and SMTP mail only.  If you want to
#   customize it, copy it to a name appropriate for your environment
```

```
#   and do the modifications there.
#

divert(0)dnl
VERSIONID(`$Id: generic-linux.mc,v 8.1 1999/09/24 22:48:05 gshapiro
            Exp $')
OSTYPE(linux)dnl
DOMAIN(generic)dnl
MAILER(local)dnl
MAILER(smtp)dnl
```

The sample file starts with a `divert(-1)` command that discards what follows. Because the following text will not appear in the output file, it is only provided as a comment or informational message. In this case, the discarded text includes a copyright notice and some general information about the file and how it should be used. The block of text ends with a `divert(0)dnl` line that redirects the output to the output file, which in effect turns m4 processing back on. In the future, when we display the contents of a macro control file we will show only the active commands and ignore the block of text at the start of the file for the sake of clearer and shorter listings. However, you should know that most sample files start with a similar block of text.

An optional VERSIONID macro is the first macro command in the generic-linux.mc file. The version control information is intended for the people who maintain this sample file. You can safely ignore it. When you create your own configuration files, you should use version control information that is meaningful to you or to the tools you use to maintain the file.

The sample OSTYPE command tells m4 to process the file ../ostype/linux.m4 for operating system attributes. No surprise here. Using Linux operating system attributes is just what you would expect in a file named generic-linux.mc. The macro configuration file must have one OSTYPE command, and it must occur before most of the other configuration commands in the file.

The DOMAIN command in Listing 4.7 processes the file ../domain/generic.m4. The configuration settings in generic.m4 are samples of the type of commands you might include in your own DOMAIN m4 source file. The DOMAIN command line is included in the generic-linux.mc file primarily as an example of how the command is used in a macro configuration file.

The generic-linux.mc file ends with two MAILER commands. These are the same two MAILER commands that were described in the preceding section. Almost all Linux Sendmail configurations have these two lines. If additional mailers, such as the UUCP mailers, are added to the configuration, they are added after these two MAILER statements.

Let's follow the advice at the beginning of the generic-linux.mc file to build our own simple configuration file.

## Building a Simple *m4* Configuration File

The problem we want to solve is very straightforward. We have installed Sendmail 8.11 on the sample system and we want a basic configuration that will work with that release. We aren't concerned yet with building a full-featured Sendmail configuration. We just want to get the system running. Let's start with the generic-linux.mc file.

Begin by changing to the cf/cf directory and copying the generic-linux.mc file to test.mc. Make sure the file permission for test.mc is 644 so that you can edit the file:

```
[root]# cd /usr/local/src/sendmail-8.11.0/cf/cf
[root]# cp generic-linux.mc test.mc
[root]# chmod 644 test.mc
```

Now edit the file to create the new configuration. Our goal is to create the simplest possible configuration in order to get the system running. To do that, remove the DOMAIN(generic) line from the test.mc macro configuration file; it is primarily included as an example and has not been customized for our domain. While editing the file, don't forget to update the VERSIONID macro to reflect the fact that this is a new configuration file. The following tail command shows the macros in the file after the edits:

```
[root]# tail -5 test.mc
divert(0)dnl
VERSIONID(`test.mc, v1.0')
OSTYPE(linux)dnl
MAILER(local)dnl
MAILER(smtp)dnl
```

The new test.mc file is even simpler than the generic-linux.mc file.

### The *m4* Command Line

The new test.mc configuration file cannot be used by Sendmail directly. The test.mc file is an input file for the m4 command. The next step in creating the new Sendmail configuration is to process the test.mc file through m4 as shown in Listing 4.8.

**Listing 4.8**  Running m4

```
[root]# m4 ../m4/cf.m4 test.mc > test.cf
```

The example shows the m4 command format used to build a sendmail.cf file. The path-name ../m4/cf.m4 is the path to the m4 source tree required to build a sendmail.cf file. This must be specified on the m4 command line if it is not included in the macro configuration file with an include command. Notice that the pathname is a relative pathname starting with ../. Older versions of m4 actually required a relative pathname. Changing to the cf/cf directory was not just a convenience; it was a necessary part of running m4 with the correct source tree path. This is no longer necessary on Linux systems. The GNU m4 program used with Linux can accept an absolute pathname for this argument, which means that the macro configuration file can be stored anywhere on the system. Red Hat takes advantage of this fact when installing Sendmail via RPM. RPM places a copy of the Red Hat macro configuration file in /etc/mail and includes an absolute pathname to cf.m4 inside the macro configuration file.

The second command-line argument is the name of the new macro configuration file, test.mc. m4 reads the source files ../m4/cf.m4 and test.mc, and it outputs the file test.cf. The file output by the m4 command is in the correct format for a sendmail.cf file.

### Testing the Configuration File Compatibility

The test.cf file is in the correct format to become the sendmail.cf file, but before moving it to /etc/mail/sendmail.cf, you should make sure it works. A quick test will tell you, as shown in Listing 4.9.

**Listing 4.9**   Testing Compatibility

```
[root]# sendmail -v -t -C /etc/sendmail.cf
Warning: .cf file is out of date: sendmail 8.11.0 supports
         version 9, .cf file is version 8
^D
No recipient addresses found in header
[root]# sendmail -v -t -C ./test.cf
^D
No recipient addresses found in header
```

As Listing 4.9 shows, the new test.cf configuration file resolves the compatibility problem that appears when we upgraded Sendmail by compiling new source code. The test doesn't prove anything else, and I won't pretend this simple configuration is the best possible configuration, but it meets the goal we set of getting Sendmail up and running.

### Installing the New Configuration

Once you decide to use the new configuration file, move it to the location where Sendmail expects to find its configuration file. The name of the configuration file for Sendmail 8.11

defaults to /etc/mail/sendmail.cf. On most Linux systems, the configuration file is /etc/sendmail.cf. Put the new file in the appropriate location for your system. In this example, we compiled Sendmail 8.11 from source code with the default setting, so we need to move test.cf to /etc/mail/sendmail.cf, which we do in Listing 4.10.

**Listing 4.10**   Putting a New Configuration File in Place

```
[root]# mv /etc/mail/sendmail.cf /etc/mail/sendmail.cf.hold
mv: /etc/mail/sendmail.cf: No such file or directory
[root]# cp test.cf /etc/mail/sendmail.cf
[root]# sendmail -v -t
To: craig@wren.foobirds.org
From: craig
Subject: Test
Please ignore this test.
^D
craig@wren.foobirds.org... Connecting to wren.foobirds.org. via esmtp...
220 wren.foobirds.org ESMTP Sendmail 8.11.0/8.11.0;
    Tue, 29 Aug 2000 20:42:44 -0
400
>>> EHLO ibis.foobirds.org
250-wren.foobirds.org Hello root@almond.nuts.com [172.16.12.1],
    pleased to meet you
>>> MAIL From:<craig@ibis.foobirds.org> SIZE=78
250 2.1.0 <craig@ibis.foobirds.org>... Sender ok
>>> RCPT To:<craig@wren.foobirds.org>
250 2.1.5 <craig@wren.foobirds.org>... Recipient ok
>>> DATA
354 Enter mail, end with "." on a line by itself
>>> .
250 2.0.0 e7U0fRg00818 Message accepted for delivery
craig@wren.foobirds.org... Sent (e7U0fRg00818 Message
    accepted for delivery)
Closing connection to wren.foobirds.org.
>>> QUIT
221 2.0.0 wren.foobirds.org closing connection
```

The first step is to move the current sendmail.cf file to a backup file, called sendmail.cf.hold in Listing 4.10. In this case, the move is unsuccessful because we just installed Sendmail from source files and there was no /etc/mail/sendmail.cf file. Still, I always run mv first just to make sure I don't overwrite a file that I later want to recover.

Next, we copy the `test.cf` file to `/etc/mail/sendmail.cf` and run a test to make sure everything is working. This time we don't need to use the -C argument with the `sendmail` command because the Sendmail configuration file is in the correct location. Also, this time we run a complete test and actually send a piece of mail. The mail is delivered correctly and is properly formatted.

We have a complete, working Sendmail 8.11 system. Of course, we're not going to leave it at this—we wouldn't have much of a book if we did. In the following chapters we will add to this basic configuration to create a more advanced custom configuration. To create an advanced configuration, we will use additional m4 configuration commands.

## More *m4* Commands

This is a chapter about basic configuration. But as you might imagine, the basic commands covered in this chapter are not the whole story. Several other m4 commands must be understood just to read all of the sample macro configuration files that come with the Sendmail distribution. Table 4.3 identifies and describes the other commands found in the sample files. The one command listed in lowercase is a built-in m4 command. All of the other commands, which are listed in uppercase, are macros the Sendmail development team created for Sendmail configuration.

**Table 4.3**    More m4 Commands

| Command | Purpose |
| --- | --- |
| EXPOSED_USER | Overrides masquerading for specific users. |
| HACK | Processes a file that contains temporary fixes. |
| include | Incorporates an external m4 file into this file by reference. |
| LOCAL_CONFIG | Marks the start of a section that contains `sendmail.cf` commands. |
| LOCAL_RULE_*n* | Marks the start of a section that contains rewrite rules. The *n*, which must be 0, 1, 2, or 3, identifies the ruleset that the rewrite rules are added to. |
| LOCAL_RULESETS | Marks the start of a ruleset to be added to the configuration. |
| MASQUERADE_AS | Defines a domain name that is used to rewrite the host part of sender addresses. |

**Table 4.3**   More m4 Commands *(continued)*

| Command | Purpose |
|---|---|
| MODIFY_MAILER_FLAGS | Defines mailer flags used to override the current mailer flag settings. |
| SITE | Identifies the names of UUCP sites connected to the server. |
| SITECONFIG | Points to the file that contains the SITE commands for the UUCP mail server. |
| UUCPSMTP | Maps a UUCP hostname to an Internet hostname. |

The first and most important thing to realize about the commands in Table 4.3 is that there are some you will never use. Just because a command shows up in a sample file, it doesn't mean that it is the correct command for you or even a recommended command. Some of the sample files that come with Sendmail are very old. Some of the commands used in these files are obsolete and can be ignored. The last three commands in Table 4.3 are good examples. SITE, SITECONFIG, and UUCPSMTP are obsolete techniques for configuring the system to handle UUCP mail. These functions have been replaced by the databases described in Chapter 6.

Another command you can safely ignore is HACK. As the name implies, it is intended to process a file that contains a hack to fix a mail problem. All normal mail problems can be addressed through the normal configuration. A hack is supposed to be something temporary, a fix that needs to be addressed in the configuration but that you know will not be required in the near future. The idea is that the fix can be put in a separate file in the cf/hack directory and then discarded when no longer needed. The problem with hacks is that they tend to develop a life of their own. The duration of a problem is rarely known. A hack that seems temporary soon becomes permanent. Generally it is better to permanently fix all problems in the "regular" configuration instead of creating a hack. A "permanent" fix can be removed as easily as a hack when it is no longer needed.

Use the include command to simplify the m4 command line. In Listing 4.8, the m4 command line begins with the argument ../m4/cf.m4 to ensure that the macro definitions and header files in the cf/m4 directory are available to the m4 process. This argument must be added to the command line every time m4 is run. It is possible to include the cf.m4 file inside the macro configuration file so that it doesn't have to be specified on the command line. If the following line is added to the beginning of the test.mc file:

```
include '../usr/local/src/sendmail-8.11.0/cf/m4/cf.m4'
```

the `test.mc` file can be processed with the following `m4` command:

[root]# **m4 test.mc > test2.cf**

Readers who use `include` commands in other languages generally think the `include` command can be used to separate a complex configuration into several files and then bring those files together for processing. While that is true for `m4` in general, it is not true for Sendmail configuration. All macro configuration files are short files that do not benefit from being segmented. The only time you'll see `include` used in the files provided with the Sendmail distribution is when `cf.m4` itself includes the large and complex `cfhead.m4` file. And the only time you will use `include` is when you want to include the `cf.m4` file into your macro configuration file to simplify the `m4` command line.

The `LOCAL_CONFIG`, `LOCAL_RULESET`, and `LOCAL_RULE_n` commands allow you to put raw `sendmail.cf` configuration commands directly in the `m4` source file. These commands, and other related commands, mean that everything that can be done in the `sendmail.cf` file can be done in the `m4` macro source files. (`sendmail.cf` configuration commands are discussed in Chapter 7.) We use the `LOCAL_CONFIG`, `LOCAL_RULESET`, and `LOCAL_RULE_n` commands several times in this text to define complex `sendmail.cf` configurations.

The `MODIFY_MAILER_FLAGS` command is used to override the flags set for a mailer. Mailer flags are described in Chapter 7, "The `sendmail.cf` File," and a listing of all of the mailer flags is found in Appendix C, "Sendmail Variables, Options, and Flags." The `MODIFY_MAILER_FLAGS` command has two arguments: the name of the mailer and the flag to be modified. The flag is preceded by a + if it is to be added to the existing set of flags or by a - if an existing flag is to be removed.

The `MASQUERADE_AS` and `EXPOSED_USER` commands both deal with masquerading. Frequently, an organization wants all of its outbound mail to appear as if it came from one source. This is done to create clean and consistent e-mail addresses, and to hide the names of internal systems that should not be directly receiving mail. *Masquerading* is the name for this type of mail rewriting. `MASQUERADE_AS` defines the hostname that is used as the hostname part for all outbound mail. If `MASQUERADE_AS('foobirds.org')` is set in the configuration, mail from `craig@wren.foobirds.org` goes out as mail from `craig@foobirds.org`.

`EXPOSED_USER` addresses a problem created by masquerading. Assume that mail from `root@wren.foobirds.org` and `root@ibis.foobirds.org` is passed through the server with the `MASQUERADE_AS('foobirds.org')` setting. If both addresses are rewritten to `root@foobirds.org`, you have a problem. There is no way for the recipient to know exactly where the message really originated, and the remote user could not reply to the correct address. Usernames, like root, that are found on every system should not be masqueraded. The EXPOSED_USER command is used to define the usernames that should not be masqueraded.

Masquerading is covered extensively in Chapter 9, "Special m4 Configurations." There are several more m4 commands that relate to masquerading, all of which will be covered in that chapter.

The commands in Table 4.1 and Table 4.3 are just the tip of the m4 iceberg. Many more commands are covered in Part 2 of the text as examples of advanced configurations, and all of the m4 commands are covered in Appendix A. This chapter does not provide exhaustive coverage of the m4 language. It is an introduction to m4 that helps you understand the m4 commands contained in the sample files. Understanding these basic commands should help you read the macro configuration file provided by your vendor, which is a topic we tackle in Chapter 5, "Understanding a Vendor's Configuration."

# In Sum

Sendmail reads its configuration from the sendmail.cf file. However, this file is not directly configured by the Sendmail administrator. Instead the file is constructed indirectly from m4 macros.

The Sendmail distribution provides the m4 source files necessary to build a Sendmail configuration. The m4 source files are contained in the nine subdirectories of the cf directory. For most configurations, eight of the nine subdirectories can be ignored because they are either unused or they contain source files that are never modified by the system administrator. The only subdirectory that the administrator needs to work with for most configurations is the cf/cf directory.

The cf/cf directory contains the macro configuration files. The Sendmail administrator creates a macro configuration file that selects the source files that provide the features necessary for the Sendmail configuration. Most macro configuration files are not built from scratch. The Sendmail distribution provides about 20 different sample macro configuration files. You select a macro configuration file that matches your needs and only make small adjustments if they are necessary.

The macro configuration file is then processed through m4 to produce the sendmail.cf file. But even this step may not be necessary if you don't need to change the sample macro configuration file for your configuration. Several Sendmail configuration files built from sample macro configuration files are included in the cf/cf directory.

To select and modify the correct macro configuration file, you must have a basic understanding of the m4 Sendmail macro configuration language. Use the tables in this chapter and the list of configuration commands in Appendix A to help you read and modify the macro configuration file. Don't bother memorizing the details of the Sendmail configuration language; you won't build new configurations often enough to make that skill worthwhile. Instead, learn the basic commands in Table 4.1 and look up the details in a reference like Appendix A.

A configuration can be built by starting with a sample file and modifying it for your configuration, as was done in this chapter. But an even more common way to configure Sendmail is to use the macro configuration file provided with your Linux distribution. In the next chapter, we examine the default mail server configuration that comes with Red Hat Linux.

# 5

# Understanding a Vendor's Configuration

Legend has it that Sendmail configuration is one of the most difficult tasks a system administrator will ever face. Like most legends, this one is only partly true. For the vast majority of Linux systems, the administrator's role in Sendmail configuration is so simple it is almost trivial. The reason is plain: Someone else has already done the difficult parts of the configuration for you. In the Linux world, that someone is the vendor who created your Linux distribution.

Of course, this is a book for professional system administrators. If you're reading this book, you don't need help mastering a trivial task. So in this chapter we analyze the configuration that the vendor provides you. We look in detail at a basic configuration that comes with the Sendmail source code distribution and at the configuration included in the RPM for the Red Hat Linux distribution. We look at the decisions made by the developers of these configurations and at the effect that those decisions have on the systems we manage. We will use the insight we gain here to enhance our own custom configuration. Let's begin by looking at the problems we have had with the source code installation and at the `generic-linux.m4` configuration that comes with the Sendmail distribution.

# The Generic Linux Configuration

The challenge in Chapter 4, "Creating a Basic Sendmail Configuration," was to find or create a sendmail.cf file that is compatible with Sendmail 8.11. Because the Sendmail 8.11 distribution comes with a file named generic-linux.cf that is already in the proper format to be used as a sendmail.cf file, the first thing we tried was to use the generic-linux.cf file without modification. The result was this error:

```
[root]# sendmail -v -t -C./generic-linux.cf

./generic-linux.cf: line 66: fileclass:

        cannot open '/etc/mail/local-host-names'

: No such file or directory
```

The generic.linux.mc file that created the generic-linux.cf file has only five significant command lines:

**Listing 5.1**   The Commands Contained in generic-linux.mc

```
[craig]$ tail -5 generic-linux.mc
VERSIONID(`$Id: generic-linux.mc,v 8.1 1999/09/24 22:48:05 gshapiro Exp $')
OSTYPE(linux)dnl
DOMAIN(generic)dnl
MAILER(local)dnl
MAILER(smtp)dnl
```

We know that the VERSIONID macro has no effect other than holding user-defined version control information. We also know that the OSTYPE macro and the two MAILER macros are required for a functioning system. This leads us to guess that removing the optional DOMAIN macro is the best place to start attacking the problem. Therefore, in Chapter 4 we created a simple m4 macro configuration file that did not contain the DOMAIN macro and used it to produce a sendmail.cf file compatible with Sendmail 8.11. It worked, and we got Sendmail up and running.

Sometimes a quick solution based on an educated guess is all that you have time for. But when you get some free time you are drawn back to the problem to find out why that guess worked and to figure out if there is a better long-term solution to the problem. We need to know more about the macro source files called by the generic-linux.mc file in order to:

- find out why the simple change worked for our problem
- see if there is a better way to solve our problem
- find out what features were lost by our quick and dirty solution
- learn more about configuring Sendmail

The first source file called by the `generic-linux.mc` file is, predictably enough, the `linux.m4` OSTYPE file. The contents of the `linux.m4` file must be analyzed to fully understand the generic Linux Sendmail configuration.

## The Linux *OSTYPE* File

The OSTYPE file contains operating system–specific configuration values. The biggest configuration variation between the different operating systems that run Sendmail is the location of files. Variables that define pathnames are commonly stored in the OSTYPE file. Since this file is specific to the Linux operating system and this book is about running Sendmail on Linux, let's take a close look at the Linux OSTYPE file.

The command OSTYPE(`linux`) loads a file named `linux.m4` from the `ostype` directory. Listing 5.2 shows the contents of this OSTYPE file:

**Listing 5.2**   The `linux.m4` OSTYPE File

```
[craig]$ cat ../ostype/linux.m4
divert(-1)
#
# Copyright (c) 1998, 1999 Sendmail, Inc. and its suppliers.
#        All rights reserved.
# Copyright (c) 1983 Eric P. Allman.  All rights reserved.
# Copyright (c) 1988, 1993
#        The Regents of the University of California.  All rights reserved.
#
# By using this file, you agree to the terms and conditions set
# forth in the LICENSE file which can be found at the top level of
# the sendmail distribution.
#
#

divert(0)
VERSIONID(`$Id: linux.m4,v 8.11.16.1 2000/05/09 18:48:58 gshapiro
        Exp $')
define(`confEBINDIR', `/usr/sbin')
ifdef(`PROCMAIL_MAILER_PATH',,
        define(`PROCMAIL_MAILER_PATH', `/usr/bin/procmail'))
FEATURE(local_procmail)
```

The file begins with a copyright notice. The copyright notice is bracketed by a `divert(-1)` statement and a `divert(0)` statement, so it is treated as a comment and can be safely ignored. The VERSIONID macro can also be ignored.

Essential Configuration

PART 2

---

**NOTE** In the rest of this chapter, to reduce the size of the listings, the copyright statements that start the files are not printed, but you should be aware that they are there.

---

The first real configuration command in the file is a `define` statement that assigns a value to the `confEBINDIR` parameter. This parameter stores the path of the directory that holds certain executable binary files. The Sendmail 8.11 default for `confEBINDIR` is `/usr/libexec`. This `define` changes the setting to `/usr/sbin`. Both of these directories exist on Linux systems, but the `/usr/sbin` directory is the one that is more commonly used to hold system binary files, and in this case it is the correct setting. The `confEBINDIR` path is used to locate the `smrsh` mailer, which is frequently used as the `prog` mailer on Linux systems. (The `prog` mailer, which is used to send mail files to programs, uses an unrestricted shell by default. Chapter 12, "Sendmail Security," describes the advantages of using the `smrsh` mailer.) A couple of quick `ls` commands on our sample Linux system show that the correct value for `confEBINDIR` is `/usr/sbin`:

```
[craig]$ ls /usr/libexec/smrsh
ls: /usr/libexec/smrsh: No such file or directory
[craig]$ ls /usr/sbin/smrsh
/usr/sbin/smrsh
```

The second configuration command is also a `define`. This one is a little more complex. This `define` is contained inside an `ifdef`. The `ifdef` has nothing to do with configuring Sendmail. It is a built-in m4 conditional command that checks whether or not a variable has already been set to a value. The `ifdef` command has three fields:

- the name of the variable that is being tested
- the action to take if the variable has been set
- the action to take if the variable has not been set

In Listing 5.2, the `ifdef` tests the variable `PROCMAIL_MAILER_PATH`. If the variable has already been defined, nothing is done. We know this by the fact that the second field of the `ifdef` is empty—notice the two commas right in a row ( , , ). If the variable has not yet been set, the `define` contained in the third field of the `ifdef` is executed. This is exactly what happens on our sample system, because we did not assign any value to `PROCMAIL_MAILER_PATH` in the macro configuration file.

The `define` assigns the variable `PROCMAIL_MAILER_PATH` the path value `/usr/bin/procmail`. This overrides the Sendmail default for `PROCMAIL_MAILER_PATH`, which is

/usr/local/bin/procmail. A quick ls shows that the new value is correct for our sample system:

```
[craig]$ ls -l /usr/bin/procmail
-rwxr-xr-x   1 root    root       68276 Aug 10   1999 /usr/bin/procmail
```

### Don't *ifdef*

I have a philosophical objection to having an ifdef inside the OSTYPE file. I understand why it had to be done: it was done to create an OSTYPE file that would work for all versions of Linux. However, that is my basic objection. If different Linux distributions require different OSTYPE settings, the developers of those distributions should create an OSTYPE file for their distribution that contains the correct setting. After all, that is what the OSTYPE file is for. There is no reason why there shouldn't be an ostype/redhat.m4 file, and an ostype/suse.m4 file, and an ostype/slackware.m4 file, and a file for any other distribution you can imagine. You'd think that distribution developers would want to put their names in the ostype directory, but the fact is that not a single Linux distribution developer has added an OSTYPE file to the ostype directory of the Sendmail source code distribution.

As Listing 5.2 shows, the last line in linux.m4 is a FEATURE macro. The feature that this macro adds to the configuration is local_procmail, which specifies that procmail will be used as the local mailer. As you'll see in Chapter 11, "Stopping Spam," procmail is a very powerful mailer. The fact that Linux uses procmail as the local mailer is a plus. The local_procmail feature accepts up to three optional arguments:

- The path to the mailer. This defaults to the path value assigned to PROCMAIL_ MAILER_PATH, which in Listing 5.2 is /usr/bin/procmail. The same effect could have been obtained with the following FEATURE command:

   ```
   FEATURE(`local_procmail', `/usr/bin/procmail')
   ```

- The command line for executing the mailer. The default is procmail -Y -a $h -d $u, where $h is replaced by the *detail* value if the *user+detail* addressing syntax is used, and $u is replaced by the username from the recipient address. $h and $u are the Sendmail variables that hold the remote hostname and the remote user's address in a standard delivery triple. In this case, however, procmail is being used as a local mailer, so there is no remote hostname and the $h variable is used to hold the *detail* value. (See Appendix C, "Sendmail Variables, Options, and Flags," for a full listing of the Sendmail variables.)

- The flags for this mailer. The default is SPfhn9. (See Appendix C, "Sendmail Variables, Options, and Flags," for a full listing of mailer flags.)

---

**NOTE**   With the local_procmail feature, procmail is being used as the local mailer. The command-line arguments and the mailer flags affected are those set by LOCAL_MAILER_FLAGS and LOCAL_MAILER_ARGS, not those set by PROCMAIL_MAILER_FLAGS and PROCMAIL_MAILER_ARGS, which are used by the MAILER (procmail) command—this despite the fact that local_procmail uses the path from PROCMAIL_MAILER_PATH instead of the path from LOCAL_MAILER_PATH. Oh well, no one said Sendmail was easy to understand.

---

The linux.m4 OSTYPE file defines the directory path for the smrsh program, the path for procmail, and a feature that uses procmail as the local mailer. Clearly, the OSTYPE file is a good place to look for file pathnames and mailer options. None of the settings in linux.m4 relate to the problem we saw when we tried to use the generic-linux.cf file on our sample system, but everything in the linux.m4 file is worth understanding because all of these settings affect the configuration of a Linux system.

The second m4 source file loaded by generic-linux.mc, as shown in Listing 5.1, is the generic.m4 file from the domain directory. Let's look at that file in detail.

## The Generic *DOMAIN* File

The DOMAIN command is optional. It loads the m4 source file that you create to configure values specific to your domain or network. You don't have to create a DOMAIN source file, but it is highly recommended that you do if you have any domain-specific processing.

Host and username processing, domain name masquerading, mail relaying, and anti-spam features are the types of information normally found in a DOMAIN source file. Listing 5.3 shows the generic.m4 DOMAIN file used by the generic-linux.mc macro configuration file.

**Listing 5.3**   The Configuration Commands in domain/generic.m4

```
[craig]$ tail -6 generic.m4
VERSIONID(`$Id: generic.m4,v 8.15 1999/04/04 00:51:09 ca Exp $')
define(`confFORWARD_PATH', `$z/.forward.$w+$h:$z/.forward+$h:$z/
.forward.$w:$z/.
forward')dnl
define(`confMAX_HEADERS_LENGTH', `32768')dnl
FEATURE(`redirect')dnl
FEATURE(`use_cw_file')dnl
EXPOSED_USER(`root')
```

The generic.m4 file contains six m4 commands after the copyright notice. The first is a VERSIONID macro that can be ignored. The first significant command is a define command.

### Defining the *.forward* Path

The first define command assigns a value to the confFORWARD_PATH variable. This variable holds a colon-separated list of the paths that Sendmail searches when looking for a .forward file. (Chapter 2, "Understanding E-Mail Architecture," explains the purpose of the .forward file.)

The default value of confFORWARD_PATH is $z/.forward.$w:$z/.forward, where $z is the recipient's home directory and $w is a valid name for this host. (See Appendix C for a full list of the Sendmail variables, including $z and $w.) Thus if the recipient's home directory is /home/jill and the hostname is gull, the path list is interpreted as /home/jill/.forward.gull:/home/jill/.forward.

The first define in Listing 5.3 increases the complexity of the .forward path list. It retains the two paths from the default search list and inserts in front of them the value $z/.forward.$w+$h:$z/.forward+$h. The $z and $w variables serve the same purpose as before. The $h variable contains the *detail* value when the *user+detail* addressing syntax is used and procmail is used as the local mailer. We know that procmail is being used as the local mailer because we saw the local_procmail feature in the linux.m4 OSTYPE file. Given this specific configuration, local mail on a host named egret addressed to craig+sybex would prepend the following .forward search path to the standard path: /home/craig/.forward.egret+sybex:/home/craig/.forward+sybex.

Essential Configuration

PART 2

### The *+detail* Syntax

The +*detail* syntax is an adaptation of the mailbox syntax used in the Cyrus mailers. The Cyrus mailers allow mail to be addressed to a specific mailbox. In a Cyrus address, the *detail* is a mailbox name. Thus mail addressed to rebecca+inbox is placed in a mailbox named inbox owned by the user rebecca.

The problem with this is that neither Sendmail nor Linux uses a mailbox architecture. Sendmail writes mail to a single spool file for each user, and Linux user mail agents read mail from a single spool file for each user. Thus, mail bound for user rebecca is written to and read from the file /var/spool/mail/rebecca. Mailboxes exist on Linux systems, but they exist because the user mail agent reads the mail from the single spool file and then routes it to different mailboxes based on some filtering rules defined inside the user mail agent.

The +*detail* syntax is rarely used in the addresses entered by users. It requires an odd form of addressing that most users don't like, and it solves a problem that user mail agents have already solved to the satisfaction of most users. If used at all, the +*detail* syntax is used internally to sendmail or procmail in the same way the pseudo-domains are used to help the mail programs route the mail. (Not sure what a pseudo-domain is? Don't worry—you'll see one in a second.)

Defining the confFORWARD_PATH variable seems more like a command that should happen in the OSTYPE source file than in the DOMAIN source file. It defines a file path, which is something that commonly happens in the OSTYPE file, and this specific path is directly related to using procmail as the local mailer, which is also defined in the OSTYPE file. This just goes to show you that you really cannot tell where something will be defined in a Sendmail configuration. The only way to know the complete configuration is to look at all of the files.

The definition of the .forward search path is the most complex define in the generic.m4 file. The second define is much easier to understand. It sets the maximum number of bytes allowed for all headers. By default no limit is set. In the generic.m4 file shown in Listing 5.3, the maximum length is set to 32,768 bytes (32KB). That is more than enough for any reasonable set of headers. Headers longer than that might indicate a mail problem or some form of mail abuse. So perhaps this limit is being set to detect mail problems or abuse. But most likely this value is being set in the generic.m4 file to provide another example of define command syntax.

The two define commands that open the generic.m4 DOMAIN file are followed by two FEATURE commands that add optional capabilities to the Sendmail configuration.

## Adding Support for the .*REDIRECT* Pseudo-Domain

The FEATURE(redirect) macro adds support for the .REDIRECT pseudo-domain. A pseudo-domain is a domain-style extension added to an e-mail address by Sendmail to define special handling for the address. The .REDIRECT pseudo-domain works together with the aliases database to handle mail for people who no longer read mail at your site but who still get mail sent to an old address.

After enabling this feature, add aliases for each obsolete mailing address in the form:

```
old-address        new-address.REDIRECT
```

For example, assume that Jay Henson is no longer a valid e-mail user in your domain. His old username, jay, should no longer accept mail. His new mailing address is HensonJ@industry.com. Enter the following alias in the /etc/aliases file:

```
jay                     HensonJ@industry.com.REDIRECT
```

Now when mail is addressed to the jay account, the following error is returned to the sender telling them to try a new address for the recipient:

```
551 User not local; please try <HensonJ@industry.com>
```

This is a useful feature for any site that is small enough, or organized enough, to keep track of the e-mail address of employees who have moved on to new jobs. It is a courtesy to the ex-employee and, better yet, it cuts down on the number of requests the postmaster receives asking for the ex-employee's new e-mail address.

The second FEATURE command also specifies a useful feature.

## Adding Support for Local Host Aliases

The FEATURE(use_cw_file) command loads the class w variable from a file. The name of the file is defined with the confCW_FILE variable. Unless modified with the confCW_FILE variable, the default file used to load class w is /etc/mail/local-host-names.

Class w holds a list of valid hostnames for which the local computer will accept mail. Normally, if a system running Sendmail receives mail addressed to another hostname, it assumes the mail belongs to that host and forwards the mail to that host if the local host is configured as a relay, or discards the mail if it is not configured as a relay. If your system should accept mail that is addressed to another host, the name of the other host should be added to class w. Class w contains a list of acceptable hostnames even if neither the use_cw_feature nor the local-host-names file is used. Anything you put in the local-host-names file is added to those names when the use_cw_file feature is used. Listing 5.4 shows the default contents of class w on a computer named ibis.foobirds.org.

**Listing 5.4**   Examining Class w

```
[root]# sendmail -bt
ADDRESS TEST MODE (ruleset 3 NOT automatically invoked)
Enter <ruleset> <address>
> $=w
[172.16.12.1]
ibis.foobirds.org
ibis
localhost
[127.0.0.1]
> ^D
```

Chapter 10, "Testing Sendmail," describes Sendmail test mode in detail. For now, it is sufficient to understand that the -bt option puts Sendmail into test mode and that you can ask Sendmail to display the contents of a variable when it is running in test mode. In this case, we ask for the contents of the class w variable ($=w). ibis is not configured with the use_cw_file feature. The contents of the class w variable on ibis are the default values set by the system. By default, class w includes the IP address of the local system and the local computer's full domain name and unqualified domain name. It also includes the special name localhost and the special address, 127.0.0.1, that is assigned to that name.

The default values are adequate for most Sendmail systems. Most systems that run Sendmail do so to provide mail for the users that log onto that system. Only a subset of the systems running Sendmail are configured to provide mail services for other computers. If you run Sendmail on a desktop system, you probably don't need the use_cw_file feature, but when you run Sendmail as a server for a group of computers, you will probably use this feature.

The primary use for the local-host-names file is to hold the names of computers that use the local system as their MX server. This means that the MX server needs to know the names of the systems for which it is providing mail exchange services. You can't just pick a remote system as an MX server. Prior agreement between the server administrator and the client administrator is needed to ensure that mail won't be rejected by the server.

### Eureka!

FEATURE(use_cw_file) is clearly the cause of the problem we had using the generic-linux.cf configuration file. The error message "cannot open '/etc/mail/local-host-names': No such file or directory" makes this crystal clear. Recall that one of the first problems we encountered with the Sendmail 8.11 upgrade was that the sendmail.cf file was in the wrong directory. The Linux sample system kept the Sendmail configuration files in the /etc directory and 8.11 wants those files in /etc/mail. Considering the fact that Sendmail 8.11 introduced the /etc/mail directory, the problem could simply be that the local-host-names file is located in the wrong directory. But it goes beyond that. A quick check of the /etc directory shows that there is no file named local-host-names:

```
[craig]$ ls /etc/local-host-names
ls: /etc/local-host-names: No such file or directory
```

Prior to Sendmail 8.11, the file that added hostnames to class w was called
`sendmail.cw`. As shown below, copying the /etc/sendmail.cw file that already existed on the sample system to /etc/mail/local-host-names solves the problem
created by the Sendmail 8.11 upgrade:

```
[root]# sendmail -v -t -Cgeneric-linux.cf

generic-linux.cf: line 66: fileclass: cannot open '/etc/mail/
local-host-names':

No such file or directory

[root]# cp /etc/sendmail.cw /etc/mail/local-host-names

[root]# sendmail -v -t -Cgeneric-linux.cf

To: craig@wren.foobirds.org

From: root

Subject: Discard this test

^D
```

This simple problem is the kind of thing that drives experienced system administrators crazy. The filename `local-host-names` may be more logical than the name
`sendmail.cw`, but since when did logic have anything to do with Sendmail configuration! Once you have learned that class w values are stored in `sendmail.cw`, you
don't really want to learn that they are now stored in `local-host-names`. It would be
much simpler if things just stayed the same. But things are always changing and you
need to be prepared for it.

All I can do is recommend that you carefully read the release notes that come with every new Sendmail source code distribution. Even when you do, things will escape
your attention and problems will appear. However, applying the knowledge this book
gives you about Sendmail should make it much easier for you to handle these problems.

## Protecting the *root* Account from Masquerading

Masquerading, which is covered in Chapter 9, "Special m4 Configurations," hides the real
hostname in outbound mail and replaces it with the hostname you wish to advertise to the
outside world. The name that replaces the real hostname is usually the name of the mail
server, or the domain name if a single server handles mail for an entire domain. Refer

back to Listing 5.3. The last line in the generic.m4 file is the EXPOSED_USER macro. The EXPOSED_USER macro adds usernames to class E. The users listed in class E are not masqueraded, even when masquerading is enabled.

Some usernames, such as root, occur on many systems and are therefore not unique across a domain. For those usernames, converting the host portion of the address makes it difficult to sort out where the message really came from and makes replies impossible. For example, assume that mail from root@wren.foobirds.org and root@ibis.foobirds.org is passed through a server that converts both addresses to root@foobirds.org. There is no way for the recipient to know exactly where the message really originated, and the remote user could not reply to the correct address. The EXPOSED_USER command in Listing 5.3 prevents that from happening by ensuring that root is not masqueraded.

The primary reason this macro is included in the generic.m4 DOMAIN source file is to serve as a warning to the experienced Sendmail administrator that something has changed. Experienced Sendmail administrators may think that root is already part of class E, because prior to Sendmail 8.10 root was the default value for class E. In Sendmail 8.11, there are no default values in class E. The EXPOSED_USER(root) command must be added to the configuration if you want to protect root from masquerading. Of course, this command has no real effect in the generic configuration because this configuration does not include any commands to enable masquerading. But the message is clear. If you want to protect the root user from masquerading, include the EXPOSED_USER command in your configuration.

This command illustrates the main purpose of the generic.m4 file—it is intended as a training tool. The file is designed to show you the type of commands you should include in your own DOMAIN source file. The generic.m4 file is really just an example. The DOMAIN source file should be specific to your environment. If you use one, you're expected to create it yourself.

This concludes the DOMAIN file, but it does not conclude the generic-linux.mc macro control file shown in Listing 5.1. There are still two more macros in that file left to explain. The last two source files invoked by the generic-linux.mc macro configuration file are MAILER source files. As the "Eureka!" sidebar explains, we know those files didn't cause the problem we had using the generic-linux.cf file, but because they are an essential part of every Linux configuration, let's take a look at what they do.

## The Essential Mailers

The two MAILER commands in the generic-linux.mc file are found in most Sendmail configurations. These commands identify the sets of mailers included in the Sendmail configuration.

The MAILER(local) macro includes the local mailer that is used to deliver local mail between users of the system and the prog mailer that is used to send mail files to programs running on the system. Even though these mailers will be added by default, the MAILER(local) macro is traditionally included in the configuration. In part this tradition arises from the fact that most configurations are built from a sample configuration file, and all of the generic macro configuration files include the MAILER(local) macro. It takes more effort to remove the macro than it does to leave it in, and it costs nothing to leave it in the configuration. In fact, it provides the slight benefit of making the configuration more "self-documenting."

The MAILER(smtp) macro includes all of the mailers needed to send SMTP mail over a TCP/IP network. The mailers included in this set are:

**smtp**    This mailer can handle only traditional seven-bit ASCII SMTP mail. It is outmoded because most modern mail networks handle a variety of data types.

**esmtp**    This mailer supports Extended SMTP (ESMTP). It understands the ESMTP protocol extensions and it can deal with the complex message bodies and enhanced data types of MIME mail. This is the default mailer used for SMTP mail.

**smtp8**    This mailer sends eight-bit data to the remote server, even if the remote server does not indicate that it can support eight-bit data. Normally, a server that supports eight-bit data also supports ESMTP and thus can advertise its support for eight-bit data in the response to the EHLO command. (See Chapter 1, "Internet Mail Protocols," for a description of the SMTP protocol and the EHLO command.) It is possible, however, to have a connection to a remote server that can support eight-bit data but does not support ESMTP. In that rare circumstance, this mailer is available for use.

**dsmtp**    This mailer allows the destination system to retrieve mail queued on the server. Normally, the source system sends mail to the destination in what might be called a "push" model, where the source pushes mail out to the destination. On demand SMTP allows the destination to "pull" mail down from the mail server when it is ready to receive the mail. This mailer implements the ETRN command that permits on-demand delivery. (See Chapter 1 for a description of the ETRN protocol command.)

**relay**    This mailer is used when SMTP mail must be relayed through another mail server. Several different mail relay hosts can be defined.

Every server that is connected to or communicates with the Internet uses the MAILER(smtp) set of mailers, and most systems on isolated networks use these mailers because they use TCP/IP on their enterprise network. Despite the fact that the vast majority of Sendmail systems require these mailers, installing them is not the default. To support SMTP mail, you must add the MAILER(smtp) macro to your configuration.

In addition to these two important sets of mailers, there are nine other sets of mailers available with the MAILER command, all of which are covered in Appendix A, "m4 Macro Command Reference." Most of them are of very little interest for an average Linux configuration. The two sets of mailers included in the generic-linux.mc configuration are the only ones that most administrators ever use.

### Tweaking the Mailer Configurations

Let's diverge for a moment from the discussion of the generic-linux.mc configuration file to talk about mailer configuration. You're strongly encouraged to create your own DOMAIN source file in the domain directory. You might even be bold enough to create an OSTYPE file for your Linux distribution in the ostype directory. But MAILER source files are different. The mailers loaded by the MAILER macros are defined in the mailer directory. You will never directly edit a file in that directory or add your own files to that directory. To modify the settings of a specific mailer, use the configuration variables created for this purpose. Table 5.1 lists the variables used to tune the local and prog mailers and all of the mailers included in the set of SMTP mailers.

**Table 5.1**   Mailer Configuration Variables

| Variable | Purpose |
| --- | --- |
| DSMTP_MAILER_ARGS | dsmtp mailer arguments. |
| ESMTP_MAILER_ARGS | esmtp mailer arguments. |
| LOCAL_MAILER_ARGS | Arguments for local mail delivery. |
| LOCAL_MAILER_CHARSET | Character set for local 8-bit MIME mail. |
| LOCAL_MAILER_DSN_DIAGNOSTIC_CODE | Delivery status notification code used for local mail. |
| LOCAL_MAILER_EOL | End-of-line character for local mail. |
| LOCAL_MAILER_FLAGS | Local mailer flags added to "lsDFMAw5:/|@q". |
| LOCAL_MAILER_MAX | Maximum size of local mail. |
| LOCAL_MAILER_MAXMSG | Maximum number of messages delivered with a single connection. |

**Table 5.1**     Mailer Configuration Variables *(continued)*

| Variable | Purpose |
| --- | --- |
| LOCAL_MAILER_PATH | Local mail delivery program. |
| LOCAL_SHELL_ARGS | Arguments for prog mail. |
| LOCAL_SHELL_DIR | Directory in which the shell should run. |
| LOCAL_SHELL_FLAGS | Flags added to lsDFM for the shell mailer. |
| LOCAL_SHELL_PATH | Shell used to deliver piped e-mail. |
| RELAY_MAILER_ARGS | Relay mailer arguments. |
| RELAY_MAILER_FLAGS | Flags added to "mDFMuX" for the relay mailer. |
| RELAY_MAIL_MAXMSG | Maximum number of messages for the relay mailer delivered by a single connection. |
| SMTP8_MAILER_ARGS | smtp8 mailer arguments. |
| SMTP_MAILER_ARGS | smtp mailer arguments. |
| SMTP_MAILER_CHARSET | Character set for SMTP 8-bit MIME mail. |
| SMTP_MAILER_FLAGS | Flags added to "mDFMuX" for all SMTP mailers. |
| SMTP_MAILER_MAX | Maximum size of messages for all SMTP mailers. |
| SMTP_MAIL_MAXMSG | Maximum number of SMTP messages delivered by a single connection. |

**Essential Configuration**

**PART 2**

It is very unlikely that you will need to change a mailer setting. But if you do, use the appropriate variable. Don't directly edit the MAILER source files. For example, if you want to limit the size of messages handled by the SMTP mailers to 2,000,000 bytes, you could add the following define to your configuration:

```
define(`SMTP_MAILER_MAX', `2000000')
```

Variable definitions, like those shown in Table 5.1, are available for all mailers. See the "OSTYPE" section of Appendix A for a complete list of these variables.

> *NOTE* Appendix A lists these variables in the discussion of the OSTYPE file
> because that is where mailer and path information is supposed to be stored. How-
> ever, most Sendmail administrators don't want to take it upon themselves to cre-
> ate their own OSTYPE file. Most administrators add commands like these directly
> to the macro configuration file.

The linux.m4 OSTYPE file shown in Listing 5.2 tweaked the mailer path setting for
PROCMAIL_MAILER_PATH. That is the only mailer setting touched by the generic-
linux.mc configuration, and it is indicative of how rarely mailer settings need to be
changed.

The analysis of the generic-linux.mc has shown us several things. We have discovered
the interrelationships of the various m4 source files and we have learned the purpose and
syntax of several different configuration commands. Also, we discovered that the
generic-linux.cf file delivered with the Sendmail 8.11 source code distribution works
fine for our sample Linux system once the various files required by Sendmail are placed
in the correct directories under the correct names.

Next we analyze the Sendmail configuration that was installed as part of the RPM package on our sample Red Hat system. That configuration worked fine from the start. The
analysis of the Red Hat configuration is not to debug a problem: it is to learn about the
configuration provided by the vendor and to see what we can do to improve it.

# The Red Hat Configuration

In Chapter 3, "Running Sendmail," Sendmail 8.11 was installed on a sample Red Hat system using the rpm command. Three RPM packages were installed in this way: the documentation, the configuration files, and the Sendmail program. The Sendmail
configuration file examined in this section is the file that was installed as part of
sendmail-cf-8.11.0-1.i386.rpm.

The RPM package creates a directory structure in /usr/lib/sendmail-cf that is very
similar to the cf directory structure from the Sendmail source code distribution. An ls of
/usr/lib/sendmail-cf shows the following directories:

```
[craig]$ ls /usr/lib/sendmail-cf
README  cf  domain  feature  hack  m4  mailer  ostype  sh  siteconfig
```

This directory contains the same cf, m4, ostype, feature, mailer, and domain subdirectories we saw in Chapter 4, and they perform the same functions. The macro control

file for the Red Hat configuration is found in the /usr/lib/sendmail-cf/cf subdirectory. It is pretty easy to locate. Among the numerous generic files is one file simply named redhat.mc. This is the file we are looking for. Change to /usr/lib/sendmail-cf/cf and cat that file.

```
[craig]$ cd /usr/lib/sendmail-cf/cf
[craig]$ cat redhat.mc
divert(-1)
dnl This is the macro config file used to generate the
dnl /etc/ sendmail.cf file. If you modify the file you will have to
dnl regenerate the /etc/sendmail.cf by running this macro config
dnl through the m4 preprocessor:
dnl
dnl          m4 /etc/sendmail.mc > /etc/sendmail.cf
dnl
dnl You will need to have the sendmail-cf package installed for this
to work.
include(`/usr/lib/sendmail-cf/m4/cf.m4')
VERSIONID(`linux setup for Red Hat Linux')dnl
OSTYPE(`linux')
define(`confDEF_USER_ID',``8:12'')dnl
undefine(`UUCP_RELAY')dnl
undefine(`BITNET_RELAY')dnl
define(`confAUTO_REBUILD')dnl
define(`confTO_CONNECT', `1m')dnl
define(`confTRY_NULL_MX_LIST',true)dnl
define(`confDONT_PROBE_INTERFACES',true)dnl
define(`PROCMAIL_MAILER_PATH',`/usr/bin/procmail')dnl
define(`ALIAS_FILE',`/etc/aliases')dnl
define(`UUCP_MAILER_MAX', `2000000')dnl
define(`confUSERDB_SPEC', `/etc/mail/userdb.db')dnl
dnl define(`confPRIVACY_FLAGS', `authwarnings,novrfy,noexpn')dnl
dnl define(`confTO_QUEUEWARN', `4h')dnl
dnl define(`confTO_QUEUERETURN', `5d')dnl
```

```
dnl define(`confQUEUE_LA', `12')dnl
dnl define(`confREFUSE_LA', `18')dnl
FEATURE(`smrsh',`/usr/sbin/smrsh')dnl
FEATURE(`mailertable',`hash -o /etc/mail/mailertable')dnl
FEATURE(`virtusertable',`hash -o /etc/mail/virtusertable')dnl
FEATURE(redirect)dnl
FEATURE(always_add_domain)dnl
FEATURE(use_cw_file)dnl
FEATURE(local_procmail)dnl
FEATURE(`access_db')dnl
FEATURE(`blacklist_recipients')dnl
dnl We strongly recommend to comment this one out if you want to
dnl protect yourself from spam. However, the laptop and users on
dnl computers that do not have 24x7 DNS do need this.
FEATURE(`accept_unresolvable_domains')dnl
dnl FEATURE(`relay_based_on_MX')dnl
MAILER(smtp)dnl
MAILER(procmail)dnl
```

Wow! This is one of the largest macro configuration files I have ever seen! The first thing we need to do is cut this monster down to size and attack it piecemeal. One thing we can do is eliminate the comments. Every line that begins with dnl is a comment that can be ignored for this exercise. Use grep to weed out every line that begins with dnl. Listing 5.5 shows the result.

**Listing 5.5**   The Active Commands in the Red Hat Macro Control File

```
[craig]$ grep -v '^dnl' redhat.mc
divert(-1)
include(`../m4/cf.m4')
VERSIONID(`linux setup for Red Hat Linux')dnl
OSTYPE(`linux')
define(`confDEF_USER_ID',``8:12'')dnl
undefine(`UUCP_RELAY')dnl
undefine(`BITNET_RELAY')dnl
define(`confAUTO_REBUILD')dnl
define(`confTO_CONNECT', `1m')dnl
define(`confTRY_NULL_MX_LIST',true)dnl
```

```
define(`confDONT_PROBE_INTERFACES',true)dnl
define(`PROCMAIL_MAILER_PATH',`/usr/bin/procmail')dnl
define(`ALIAS_FILE',`/etc/aliases')dnl
define(`STATUS_FILE', `/var/log/sendmail.st')dnl
define(`UUCP_MAILER_MAX', `2000000')dnl
define(`confUSERDB_SPEC', `/etc/mail/userdb.db')dnl
FEATURE(`smrsh',`/usr/sbin/smrsh')dnl
FEATURE(`mailertable',`hash -o /etc/mail/mailertable')dnl
FEATURE(`virtusertable',`hash -o /etc/mail/virtusertable')dnl
FEATURE(redirect)dnl
FEATURE(always_add_domain)dnl
FEATURE(use_cw_file)dnl
FEATURE(local_procmail)dnl
FEATURE(`access_db')dnl
FEATURE(`blacklist_recipients')dnl
FEATURE(`accept_unresolvable_domains')dnl
MAILER(smtp)dnl
MAILER(procmail)dnl
```

Okay, it is still surprisingly large, but it is not as bad as it looks. We have already covered many of the lines in this file and don't need to cover them again. divert and include were covered in Chapter 4. We know what the VERSIONID macro does and can ignore it. The OSTYPE(`linux') macro is the same one covered earlier in this chapter, and during that discussion of the linux.m4 file we covered PROCMAIL_MAILER_PATH and FEATURE(local_procmail). We also covered FEATURE(redirect), FEATURE(use_cw_file), and MAILER(smtp) during the discussion of the generic-linux.mc configuration. So we've made a good start. Still, there are lots of commands to discuss.

### Understanding the Defines and Undefines

The first new command in this configuration is a define command that overrides the default setting of confDEF_USER_ID, which is the variable that holds the user ID and group ID used by Sendmail. By default confDEF_USER_ID is set to 1:1, which on a Red Hat system is user bin and group bin. In the redhat.mc configuration file this is changed to 8:12, which is user mail and group mail. Having a specific user ID and group ID for Sendmail is a good idea. The bin user can be used for a wide variety of programs. Creating a specific mail user and group makes it easier to track actions back to Sendmail and to control the access Sendmail is given to the rest of the system.

The next two lines are undefine commands that clear the names of the relay servers from the UUCP_RELAY and the BITNET_RELAY variables. Clearing these variables means that all UUCP sites must be directly connected and that the .BITNET pseudo-domain will not work on this system. (BITNET is an outdated mail network that is no longer used.) However, in this specific configuration there aren't any server names to clear from UUCP_RELAY or BITNET_RELAY. By default, UUCP_RELAY and BITNET_RELAY are empty, so there are no default values to clear. We know the commands that have been executed so far in the macro configuration file and in the linux.m4 file, and none of those have set any relay server names. Therefore these two commands are unnecessary for this configuration.

Next comes a series of nine define commands. We know that PROCMAIL_MAILER_PATH specifies the path to the procmail program. The other eight define variables, however, are new. They are:

**confAUTO_REBUILD**   This boolean tells Sendmail whether or not it should automatically rebuild the aliases database. It defaults to false, meaning that the aliases database must be manually rebuilt as described in Chapter 6, "Using Sendmail Databases." If set to true, Sendmail checks to see if the aliases source file is newer than the aliases.pag, aliases.dir, and aliases.db database files. If it is, Sendmail automatically rebuilds the database. This capability can be exploited in a denial of service attack. A fix was added to address this vulnerability prior to Sendmail version 8.10, but the Sendmail developers have deprecated this option and strongly recommend that you not use it.

**confTO_CONNECT**   This parameter defines the amount of time Sendmail will wait for the TCP connection to complete. By default, Sendmail sets no time limit and counts on the TCP/IP parameters configured in the kernel to handle this time out. The Red Hat configuration shown in Listing 5.5 sets this timeout to one minute (1m), which seems like plenty of time to wait for a network connection to complete.

**confTRY_NULL_MX_LIST**   This boolean tells Sendmail whether or not it should attempt to deliver mail directly to hosts that list this server as their best mail exchange server. The Red Hat configuration sets this to true, so the server will attempt to deliver mail to its own MX clients. By default, this is set to false, which causes mail outbound for an MX client to be flagged as a configuration error. The default is correct for most configurations. As Chapter 2 explained, the MX server collects mail for its clients and either waits for the client to pull down the mail with a protocol such as POP or routes the mail to the correct destination using one of the Sendmail databases. It doesn't, however, forward mail on to a client using the same address that originally delivered the mail to the server. However, as we saw in the discussion of class w earlier in this chapter, the MX server only knows who its clients are if it is properly configured. If it receives mail that MX records say it should accept but that class w says it should not accept, it has a configuration error. The Red Hat configuration forgives this configuration error and attempts to deliver the mail directly to the client.

**confDONT_PROBE_INTERFACES**   This boolean tells Sendmail whether or not it should add the names and addresses of all of the network interfaces to class w. The default is false, which means that Sendmail *does* probe all network interfaces and automatically adds the names and addresses of those interfaces to class w. With the default setting, a second interface installed in the server is automatically detected and considered an acceptable e-mail address. The Red Hat configuration sets this to true, which means that only the names and addresses associated with the primary network interface are added to class w. If another interface is installed in the Red Hat system, it must be manually added to class w before it will be considered an acceptable e-mail address.

**ALIAS_FILE**   This parameter defines the path of the aliases file. The default path is /etc/mail/aliases. The Red Hat configuration sets this to /etc/aliases, which was the default prior to Sendmail 8.11 and is the most common location for the aliases file on Linux systems.

**STATUS_FILE**   This parameter defines the path to the statistics file. The default is /etc/mail/statistics. This default is new as of Sendmail 8.11, which changes the name of the file from the previous default of sendmail.st to statistics. The Red Hat configuration maintains the traditional name and places the file in the Linux /var/log directory.

**UUCP_MAILER_MAX**   This parameter defines the maximum acceptable size of a UUCP mail message. The default is 100,000 bytes. The Red Hat configuration sets this to 2,000,000 bytes.

**confUSERDB_SPEC**   This parameter defines the path to the user database and determines whether or not the database is used. By default no path to the user database is defined. When no path is defined, the user database is not used in processing mail addresses. The Red Hat configuration declares that the path to the user database is /etc/mail/userdb.db. This means that Sendmail will check for the existence of that file and will use it to process addresses after the aliases database is applied to the address and before the user's .forward file is applied. The user database is covered in detail in Chapter 6.

### Understanding the Features

The `redhat.mc` macro configuration file shown in Listing 5.5 also includes 10 FEATURE commands. We have already discussed the `redirect`, `use_cw_file`, and `local_procmail` features, but there are seven new features that we haven't seen before. These are:

**smrsh**  The smrsh feature tells Sendmail to use `smrsh` instead of `/bin/sh` as the program for the `prog` mailer. This is a highly recommended feature. The SendMail Restricted Shell (`smrsh`) limits what can be run via the `prog` mailer, which is an important improvement to Sendmail security.

The argument associated with the `smrsh` feature is the pathname of the `smrsh` program. The default is to look for a program named `smrsh` in the directory defined by the `confEBINDIR` variable. In the `redhat.mc` file, the path of the `smrsh` program is explicitly set to `/usr/sbin/smrsh`. As we saw earlier, the `smrsh` directory path is set to `/usr/sbin` with the `confEBINDIR` variable in the `linux.m4` OSTYPE file. Because of that, an explicit path was not really required for the `redhat.mc` configuration and is probably only used to make the configuration self-documenting.

**mailertable**  This feature tells Sendmail to use the `mailertable` database to route specific domain names to specific mailers. The argument for the `mailertable` feature defines the database type and the path to the database. The default database type is `hash` and the default path is `/etc/mail/mailertable`. The `redhat.mc` configuration explicitly identifies the database type as `hash` and the path as `/etc/mail/mailertable`. Since these are the defaults, the argument provided with the `mailertable` feature is not really required for the `redhat.mc` configuration and is probably only used to make the configuration self-documenting. Chapter 6 covers the `mailertable` database in detail.

**virtusertable**  This feature tells Sendmail to use the `virtusertable` database to map domain names and hostnames to specific e-mail addresses. This database is an extended alias database that accepts incoming mail that has a domain name or hostname found in class w or class {VirtHost} and routes that mail as directed by the `virtusertable` database. Chapter 6 describes how this database is used.

The argument for the `virtusertable` feature defines the database type and the path to the database. The default database type is `hash` and the default path is `/etc/mail/virtusertable`. The argument provided with the `virtusertable` feature in the `redhat.mc` configuration is not really required because it reiterates the defaults. It is probably only used to make the configuration self-documenting.

**always_add_domain**   This feature tells Sendmail to add the domain name to locally delivered mail. By default, a username is sufficient for local delivery. A quick test illustrates the effect always_add_domain has on a local address:

```
[root]# sendmail -bt -Cgeneric-linux.cf
ADDRESS TEST MODE (ruleset 3 NOT automatically invoked)
Enter <ruleset> <address>
> /tryflags HS
> /try local craig
Trying header sender address craig for mailer local
canonify          input: craig
Canonify2         input: craig
Canonify2         returns: craig
canonify          returns: craig
1                 input: craig
1                 returns: craig
HdrFromL          input: craig
AddDomain         input: craig
AddDomain         returns: craig
MasqHdr           input: craig
MasqHdr           returns: craig
HdrFromL          returns: craig
final             input: craig
final             returns: craig
Rcode = 0, addr = craig
> ^D
[root]# sendmail -bt -Credhat.cf
ADDRESS TEST MODE (ruleset 3 NOT automatically invoked)
Enter <ruleset> <address>
> /tryflags HS
> /try local craig
Trying header sender address craig for mailer local
```

```
canonify          input: craig
Canonify2         input: craig
Canonify2         returns: craig
canonify          returns: craig
1                 input: craig
1                 returns: craig
HdrFromL          input: craig
AddDomain         input: craig
AddDomain         returns: craig < @ *LOCAL* >
MasqHdr           input: craig < @ *LOCAL* >
MasqHdr           returns: craig < @ wren . foobirds . org . >
HdrFromL          returns: craig < @ wren . foobirds . org . >
final             input: craig < @ wren . foobirds . org . >
final             returns: craig @ wren . foobirds . org
Rcode = 0, addr = craig@wren.foobirds.org
> ^D
```

We run two tests using Sendmail in -bt mode. In both cases we ask Sendmail to process a header/sender address, and we give it the address craig to process through the local mailer. The first test uses the generic-linux.cf configuration, which does not use the always_add_domain feature. The address goes in as craig and comes out as craig. In the second test we use the redhat.cf configuration, which uses the always_add_domain feature. In the second test, craig is converted to craig@wren.foobirds.org. The effect of always_add_domain is clearly shown.

This is a good feature to use. The address shown, even on local mail, is valid everywhere. This helps avoid confusion among your users, and confused users are something you want to avoid!

**access_db** This feature tells Sendmail to use the access database to decide what hosts, domains, and networks are acceptable sources of e-mail. An optional argument that defines the database type and path can be used with the access_db feature. The default database type is hash and the default path is /etc/mail/access. The access database is described in Chapter 6. Its use in fighting spam is covered in Chapter 11.

**blacklist_recipients** This feature allows the access database to be used to block mail to specific recipients. Normally, the access database is used to control mail from undesirable sources. With this feature, the access database also can be used to control mail bound for certain destinations. The `blacklist_recipients` feature is covered in detail in Chapter 11.

`accept_unresolvable_domains`    This feature tells Sendmail to accept mail from a source even if the domain name of the source cannot be resolved by DNS. By default, Sendmail takes the hostname in the MAIL FROM: header and asks DNS to map that name back to an address before it will accept incoming mail. This option overrides that default behavior.

Allowing mail from unresolvable domains is a potential security problem, but this feature is often necessary for systems that do not have full-time DNS service. Such systems are laptops that might be disconnected from the network or systems sitting behind a firewall that are not given full DNS access. The Red Hat configuration includes this feature because Red Hat must create a configuration that will work with the widest range of systems. If you have full-time DNS service for your network—and you should—you should remove this feature from your configuration.

Following this batch of FEATURE commands are two MAILER commands. The first is the MAILER(smtp) command that we have already discussed. The second is the MAILER(procmail) command. Looking at this command, you might think it has something to do with the `local_procmail` parameter described earlier. It doesn't. `local_procmail` means that the mailer named `local` will use the program `procmail`. MAILER(procmail) means that a mailer named `procmail` that uses the `procmail` program will be added to the configuration. These two are unrelated. The mailer installed by MAILER(procmail) is used only if you configure entries in the `mailertable` to use it.

That's it—a big complex configuration that includes important capabilities, such as `smrsh`, and not so important capabilities, like MAILER(procmail). As we saw in Chapter 4, this configuration works fine and delivers mail for our Red Hat system. But it is only a start. As the discussion of the `accept_unresolvable_domains` feature and the comments inside the `redhat.mc` file make clear, we are expected to create our own configuration that suits our needs. In the next section we do just that. Starting with the `redhat.mc` file, we create our own Red Hat configuration.

# Modifying the Red Hat Configuration

There are lots of good things in the `redhat.mc` configuration, a couple of undesirable things, and a few redundancies. Since we are going to rewrite the configuration, I think we should also reorganize it to move some things out of the macro configuration file into macro source files where those items are a better fit. As a result, we will edit the `redhat.mc` file, create a new OSTYPE file, and create a new DOMAIN file. To do this we first copy redhat.mc to redhat811.mc, ostype/linux.m4 to ostype/redhat7.0.m4, and domain/generic.m4 to domain/foobirds.m4.

Next we edit the files. First I edited the macro configuration file, redhat811.mc, changing the DOMAIN command to load foobirds.m4 instead of generic.m4. Then I moved the confDEF_USER_ID parameter to the new OSTYPE file because I consider the user ID and group ID setting specific to Red Hat Linux. Next I deleted the two undefines because they serve no purpose. I also deleted confAUTO_REBUILD because it is a deprecated option.

I considered moving confTO_CONNECT to the OSTYPE file because it is designed to override the default TCP timeout settings used by the Linux operating system. Instead, I decided to delete it because I have not had any TCP timeout problems and don't anticipate any. Likewise I considered moving confTRY_NULL_MX_LIST to the DOMAIN file because this option is clearly related to how domain MX records are handled. But I decided to delete the option instead because it causes Sendmail to handle MX records in a non-standard way. Unless I must break a standard to get things running, I don't want to.

I deleted the confDONT_PROBE_INTERFACES option because I want Sendmail to include all of the server's interfaces as part of class w. The confDONT_PROBE_INTERFACES option is primarily useful on laptop systems where PCMCIA interfaces may be added or removed from a running system. Since I'm not running my server on a laptop, I don't want this option. For the same reason, I deleted the accept_unresolvable_domains feature from the configuration, which is primarily used on laptops. I have good DNS service and therefore should not use that feature.

Some lines required no decision. PROCMAIL_MAILER_PATH and local_procmail are already in the OSTYPE file, and redirect and use_cw_file are already in the DOMAIN file. However, the confMAX_HEADERS_LENGTH option that came from the generic.m4 file seemed unnecessary to me, so I deleted it from the new DOMAIN file. I also deleted the ifdef conditional from the OSTYPE file to set PROCMAIL_MAILER_PATH unconditionally.

I moved ALIAS_FILE, STATUS_FILE, and smrsh to the OSTYPE file because file locations and mailer options are usually stored there. I deleted the UUCP_MAILER_MAX setting because the configuration does not define any UUCP mailers. I moved confUSERDB_SPEC, always_add_domain, access_db, and blacklist_recipients to the new DOMAIN file because I decided to put all domain, masquerading, and anti-spam configuration in that file. The remaining configuration commands I left in the macro configuration file. Confused? Take a look at Table 5.2. It lists every line from the original redhat.mc configuration file and tells what we did with it.

**Table 5.2**    Rewriting the Red Hat Configuration File

| Command | Disposition |
| --- | --- |
| OSTYPE | Kept in the macro configuration file. |
| confDEF_USER_ID | Moved to the OSTYPE file. |
| UUCP_RELAY | Deleted. |
| BITNET_RELAY | Deleted. |
| confAUTO_REBUILD | Deleted. |
| confTO_CONNECT | Deleted. |
| confTRY_NULL_MX_LIST | Deleted. |
| confDONT_PROBE_INTERFACES | Deleted. |
| PROCMAIL_MAILER_PATH | Located in the OSTYPE file. |
| ALIAS_FILE | Moved to the OSTYPE file. |
| STATUS_FILE | Moved to the OSTYPE file. |
| UUCP_MAILER_MAX | Deleted. |
| confUSERDB_SPEC | Moved to the DOMAIN file. |
| smrsh | Moved to the OSTYPE file. |
| mailertable | Kept in the macro configuration file. |
| virtusertable | Kept in the macro configuration file. |
| redirect | Located in the DOMAIN file. |
| always_add_domain | Moved to the DOMAIN file. |
| use_cw_file | Located in the DOMAIN file. |
| local_procmail | Located in the OSTYPE file. |
| access_db | Moved to the DOMAIN file. |

**Essential Configuration**

**PART 2**

**Table 5.2** Rewriting the Red Hat Configuration File *(continued)*

| Command | Disposition |
| --- | --- |
| blacklist_recipients | Moved to the DOMAIN file. |
| accept_unresolvable_domains | Deleted. |
| MAILER(smtp) | Kept in the macro configuration file. |
| MAILER(procmail) | Kept in the macro configuration file. |

Listing 5.6 shows the contents of all three files for the new configuration. Examining the listing will make it clear what went where.

**Listing 5.6** Custom DOMAIN, OSTYPE, and Macro Control Files

```
[root]# cat redhat811.mc
VERSIONID(`Red Hat Linux Configuration for Sendmail 8.11')dnl
OSTYPE(`redhat7.0')
DOMAIN(`foobirds')
FEATURE(`mailertable',`hash -o /etc/mail/mailertable')dnl
FEATURE(`virtusertable',`hash -o /etc/mail/virtusertable')dnl
MAILER(smtp)dnl
MAILER(procmail)dnl
[root]# cat ../ostype/redhat7.0.m4
VERSIONID(`Red Hat Linux release 7.0')dnl
define(`confDEF_USER_ID',``8:12'')dnl
define(`ALIAS_FILE',`/etc/aliases')dnl
define(`STATUS_FILE', `/var/log/sendmail.st')dnl
define(`confEBINDIR', `/usr/sbin')
FEATURE(`smrsh')dnl
define(`PROCMAIL_MAILER_PATH', `/usr/bin/procmail'))
FEATURE(local_procmail)
[root]# cat ../domain/foobirds.m4
VERSIONID(`Setting for the foobirds.org domain')dnl
define(`confFORWARD_PATH',
`$z/.forward.$w+$h:$z/.forward+$h:$z/.forward.$w:$z/.
forward')dnl
define(`confUSERDB_SPEC', `/etc/mail/userdb.db')dnl
FEATURE(always_add_domain)dnl
FEATURE(`access_db')dnl
```

```
FEATURE(`blacklist_recipients')dnl
FEATURE(`redirect')dnl
FEATURE(`use_cw_file')dnl
EXPOSED_USER(`root')
```

The `redhat811.mc` macro control file has been reduced to a more readable seven lines. The `OSTYPE` command was edited to call the new `redhat7.0.m4` `OSTYPE` source file and the `DOMAIN` command was added to call the new `foobirds.m4` `DOMAIN` source file. These three files combine all of the desirable features that we saw in the `generic-linux.mc` configuration and in the `redhat.mc` configuration.

# In Sum

A Sendmail configuration is not built from scratch. Start from one of the sample files that is provided as part of the Sendmail source code distribution or start with the configuration file that comes from your distribution vendor. Read and understand the vendor's configuration before modifying it to create your own. Don't assume the vendor's configuration is right for you. A vendor often must make compromises to create a configuration that runs on a wide variety of systems. Focus the configuration you create on those capabilities that you actually need.

Starting from a sample configuration can simplify the creation of your configuration, but the sample configurations carry their own level of complexity. Some, like `generic-linux.mc`, are reasonably simple, but may not provide the features you need. Others, like `redhat.mc`, are more complex than necessary. The way to attack the complexity of the sample configuration files is one line at a time. Even a very large macro configuration file probably has fewer than 30 lines. Using a reference, such as this book, get a general idea of what each line does. Discard those lines that are clearly unnecessary for your configuration. Then research the others in more detail to select those that you want to keep.

The analysis of the configurations in this chapter have shown that Sendmail relies heavily on database files to route mail, convert addresses, and control spam. In the next chapter, we look at the databases used by Sendmail and describe how you can use those databases to configure your system.

# 6

# Using Sendmail Databases

**M**ention Sendmail configuration to a group of Linux administrators. The first thing that most of them will think of is a large `sendmail.cf` file filled with terse configuration commands that are difficult to read. Some think of an `m4` macro control file built from a complex configuration language that has hundreds of options. A very few think of database files. Yet database files play an important role in Sendmail configuration—a bigger role for the average system administrator than either the `sendmail.cf` or the macro configuration files.

The reason that the databases play such a big role for the average administrator is not that the databases are more important than the other files; they're not. The reason is that many administrators use the `sendmail.cf` provided by the Linux distribution vendor and never change it. Or they build a custom configuration when they install Sendmail and never change that. They then use the Sendmail databases for day-to-day configuration changes and to control the way in which Sendmail processes mail.

Sendmail uses several databases. In this chapter you'll learn about all of them. I use the term "databases" loosely. Some of the files described here are flat files; others are true databases. Regardless of their structure, all of these files are used to control the operation of Sendmail. Understanding the role of the databases and using them to your advantage are essential parts of becoming an effective Sendmail administrator. Let's begin by understanding how database support is incorporated in Sendmail and specified in the Sendmail configuration.

# Adding Database Support

The aliases database is the only database included in every configuration. If you want to use any other database, you need to add that database to your Sendmail configuration. There are two levels of configuration required for database support:

- First, the Sendmail program must be compiled with database support. Several compiler options are available to select the database support appropriate for your server.
- Second, the Sendmail configuration must be built with database support. Various features and defines are available to include database support in your server's configuration.

Understanding the various database compiler options, how they are set, and how you can tell which ones are set for your server is essential. These options tell you what database types are supported by your system and should be checked before you attempt to implement any new database feature. The database compiler options are covered next.

## Database Compiler Options

If you have experience with compiling Sendmail, you may be tempted to look for the database compiler options in the Makefile in the Sendmail distribution's source code directory. You may even remember, or have read, that the database compiler options are set in the Makefile with the DBMDEF= directive—e.g., DBMDEF= -DNEWDB -DNIS. But all that has changed. Now, compiler options are set in the files located in the devtools directory of the Sendmail source code distribution. See Chapter 3, "Running Sendmail," for details about the devtools directory.

The default database compiler options are normally changed in an operating system–specific file in the devtools/OS directory or in a file you create specially for your server in the devtools/Site directory. The command that is used in those files to select support for different database types is confMAPDEF. The default devtools/OS/Linux file does not contain a confMAPDEF command because the default database types determined by the build process are generally correct for Linux. Create your own file in devtools/Site only if you want to define optional database types. The function of the confMAPDEF command parallels that of the old DBMDEF= Makefile variable, and it accepts the same values, which are shown in Table 6.1.

**Table 6.1** Available confMAPDEF Database Options

| Option | Usage |
|---|---|
| AUTO_NIS_ALIASES | Searches the NIS server for aliases. |
| AUTO_NETINFO_ALIASES | Searches the netinfo server for aliases. |
| AUTO_NETINFO_HOSTS | Searches the netinfo server for host addresses. |
| HESIOD | Adds support for Hesiod databases. |
| LDAPMAP | Adds support for LDAP databases. |
| MAP_NSD | Adds support for Irix NSD databases. |
| MAP_REGEX | Allows database searches using regular expressions. |
| NDBM | Adds support for Unix ndbm databases. |
| NETINFO | Adds support for NeXT netinfo databases. |
| NEWDB | Adds support for the hash and btree databases. |
| NIS | Adds support for Sun NIS databases. |
| NISPLUS | Adds support for Sun NIS+ databases. |
| OLD_NEWDB | Adds support for an outdated form of the db databases. |
| PH_MAP | Adds support for a CCSO phonebook database. |
| UDB_DEFAULT_SPEC | Specifies the default path used for the user database. |
| USERDB | Adds support for the user database. |
| YPCOMPAT | Adds support for an outdated SunOS version of NIS. |

Essential Configuration

PART 2

The Table shows a large number of database options, many more than you will ever use. No system uses all of these database types. They are included as options to support a wide range of operating systems. For example, three options, AUTO_NETINFO_ALIASES, AUTO_NETINFO_HOSTS, and NETINFO, support a database specific to the NeXT operating system, and another, MAP_NSD, is specific to Irix. Two options, OLD_NEWDB and YPCOMPAT, are described as outdated. Clearly, a Linux system administrator can ignore many of these options. All of the options are there if you ever need them; it is just unlikely that you ever will. The options that are most useful to a Linux administrator are:

**NEWDB**   This option adds the basic database support used on Linux systems. It provides both hash and btree databases. This one option provides all you need to build and access most local Sendmail databases.

**MAP_REGEX**   This option adds a new feature to Sendmail that permits databases to be searched with regular expressions. Anyone who has used regular expressions with grep knows that they are much more powerful than simple wildcard characters. This added power is useful when you need to create complex rules to block spammers.

**USERDB**   This option adds support for the user database, which can be used to process e-mail addresses on both inbound and outbound e-mail. A related option is UDB_DEFAULT_SPEC, which defines the default path to the user database. The path can also be set with the confUSERDB_SPEC define in the Sendmail configuration, as we saw in the redhat.mc file in Chapter 5, "Understanding a Vendor's Configuration." I prefer setting the path value in the configuration instead of compiling it into Sendmail because it is more easily changed when it is set in the configuration. However, some path value must be explicitly defined before Sendmail can use the user database.

**NIS**   This option provides access to Network Information System (NIS) databases. These are administrative databases, such as /etc/mail/aliases and /etc/hosts, stored on the NIS server. The related database options NISPLUS and YPCOMPAT are rarely used on Linux systems. NIS+, which is an upgraded version of NIS, is not often used in Linux environments; YPCOMPAT creates compatibility with a version of NIS that has not been produced in several years. YPCOMPAT permits use of the old "plus syntax," in which a + is placed at the end of a local administrative database to tell the system to first search the local database and then search the database on the NIS server. Thus, with YPCOMPAT and a + at the end of the /etc/mail/aliases database, Sendmail first checks the local aliases database and then checks the one on the NIS server. Sounds like a good idea, but it is completely unnecessary. The AUTO_NIS_ALIASES option does exactly the same thing. It tells Sendmail to check the local aliases database first and then check the NIS server, and it does it without the outdated plus syntax. (Details of setting up an NIS server on a Linux system are covered in the *Linux DNS Server Administration* book of this series.)

To force Sendmail to use these four database options, you could either edit the devtools/OS/linux.m4 file or create a file in the devtools/Site directory that contained the following line:

```
define(`confDEFMAP', `-DNEWDB -DNIS -DMAP_REGEX -DUSERDB')
```

Once the line is inserted in the file of your choice, recompile Sendmail to put the options into effect. (See Chapter 3 for instructions on compiling Sendmail.)

However, before going to all this trouble, check which options your Sendmail program is already using. The default database option settings vary based on the database libraries detected by the Sendmail source distribution's build routine. On a Linux system, the default is usually -DNEWDB. But build does a good job of detecting the capabilities of your system, so your Sendmail program could include additional options. Listing 6.1 shows the options compiled into the Sendmail program delivered with the sendmail-8.11.0.i386.rpm RPM file.

**Listing 6.1**  Checking the sendmail Compile Options

```
[root]# sendmail -bt -d0.4
Version 8.11.0
 Compiled with: MAP_REGEX LOG MATCHGECOS MIME7TO8 MIME8TO7 NAMED_BIND
                NETINET NETUNIX NEWDB NIS QUEUE SASL SCANF SFIO SMTP
                STARTTLS USERDB
canonical name: wren.foobirds.org
        a.k.a.: wren
 UUCP nodename: wren.foobirds.org
        a.k.a.: wren
        a.k.a.: [172.16.12.3]

============ SYSTEM IDENTITY (after readcf) ============
      (short domain name) $w = wren
  (canonical domain name) $j = wren.foobirds.org
         (subdomain name) $m = foobirds.org
              (node name) $k = wren.foobirds.org
========================================================

ADDRESS TEST MODE (ruleset 3 NOT automatically invoked)
Enter <ruleset> <address>
> ^D
```

Listing 6.1 shows Sendmail being run in -bt test mode. Sendmail is also being passed the debug value -d0.4. This debug value causes Sendmail to display several lines of information before accepting input. We don't really have any input for Sendmail to process; we just want to see the display so we enter Ctrl+D to exit.

The first line displayed by the Sendmail program tells us this is Sendmail 8.11.0. The second line is the one we're interested in. It lists all of the options that Sendmail was compiled with. Four of these, MAP_REGEX, NEWDB, NIS, and USERDB, are related to databases, and they are the four options we want. This display makes it clear that there is no need for us to recompile Sendmail to set database options. If your system doesn't have the options you want, make sure you have all of the necessary database libraries before setting the compiler options and recompiling Sendmail.

Listing 6.1 shows that the Sendmail delivered with the Red Hat RPM is ready to run all of the databases we could want, assuming support for the databases is included in the Sendmail configuration. The configuration options used to add support for Sendmail databases is the next topic.

## Configuration Options

As noted at the beginning of this section, the `aliases` database is the only database that is available to Sendmail by default. All of the other databases described in this chapter must be added to the Sendmail configuration before they can be used. The following defines and features are used to configure support for the optional databases, as well as some important files:

**define(`confUSERDB_SPEC', `path')**   The confUSERDB_SPEC option tells Sendmail to apply the user database to local addresses after the `aliases` database is applied and before the `.forward` file is applied. The *path* argument given with this option is the full pathname of the database. There is no default for the path unless Sendmail is compiled with UDB_DEFAULT_SPEC. Setting the path with the confUSERDB_SPEC option is much simpler and more flexible than using UDB_DEFAULT_SPEC. The following `define` command enables the user database and tells Sendmail that it can be found in /etc/mail/userdb.db.

        define(`confUSERDB_SPEC', `/etc/mail/userdb.db')

**define(`confCR_FILE'[, `path'])**   The confCR_FILE option tells Sendmail to add the list of hosts permitted to relay mail from the specified file to the class R variable. The full pathname of the file can be provided as an argument to the option. If the pathname is not provided, it defaults to /etc/mail/relay-domains for Sendmail 8.11.

**FEATURE(`use_ct_file'[, `path'])**   The use_ct_file feature tells Sendmail to add trusted usernames from the file to the class variable t. The full pathname of the file is an optional argument. If the pathname is not provided, Sendmail 8.11 defaults to /etc/mail/trusted-users.

**FEATURE(`use_cw_file'[, `path'])**   The use_cw_file tells Sendmail to add hostname aliases from the file to the class variable w. The full pathname of the file is an optional argument. If the pathname is not provided, Sendmail 8.11 uses /etc/mail/local-host-names as the default.

**FEATURE(`access_db'[, `*specification*'])** The access_db feature tells Sendmail to use the access database to control mail relaying and mail delivery based on the source of the mail. An optional database specification can be provided to define the database type and the full pathname of the database. By default, the database type is hash and the database path is /etc/mail/access.

**FEATURE(`mailertable'[, `*specification*'])** The mailertable feature tells Sendmail to use the mailer table to map the domain name in a delivery address to a specific mailer and host for delivery. An optional database specification can be provided to define the database type and the full pathname of the database. By default, the database type is hash and the database path is /etc/mail/mailertable.

**FEATURE(`virtusertable'[, `*specification*'])** The virtusertable feature tells Sendmail to use the virtusertable database to map the recipient address in incoming e-mail to a different recipient address. This function is similar to the one performed by the aliases database, except that the virtusertable aliases domain names, not just usernames. An optional database specification can be provided to define the database type and the full pathname of the database. By default, the database type is hash and the database path is /etc/mail/virtusertable.

**FEATURE(`genericstable'[, `*specification*'])** The genericstable feature tells Sendmail to use the genericstable database to map the sender address on outbound mail to a different sender address. An optional database specification can be provided to define the database type and the full pathname of the database. By default, the database type is hash and the database path is /etc/mail/genericstable.

**FEATURE(`domaintable'[, `*specification*'])** The domaintable feature tells Sendmail to use the domain table to map one domain name to another. An optional database specification can be provided to define the database type and the full pathname of the database. By default, the database type is hash and the database path is /etc/mail/domaintable.

**FEATURE(`uucpdomain'[, `*specification*'])** The uucpdomain feature tells Sendmail to use the uucpdomain database to map UUCP site names to Internet domain names. An optional database specification can be provided to define the database type and the full pathname of the database. By default, the database type is hash and the database path is /etc/mail/uucpdomain.

**FEATURE(`bitdomain'[, `*specification*'])** The bitdomain feature tells Sendmail to use the bitdomain database to map BITNET hostnames to Internet domain names. (BITNET is an outdated IBM network that you won't use.) An optional database specification can be provided to define the database type and the full pathname of the database. By default, the database type is hash and the database path is /etc/mail/bitdomain.

Essential Configuration

PART 2

There are more databases available for Sendmail than you will ever use. A couple are of little or no value to Linux sites—the `bitdomain` database converts addresses for a network that no Linux site uses and the `uucpdomain` database converts UUCP "bang" addresses, the old *host!user* e-mail addresses, that almost no one uses anymore. Other available databases have overlapping functions that might mean you don't need to use both of them at your site. The `redhat.mc` configuration delivered with the RPM contains fewer than half of the defines and features listed above, and that configuration probably has more database capabilities than you will really need. To help you evaluate which databases you do need, we'll examine all of them in more detail.

# The Cr, Cw, and Ct Files

The first three databases we cover are not, in the strict sense of the word, databases. They are disk files used to load `sendmail.cf` class variables. The "cr" and "cw" files perform important roles in configuring Sendmail, but changes in the security atmosphere of the network mean that the "ct" file no longer has a useful role.

The file that loads the t class variable is often called the "ct" file because the traditional name of this file was `/etc/sendmail.ct`. In Sendmail 8.11 the default name of this file is `/etc/mail/trusted-users`, but the function of the file remains the same. It is used to add usernames to the list of users that are trusted to send mail under another user's name. By default, class t contains the usernames daemon, root, and uucp.

You will never use the `/etc/mail/trusted-users` file, and there are some good reasons why you won't. First, it is a bad idea to let people send out mail under other people's names. So in general, you don't want to expand the list of trusted users. Second, if you decide you absolutely must add usernames to the trusted user list, you won't add enough names to justify putting them in a separate file. For example, assume you want to add the username "mail" to the trusted user list. You could edit the macro configuration file to add the `FEATURE(use_ct_file)` command, rebuild the `sendmail.cf` file, and create a `trusted-users` file containing the single word `mail`. But why would you? You could just as easily edit the macro configuration file to add the `define(`confTRUSTED_USERS', `mail')` command, rebuild the `sendmail.cf` file, and be done with it. Not only is this second approach slightly easier, it is safer because there is one fewer file created and thus one fewer file where the permissions could be set incorrectly.

---

**WARNING** Despite this example, neither confTRUSTED_USERS nor use_ct_file is recommended because you shouldn't add any users to the trusted user list. Trusting users is a bad idea in this age of spammers and security crackers.

Unlike the "ct" file, which is never used, the "cr" file is always used. The "cr" file is really named the `relay-domains` file. Sendmail always uses the data it finds in the `relay-domains` file. The purpose and structure of that file is the next topic.

## The *relay-domains* File

When mail arrives at a Sendmail server, it is either accepted, rejected, or relayed. If it is addressed to the server itself, by any name that the server accepts as its own, the mail is accepted for local delivery, meaning that the mail is either placed in the mailbox of a local user or routed as directed by one of the Sendmail databases. If the mail is not addressed to the server itself, the mail is either rejected or relayed. Mail is relayed by re-sending it to the delivery address. Prior to Sendmail 8.9, all mail addressed to another host that was received by a Sendmail server was relayed. Now, no mail is relayed unless you explicitly tell Sendmail to relay it. This change was a big headache for many system administrators who were using a Sendmail server to relay outbound mail for their PCs. But the change was necessary. Spammers were exploiting the relaying feature of Sendmail to hide the true source of spam. Now all administrators must pay the price of spam, and that price is the extra work necessary to create an explicit relay configuration.

One way to explicitly enable relaying is to list the names of hosts allowed to relay mail in the /etc/mail/relay-domains file. Sendmail copies anything written in that file to the class variable R. Any host listed in class variable R is allowed to relay mail. Listing 6.2 shows the contents of a simple `relay-domains` file.

**Listing 6.2**   Using the `relay-domains` File

```
[root]# cat /etc/mail/relay-domains
ibis.foobirds.org
[root]# ps -ax | grep sendmail
  542 ?        S       0:00 sendmail: accepting connections
[root]# kill -HUP 542
[root]# sendmail -bt
ADDRESS TEST MODE (ruleset 3 NOT automatically invoked)
Enter <ruleset> <address>
> $=R
ibis.foobirds.org
> ^D
```

A SIGHUP signal is passed to the Sendmail process to ensure that it reads the hostnames from `relay-domains` into class R. The test in Listing 6.2 shows that class R was successfully modified.

> **NOTE**  The hosts listed in `relay-domains` and in class R are the sources of relayed mail; they are not the destinations. Class w, covered in the next section, contains destination hostnames. Class R contains source hostnames.

Listing 6.2 adds only one domain name to class R. It is possible to add a limited number of domains to class R from inside the Sendmail configuration by using the `RELAY_DOMAIN` macro. For example, the following command placed inside the Sendmail configuration file would have the same effect as the `relay-domains` file shown in Listing 6.2:

```
RELAY_DOMAIN(`ibis.foobirds.org')
```

However, using the `relay-domains` file is simpler than using the `RELAY_DOMAIN` macro. The `RELAY_DOMAIN` command requires modifying the Sendmail macro configuration and rerunning m4 to build the new `sendmail.cf` file. Using the `relay-domains` file does not. By default, Sendmail checks for a file named `/etc/mail/relay-domains` and adds the names it finds there to class R. No modifications to the configuration are required. You would need to place a command in the macro configuration only if you wanted to change the default filename of the `relay-domains` file. There are two ways this can be done:

**`define(`confCR_FILE'[, `path'])`**  This `define` command sets the path to the file loaded into class R. It defaults to `/etc/mail/relay-domains`, which means that even if you have not explicitly set any value for this file in your configuration, Sendmail uses a file with that name to load class R. The `confCR_FILE` option is only needed if you want to change the default filename. For example, the following command causes Sendmail to load class R from a file named `/etc/relay-hosts`:

```
define(`confCR_FILE', `/etc/relay-hosts')
```

**`RELAY_DOMAIN_FILE(`path')`**  This macro can be used to specify the path to the file that loads class R. For example, the following command loads class R from a file named `/etc/relay-for`:

```
RELAY_DOMAIN_FILE(`/etc/relay-for')
```

There are three commands relating to setting relay values for class R, `RELAY_DOMAIN`, `RELAY_DOMAIN_FILE`, and `confCR_FILE`. But you don't need to use any of them. Just create a file named `/etc/mail/relay-domains` and put the names of the hosts for which your server should relay mail in that file. That's all there is to it.

The "cr" file is a default feature of the Sendmail configuration. Nothing needs to be done to the Sendmail configuration to add it. On the other hand, the "cw" file, which is discussed next, must be specifically added to the configuration even though its role is as important as that of the "cr" file.

## The *local-host-names* File

In Chapter 5, both the generic Linux configuration and the Red Hat configuration contain the FEATURE(use_cw_file) command. That feature reads the /etc/mail/local-host-names file and adds the hostnames listed there to the hostnames and addresses defined in class w. Listing 5.4 in Chapter 5 shows that, by default, class w contains the special name localhost, the special address 127.0.0.1, and the system's IP addresses, full domain names, and unqualified hostnames. Anything you put in local-host-names is added to these default values.

The system checks class w to decide whether or not it should accept inbound mail for local delivery. The Sendmail server only accepts mail for local delivery that is addressed to the server. Yet many systems might use the Sendmail server as a mailbox server to collect and hold their mail. If the mail that the server should collect and hold is literally addressed to another system, the name of that system needs to be added to class w. Once added to class w, the other system's hostname is treated by Sendmail as if it were a hostname alias for the server. Mail addressed to systems listed in class w is accepted as if it were mail addressed to the server. An example will make this clear.

Assume that robin.foobirds.org is a PC that uses the server wren.foobirds.org as a mailbox to collect and hold mail. An MX record is placed in the DNS server that directs robin's mail to wren. Listing 6.3 shows what happens when logan on bear.mammals.org sends mail to jill on robin before class w is updated.

**Listing 6.3**  A Failed Test of Class w

```
[craig@ibis]$ sendmail -v -t
To: jill@robin.foobirds.org
From: logan
Subject: Class w test
^D
jill@robin.foobirds.org... Connecting to wren.foobirds.org.
   via esmtp...
220 wren.foobirds.org ESMTP Sendmail 8.11.0/8.11.0;
   Thu, 21 Sep 2000 16:27:59 -0400
>>> EHLO bear.mammals.org
250-wren.foobirds.org Hello root@bear.mammals.org [172.16.12.1],
   pleased to meet you
>>> MAIL From:<logan@bear.mammals.org> SIZE=62
250 2.1.0 <logan@bear.mammals.org>... Sender ok
>>> RCPT To:<jill@robin.foobirds.org>
550 5.7.1 <jill@robin.foobirds.org>... Relaying denied
```

Essential Configuration

PART 2

```
>>> RSET
250 2.0.0 Reset state
/home/logan/dead.letter... Saved message in /home/logan/dead.letter
Closing connection to wren.foobirds.org.
>>> QUIT
221 2.0.0 wren.foobirds.org closing connection
```

Other than deleting several lines from the EHLO response to save a few trees, the test in Listing 6.3 appears exactly as it happened. Sendmail was invoked with -v and -t so that I could type the test in from the keyboard and receive verbose responses. The first four lines, which are shown in bold, are what I typed in. The remainder is the response from the remote e-mail server. As the To: line clearly shows, the mail was addressed to jill@robin.foobirds.org. The first line displayed by Sendmail says that it is connecting to wren.foobirds.org via the esmtp mailer. Mail addressed to robin.foobirds.org is being sent to wren.foobirds.org, which means that wren must be the preferred mail exchange server for robin. Great, except that apparently nobody told the administrator of wren! The 550 response line, shown in bold italics, is an error message saying that wren will not relay mail from bear to robin. Well, we didn't want it to relay mail, but we did want it to accept mail for robin, which it clearly won't do. What is wrong is that the name robin.foobirds.org is not a valid alias for wren.foobirds.org, so wren will not accept mail for robin.

To correct this, robin must be added to class w. There are two ways this can be done. One way is to add the value directly to class w in the Sendmail configuration using the LOCAL_DOMAIN macro command, as in this example:

```
LOCAL_DOMAIN(`robin.foobirds.org')
```

This works well if there are only a few hosts to add. It is straightforward and everything is contained in the Sendmail configuration file.

The other way to add hostnames to class w is to put them in the local-host-names file. Putting the hostname aliases in the local-host-names file is better whenever there are several names to add or the list of names changes over time. In the case of both the generic-linux.mc and redhat.mc configurations, using the local-host-names file is also simpler because the FEATURE(use_cw_file) command is already in the configuration. Thus there is no need to add a LOCAL_DOMAIN command or to rebuild the sendmail.cf file. Listing 6.4 shows the local-host-names file with two entries for robin and it shows a SIGHUP signal being sent to Sendmail to make sure Sendmail loads the new values.

**Listing 6.4**    Entries in the `local-host-names` File

```
[root]# cat local-host-names
# local-host-names - include all aliases for your machine here.
#
robin.foobirds.org
robin
[root]# ps -ax | grep sendmail
  542 ?         S       0:00 sendmail: accepting connections
[root]# kill -HUP 542
[root]# sendmail -bt
ADDRESS TEST MODE (ruleset 3 NOT automatically invoked)
Enter <ruleset> <address>
> $=w
robin.foobirds.org
wren.foobirds.org
[172.16.12.3]
wren
localhost
robin
> ^D
```

Now `wren` will accept mail for `robin`, although it won't necessarily know what to do with it. If Jill will be downloading her mail from a mailbox on `wren`, you must create a valid user account for Jill to allow Sendmail to create the necessary spool directory to hold her mail and to allow her to download the mail via POP or IMAP. If Jill's mail is supposed to be forwarded to another system, mail routing instructions need to be given to Sendmail through the `aliases` database or another appropriate database. Clearly, while adding hostnames to class `w` is essential, it is only a first step. A possible next step is to configure the `aliases` database.

# The *aliases* Database

Once mail is accepted by the Sendmail server for local delivery, Sendmail must decide *how* to deliver the mail. It must determine whether the user identified in the recipient address is a local user with a local mailbox, or a user alias whose mail must be forwarded on to the real recipient. The primary database used to make this determination is the `aliases` database.

Sendmail aliases perform important functions that are an essential part of creating a mail server. Mail aliases do the following:

**Specify nicknames for individual users.**   Nicknames can be used to direct mail addressed to special names, such as `postmaster` or `root`, to the real users that do those jobs. Aliases can simplify creation of a standard e-mail address structure for a domain because mail aliases have a more flexible structure than login usernames.

**Forward mail to other hosts.**   Sendmail aliases automatically forward mail to the host address included as part of the recipient address.

**Define mailing lists.**   An alias with multiple recipients is a mailing list.

Mail aliases are defined in the `aliases` file. The location of the `aliases` file is set by the `ALIAS_FILE` define in the Sendmail configuration. The `redhat.mc` configuration file in Chapter 5 uses `ALIAS_FILE` to set the location of the `aliases` file to `/etc/aliases`. By default, Sendmail 8.11 locates the file in the `/etc/mail` directory (`/etc/mail/aliases`). Regardless of where it is located, the basic format of entries in the `aliases` file is:

```
alias: recipient
```

The `alias` is the username from the e-mail address, and `recipient` is the name to which the mail should be delivered. The `recipient` field can contain a username, another alias, or a full e-mail address containing both a username and a hostname. Additionally, there can be multiple recipients for a single alias to create a mailing list. The `aliases` file delivered with a Red Hat system, with a few additions to illustrates the full range of uses for aliases, is shown in Listing 6.5.

**Listing 6.5**   The Basic Red Hat `aliases` Database

```
#
#       @(#)aliases     8.2 (Berkeley) 3/5/94
#
#  Aliases in this file will NOT be expanded in the header from
#  Mail, but WILL be visible over networks or from /bin/mail.
#
#       >>>>>>>>>>      The program "newaliases" must be run after
#       >> NOTE >>      this file is updated for any changes to
#       >>>>>>>>>>      show through to sendmail.
#

# Basic system aliases -- these MUST be present.
MAILER-DAEMON:  postmaster
postmaster:     root
```

```
# General redirections for pseudo accounts.
bin:            root
daemon:         root
games:          root
ingres:         root
nobody:         root
system:         root
toor:           root
uucp:           root

# Well-known aliases.
manager:        root
dumper:         root
operator:       root
webmaster:      root

# trap decode to catch security attacks
decode:         root

# Person who should get root's mail
root:           staff

# System administrator mailing list
staff: kathy, craig, david@parrot, sara@hawk, becky@parrot
owner-staff: staff-request
staff-request: craig

# User aliases
jill: jill@egret.foobirds.org
norman.edwards: norm
edwardsn: norm
norm: norm@hawk.foobirds.org
rebecca.hunt: becky@parrot
andy.wright: andy
sara.henson: sara
kathy.McCafferty: kathy
kathleen.McCafferty: kathy
```

The Red Hat `aliases` file opens with several comment lines, which begin with a pound sign (#). Ignore the information about which mail programs display aliases in the headers of mail messages; it is not really significant. The comment that is significant is the one that tells you to run `newaliases` every time you update this file. Sendmail does not read the aliases file directly. Instead, it reads a database file produced from this file by the newaliases command.

---

> **NOTE**    newaliases is not really a program; it is a link to Sendmail. The aliases database can also be built by running sendmail with the -bi argument—e.g., sendmail -bi.

---

The next 15 lines in Listing 6.5 define aliases for special names. All of these, except the webmaster alias that I added, come pre-configured in the Red Hat aliases file. The first two, MAILER-DAEMON and postmaster, are aliases that people expect to find on any system running Sendmail. Most of the others are aliases assigned to the daemon usernames that are found in the /etc/passwd file. No one can actually log on using the daemon usernames, so any mail that might be directed to these pseudo accounts is forwarded to a real user account. In the example, this mail is forwarded to the root user account.

Of course you don't really want people logging onto the root account just to read mail, so the aliases file also has an alias for root. In the example, I edited the root entry to forward all mail addressed to root to staff, which is another alias. Notice how often aliases point to other aliases. Doing so is very useful because it allows you to update one alias instead of many when the real user account that the mail is delivered to changes.

The staff alias is a mailing list. A mailing list is simply an alias with multiple recipients. In the example, several people are responsible for maintaining this mail server. Messages addressed to root are delivered to all of these people through the staff mailing list.

Two special aliases are associated with the mailing list. The owner-staff alias is a special alias used by Sendmail for error messages relating to the staff mailing list. The format that Sendmail requires for this special alias is owner-list, where list is the name of the mailing list. The other special alias, staff-request, is not required by Sendmail but it is expected by remote users. By convention, manual mailing list maintenance requests, such as being added to or deleted from a list, are sent to the alias list-request, where list is the name of the mailing list.

The last nine lines are user aliases I added to the file. These lines direct mail received at the mail server to the computers where the users read their mail. The first alias directs the mail this server receives for Jill. (Refer back to Listing 6.3.) Remember that when we discussed class w, it was pointed out that simply adding a hostname to class w does not mean that the server will be able to handle the mail for a specific user on that remote host. The user needs either an account on the server or an alias in the aliases database. This alias means that it is not necessary to create a user account for Jill on the mail server because her mail is forwarded to egret.foobirds.org. It is egret's job to see that Jill gets her mail.

Aliases can be in a variety of formats to handle the various ways that e-mail is addressed to a user. The next three lines, which forward mail to norm@hawk.foobirds.org, all illustrate this. Mail addressed to norman.edwards or to edwardsn is mapped to the alias norm, and the alias norm forwards the mail to norm@hawk.foobirds.org. Thus the server will accept mail addressed in any of three different formats and make sure it gets to the correct recipient on the remote system hawk.foobirds.org.

The last five lines all have the same alias format: first name, dot, last name. This format is a popular one for e-mail addressing. When combined with an MX record in DNS that says that this server is the mail exchanger for the entire domain, it creates the simplified mail-addressing schemes used at many organizations. Assume the MX record for the domain foobirds.org points to this server. Mail addressed to Rebecca.Hunt@foobirds.org would actually be delivered to becky@parrot.foobirds.org. Notice that e-mail addresses are not case sensitive.

The aliases database is used on every system to specify how mail is forwarded. The aliases database handles mail forwarding for the entire system. It is also possible for individual users to define personal forwarding for their own mail in the .forward file. While the .forward file is not strictly a database, its close relationship to systemwide aliases make this a good time to take a quick look at the .forward file.

## Defining Personal Mail Aliases

As some of the lines in the aliases file in Listing 6.5 illustrate, one of the main functions of the aliases file is to forward mail to other accounts or other computers. The aliases file, because it impacts the entire system, must be maintained by the system administrator. Thus, if a user wants to set up forwarding for their account through the aliases file, they need to ask the system administrator for help. The .forward file, which can be created in any user's home directory, defines mail forwarding for an individual user and is completely under the control of the user. Often, the .forward file is the most convenient place to set up forwarding.

It is possible to use the .forward file to do something that can be done in the aliases file. For example, if Norman Edwards had an account on a system but didn't really want to read his mail on that system, he could create the following .forward file:

```
norm@hawk.foobirds.org
```

The function of this entry is very similar to the norm alias line in Listing 6.5. It forwards all mail received in this user's account on the local system to the norm account at hawk.foobirds.org.

However, simple forwarding is not the primary use for the .forward file. A much more common use for this file is to invoke special mail processing before mail is delivered to your personal mail account. Chapter 11, "Stopping Spam," illustrates this when procmail and mail filtering are discussed.

The aliases database and the .forward file are the default files used to process user addresses. Sendmail will use both of these files if it finds them. There is no need to define them inside the Sendmail configuration; they are used by default. There is also an optional database that can be used to process users' addresses. It is the user database, and it is our next topic.

# The User Database

The user database is available to Sendmail only if Sendmail is compiled with the USERDB compiler flag and the path to the user database is defined inside the Sendmail configuration using the confUSERDB_SPEC option. Listing 6.1 shows that the Sendmail delivered with the Red Hat RPM has the USERDB compiler flag set, and in Chapter 5 we saw that the redhat.mc file contained the following define command:

```
define(`confUSERDB_SPEC', `/etc/mail/userdb.db')
```

From these things, we know that we can use the user database on our sample Red Hat system. If your system doesn't meet both of these conditions, you can't use this database until you update the configuration.

Sendmail applies the user database to inbound mail after the aliases database and before the .forward file. But unlike the aliases and .forward files, the user database can also be applied to outbound mail to transform the sender address and, in effect, create a reverse alias. Listing 6.6 shows a realistic user database file based on the last four lines of the aliases database in Listing 6.5.

**Listing 6.6**  A Sample User Database File

```
[root]# cd /etc/mail
[root]# cat userdb
andy.wright:maildrop andy
andy:mailname andy.wright@foobirds.org
sara.henson:maildrop sara
sara:mailname sara.henson@foobirds.org
kathy.McCafferty:maildrop kathy
kathleen.McCafferty:maildrop kathy
kathy:mailname katheleen.mccafferty@foobirds.org
[root]# makemap btree userdb.db < userdb
```

In Listing 6.6, we change to the /etc/mail directory and display the contents of the user database file we have created. We arbitrarily named this file userdb. Like the aliases file, the user database file must be converted to a true database before it can be used by Sendmail. Use the makemap command to build the database. The makemap program reads the standard input and writes out the specified database of the type selected. The makemap command is fully described later in this chapter. In Listing 6.6, the command has two arguments: the database type and the name of the database to be written. The user database must be of the btree type, and the name of the user database must be the one defined inside the Sendmail configuration.

The entries in the user database look something like the entries in the aliases database except for the addition of a keyword, either maildrop or mailname. The entries that use the keyword maildrop are almost exactly like entries in the aliases database. The value before the colon (:) is the user alias and the value after the keyword maildrop is the recipient address. The first entry in the sample userdb file:

    andy.wright:maildrop andy

performs exactly the same function as this line from the aliases database:

    andy.wright: andy

Both of these take mail addressed to andy.wright and deliver it to the user account andy. The similarity between entries in the aliases database and maildrop entries in the user database are so strong that the following lines from the aliases file shown in Listing 6.5:

    staff: kathy, craig, david@parrot.foobirds.org, sara@hawk.foobirds.org
    owner-staff: staff-request
    staff-request: craig

can be rewritten in the user database as follows:

    staff:maildrop kathy,craig,david@parrot.foobirds.org,sara@hawk.foobirds.org
    owner-staff:maildrop craig
    staff-request:maildrop craig

This shows that just like an alias database entry, a maildrop entry can accept multiple delivery addresses, which in effect creates a mailing list. The only difference in these three entries, other than the addition of the keyword maildrop, is that maildrop entries cannot point to aliases. The recipient address in a maildrop entry must be a real address—thus the change that maps owner-staff to the real address craig instead of the alias staff-request.

---

> *NOTE*   The fact is that none of the maildrop lines shown in Listing 6.6 is needed if this system has the aliases file shown in Listing 6.5. That aliases file would have already done the mapping of inbound addresses before the user database was even called. The maildrop lines are shown in Listing 6.6 as examples. If you decide to use maildrop entries, don't duplicate entries already in the aliases database. Some administrators prefer using maildrop entries over aliases when they also want to take advantage of the mailname entries so that everything can be done in one file.

---

The mailname entries provide a feature that is not available in the aliases database. The mailname entries rewrite outbound addresses. The value before the colon (:) is the local username. The value following the keyword mailname is the sender address that should be used on mail originating from the user. Thus the line

 andy:mailname andy.wright@foobirds.org

converts the sender address on all mail from the user andy to

 andy.wright@foobirds.org.

Converting outbound addresses is a very important function because it balances the way addresses are treated. Remote users send mail to the address andy.wright@foobirds.org. The MX record for foobirds.org directs the mail to a server—say, wren.foobirds.org. wren maps andy.wright through the aliases database and delivers the mail to andy. Without the mailname entry and the user database, when andy replies to the mail his address goes out as andy@wren.foobirds.org. Not very neat! With the mailname entry shown above, his mail goes out with the address andy.wright@foobirds.org, which is just what the remote user expects. Nice!

However, the user database is not the only way to rewrite outbound addresses, as we will see later. The decision to use the user database is primarily a matter of taste based on the database that you like best and find most understandable. While using the user database is largely a matter of choice, using the access database is often a matter of necessity, particularly in a world full of spammers.

# The *access* Database

The access database is a powerful configuration tool for mail relay servers. It provides much finer control over the relay process than is provided by the relay-domains file. Unlike the relay-domains file, the access database is not a default part of the Sendmail configuration. If you want to use the access database, you must add the access_db feature to your configuration. The generic-linux.mc configuration did not include support for the access database, but the redhat.mc configuration did with the following command:

```
FEATURE(`access_db')dnl
```

This command uses the default database type hash and the default pathname /etc/mail/access.db. You could change these values by providing an optional argument field to the command, as in this example:

```
FEATURE(`access_db', `btree /var/mail/access')
```

However, I recommend against changing these defaults. The hash type is supported on all Linux systems and all administrators expect to find the access database in /etc/mail. Changing these values doesn't gain you anything and it can cause confusion. Add the access_db feature to your configuration, but use the default arguments.

Use the access database to accept or reject mail based on the source or destination of the mail. Each line in the database contains two fields: the address field and the action field. The address field is the key to the database and the action field is the value returned from the database that specifies the action that Sendmail should take in regard to mail to or from the specified address.

## The Address Field

The address field can define a user, an individual e-mail address, a source IP address, a network address, or the name of a domain. The address field can begin with an optional tag to tell Sendmail to limit checks for that address field to certain conditions. Three optional tag keywords are available:

**To:**    The action is taken only when mail is being sent to the specified address.

**From:**    The action is taken only when mail is received from the specified address.

**Connect:**    The action is taken only when the specified address is the address of the system at the remote end of the SMTP connection.

The tag field is not required. It provides finer control over e-mail access, but fine control is not always needed. In many cases, you want broader control over relaying, not finer control, because you don't want to accept mail from a bad source and you don't want to send them mail, either. If no tag field is included, the default is to treat the address as the source of the mail. Thus, by default, the action is taken only if the mail comes from the specified address. Add the following blacklist_recipient feature to the Sendmail configuration:

```
FEATURE(`blacklist_recipients')
```

to make Sendmail apply the rules defined in the `access` database to both source and destination addresses.

The address in the address field can define an individual, a host, a domain, or a network:

- An individual is defined using either a full e-mail address in the form *user@host.domain* or a username in the form *username@*.
- A host is identified by its hostname or its IP address.
- A domain is identified by a domain name.
- A network is identified by the network portion of an IP address.

Listing 6.7 illustrates the various possible address fields. The listing is a contrived example that includes each tag type and each address type.

**Listing 6.7** Address Formats for the access Database

```
spammer@bigisp.com                REJECT

makemoneyfast@                    REJECT

wespamu.com                       REJECT

172.18                            REJECT

[172.20.12.6]                     REJECT

From:weselljunk.com               REJECT

To:bigmoney@foolsgetrich.com      REJECT

Connect:wepushporn.com            REJECT
```

The first two lines in this `access` database define two individual users. These lines tell Sendmail to reject any mail from the e-mail address `spammer@bigisp.com` and any mail from a user named `makemoneyfast`. The third line defines an entire domain. It rejects mail from any host in the domain `wespamu.com`. The fourth line defines an entire network. It rejects mail from any computer whose IP address begins with network number 172.18. The fifth line defines a specific computer with the address 172.20.12.6. The square brackets surrounding the individual address mean that this IP address is literally in the e-mail address because it doesn't resolve to a hostname or is flagged by Sendmail as "might be forged."

---

**NOTE** Addresses that don't map to hostnames are rejected by default, so normally there would be no need to have an entry that rejects [172.20.12.6] in the access database. But as noted above, Listing 6.7 is a contrived example meant to show different address formats.

The last three entries have optional tag fields. Mail from the domain `weselljunk.com` is rejected but users are allowed to send mail to that domain. Mail is accepted from the user `bigmoney@foolsgetrich.com` but local users are not allowed to reply to that address. Any connection to the domain `wepushporn.com` is rejected.

All of the examples in Listing 6.7 tell Sendmail to reject the mail. Rejecting the mail is only one of the actions available through the `access` database.

## The Action Field

The second field in each entry in the `access` database is a keyword that tells Sendmail what action to take. Table 6.2 lists the valid keywords and the actions they cause.

**Table 6.2**    access Database Actions

| Keyword | Action |
| --- | --- |
| **DISCARD** | Drops any message from or to the specified address. |
| **OK** | Absolutely accepts messages from or to the specified address. |
| **REJECT** | Issues an error message and drops any mail from or to the specified address. |
| **RELAY** | Relays mail coming from the specified address. |
| **[ERROR:**[*dsn:*]]*code  text* | Returns the specified RFC 821 response *code* and the *text* to the source of the mail. Optionally, the string `ERROR:` or `ERROR:` and an RFC 1893 DSN code can be used. |

> **NOTE**  The actions in Table 6.2 are described as affecting mail "from or to" an address. This is only true if the `blacklist_recipients` feature is used. If that feature is not used, the actions only affect mail coming from a source address unless the address is modified by an optional tag.

The access database shown in Listing 6.8 illustrates how the various action field values are used.

**Listing 6.8**   Specifying Different Actions in the access Database

```
wespamu.com             REJECT
172.18                  DISCARD
weselljunk.com          550 Junk mail is not accepted
wepushporn.com          ERROR:5.7.1:550 Relaying denied to spammers
friendly.org            OK
129.6                   RELAY
```

The REJECT command causes Sendmail to return a standard error message to the source and then discard the mail. The DISCARD command drops the mail without sending any message back to the source. Most anti-spam authorities discourage silently discarding mail because they feel it does not discourage the spammer. For all the spammer knows, you received the mail, so they just keep sending more junk.

The action taken for weselljunk.com and wepushporn.com is similar to the action taken when a REJECT action command is specified, except that in these two cases you define the error messages sent. In both cases, mail from these domains is rejected and an error message is returned to the sender. In the case of weselljunk.com, the error message returned to the sender is "550 Junk mail is not accepted." In the case of wepushporn.com, the error message returned to the sender is "550 5.7.1 Relaying denied to spammers." This error message includes delivery status notification code 5.7.1. If you use a DSN code in your error message, use a valid DSN code from RFC 1893 that is compatible with the RFC 821 error code and the message you send. The action field for this error message starts with the keyword ERROR:. If you use this keyword with a DSN code, you must use the format **ERROR:**dsn:code, where dsn is a valid DSN code and code is a valid RFC 821 code. This format is used as an example. It is not required. You could have just as easily specified this error with the following entry:

```
wepushporn.com              550 5.7.1 Relaying denied to spammers
```

The OK command in Listing 6.8 causes Sendmail to accept mail from friendly.org regardless of other conditions. For example, if mail arrives from a hostname that includes the friendly.org domain and cannot be resolved by DNS, Sendmail accepts that mail even though the accept_unresolvable_domains feature has not been enabled. To allow this you must, of course, fully trust friendly.org.

The RELAY command causes Sendmail to relay mail for network 129.6 even if basic relaying is not enabled on the system. Like the OK command, using the RELAY command means that you fully trust every host on network 129.6.

> **TIP** If you don't have anything else in your database, you probably want an entry like the one for network 129.6 for your own network. As discussed above, Sendmail blocks all mail relaying, even mail from your clients. Use the access database and an entry like 129.6 RELAY to enable relaying for every host attached to your local network.

Once you build your access list, it must be converted into a database before Sendmail can use it. Use the makemap command to do the job, as shown below.

```
makemap hash /etc/mail/access.db < /etc/mail/access.txt
```

This command reads the entries in a text file named /etc/mail/access and uses them to build a hash type database in the file named /etc/mail/access.db.

The local-host-names and relay-domains files and the aliases and access databases are probably the most important databases that were configured in the redhat.mc configuration file. But they are not the only databases configured there. Two others, virtusertable and mailertable, are configured in redhat.mc. Of these, virtusertable is the most useful.

# The *virtusertable*

The virtusertable is a database that routes mail for virtual mail domains. A virtual mail domain is similar to a virtual host in the Apache Web server. In the same way that a Web server can be configured to serve Web pages for host computers that do not physically exist, the Sendmail server can be configured to provide mail service for mail domains that do not have any existence beyond the Sendmail server itself. Creating a virtual mail domain allows you to advertise a meaningful domain name to the outside world without having to create all of the services necessary to support a full domain.

## Defining a Virtual Domain

Each entry in the virtusertable has two fields: a virtual domain and a delivery address. The first field contains the virtual domain name found in the e-mail address. The second field contains the address to which the mail is really delivered. The virtual domain name contained in the first field can be a complete address in the form of *user@domain* or it can be a partial address in the form *@domain*. When the *@domain* format is used, mail to any user in the specified domain is routed to the mail address contained in the second field. Some sample virtusertable entries are shown in Listing 6.9.

**Listing 6.9**  Sample Virtual Domains

```
sales@bridal-gowns.com    jill
info@patient-rights.org   sara@hawk.foobirds.org
@imaginary.com            david@lion.mammals.org
```

These three sample entries show basic virtual domains and delivery addresses. Mail addressed to `sales@bridal-gowns.com` is really delivered to the `jill` account on the Sendmail server. (Looks like Jill is in the business of selling bridal gowns.) Requests e-mailed to `info@patient-rights.org` are forwarded to `sara@hawk.foobirds.org`. Mail sent to any username in the `imaginary.com` domain is forwarded to `david@lion` `.mammals.org`.

Sendmail must be configured to accept mail addressed to the virtual domains. In Listing 6.9, Sendmail must either accept `bridal-gowns.com`, `patient-rights.org`, and `imaginary.com` as aliases for the local host or recognize them as virtual domains. You know from the discussion of the `local-host-names` file earlier in this chapter that Sendmail accepts any name contained in class w as an alias for the local host. From that earlier discussion, you know how to add the three virtual domains to class w. But it is not necessary to turn a virtual domain into a hostname alias to get the `virtusertable` working. An alternative is to tell Sendmail that the virtual domain is a virtual domain by storing the domain name in the {VirtHost} class.

Domain names can be added to the {VirtHost} class one at a time using the VIRTUSER_ DOMAIN macro inside the Sendmail configuration. For example, the three domains from Listing 6.9 could be added with the following three macros:

```
VIRTUSER_DOMAIN(`bridal-gowns.com')

VIRTUSER_DOMAIN(`patient-rights.org')

VIRTUSER_DOMAIN(`imaginary.com')
```

Once these lines are inserted in the macro configuration file, rerun `m4` to build the new `sendmail.cf` file and reload Sendmail to load the new configuration. This technique is complex and not very flexible, so the VIRTUSER_DOMAIN macro is only suitable if you have few virtual domains and they do not change often.

An alternate way to load the {VirtHost} class is from a file. Use the VIRTUSER_DOMAIN_ FILE macro to specify the path to the file that contains the list of virtual domains. For example, the following command tells Sendmail to copy /etc/mail/virtual-domains to class {VirtHost}:

```
VIRTUSER_DOMAIN_FILE(`/etc/mail/virtual-domains')
```

After adding the VIRTUSER_DOMAIN_FILE command to the macro configuration file, rerun m4 to build the new sendmail.cf file. Then add the virtual domains from Listing 6.9 to the new virtual-domains file, one domain per line, as shown below:

```
[craig]$ cat /etc/mail/virtual-domains
bridal-gowns.com
patient-rights.org
imaginary.com
```

Whenever new virtual domains are added to the file, send Sendmail the SIGHUP signal to make sure it reads the new values and loads them into class {VirtHost}.

> **TIP**  Both the VIRTUSER_DOMAIN and VIRTUSER_DOMAIN_FILE macros require changing and rebuilding the sample configuration. Because we already had the local-host-names file in our configuration, it would be easier to add the virtual domains to that file. It works just as well because Sendmail checks both class w and class {VirtHost} when processing virtual domains.

## Defining *virtusertable* Delivery Addresses

The delivery address in all three sample entries in Listing 6.9 is a simple e-mail address. It doesn't have to be. The second field can contain a dynamic address that uses values from the input address or an error message that Sendmail returns to the sender. Listing 6.10 shows a larger virtusertable with a variety of values in the delivery address field.

**Listing 6.10**   A Sample virtusertable

```
sales@bridal-gowns.com    jill
info@patient-rights.org   sara@hawk.foobirds.org
@imaginary.com            david@lion.mammals.org
sales@outofbusiness.com   error:nouser User address is not valid
sales@weRbroke.com        error:5.1.5 Destination address invalid
@other.org                %1@local.org
+*@thatplace.com          %2@newplace.com
```

The first three entries have already been explained. Mail is accepted with a virtual domain address and routed to a real e-mail address. The e-mail address in the second field must be a real address; it cannot be another virtual domain address. For example, the following `virtusertable` entries would not work as you might think:

```
sales@bridal-gowns.com    sales@imaginary.com

@imaginary.com            david@lion.mammals.org
```

This cannot be used to forward mail addressed to `sales@bridal-gowns.com` to `david@lion.mammals.com`. Unlike aliases that can point to other aliases, virtual domains cannot point to other virtual domains.

The next two lines in Listing 6.10 illustrate the use of error messages. Mail addressed to `sales@outofbusiness.com` is not delivered. Instead, an error message that says "User address is not valid" is returned to the sender. Mail sent to `sales@weRbroke.com` returns the error message "Destination address invalid" to the sender.

Error messages must start with the keyword `error`, which is the name of a special mailer that is built into Sendmail. Separated by a colon from the keyword `error` is an error condition, specified either as a keyword or as a DSN code. The DSN code can be any valid code defined in RFC 1893. The error condition keyword must be a keyword recognized by the `error` mailer. A list of valid error condition keywords is found in Chapter 8, "Understanding Rewrite Rules," in the discussion of the error mailer.

---

**TIP** Use DSN codes. They are an Internet standard and are well defined in the RFC. The error condition keywords are internal to Sendmail and subject to change in future releases.

---

The last two lines in Listing 6.10 provide examples of how values from the input address can be used in the outbound address. The `@other.org` entry provides the classic example. The username part of the input address is passed in the `%1` variable, so that `%1` in the outbound address is replaced by the username from the input address. Using the `virtusertable` shown in Listing 6.10, mail addressed to `pat@other.org` would be delivered to `pat@local.org` and mail sent to `doris@other.org` would be forwarded to `doris@local.org`.

This is a powerful feature. Obviously, it can be used to ease the transition when you change domain names, but that is a rare occurrence. More importantly, this feature can be used when the products you sell are not clearly associated with your official domain name. Assume you have an online mall that sells party products. The real name of your domain is `stuffycorporation.com`, but you also own the domains `funstuff.com` and happythings.com. The following two lines in the virtusertable would route mail to the correct employee regardless of the domain to which it was addressed:

```
@funstuff.com          %1@stuffycorporation.com
@happythings.com       %1@stuffycorporation.com
```

The last line in Listing 6.10 shows that the *detail* value in the *+detail* syntax can be passed to the outbound address as %2. Mail sent to sales+info@thatplace.com would be delivered to info@newplace.com and mail to sales+orders@thatplace.com would be delivered to orders@newplace.com. Notice that the use of *+detail* syntax must be indicated in the first field of the virtusertable entry by placing +* before the @ in the virtual domain address. Users find e-mail addresses complex enough without using the *+detail* syntax. For this reason, the syntax is rarely used unless you have a program that automatically generates this syntax for the user. It is covered here for the sake of completeness, but you will probably not use it in your configuration.

Before the virtusertable can be used by Sendmail, it must be turned into a hash database using makemap. Listing 6.11 shows a successful build and test of the virtusertable database.

**Listing 6.11**   Building and Testing the virtusertable

```
[root]# cat local-host-names
# local-host-names - include all aliases for your machine here.
#
robin.foobirds.org
robin
bridal-gowns.com
patient-rights.org
imaginary.com
outofbusiness.com
weRbroke.com
other.org
thatplace.com
[root]# cat virtusertable
sales@bridal-gowns.com      jill
info@patient-rights.org     sara@hawk.foobirds.org
@imaginary.com              david@lion.mammals.org
sales@outofbusiness.com     error:nouser User address is not valid
sales@weRbroke.com          error:5.1.5 Destination address invalid
@other.org                  %1@local.org
+*@thatplace.com            %2@newplace.com
```

```
[root]# makemap hash virtusertable < virtusertable
[root]# sendmail -bv sales@bridal-gowns.com
sales@bridal-gowns.com... deliverable: mailer local, user jill
```

The virtusertable database is built with the makemap command and then tested using sendmail with the -bv argument. The -bv argument causes the sendmail command to process the address entered on the command line as a delivery address. The test shows that the address sales@bridal-gown.com will be delivered via the local mailer to the user account jill. This is just what we expected based on the first line of the virtusertable file.

In Listing 6.11 we examine the contents of the local-host-names file and the virtusertable source file. The local-host-names file shows that all of the virtual domains have been added to class w. If the virtual domains are not added to class w or class {VirtHost}, the sendmail -bv test produces the following result:

```
[root]# sendmail -bv sales@bridal-gowns.com
sales@bridal-gowns.com... deliverable: mailer esmtp,
    host bridal-gowns.com, user sales@bridal-gowns.com
```

This test shows that Sendmail believes that bridal-gowns.com is an external domain that can be reached through the esmtp mail. If we defined the virtual domain in the local-host-names file and forgot to provide the mapping in the virtusertable, either by not including it in the file or not running makemap, sendmail -bv produces the following result:

```
[root]# sendmail -bv info@patient-rights.org
info@patient-rights.org... deliverable: mailer local, user info
```

Here the virtual domain is accepted, but the address is not mapped to the external host as we wished. A simple sendmail -bv test can tell you if the virtusertable is working and can indicate what's wrong if it isn't.

There are many good reasons to use the virtusertable, particularly if you run an ISP that provides service to a large number of customers or you run an e-business site. It is easy to see why Red Hat includes this in their default Sendmail configuration. The last database included in the redhat.mc file, the mailertable, is more rarely used.

# The *mailertable*

The mailertable is rarely needed. It maps domain names to the internal mailer that should handle mail bound for that domain. The reason that this database is rarely needed is that Sendmail usually routes mail to the correct mailer without any help from you. You only need this table to handle exceptional circumstances. An exceptional case might be a remote server that cannot handle standard mail. For example: From the discussion of the MAILER(smtp) command in Chapter 5, you know that Sendmail sends out SMTP mail using the esmtp mailer and that there are several other mailers available to handle SMTP mail in special ways. One of these is the smtp8 mailer that is designed to send eight-bit MIME data to outdated mail servers that support MIME but cannot understand Extended SMTP. If the domain cluelesscollege.edu used such a mail server, you could put the following entry in the mailertable to handle the mail:

```
.cluelesscollege.edu        smtp8:oldserver.cluelesscollege.edu
```

A mailertable entry contains two fields. The first field is the key. It contains the host portion of the delivery address. It can contain either the full name of the host—e.g., emma.cluelesscollege.edu—or just the domain name. To specify a domain name, start the name with a dot, as in the example above. If a domain name is used, it matches every host in the domain.

The second field in the entry is the value returned for the key. It normally contains the name of the mailer that should handle the mail and the name of the server to which the mail should be sent. Optionally, a username can be specified with the server address in the form *user@server*. Additionally, the mailer that is specified can be the internal error mailer. If the error mailer is used, the value following the mailer name is an error message instead of a server name. Here is an example of each of these alternative entries:

```
.cluelesscollege.edu        smtp8:oldserver.cluelesscollege.edu
booby.foobirds.org          esmtp:postmaster@wren.foobirds.org
dodo.foobirds.org           error:nohost This host is extinct
```

Normally, mail passing through the mailertable is sent to the user to which it is addressed. For example, mail to jane@emma.cluelesscollege.edu is sent through the smtp8 mailer to the server oldserver.cluelesscollege.edu addressed to the user jane@emma.cluelesscollege.edu. Adding a username to the second field, however, changes this normal behavior and causes Sendmail to route the mail to an individual instead of a mail server. For example, mail sent to any user at booby.foobirds.org is sent instead to postmaster@wren.foobirds.org. There, presumably, the mail is handled manually. Finally, mail handled by the mailertable does not have to be delivered at all. Instead, an error message can be returned to the sender. Any mail sent to dodo.foobirds.org returns the error message "This host is extinct" to the sender. The error message is constructed exactly as it is for the virtusertable, using either the Sendmail error condition keywords or the DSN error codes.

Returning error messages is not the only thing that can be done with the `mailertable` that replicates a feature of the `virtusertable`. It is possible to use the `mailertable` to route mail for a virtual domain. For example, the following entry routes mail addressed to anyone in the `bridal-gowns.com` virtual domain to the user account `jill`:

```
.bridal-gowns.com    local:jill
```

The advantage of using the `mailertable` for virtual domains is that, if you are already using the `mailertable` for some other purpose, you can do everything in one configuration file. The disadvantage is that you cannot specify individual users in the virtual domain, only domain names, and you don't get the cool features of the `virtusertable`, such as the ability to capture and reuse usernames with the %1 variable. Personally, I prefer `virtusertable`.

One other interesting thing you can do with the `mailertable` is to use it to route all of the mail on a client system to a central mail server. Suppose you had a Red Hat Linux client system that you wanted to configure to send all of its mail to `mailserver.foobirds.org` for processing. You could create a custom macro configuration on the client with a `define` command that sets SMART_HOST to `mailserver.foobirds.org`, or you could simply create a `mailertable` with a single entry:

```
esmtp:mailserver.foobirds.org
```

SMART_HOST is a variable in the macro configuration file that can be set to the name of a mail server that handles all outbound mail for the client. The `mailertable` entry does essentially the same thing. The dot (.) in the first field matches all domain names. This means that all non-local mail will be sent through the `esmtp` mailer to `mailserver.foobirds.org` for delivery. This is exactly what we want for our imaginary client, and it is exactly what the SMART_HOST define would have given us. But this is simpler.

Once a `mailertable` source file is built, it must be processed through `makemap`. By default, Sendmail expects the `mailertable` database to be in `hash` database format.

The likelihood that you will need to deal with a server that cannot handle standard Internet mail is remote. Time has already solved most of the incompatibilities that made the `mailertable` and the wide variety of mailers necessary. The other uses of the `mailertable` can be performed by other databases. So why is the `mailertable` database included in the default `redhat.mc` configuration? It is there to provide access to the `procmail` mailer. The `redhat.mc` file contains the command MAILER(procmail). This command has nothing to do with the FEATURE(local_procmail) command. The `local_procmail` feature causes Sendmail to use `procmail` as the `local` mailer. The MAILER(procmail) macro makes `procmail` available for mail other than local mail, but it does not add any rewrite rules to use `procmail`. To make use of the `procmail` mailer for non-local mail, you need to add it to the `mailertable`, as in this example:

```
.fishorfowl.org          procmail:fishorfowl.org
```

This example sends mail for the domain `fishorfowl.org` through `procmail`. The primary reason for using `procmail` is that it offers powerful tools for filtering mail. (The filtering features of `procmail` are covered in Chapter 11.) In the case of the sample entry shown above, we must assume that mail bound for `fishorfowl.org` requires special filtering.

Of the databases defined in the default Red Hat configuration, `mailertable` is the one you are least likely to use. Unless you need `procmail` to filter outgoing mail or you must send mail to a server that can't handle standard mail, you won't create any entries in this database.

Despite the large number of databases configured in `redhat.mc`, there are four more databases not included in that configuration. Of these four databases, only `genericstable` gets much use.

# The *genericstable*

The `genericstable` database rewrites sender addresses. A `genericstable` entry is composed of two fields: the original sender address, which acts as the key, and the rewritten sender address, which is the value returned for the key. Like other databases, the `genericstable` source file must be processed through `makemap` to build a `hash` database before Sendmail can use it. Listing 6.12 shows a reasonable `genericstable` source file.

**Listing 6.12**   Mapping Sender Addresses with `genericstable`

```
andy     andy.wright@foobirds.org
sara     sara.henson@foobirds.org
kathy    katheleen.mccafferty@foobirds.org
```

Given the `genericstable` shown in Listing 6.12, mail sent from the user account `andy` is sent out with a sender address of `andy.wright@foobirds.org`. If you remember the discussion of the user database earlier in the chapter, this probably sounds familiar. Entries in the `genericstable` perform exactly the same function as the `mailname` entries in the user database—both types of entries rewrite sender addresses.

The `genericstable` database has one small feature not found in the user database. It can accept *+detail* syntax in the original address and pass the *detail* part of the address as variable %1 to the output address, in the following manner:

```
sales+*@insects.org       %1@sales.insects.org
```

Of course, the *+detail* syntax is only important if you actually use it, and it is rarely used.

If a domain name is included in the first field of a `genericstable` entry, that domain name must be defined in class G. Values can be stored in class G using the GENERICS_DOMAIN macro or they can be loaded into class G from the file identified by the GENERICS_DOMAIN_FILE. For example, the following command stores the domain name `insects.org` in class G:

```
GENERICS_DOMAIN(`insects.org')
```

While the next command loads class G from a file named `/etc/mail/generics-domains`:

```
GENERICS_DOMAIN_FILE(`/etc/mail/generics-domains')
```

The domain names in class G normally require an exact match. Using the GENERICS_DOMAIN(`insects.org') macro shown above, *user*@insects.org would match the requirements set by class G but *user*@fly.insects.org would not match, even though fly.insects.org is part of the insects.org domain. To get Sendmail to match all hosts and subdomains within a domain defined in class G, use FEATURE(`generics_entire_domain').

The similarities between the user database and the `genericstable` mean that you can use either one of these databases to rewrite sender addresses. The syntax of `genericstable` entries is a little simpler because `genericstable` does not use keywords like mailname. But the `genericstable` only handles sender addresses. Recipient addresses must be handled in a separate database, either /etc/aliases or the user database. Some administrators like the simplicity of the `genericstable` database; others prefer the user database so they can have everything in one file. It is primarily a matter of taste. Both files work in the same way.

I generally prefer to use aliases for recipient addresses and the `genericstable` for sender addresses because that's what I'm used to. I have several configurations already set up this way. However, the redhat.mc file does not have `genericstable` support in the configuration. To use `genericstable` with that configuration, I must add the FEATURE(`genericstable') command to the macro configuration and rerun m4 to build a new sendmail.cf file. In the case of the redhat.mc configuration, it is probably just easier to use the user database.

The `genericstable` is the only database that I use that Red Hat did not include in the configuration. The other three databases that Red Hat did not configure are very seldom used.

# Little-Used Databases

The three remaining databases have very little use in current configurations because they deal with outdated networks, outmoded syntax, or rare situations. These three databases are:

**`domaintable`**    The `domaintable` is intended to ease the transition from an old domain name to a new domain name by translating the old name to the new name on all mail. You are rarely in the situation where you must change domain names, but if you are this database can help. The old domain name is the key and the new domain name is the value returned for the key. For example, assume we changed the domain name for the sales division from `sales.business.com` to `marketing.business.com`. We could put the following line in the `domaintable` to handle the address mapping:

```
sales.business.com        marketing.business.com
```

The `domaintable` source file must be converted to a `hash` type database with `makemap` before Sendmail can use it. Also, support for the `domaintable` must be added to the configuration with the `FEATURE(`domaintable')` command before Sendmail will even attempt to use the file.

**`uucpdomain`**    The `uucpdomain` database converts e-mail addresses from the `.UUCP` pseudo-domain into old-fashioned UUCP bang addresses. The key to the database is the hostname from the `.UUCP` pseudo-domain. The value returned for the key is the bang address. It is very unlikely that you will use this database. Most sites no longer use UUCP for mail, and those that do don't use bang addresses. Bang addresses are almost never used anymore because current UUCP mailers handle e-mail addresses that look just like Internet addresses.

**`bitdomain`**    BITNET is an IBM-mainframe-to-IBM-mainframe network that was created at a time when IBM did not offer TCP/IP protocols for their mainframes. The `bitdomain` database converts BITNET hostnames to legal Internet hostnames. BIT-NET is outdated. You will not use it at your site.

Well, that's finally it: almost a dozen different files and databases, more databases than you will ever want or use. And most of them are built using the `makemap` command.

# The *makemap* Command

The makemap command is included with Sendmail as a tool to help you build databases. Of all the true databases discussed in this chapter, only one, the aliases database—which is built by the newaliases command—is not built by the makemap command.

The makemap command reads the standard input and writes out a database according to the instructions you provide on the command line. The command line accepts three arguments: the command options, the database type, and the name of the output database file.

The name of the file is obvious. It must match the name of the database that is configured in Sendmail. One minor point: It is not necessary to include the filename extension, either in the Sendmail configuration or on the makemap command line. If you don't provide a filename extension, makemap will apply the correct extension to the filename based on the database type. Since Sendmail knows the database type from its configuration, it will search for a file with the correct extension. For example, we used this command to build the virtusertable:

```
[root]# makemap hash virtusertable < virtusertable
```

A simple reading of this command might imply that we read and wrote a file named virtusertable. In fact, we read a file named virtusertable and wrote a file named virtusertable.db, because makemap adds the correct .db extension to the output filename for hash type databases.

The type field of the makemap command can accept many different database types to support the wide variety of different databases used on different computers. On Linux systems, however, the database type will be either hash or btree, the two database types provided by the NEWDB compiler option. The type selected must match the database type defined for the specific database in the Sendmail configuration. All of the databases built by makemap, except for the user database, default to hash type databases in the Sendmail configuration. The user database defaults to btree.

In this chapter, none of the makemap examples included command line options because they are not generally required. Table 6.3 lists all available makemap command line options.

**Table 6.3**    makemap Command Line Options

| Option | Purpose |
| --- | --- |
| –d | Permit duplicate keys in the database. |
| –f | Allow uppercase characters in the database keys. |
| –N | Append a null character to the end of each key. |
| –o | Append the new entries to an existing database. |
| –r | Overwrite duplicate keys. |
| –v | Run in verbose mode. |

The –d option forces makemap to accept duplicate keys. Normally, duplicate keys produce an error. Don't use duplicate keys. The key is the value looked up in the database. Duplicates can cause unpredictable results and they are not supported in most types of databases.

Also, don't add null characters to the end of keys. This was necessary for some systems, like the old SunOS system, but it is not necessary for Linux. You don't need the –N option on a Linux system.

Normally, e-mail addresses are case-insensitive. Craig.Hunt@foobirds.org is the same as craig.hunt@foobirds.org. makemap eliminates case by converting everything to lowercase characters. The –f option overrides the standard behavior and forces makemap to maintain case. Because e-mail addresses are supposed to be case insensitive, maintaining case is probably not a good idea.

The –o and –r options are related. Normally, makemap reads the source file and replaces the old database with an entirely new file. The –o option tells makemap to save the old database and add the entries from the source file to it. Adding entries to the database increases the possibility of duplicate keys. The –r option tells makemap that if an entry from the source file duplicates a key already in the database, it should replace the database entry with the new entry. The –r option only make sense when the –o option is used.

The –v option produces verbose output. It lets you watch the progress of the makemap command. Listing 6.13 shows the result of the –v option.

**Listing 6.13**  Using –v with the makemap Command

```
[root]# makemap -v hash virtusertable < virtusertable
key=`info@patient-rights.org', val=`sara@hawk.foobirds.org'
key=`@imaginary.com', val=`david@lion.mammals.org'
key=`sales@outofbusiness.com', val=`error:nouser User address is not valid'
key=`sales@weRbroke.com', val=`error:5.1.5 Destination address invalid'
key=`@other.org', val=`%1@local.org'
key=`+*@thatplace.com', val=`%2@newplace.com'
```

makemap is an important tool needed to build most Sendmail databases. It is simple to use, but you need to understand how it is used and remember to use it every time a database is modified. Whenever you edit a database source file, rerun makemap and then run a simple test to make sure Sendmail is properly using the new database.

# In Sum

At most sites, the Sendmail macro configuration file and the sendmail.cf file are built just once. The bulk of the configuration, and particularly the bulk of the ongoing configuration maintenance, takes place in the Sendmail databases. The Sendmail databases are a powerful tool for bypassing the complexity of the Sendmail configuration files. There is no need to add a RELAY_DOMAIN macro and rebuild the Sendmail configuration when a line added to the relay-domains file does the same job. There is no need to set SMART_HOST and rebuild the Sendmail configuration when a single line in the mailertable will do the same thing. The databases simplify Sendmail configuration.

Unfortunately, like everything else about Sendmail, the databases themselves have too much complexity. There are too many ways to do the same thing. The user database replicates functions done by /etc/aliases and the genericstable. The mailertable can be made to do the same thing as the virtusertable. Entries in class w can have the same effect as entries in class {VirtHost} and there are a couple of different ways to get entries into both of these classes. In order to troubleshoot configurations created by others, you need to understand the role of every database and you need to understand the fact that these overlapping functions exist. But in your own configuration, you need to eliminate this overlap by focusing on a subset of databases and by using those databases for specific purposes. Here are a few suggestions, in no particular order, to help you choose the correct database for the job.

- Define all of your server's hostname aliases in the local-host-names file.

- Use the aliases database to process recipient addresses. It is available on every system and is already configured.

- Use either the `genericstable` or the user database to process sender addresses, but do not use both. If you use the user database, don't use `maildrop` commands to replicate recipient names already covered by the `aliases` database.

- Use the `access` database to control mail delivery and relaying. It provides finer control than the `relay-domains` file. Only use `relay-domains` where it is adequate to the task, such as on small departmental systems that don't need the full range of services provided by the `access` database.

- Use the `virtusertable` only if you truly need to support virtual domains. This database probably only applies to e-business sites and ISPs.

- Use the `mailertable` only if you use `procmail` for non-local mail. Most other uses of the `mailertable` are less than optimal solutions for real problems. For example, upgrading the external system to accept Extended SMTP is a better solution than using the `mailertable` to force mail through `smtp8`.

- Solve DNS transition problems with proper DNS configuration. Avoid using `domaintable` as anything other than a short-term fix.

- Don't use the `trusted-users` file, the `bitdomain` database, or the `uucpdomain` database.

The Sendmail databases are the final topic in Part 2, "Essential Configuration," and they are the most frequently used tools of basic configuration. The next chapter, "The `sendmail.cf` File," begins Part 3, "Advanced Configuration." Considering the complexity we have already seen, and the advanced nature of the skills needed to master this complexity, it might be hard to believe things could get more advanced. But they can. In the next part of this book, we drill deeper into the configuration and look at ways we can customize Sendmail at this deep level.

# Part 3

## Advanced Configuration

**Featuring:**

- The structure of the `sendmail.cf` file and the commands used to build it
- How values are set for `sendmail.cf` variables and classes
- How databases and mailers are defined in `sendmail.cf`
- Editing and testing `sendmail.cf`
- Special rulesets and when they are invoked
- All of the rulesets used by Sendmail and what they do
- Pattern matching in rewrite rules
- Transforming e-mail addresses with rewrite rules
- What address masquerading is and when it is used
- Rewriting the user portion of addresses
- Creating your own rewrite rules
- Building a relay client configuration

# The *sendmail.cf* File

# 7

**Y**ou use the m4 commands covered in the previous part of this book to create the Sendmail configuration. The file you build to hold those commands is the macro configuration file. However, Sendmail does not use the macro configuration file that you create. That file must be processed by m4 to build Sendmail's runtime configuration. The file that defines the Sendmail runtime configuration is sendmail.cf.

The sendmail.cf file is a large complex file divided into seven different sections. All Linux sendmail.cf files have the same structure, because they are all created from the m4 macros that come in the Sendmail distribution. The section labels from the sendmail.cf files provide an overview of the structure and the functions of this file. The sections are:

**Local Info**   This section defines the configuration information specific to the local host.

**Options**   This section sets the options that define the Sendmail environment.

**Message Precedence**   This section defines the Sendmail message precedence values.

**Trusted Users**   This section defines the users who are allowed to change the sender address when they are sending mail.

**Format of Headers**   This section defines the headers that Sendmail inserts into mail.

**Rewriting Rules**   This section holds the commands that rewrite e-mail addresses from user mail programs into the form required by the mail delivery programs.

**Mailer Definitions**   This section defines the programs used to deliver the mail. The rewrite rules used by the mailers are also defined in this section.

Each section is examined in detail in this chapter. It is unlikely that you will directly modify the `sendmail.cf` file except for the smallest of changes. Changing the macro configuration and rebuilding a new `sendmail.cf` is the preferred technique for making configuration changes. Yet understanding the structure of the `sendmail.cf` file, and the syntax and purpose of the configuration commands it contains, is an essential skill for every Sendmail administrator. Understanding the `sendmail.cf` file helps you better understand the purpose of the macro configuration commands and lets you observe their impact on the underlying configuration. More importantly, the Sendmail test tools run with the `sendmail.cf` configuration file. To effectively monitor a test, you need to understand the test output, which is often based on the structure of the `sendmail.cf` file.

Our analysis of the `sendmail.cf` file begins at the beginning with the first section, Local Info, and moves section by section through the entire file. The Local Info section contains the widest variety of configuration statements, and it is the part of the `sendmail.cf` file that is most often modified by system administrators.

## The Local Info Section

The first section in the `sendmail.cf` file contains information that is specific to the local host: information such as the hostname, the names of any mail relay hosts, and the mail domain name. It also contains information specific to your copy of Sendmail, such as the name that Sendmail uses to identify itself when it returns error messages, and the version number of the Sendmail distribution you're running. Additionally, the Local Info section contains the definitions of the optional databases used by Sendmail. This collection of diverse information is gathered together at the beginning of the `sendmail.cf` file to make it easier to locate in case manual editing is required.

The Local Info section of the `sendmail.cf` file generated for Sendmail 8.11 from the `redhat.mc` file is shown in Listing 7.1. It has been edited to reduce the number of unneeded lines. It should be largely identical to the Local Info section on your Linux system, but it won't be exactly the same. Don't worry about the differences; they are all related to comments and the number of blank lines. The commands are unchanged.

**Listing 7.1**   The Full Local Info Section

```
##################
#   local info   #
##################

Cwlocalhost
# file containing names of hosts for which we receive email
```

```
Fw/etc/mail/local-host-names
# my official domain name
#Dj$w.Foo.COM

CP.

# "Smart" relay host (may be null)
DS
# operators that cannot be in local usernames
CO @ % !
# a class with just a dot (for identifying canonical names)
C..
# a class with just a left bracket (for identifying domain literals)
C[[
# access_db acceptance class
C{Accept}OK RELAY
# Hosts that will permit relaying ($=R)
FR-o /etc/mail/relay-domains
# arithmetic map
Karith arith
# possible values for tls_connect in access map
C{tls}VERIFY ENCR
# who I send unqualified names to (null means deliver locally)
DR
# who gets all local email traffic
DH
# dequoting map
Kdequote dequote
# class E: names that should be exposed as from this host, even
   if we masquerade
# class L: names that should be delivered locally
# class M: domains that should be converted to $M
# class N: domains that should not be converted to $M
#CL root
# who I masquerade as (null for no masquerading) (see also $=M)
DM
# my name for error messages
DnMAILER-DAEMON
# Mailer table (overriding domains)
Kmailertable hash -o /etc/mail/mailertable
```

```
# Virtual user table (maps incoming users)
Kvirtuser hash -o /etc/mail/virtusertable

CPREDIRECT

# Access list database (for spam stomping)
Kaccess hash /etc/mail/access
# Configuration version number
DZ8.11.0
```

Blank lines are ignored. Lines that begin with # are comments. Comments are invaluable aids to understanding the arcane `sendmail.cf` file. Lines that begin with an uppercase character are configuration commands. Listing 7.1 contains the commands D, C, F, and K.

The local information is defined by D commands that define macro variables, C commands that define class variables, F commands that load class values from files, and K commands that define databases of information. The `sendmail.cf` command syntax is very terse. The commands are only one character long and many variables also have one-character names. Add to this the fact that the value assigned to the variable is crammed right next to the variable name and you have configuration commands that are terse and hard to read. Let's take a closer look at the D, C, F, and K commands so that we can decipher what is happening in the Local Info section.

## The Define Macro Command

The define macro command (D) defines a variable and assigns a value to it. Once the variable is defined, the stored value is used by other `sendmail.cf` commands and directly by Sendmail itself. Variables provide the flexibility that permits the same basic `sendmail.cf` configurations to run on many different systems, simply by modifying a few system-specific macro variables.

Traditional variable names are a single ASCII character, with user-created macro variables using uppercase letters as names and Sendmail internal macros using lowercase letters and special characters as names. These rules have changed. Now Sendmail predefines the meaning of several variables with uppercase names, and in Sendmail version 8 variable names are not restricted to a single character. Long variable names are enclosed in curly braces—e.g., {VirtHost} is a valid variable name. However, a quick check of the `sendmail.cf` delivered with the Red Hat RPM shows that not a single long variable name was used with a define macro command. Listing 7.2 shows a `grep` that displays every D command contained in the entire `sendmail.cf` file.

**Listing 7.2**  The Define Macro Commands Found in `sendmail.cf`

```
[craig]$ grep '^D' /etc/sendmail.cf
DS
DR
DH
DM
DnMAILER-DAEMON
DZ8.11.0
```

Listing 7.2 shows some interesting things. First, most of the macro variables are not set. The first three D commands set values for the S, R, and H variables. Each of these variables identifies an external mail relay server.

- The S variable stores the name of the relay host defined by the SMART_HOST variable in the m4 macro configuration. The SMART_HOST relay is a central mail server that handles all outgoing mail.

- The R variable holds the name of a relay host that handles local mail. The LOCAL_ RELAY `define` command in the m4 macro configuration sets the value for R. When R is set, the local computer does not handle its own local mail. Mail addressed from local user `craig` to local user `kathy` is not handle by the `local` mailer; it is relayed through the server specified by the R variable.

- The H variable stores the mail server name defined by the MAIL_HUB command in the m4 macro configuration. The MAIL_HUB server handles all local mail in which the recipient address includes the name of the local host. Therefore, while mail addressed to `kathy` might be handled by the LOCAL_RELAY, mail from any user logged into `chicken.foobirds.org` that was addressed to `kathy@chicken.foobirds.org` would be relayed through the MAIL_HUB server.

It is easy to see why these variables are not set on our sample system. These external relays are used only when the local system does not handle its own e-mail—for example, in a client configuration. So far we have been creating server configurations.

The fourth variable that is not set is M. It has nothing to do with relaying. The M variable holds the masquerade value. We will play with variable M later in this chapter and hear much more about masquerading in Chapter 9, "Special m4 Configurations."

Only two of the variables in Listing 7.2 have a value assigned to them. The n variable holds the sender name that Sendmail uses to send generated error messages. This value can be set in the macro configuration with the confMAILER_NAME option. But if it is not set, it defaults to MAILER-DAEMON, which is exactly what happened in our sample configuration.

**Advanced Configuration**

**PART 3**

The Z variable is set to `8.11.0` in Listing 7.2. By default, Z is set to the Sendmail version number. The default can be overridden in the macro configuration file by setting a value with the `confCF_VERSION` option, but it rarely is. About the only time anyone ever changes the Z variable is when they manually update the `sendmail.cf` file and they want to signal the update to others. People who edit the `sendmail.cf` file directly will place detailed comments right next to the changes they make, modify the Z variable, and place comments explaining the change near the Z variable declaration. For example, assuming you edited the `sendmail.cf` file to set a value for M, in addition to placing comments next to the DM command you might make the following modifications to notify others of the change:

```
# Configuration version number
DZ8.11.0/20001004
# Notes on locally made configuration changes
# 20001004 - set the M macro variable to foobirds.org.
#       Change made by Craig Hunt x4096.
```

Again, changes like this are rarely made. Most system administrators maintain the Sendmail configuration through the macro configuration file, not through directly editing the `sendmail.cf` file. The macro configuration file provides a hook into your revision control system with the `VERSIONID` macro, making it unnecessary to modify `confCF_VERSION` to set Z when the macro configuration file is used.

The last two D commands clearly show the run-together nature of `sendmail.cf` configuration commands. Look at the command

```
DnMAILER-DAEMON
```

D is the command. n is the name of the macro variable. And `MAILER-DAEMON` is the value being assigned to the variable. The uninitiated find these run-together commands hard to read. When macro variables reference other macro variables, they become even more difficult to read.

To use the value stored in a variable, reference it as $x, where x is the variable name. Variable references can be used in pattern matching—for example, to test if the username in the sender address was equal to $n. They can also be used to assign values to other variables.

> **NOTE** Macro variables are normally expanded when the `sendmail.cf` file is read. A special syntax, $&x, is used to expand macro variables when they are referenced. The $&x syntax is used only with certain internal variables that change at runtime.

None of the define macro commands shown in Listing 7.2 use other macro variables to assign values. In fact, the only D command in the `sendmail.cf` file on our sample Red Hat system that does use another variable is commented out, as the following `grep` command shows:

```
[craig]$ grep '^#D' /etc/sendmail.cf
#Dj$w.Foo.COM
```

If this code were not commented out, it would define the value for macro variable j. It defines j as containing the value of variable w (`$w`), plus the literal string `.Foo.COM`. w contains your host's unqualified hostname. j is supposed to contain the fully qualified domain name of your host—i.e., hostname plus domain name. Clearly, if you need to define a value for j, you must remove the # that turns this line into a comment and change `.Foo.COM` into your real domain name. Luckily you never need to manually set j on a Linux system. Running under Linux, Sendmail can automatically determine the correct value for j. This line is included in the configuration only as an aid to administrators of some outdated systems that required manual configuration.

Like j, the values of most internal macro variables are not set in the `sendmail.cf` file; they are assigned internally by Sendmail. Appendix C, "Sendmail Variables, Options, and Flags," provides a complete listing of all of the predefined variables used by Sendmail.

Using a variable to set a variable is not the only variation of the D command syntax that we didn't see in the `sendmail.cf` file from our sample Red Hat system. The D command also has a conditional syntax that our sample file did not contain.

## Using Conditionals

One variation of the D command syntax that deserves special comment is the conditional format. A D command with the conditional syntax is shown below:

```
Dq$g$?x ($x)$.
```

The D is the define macro command; the q is the variable being defined; and the `$g` says to assign q the value found in g. The `$?x ($x)$.` is the conditional statement The `$?x` is a conditional test. It checks whether or not x has a value set. If x has been set, the value defined by `($x)` is assigned to q. The `$.` ends the conditional.

Given this, the assignment of q is interpreted as follows:

- q is assigned the value of g;
- if x is set, q is also assigned a literal blank, a literal left parenthesis, the value of x, and a literal right parenthesis.

So if g contains kathy@foobirds.org and x contains Kathleen McCafferty, q will contain

    kathy@foobirds.org (Kathleen McCafferty)

But if g contains sara@hawk.foobirds.org and x is empty, q will contain only

    sara@hawk.foobirds.org.

$? is the test—the "if" of the conditional. $. is the "endif." The conditional also has "else," which is $|. The full syntax of the conditional is

    **$?x** *value1* **$|** *value2* **$.**

which is interpreted as

    if ($?) *x* is set;

        use *value1*;

    else ($|);

        use *value2*;

    end if ($.).

This same conditional syntax can be used in other sendmail.cf configuration commands. We didn't see it in the D commands from our sample system, but we will see it later in the configuration file when we look at the H command.

All of the D commands shown in Listing 7.2 are found in the Local Info section of the sendmail.cf file. Another command that is almost exclusively used in the Local Info section is the C command.

## The Define Class Command

A C command defines a Sendmail class. A class is an array of values. Classes are used for anything with multiple values that are handled in the same way, such as multiple names for the local host or a list of domain names for which mail will be relayed. The C command can define the values for a class variable on a single line or on multiple lines. For example, the following line:

    C{Accept}OK RELAY

performs the same function as these two lines:

    C{Accept}OK

    C{Accept}RELAY

The syntax of the C command is similar to that of the D command. The first character is the command C. It is followed by the name of the class variable, which in turn is followed by the value being assigned to the variable. If multiple values are assigned on a single line, they are separated by white space.

Like the Sendmail variables assigned by the D command, class variables traditionally had single character names, with user-created classes using uppercase letters for names and Sendmail internal classes using lowercase letters for names. Now, classes can use long names by enclosing the name inside curly braces—e.g., {Accept}. Listing 7.3 uses a grep command to show all of the C commands contained in the sendmail.cf file delivered with the Red Hat RPM:

**Listing 7.3**   The Define Class Commands Found in sendmail.cf

```
[craig]$ grep '^C' /etc/sendmail.cf
Cwlocalhost
CP.
CO @ % !
C..
C[[
C{Accept}OK RELAY
C{tls}VERIFY ENCR
CPREDIRECT
C{src}E F H U
```

The first C command in Listing 7.3 adds the value localhost to class w. From the discussion of the local-host-names file in the previous chapter, you know that class w holds all of the computer's hostname aliases. In that chapter we used sendmail –bt to view the contents of class w, so you also know that class w contains much more than just the word localhost. Unlike a D command, which overwrites the contents of a variable to set the variable to a specific value, C commands are additive. This C command doesn't replace everything in class w with the word localhost; it adds the word localhost to whatever else is there.

The class variable P is a good example of the additive nature of C commands. The second C command in Listing 7.3 stores the value . (dot) in class variable P. Later, in the second-to-last line of Listing 7.3, another C command stores the value REDIRECT in the same class variable P. After the latter command, P contains both a . (dot) and the word REDIRECT, as this sendmail –bt test shows:

```
[root]# sendmail -bt
ADDRESS TEST MODE (ruleset 3 NOT automatically invoked)
Enter <ruleset> <address>
> $=P
```

    REDIRECT

    > ^D

P holds the list of pseudo-domains. As explained earlier, pseudo-domains are not real domains found in the DNS; they are values used to request special processing from Sendmail. The dot is always defined as part of this class. The value REDIRECT is added because the redhat.mc file that built this sendmail.cf file contained the FEATURE(redirect) command. The CPREDIRECT command in this sendmail.cf file clearly demonstrates the direct impact that the macro configuration you build has on the Sendmail configuration.

The third C command assigns the values @, %, and ! to the class variable O. Class O holds tokens that are used to divide the parts of an e-mail address. These three values are characters that cannot be used in local usernames, because they have special meanings in e-mail addresses. Everyone is familiar with the role that @ plays in an address. Those who are familiar with UUCP known that ! is used in traditional UUCP bang addressing. And the % character is used in old systems as a way to forward an e-mail address to a remote system for processing. These are default values set by Sendmail that do not need to be modified.

The next two C commands, C.. and C[[, are unique for two reasons. First, they demonstrate that variables can be given names that are special characters. Here we are assigning values to the class variable . and to the class variable [. Secondly, and more surprisingly, the commands assign these variables a value that exactly matches the name of the variable. Thus variable . is assigned the value . and variable [ is assigned the value [. Strange! We know from the discussion of the D command that variables can be used in pattern matching. Class variables are only used in pattern matching. So why create a variable for . and [ when a pattern match could just as easily compare against the literal value? There are reasons.

Special symbols are used when referring to classes in a pattern. Above, we saw that the value in an individual variable is referred to as $x, where x is the variable name. The $= symbol matches any value in a class, and the $~ symbol matches any value not in a class. Thus $=P means any value in class P and $~[ means anything that is not in class [.

One reason to define classes named . and [ is that classes are expandable. The characters . and [ have special meaning in addresses. The . character separates the parts of a domain name. The [ character encloses raw IP addresses that are being used in place of hostnames in e-mail addresses. Classes allow Sendmail to compare a value against a list of values, instead of against a single value. This means that if the range of possible characters that can be used to separate domain names ever increases or the range of characters used to enclose special addresses ever changes, values could be added to the . and [ classes to handle these changes without changing the entire sendmail.cf file.

The second advantage of a class over a literal is that the $~ syntax allows Sendmail to check for a "not equal" condition. A grep of the sample sendmail.cf in Listing 7.4 shows that, at least in the case of the [ class, this capability is important.

**Listing 7.4**  Checking How Classes Are Used

```
[craig]$ grep '\$\=\.' /etc/sendmail.cf
[craig]$ grep '\$\=\[' /etc/sendmail.cf
[craig]$ grep '\$\~\.' /etc/sendmail.cf
[craig]$ grep '\$\~\[' /etc/sendmail.cf
R< $~[ : $* > $*      $>MailerToTriple < $1 : $2 > $3  check -- resolved?
R$* <$~[ : $* > $*    $>MailerToTriple < $2 : $3 > $4  check -- resolved?
R< $~[ : $* > $*      $>MailerToTriple < $1 : $2 > $3  "." found?
```

Listing 7.4 shows some interesting things. When used in the configuration, class variable . must be referenced as either $=. or $~., and class variable [ must be referenced as either $=[ or $~[. Using grep to search for these values shows how these class variables are used. First off, class . is not used at all, and there are no tests using $=[ to see if a value exists in the [ class variable. However, $~[ is used to select addresses that do not start with a [. This is not the time to discuss the exact details of the pattern matching. Pattern matching is covered in detail in Chapter 8. The thing to understand here is that even inexplicable commands such as C[[ might have a valid use.

> **NOTE**  Remember that your system might be different. These same class names may be used for other purposes on your system. This only shows how they are used in our example sendmail.cf. Carefully read the comments in your sendmail.cf file for guidance as to how classes and variables are used in your configuration.

The next two lines in Listing 7.3 are:

```
C{Accept}OK RELAY
C{tls}VERIFY ENCR
```

These two C commands both use long class variable names, {Accept} and {tls}, and both define keywords used to configure some aspect of Sendmail. You recognize the OK and RELAY keywords from the discussion of the access database in Chapter 6, "Using Sendmail Databases." You'll see the VERIFY and ENCR keywords in the discussion of STARTTLS in Chapter 12, "Sendmail Security."

The last line in Listing 7.3 is C{src}E F H U. It does essentially the same thing as the two commands just described above. It defines a long class variable name, {src}, and it assigns a list of values to that class that are used in the Sendmail syntax. In this case, the values are tags internally assigned by Sendmail to addresses to aid it in processing the various types of addresses that can be found in the Sendmail databases. What is unique about this C command is that it occurs outside of the Local Info section. All of the other C commands are found in Local Info. This illustrates the fact that, while most variables are declared in the Local Info section, they can be declared anywhere in the sendmail.cf file as long as they are declared before they are used. This C command occurs immediately before the ruleset that uses it. On the other hand, all active F commands in our sample sendmail.cf file are located in the Local Info section.

## Loading a Class Variable from a File

The F command loads values into a class variable from a file. The Local Info section from the sample sendmail.cf file contains only two F commands, which are shown in Listing 7.5.

**Listing 7.5**  Commands that Load Class Variables from a File

```
[root]# grep '^F' /etc/sendmail.cf
Fw/etc/mail/local-host-names
FR-o /etc/mail/relay-domains
```

The first F command is the simplest form of the command syntax—the F command followed by the variable name, in this case w, and the pathname of the file that is to be loaded into the variable, which in this case is /etc/mail/local-host-names. This simple form of the F command is the most commonly used, but it is not the only format. The F command syntax accepts an optional switch value before the pathname of the file and an optional scanf pattern after the file pathname.

By default, Sendmail reads data from the file using the scanf pattern %s, which means it reads the first white space–delimited string from each line in the file. A different scanf pattern can be provided on the F command line if Sendmail is compiled with the SCANF compiler option. We saw from the sendmail -bt -d0.4 command in Listing 6.1 in Chapter 6 that the copy of Sendmail delivered with the Red Hat RPM does use the SCANF compiler option. Therefore, we could enter a command in the following format if we needed to:

```
Fw/etc/mail/local-host-names %.25s
```

This command reads data from local-host-names into class w but it reads no more than 25 characters from a string even if a whitespace character has not been encountered. Why would you do this? You wouldn't. This is just an example of the possible syntax. I never use a scanf pattern with the F command, and neither should you. You should not expect

Sendmail to clean up a file as it is reading it. You should present Sendmail with files that are already clean and properly formatted. Doing otherwise confuses the other system administrators who might be called in to maintain your system and introduces the possibility that you will create a bad scanf pattern that can be exploited by an intruder in a buffer-overflow attack.

> **NOTE**    scanf is a C language library routine. C programming and the details of scanf are beyond the scope of this book. For more information, see *The C Programming Language* by Brian Kernighan and Dennis Ritchie (Prentice Hall, 1988).

The second F command in Listing 7.5 loads class R from the file /etc/mail/relay-domains. As you'll recall from Chapter 6, class R holds the names of domains for which Sendmail will relay mail and the relay-domains file is the traditional way to load values into class R. The interesting thing about this F command is that the –o switch is used before the pathname. The –o switch tells Sendmail that the relay-domains file is optional. Notice that the local-host-names file used in the first F command does not have the –o switch, and therefore is mandatory. That's why we got the error "cannot open '/etc/mail/local-host-names'" in Listing 4.2 of Chapter 4 ("Creating a Basic Sendmail Configuration") when we tried to use the generic-linux.cf configuration file without a local-host-names file, but we got no complaint at all about the fact that we didn't have a relay-domains file. The –o switch is very useful because it creates a more forgiving configuration that works in a wide variety of situations.

While the –o switch is the only switch available with the F command, the K command, our next topic, has several possible switch values. The K command is the most complex command used in the Local Info section. It needs to be. Unlike the F command that works with simple flat files, the K command deals with true database files.

## The Keyed File Command

The last of the four commands from the Local Info section is the K command, which defines a Sendmail database's characteristics for the sendmail.cf file. The K command has the most complex syntax of any command in the Local Info section. The basic format of a K command is:

```
K name type switches path
```

The various pieces of the command are separated by white space, although the white space between K and *name* is optional and rarely used. K, of course, is the command. *name* is the name used inside sendmail.cf to reference this database. The *name* can be any text string you want, but the *name* should be something logical, such as the external filename of the database.

## The *K* Command Type Argument

*type* is the database type. Several database types were discussed in Chapter 6 in relationship to which compiler options add support for which database types. The long list of database types discussed in Chapter 6, however, is only part of the story. Sendmail has several internal database types. Table 7.1 lists all of the valid *type* values.

**Table 7.1**   Valid K Command Type Values

| Type | Description |
| --- | --- |
| arith | An internal routine for doing arithmetic. |
| btree | A type added by the NEWDB compiler option. |
| bestmx | An internal routine that retrieves the MX record for a host. |
| dbm | A type added by the NDBM compiler option. |
| dequote | An internal routine that removes quotation marks. |
| dns | An internal routine that retrieves the address record for a host name. |
| hash | A type added by the NEWDB compiler option. |
| hesiod | A database located on a hesiod server. |
| host | An internal table for hostnames. |
| implicit | The type used for the aliases database file. |
| ldap | A database located on an LDAP server. |
| netinfo | A database located on a NeXT netinfo server. |
| nis | A database located on an NIS server. |
| nisplus | A database located on an NIS+ server. |
| null | An internal routine that returns "Not found" for all lookups. |
| ph | A database located on a CCSO Nameserver. |
| program | Passes the query to an external program. |

**Table 7.1**    Valid K Command Type Values *(continued)*

| Type | Description |
|------|-------------|
| regex | An internal routine that handles regular expressions. |
| sequence | Defines a search list to search multiple databases. |
| switch | References an entry in the nsswitch.conf file or the host.conf file to create a database sequence. |
| text | A text file database. |
| user | The type used for the /etc/passwd file. |

On a Linux system, many of these database types are not used. The internal types are always available, but are set up by Sendmail when they are needed and thus require no intervention by you. btree and hash are the only two types you are likely to use for the external databases that you create yourself. But even in that case, you will declare the database using a FEATURE macro in the macro configuration file; you won't create your own K commands in the sendmail.cf file. As noted in Chapter 6, all of the databases created by FEATURE commands default to hash type.

### The *K* Command Switches

The *switches* that optionally follow *type* on the K command line specify optional processing. Table 7.2 lists the valid switches.

**Table 7.2**    Valid K Command Switches

| Switch | Description |
|--------|-------------|
| −A | Accepts values from duplicate keys. |
| −a | Appends the specified string to the values returned by the lookup. |
| −f | Preserves uppercase. |
| −k | Identifies the column used as the key in a flat file lookup. |
| −m | Verifies the key but doesn't return a value. |
| −N | Indicates that the keys in the database always end with a null byte. |

**Table 7.2** Valid K Command Switches *(continued)*

| Switch | Description |
|--------|-------------|
| –0 | Indicates that the keys in the database never end with a null byte. |
| –o | Specifies that the database is optional, so no error is produced if the file is not found. |
| –q | Preserves quotes in the keys, which are normally removed. |
| –s | Replaces spaces with the specified character. |
| –v | Identifies the column used as the value in a flat file lookup. |
| –z | Specifies the character used to delimit columns for flat file lookups. |

Some of these switches mirror options defined when the database is built. These are:

**–A**   This option makes sense only for a database that has duplicate keys, which means the database must be built with the makemap –d option. Recall the staff mailing list from Listing 6.5 in Chapter 6. The alias staff pointed to five recipient addresses. Assume that that mailing list was replicated as a group of five entries in some odd database that allowed duplicate keys:

```
staff   kathy
staff   craig
staff   david@parrot
staff   sara@hawk
staff   becky@parrot
```

If the K command that declared this odd database inside the sendmail.cf file did *not* have the –A switch, a query for staff would return kathy. But if the –A switch was used, Sendmail would access all of the duplicate keys and append all of the values returned for those keys. Thus, a query for staff would return kathy, craig, david@parrot, sara@hawk, and becky@parrot, which exactly matches the original mailing list. Of course, you wouldn't actually do this, because the aliases database already handles mailing lists and does a better job of it. This is just an example.

**–f**   This option preserves uppercase characters. It directly relates to the –f option used with makemap that preserves uppercase characters when the database is built. Normally, all characters are converted to lowercase characters. E-mail addresses are supposed to be case insensitive. Avoid introducing case-sensitivity into a process that is defined as case insensitive. Don't use –f.

**–N**  This option tells Sendmail that the database keys end with a null character. If the makemap command used to build the database used –N, which inserts a null character at the end of each key, the database can be read using the –N switch on the K command line. The inverse of this is the –O switch that tells Sendmail that the keys do not end with null characters. If neither the –N nor the –O switches are used, Sendmail will successfully match keys whether or not the keys end in a null character. Using either –N or –O reduces the robustness of Sendmail. –N or –O might slightly increase the performance of database lookups, but they do so at the cost of reliability.

Two switches handle embedded spaces. Spaces are not allowed inside standard RFC 822 e-mail addresses. If spaces are included, they must be enclosed in quotes or replaced with characters that are allowed. The –q switch retains the quotes, which are normally removed unless they are "escaped" by a backslash character. The –s switch converts spaces to another character. For example, –s- converts spaces to dashes. The –s switch is only used with dequote, because dequote is the internal routine that removes the quote marks that surround embedded spaces.

Three switches are used to treat traditional flat files as if they were databases. –k identifies the column of text that should be used as the key, –v identifies the column of text that should be used as the value returned for the key, and –z identifies the character that is used to separate columns in the flat file. By default, white space separates columns. The /etc/passwd file is a classic flat file that is not delimited by white spaces. Each column in /etc/passwd is separated by a colon (:). Imagine using the passwd file as a database to retrieve the home directory based on the login username. Here is the passwd entry for craig on our sample system:

```
[craig]$ grep '^craig' /etc/passwd
craig:x:500:500:Craig Hunt:/home/craig:/bin/bash
```

The first column contains the username, and the sixth column contains the home directory. The –k and –v switches count columns from zero. So the first column is 0 and the sixth column is 5. The following K command defines a database that uses /etc/passwd to convert a username to a home directory path:

```
Khomedir text -z: -k0 -v5 /etc/passwd
```

Here K is the command. homedir is the internal name used for this database, and text is the database type. –z: –k0 –v5 are the switches, and /etc/passwd is the path. Given this declaration, a rewrite rule later in the sendmail.cf file could pass the key value craig to the homedir database and receive /home/craig as a response. Would you actually do

Advanced Configuration

PART 3

this? Probably not. Sendmail already knows the home directory associated with a local username without any help from you. (It is the values stored in variable $z.) Just because Sendmail provides a configuration option doesn't mean you will ever need to use it.

Most switches fall into the category of configuration options that you will never use. The –m switch verifies that a key exists but does not return the value for the key. This is rarely used because a successful lookup in a normal database both validates the key and returns the value for the key. The –a switch appends a fixed string to the value returned for a lookup. For example, –a.foobirds.org adds the string .foobirds.org to every response from the database. This switch is rarely used, because if every value in a database needs to have a specific value appended, it can very easily be done when the database is originally built without any manual modification of the sendmail.cf file.

The most commonly used, and most important, switch is –o. –o tells Sendmail that a database is optional. With this switch, a K command can be included in sendmail.cf in anticipation of the need for a database without requiring that the database be present. Without the –o switch, Sendmail will fail on the first command that attempts to access the database if the database file cannot be found. Using –o makes Sendmail more forgiving and more robust.

We have covered most of the K command syntax: the database name, the database type, and the switches. The last field in the K command is the *path*. This is simply the pathname of the database, generally written without the filename extension. (The K command adds the correct extension—for example, .db—to the pathname based on the database type.) The *path* value is only required if the database is external to Sendmail. As the list of database types made clear, several of the databases declared by K commands are internal to Sendmail. When an internal database is used, no *path* is needed. Some sample K commands from the sendmail.cf file will make the structure of the command clear.

### Realistic *K* Commands

The sample configuration contains five K commands, all of which are shown in Listing 7.6.

**Listing 7.6**   The K Commands Found in sendmail.cf

```
[craig]$ grep '^K' /etc/sendmail.cf
Karith arith
Kdequote dequote
Kmailertable hash -o /etc/mail/mailertable
Kvirtuser hash -o /etc/mail/virtusertable
Kaccess hash /etc/mail/access
```

Let's work our way through Listing 7.6 from the bottom up. The last K command declares a database named access. The database is the standard hash type. The file that contains the database is /etc/mail/access. All of this information—the internal name, the database type, and the file that holds the database—defined by the K command is the direct result of the FEATURE(`access_db') command from our sample macro configuration file. The access database, which is used to control mail relaying and delivery, is covered in Chapter 6.

The previous two K commands define the virtuser and mailertable databases that result from the following commands found in the sample macro configuration file:

```
FEATURE(`mailertable', `hash -o /etc/mail/mailertable')
FEATURE(`virtusertable', `hash -o /etc/mail/virtusertable')
```

Both are hash type databases, and both use the –o switch, which means that Sendmail will run even if these files are not found. Notice that the K command for the access database did not use the –o switch. If the file /etc/mail/access.db is not found, Sendmail will fail if a command attempts to use the access database. Even if you don't have any entries for the access database, create an empty /etc/mail/access.db file in order to make Sendmail more robust, as in this example:

```
[root]# touch /etc/mail/access
[root]# makemap hash /etc/mail/access < /etc/mail/access
```

The mailertable, the virtusertable, and the access database are all covered in Chapter 6. The other two databases, however, were not covered in that chapter. Both the arith and dequote databases are pseudo-databases. That means that they are not real databases. Instead they are internal Sendmail routines that are accessed by rewrite rules as if they were databases. The dequote map, which has already been discussed, is used to remove quotation marks from addresses. The arith map is used to do arithmetic functions for STARTTLS security. STARTTLS is covered in Chapter 12.

The four commands, D, C, F, and K, illustrate everything that is done in the Local Info section of the sendmail.cf file. The Local Info section is the most important section of the file from the standpoint of a system administrator trying to directly configure sendmail.cf, because it defines the configuration information that varies from system to system. We have covered every command in the Local Info section of our sample system, but before moving on to the Options section, we should cover the only configuration command that occurs before the Local Info section—the version level command.

## The Version Level Command

The version level command (V) defines the version of the sendmail.cf file. This should not be confused with the Z variable that identifies the Sendmail source code release number or the m4 VERSIONID macro that defines revision control information for the macro

Advanced Configuration

PART 3

source files. The V command tells Sendmail the level of syntax and commands required to support the configuration. If the Sendmail program cannot support the requested commands and syntax, it complains about the commands it does not understand and displays the following version level error message:

```
[root]# sendmail -v -t
/etc/sendmail.cf: line 83: readcf: map arith: class arith
not available
/etc/sendmail.cf: line 211: DaemonPortOptions parameter
    "Name=MTA" unknown
/etc/sendmail.cf: line 212: DaemonPortOptions parameter
    "Name=MSA" unknown
/etc/sendmail.cf: line 212: DaemonPortOptions parameter "M=E" unknown
Warning: .cf version level (9) exceeds sendmail version 8.9.3
    functionality (8)
```

On the other hand, if the Sendmail program is newer than the configuration, the program can support more features than the configuration uses. In that case, Sendmail displays the error we first saw in Chapter 3, "Running Sendmail."

```
[root]# sendmail -v -t -C /etc/sendmail.cf
Warning: .cf file is out of date: sendmail 8.11.0 supports version 9,
    .cf file is version 8
No recipient addresses found in header
^D
```

The version level command is a key component of warning Sendmail about potential incompatibility.

You don't change the V command in the sendmail.cf file. And unlike most other things in the sendmail.cf file, you do not control the setting of the V command using an m4 macro in the macro control file. The V command is inserted into the sendmail.cf file when it is first built by m4. Listing 7.7 shows the commands that occur before the Local Info section, including the V command.

**Listing 7.7**  The V Command from the Sample sendmail.cf

```
# level 9 config file format
V9/Berkeley

# override file safeties - setting this option compromises security,
# addressing the actual file configuration problem is preferred
# need to set this before any file actions are encountered in
    the cf file
#O DontBlameSendmail=safe

# default LDAP map specification
# need to set this now before any LDAP maps are defined
#O LDAPDefaultSpec=-h localhost
```

The format of the V command is **V***level*/*vendor*. The *level* number on the V command line indicates the version level of the configuration syntax. V9 is the version supported by Sendmail 8.11.0. The *vendor* part of the V command identifies whether any vendor-specific syntax is supported. The default *vendor* value for the Sendmail distribution is Berkeley, which is the vendor value used for Linux.

Everything after the V command and before the Local Info section is a comment, as indicated by the fact that the lines start with a # character. However, two of these lines are commented-out option commands:

```
#O DontBlameSendmail=safe
#O LDAPDefaultSpec=-h localhost
```

The first one disables Sendmail's file security, which is obviously a bad idea. It is used only when absolutely required to read a given file. The second one defines the default LDAP map specification, which is only used if LDAP is used. As the O command indicates, both of these are options, and they are the only options that are located outside of the Options section of our sample sendmail.cf file. They occur before the Local Info section because they must be declared before they are used, and if they are used at all it is by file and database references that occur in the Local Info section of the file. All other options are found in the Options section.

# The Options Section

The Sendmail program uses option values to define the Sendmail environment. There are nearly 100 options, all of which are listed in Appendix C. A few samples from the sendmail.cf file are shown in Listing 7.8 to illustrate what options do.

**Listing 7.8**    Sample Option Commands from `sendmail.cf`

```
# location of alias file
O AliasFile=/etc/aliases
# Forward file search path
O ForwardPath=$z/.forward.$w:$z/.forward
# timeouts (many of these)
O Timeout.queuereturn=5d
O Timeout.queuewarn=4h
```

These options all have something to do with Sendmail functions that have already been discussed. The first O command sets the location of the `aliases` file to `/etc/aliases`. The second option defines the location of the `.forward` file. Notice the `$z` and `$w` included in this option. These are Sendmail variables in action. Given the fact that you already know that the `.forward` file is in the user's home directory, you can guess that the value of the `$z` variable is the user's home directory. The `$w` variable contains the computer's hostname, indicating that it is possible to use the computer's hostname as a filename extension on a `.forward` file.

> **NOTE**   A variable and a class variable can exist with the same name, and still be two different things. A variable is used to provide a value, as in Listing 7.8 where $w provides a hostname, and a class is used to test a value. $w is not the same as $=w. $=w holds all of the names by which the local host is known. $w holds only the primary hostname of the local host and thus returns only a single value.

The last two options in the example relate to processing the queue of undelivered mail. The first of these options tells Sendmail that if a piece of mail stays in the queue for five days (5d), it should be returned to the sender as undeliverable. The second of these options tells Sendmail to send the user a warning message if a piece of mail has been undeliverable for four hours (4h).

This section requires no direct modifications. All of the options can be set through the m4 macro configuration file. The four values shown in Listing 7.8 could be set with these m4 commands:

```
define(`ALIAS_FILE', `/etc/aliases')
define(`confFORWARD_PATH', `$z/.forward.$w:$z/.forward')
define(`confTO_QUEUERETURN', `5d')
define(`confTO_QUEUEWARN', `4h')
```

The options in the `sendmail.cf` file that comes with your Linux system are correctly defined for that system. I have never directly edited the Options section of a Linux sendmail.cf file. In fact, the last time I edited an Options section was years ago, before the development of the m4 macros. It was sometimes necessary back then to move a sendmail.cf from one operating system to another. In those cases, it was necessary to edit the options to fit the new environment. That is not necessary now, because the m4 macros build a sendmail.cf customized for the target operating system. The Message Precedence section that follows the Options section also requires no modifications.

# The Message Precedence Section

Message Precedence is used to assign priority to messages entering the queue. By default, mail is considered "first-class mail" and is given a precedence of 0. The higher the precedence number, the greater the precedence of the message. But don't get excited. Increasing priority is essentially meaningless. About the only useful thing you can do is select a negative precedence number, which indicates low-priority mail. Because error messages are not generated for mail with a negative precedence number, low priorities are useful for mass mailings. The precedence values from the sample sendmail.cf are shown in Listing 7.9.

**Listing 7.9**   Standard Message Precedence Values

```
###########################
#   Message precedences   #
###########################
Pfirst-class=0
Pspecial-delivery=100
Plist=-30
Pbulk=-60
Pjunk=-100
```

The P command defines precedence. The format of the command is:

**P**_name=number_

where P is the command. _name_ is the text name used to request the precedence and _number_ is the numeric precedence value associated with the text name.

To request a precedence, mail must include a Precedence header that specifies the name associated with the desired precedence. For example, to request a precedence of -30, add the following header to the mail message:

Precedence: list

Precedence values are rarely used, and to be of any use at all, the remote user must know the precedence names. The five precedence values included in the sendmail.cf file are the standard names that are known to all other mail systems. If you add a new precedence value, most remote users will never know the name associated with the precedence and thus will not use it. The precedence values that come with your Linux system are more than you'll ever need.

# The Trusted Users Section

Trusted users are allowed to change the sender address when sending mail. The T command defines trusted users. It syntax is:

T=*user*

where T is the command and *user* is a valid username from the /etc/passwd file.

The trusted users defined in the sendmail.cf file that comes with your Linux system are root, uucp, and daemon. The entire Trusted Users section is shown in Listing 7.10.

**Listing 7.10**   The sendmail.cf Trusted Users Section

```
#####################
#   Trusted users   #
#####################
# this is equivalent to setting class "t"
#Ft/etc/mail/trusted-users
Troot
Tdaemon
Tuucp
```

The T command is not the only way to define trusted users. Any user listed in class t is a trusted user. As described in Chapter 6, usernames can be added to class t with the confTRUSTED_USERS parameter or the use_ct_file feature in the m4 macro configuration. If use_ct_file is specified, trusted users are read from the /etc/mail/trusted-users file. In this configuration, the use_ct_file feature was not used. If it had been used, the F command located before the T commands in Listing 7.10 would not be commented out.

---

**NOTE**   Do not modify the Trusted Users list. Allowing users to send mail using another user's name is a potential security problem.

---

# The Format of Headers Section

The Format of Headers section defines the headers that Sendmail inserts into mail. Headers are defined by the H command. The header definitions from the `sendmail.cf` file are shown in Listing 7.11.

**Listing 7.11**   Header Formats in `sendmail.cf`

```
##########################
#    Format of headers   #
##########################
H?P?Return-Path: <$g>
HReceived: $?sfrom $s $.$?_($?s$|from $.$_)
    $.$?{auth_type}(authenticated$?{auth_ssf} (${auth_ssf} bits)$.)
    $.by $j ($v/$Z)$?r with $r$. id $i$?{tls_version}(using
    ${tls_version} with cipher ${cipher} (${cipher_bits} bits)
    verified ${verify})$.$?u for $u; $|; $.$b
H?D?Resent-Date: $a
H?D?Date: $a
H?F?Resent-From: $?x$x <$g>$|$g$.
H?F?From: $?x$x <$g>$|$g$.
H?x?Full-Name: $x
# HPosted-Date: $a
# H?l?Received-Date: $b
H?M?Resent-Message-Id: <$t.$i@$j>
H?M?Message-Id: <$t.$i@$j>
```

Each header line begins with the H command, which is optionally followed by header flags enclosed in question marks. The header flags control whether or not the header is inserted into mail bound for a specific mailer. If no flags are specified, the header is used for all mailers. If a flag is specified, the header is used only for a mailer that has the same flag set in the mailer's definition. (Mailer definitions are covered later in this chapter.) Header flags only control header insertion. If a header is received in the input, it is passed to the output, regardless of the flag settings.

Each line also contains a header name, a colon, and a header template. These fields define the structure of the actual header. Macros in the header template are expanded before the header is inserted in a message. The first header in Listing 7.11 contains $g, which tells Sendmail to use the value stored in the g macro. The g macro holds the sender's e-mail address. Assume that the sender is David. After the macro expansion, the header might contain:

```
Return-Path: <david@wren.foobirds.com>
```

The headers in Listing 7.11 provide examples of using the conditional syntax in header templates. The conditional syntax is an if/else construct where $? is the "if," $| is the "else," and $. is the "endif." This is exactly the same conditional syntax that was described for the D command, and it is used in the same way. An example from Listing 7.11 is:

```
H?F?Resent-From: $?x$x <$g>$|$g$.
```

H is the command. ?F? is a flag value. Resent-From: is the header name, and $?x$x <$g>$|$g$. is the template, which uses conditional syntax. This conditional template says that if ($?) macro x exists, use $x <$g> as the header template, else ($|) use $g as the template. Macro x contains the full name of the sender. Thus, if it exists, the header is

```
Resent-From: David Craig <david@wren.foobirds.org>
```

If x doesn't exist, the header is

```
Resent-From: david@wren.foobirds.org
```

The headers provided in the Linux sendmail.cf file are sufficient for a basic installation. You'll see additional header declarations in Chapter 11, "Stopping Spam," for mail filtering, but the basic declarations shown in Listing 7.11 will be found on all systems.

All five sections discussed so far—Local Info, Options, Message Precedence, Trusted Users and Format of Headers—define configuration values used by Sendmail. These sections are essentially passive, telling Sendmail things such as the structure of headers or the locations of files. These sections have not defined the actions that Sendmail should take. That changes with the next section. The Rewrite Rules section contains the instructions that Sendmail uses to process mail.

# The Rewriting Rules Section

The Rewriting Rules section defines the rules used to parse e-mail addresses from user mail programs and rewrite them into the form required by the mail delivery programs. Rewrite rules match the input address against a pattern and, if a match is found, rewrite the address in a new format using the rules defined in the command. The format of a rewrite rule is:

```
Rpattern    template
```

where R is the command. *pattern* selects the address to be modified and *template* rewrites the address.

Rewrite rules divide e-mail addresses into tokens for processing. Tokens are strings of characters delimited by operators defined in the `OperatorChars` option, and the operators themselves. The left-hand side of a rewrite rule contains a pattern defined by macro variables and literal values and by special symbols. The tokens from the input address are matched against the pattern. If the address matches the pattern, the address is rewritten using the template defined in the right-hand side of the rewrite rule. The template is also defined with literals, macro values, and special symbols.

A rewrite rule may process the same address several times because, after being rewritten, the address is again compared against the pattern. If it still matches, it is rewritten again. The cycle of pattern matching and rewriting continues until the address no longer matches the pattern. Then no further processing is done by this rewrite rule, and the address is passed to the next rule in line.

Individual rewrite rules are grouped together in rulesets so that related rewrite rules can be referenced by a single name or number. The S command marks the beginning of a ruleset and identifies it with a name and optionally a number. Therefore, the command `Sfinal=4` marks the beginning of the ruleset known as either `final` or 4, and `SLocal_check_mail` marks the beginning of the `Local_check_mail` ruleset.

> **NOTE**   Prior to Sendmail 8.11, many rulesets were known only by numbers and did not have associated names.

Rewrite rules are the heart of the `sendmail.cf` file and they make up the bulk of the command lines in the configuration file. The sample `sendmail.cf` we have been examining in this chapter contains more than 425 rewrite rules. The number of rules, the complexity of the syntax, and the importance of rewrite rules all demand that rewrite rules receive detailed coverage. For that reason, the entire following chapter is dedicated to rewrite rules.

Not all rewrite rules are found in the Rewrite Rules section. Several rulesets are associated with specific mailers defined in the Mailer Definitions section.

# The Mailer Definitions Section

The Mailer Definitions section defines the instructions used by Sendmail to invoke the mail delivery programs. Mailer definitions begin with the mailer command (`M`). Searching through the Mailer Definitions section of the sample `sendmail.cf` configuration file for lines that begin with `M` produces the mailer definitions list shown in Listing 7.12.

**Listing 7.12** The Mailers defined in sendmail.cf

```
Mesmtp,       P=[IPC], F=mDFMuXa, S=EnvFromSMTP/HdrFromSMTP,
              R=EnvToSMTP, E=\r\n, L=990,
              T=DNS/RFC822/SMTP,
              A=TCP $h
Msmtp8,       P=[IPC], F=mDFMuX8, S=EnvFromSMTP/HdrFromSMTP,
              R=EnvToSMTP, E=\r\n, L=990,
              T=DNS/RFC822/SMTP,
              A=TCP $h
Mdsmtp,       P=[IPC], F=mDFMuXa%, S=EnvFromSMTP/HdrFromSMTP,
              R=EnvToSMTP, E=\r\n, L=990,
              T=DNS/RFC822/SMTP,
              A=TCP $h
Mrelay,       P=[IPC], F=mDFMuXa8, S=EnvFromSMTP/HdrFromSMTP,
              R=MasqSMTP, E=\r\n, L=2040,
              T=DNS/RFC822/SMTP,
              A=TCP $h
Mlocal,       P=/usr/bin/procmail, F=lsDFMAw5:/|@qSPfhn9,
              S=EnvFromL/HdrFromL, R=EnvToL/HdrToL,
              T=DNS/RFC822/X-Unix,
              A=procmail -Y -a $h -d $u
Mprog,        P=/usr/sbin/smrsh, F=lsDFMoqeu9, S=EnvFromL/HdrFromL,
              R=EnvToL/HdrToL, D=$z:/,
              T=X-Unix/X-Unix/X-Unix,
              A=smrsh -c $u
Mprocmail,    P=/usr/bin/procmail, F=DFMSPhnu9,
              S=EnvFromSMTP/HdrFromSMTP,
              R=EnvToSMTP/HdrFromSMTP,
              T=DNS/RFC822/X-Unix,
              A=procmail -Y -m $h $f $u
```

The sendmail.cf file created by the redhat.mc macro configuration contains eight mailer definitions. The first five mailer commands define mailers for TCP/IP mail delivery. The first one, designed to deliver traditional seven-bit ASCII SMTP mail, is called smtp. The next mailer definition is for Extended SMTP mail and is called esmtp. (It is the default mailer used for Internet mail.) The smtp8 mailer definition handles unencoded eight-bit SMTP data bound for remote servers that can't handle Extended SMTP. The dsmtp mailer is used when the recipient server initiates the mail connection and downloads mail with the ETRN command. Finally, relay is a mailer that relays TCP/IP mail through an external mail relay host. All of these mailers were covered in Chapter 5, "Understanding a Vendor's Configuration," in relationship to the MAILER(smtp) macro configuration command that inserts this set of mailers into the `sendmail.cf` file. This set of mailers is required by every system that sends mail over a TCP/IP network, such as the Internet.

Two other mailer definitions in the list are required by Sendmail, and thus found in all configurations. The first of these defines a mailer for local mail delivery. This mailer must always be called `local`. The second definition specifies a mailer, which is always called `prog`, for delivering mail to programs. Sendmail expects to find both of these mailers in the configuration and requires that they be given the names `local` and `prog`. All other mailers can be named anything the system administrator wishes. However, in practice, that is not the case. Because the `sendmail.cf` files on all Linux systems are built from the same m4 macros, they all use the same mailer names. The m4 macro that adds `prog` and `local` to the configuration is `MAILER(local)`. This sample configuration uses `smrsh` as the `prog` mailer and `procmail` as the `local` mailer because of the `FEATURE(`smrsh', `/usr/sbin/smrsh')` and the `FEATURE(local_procmail)` commands in the m4 configuration that created this `sendmail.cf` file.

The last definition is for `procmail`. This `procmail` mailer has nothing to do with the use of `procmail` as the `local` mailer. This definition invokes `procmail` with the –m command-line argument, which allows `procmail` to be used for mail filtering. `procmail` mail filtering features are covered in Chapter 11.

## The *M* Command

The M command defines the mail delivery programs used by Sendmail. The syntax of the command is:

```
Mname, field=value, field=value, ...
```

*name* is an arbitrary name used internally by Sendmail to refer to the mailer. With the exception of the `prog` and `local` mailer names required by Sendmail, the name doesn't matter as long as it is used consistently within the `sendmail.cf` file to refer to this mailer. For example, the mailer used to deliver SMTP mail within the local domain could be called `smtp` on a Linux system, and `ether` on some other system. The function of both mailers is the same, only the names are different. The basic mailer names are the same from system to system only because they come from the same m4 macros. Customized mailers created inside the `sendmail.cf` file by adventurous Sendmail administrators can be named anything.

The mailer name is followed by a comma-separated list of *field=value* pairs that define the characteristics of the mailer. Table 7.3 shows the single character field identifiers, a text name for the field, and a description of the value associated with the field. No mailer requires all of these fields.

Advanced
Configuration

PART 3

**Table 7.3**    Mailer Definition Fields

| Field | Name | Value |
|-------|------|-------|
| P | Path | The full pathname of the mailer program. |
| F | Flags | The sendmail flags used by this mailer. |
| S | Sender | The rulesets that process sender addresses for this mailer. |
| R | Recipient | The rulesets that process recipient addresses for this mailer. |
| A | Argv | This mailer's command line. |
| E | End-of-line | The end-of-line string for this mailer. |
| M | Maxsize | The maximum message length supported by this mailer. |
| L | Linelimit | The maximum line length supported by this mailer. |
| D | Directory | The prog mailer's execution directory. |
| U | Userid | The user and group ID used to run the mailer. |
| N | Nice | The nice value used to run mailer. |
| C | Charset | The default Content-type for 8-bit MIME characters. |
| T | Type | The MIME error types this mailer supports. |

The Path (P) field contains either the path to the mail delivery program, the literal string [IPC], or the literal string [TCP]. Mailer definitions that specify P=[IPC] or P=[TCP] use Sendmail to deliver the mail. (P=[TCP] is not commonly used.) The path to a mail delivery program varies from system to system depending on where the systems store the programs.

The Flags (F) field contains the Sendmail flags used for this mailer. These are the mailer flags referenced above in the "Format of Headers" section, but mailer flags do more than just control header insertion. There are a large number of flags. All of them and their functions are described in Appendix C.

The Sender (S) and the Recipient (R) fields identify the rulesets used to rewrite the sender and recipient addresses for this mailer. Each ruleset is identified by its name or number.

Understanding the role of the S and R rulesets is important when troubleshooting the Sendmail configuration because these rulesets add the variety that is necessary to handle addresses differently for different mailers.

The Argv (A) field defines the mailer command line. It is the argument vector passed to the mailer. It contains, along with the executable command and the command-line arguments, macro expansions that provide the recipient username ($u), the recipient hostname ($h), and the sender's from address ($f). These macros are expanded before the argument vector is passed to the mailer.

Maxsize (M) defines, in bytes, the longest message that this mailer will handle, while Linelimit (L) defines, in bytes, the maximum length of a line that can be contained in a message handled by this mailer. The End-of-line (E) field defines the characters used to mark the end of a line. A newline is the default.

The Directory (D) field specifies the working directory for the prog mailer. More than one directory can be specified for the directory field by separating the directory paths with colons. The prog mailer definition in Listing 7.12 uses the recipient's home directory, which is the value returned by the $z. If that directory is not available, it then uses the root (/) directory.

You can specify the user and the group ID used to execute the mailer with the Userid (U) field. For example U=mail:mail says that the mailer should be run under the user ID mail and the group ID mail. If no value is specified for the Userid field, the value defined by the DefaultUser option is used. Note that none of the mailers in Listing 7.12 used the Userid field.

Nice (N) changes the nice value for the execution of the mailer. This allows you to change the scheduling priority of the mailer. This is rarely used. If you're interested, see the nice man page for appropriate values.

The last two fields are used for MIME mail. Charset (C) defines the character set used in the Content-type header when an eight-bit message is converted to MIME. If Charset is not defined, the value defined in the DefaultCharset option is used. If that option is not defined, unknown-8bit is used as the default value.

The Type (T) field defines the type information used in MIME error messages. MIME type information defines the mailer transfer agent type, the mail address type, and the error code type. The default is dns/rfc822/smtp.

### Analyzing a Sample M Command

Examining one of the mailer entries from Listing 7.12 explains the structure of all of the mailer definitions. The entry for the smtp mailer from Listing 7.12 is:

```
Msmtp,          P=[IPC], F=mDFMuX, S=EnvFromSMTP/HdrFromSMTP,
                R=EnvToSMTP, E=\r\n, L=990,
                T=DNS/RFC822/SMTP,
                A=TCP $h
```

Let's examine each field in this definition:

**M**   Beginning a line with an M indicates that the command is a mailer definition.

**smtp**   Immediately following the M is the name of the mailer, which in this case is smtp.

**P=[IPC]**   The P argument defines the path to the program used for this mailer. In this case it is [IPC], which means this mail is delivered by Sendmail. Other mailer definitions, such as local, have the full path of some external program in this field.

**F=mDFMuX**   The F argument defines the Sendmail flags for this mailer. Other than knowing that these are mailer flags, the meaning of each individual mailer flag is of little interest, because the flags are correctly set by the m4 macro that builds the mailer entry. In this case, m says that this mailer can send to multiple recipients at once; DFM says that Date, From, and Message-ID headers are needed; u says that uppercase should be preserved in hostnames and usernames; and X says that message lines beginning with a dot have an extra dot prepended.

**S=EnvFromSMTP/HdrFromSMTP**   The S argument defines the rulesets that process sender addresses. The ruleset names can be different for every mailer, allowing different mailers to process e-mail addresses differently. In this case, the sender address in the mail "envelope" is processed through ruleset EnvFromSMTP, and the sender address in the message is processed through ruleset HdrFromSMTP. These rulesets are also addressable as 11 and 31 respectively. So it is possible that you'll see S for the smtp mailer defined as S=11/31 on some systems.

**R=EnvToSMTP**   The R argument defines the ruleset used to process recipient addresses for this mailer. Every mailer can have a different R value to allow each mailer to handle recipient addresses differently. Like the S field described above, the R field can have two rulesets, one for the envelope header and one for the mail header, separated by a slash. In this case, one ruleset (EnvToSMTP) is applied to all recipient addresses for the smtp mailer. EnvToSMTP is also known as ruleset 21, so this could have been written as R=21.

**E=\r\n**   The E argument defines how individual lines in a message are terminated. In this case, lines are terminated with a carriage return and a line feed.

**L=990**    The L argument defines the maximum line length for this mailer. In this case, the mailer can handle messages that contain individual lines up to 990 bytes long.

**T=DNS/RFC822/SMTP**    The T argument defines the MIME types for messages handled by this mailer. In this case, the mailer uses DNS for hostnames, RFC822 for e-mail addresses, and SMTP for error codes.

**A=TCP $h**    The A argument defines the command used to execute the mailer. In this case, the argument refers to an internal Sendmail process. In other cases—the local mailer is a good example—the A argument is clearly a command line.

---

**NOTE**    One of the confusing little idiosyncrasies of Sendmail is that the path to Sendmail's internal mail delivery can be either TCP or IPC. For this version of Sendmail, TCP was used in the A argument. On your version it might be IPC.

---

It is good to know how mailer definitions are structured, but the basic mailer definitions built from the m4 macros contain all the mailers you'll need to run Sendmail in a TCP/IP network environment. You shouldn't need to modify any mailer definitions for an average configuration. In fact, nothing in the sendmail.cf files needs direct modifications for an average configuration. But this section of the book doesn't limit itself to average configurations, so in the next section we directly edit the sendmail.cf file and use test tools to observe the impact of the change.

# Editing the *sendmail.cf* File

It's important to realize how rarely the sendmail.cf file needs to be modified on a typical Linux system. The configuration file that comes with your Linux system will work. Generally, you modify the Sendmail configuration not because you need to, but because you want to. You modify the configuration to improve the way things operate, not to get them to operate, and when you do modify it, you change the m4 macro configuration—not sendmail.cf. Despite this, in this section we edit the sendmail.cf file to change the way that Sendmail works.

---

**TIP**    Before you make any change to sendmail.cf—even a minor one—copy sendmail.cf to a work file such as test.cf and edit the work file. Never edit sendmail.cf without having a backup copy.

---

Assume our Linux system is named parrot.foobirds.org. Using the default configuration, the From address on outbound e-mail is *user*@parrot.foobirds.org. This is a valid address, but it's not exactly what you want. You want to hide the hostname in outbound e-mail by using the address *user*@foobirds.org. Sendmail calls hiding the real hostname "masquerading." Chapter 9, "Special m4 Configurations," provides much more coverage on masquerading, but for now all we need to know is that we want to masquerade as foobirds.org.

To create the new configuration, you need to understand the purpose of the macro variable M, found in the Local Info section of the sendmail.cf file. The comment for the D command that sets M says "who I masquerade as." Checking Listing 7.1, you find that no value is assigned to macro M, which means that masquerading is not being used. To replace the name of the local host in outbound mail with the name of the domain, set M to the domain name, as shown below.

```
# who I masquerade as (null for no masquerading)

DMfoobirds.org
```

Given this value for M, parrot rewrites the sender addresses on outbound mail to *user*@foobirds.org.

After setting a value for the M macro in the test.cf file, run a test to see if it works. Running Sendmail with the test configuration does not affect the Sendmail daemon that was started by the boot script. A separate instantiation of Sendmail is used for the test.

# Testing Your New Configuration

To test the new configuration, run the sendmail command with the -bt option. Sendmail displays a welcome message and waits for you to enter a test. The details of testing Sendmail and of the –bt syntax are covered in Chapter 10, "Testing Sendmail." For now, all you need to know is that we want to see if the header sender address is properly rewritten to masquerade the hostname as the domain name when we send outbound SMTP mail. The /tryflags test command lets us request header sender address processing and the /try command lets us process the sender address for the smtp mailer. First, test the existing configuration to see how the address is processed by the default configuration:

```
[root]# sendmail -bt
ADDRESS TEST MODE (ruleset 3 NOT automatically invoked)
Enter <ruleset> <address>
> /tryflags HS
> /try smtp craig
Trying header sender address craig for mailer smtp
```

```
canonify           input: craig
Canonify2          input: craig
Canonify2          returns: craig
canonify           returns: craig
1                  input: craig
1                  returns: craig
HdrFromSMTP        input: craig
PseudoToReal       input: craig
PseudoToReal       returns: craig
MasqSMTP           input: craig
MasqSMTP           returns: craig < @ *LOCAL* >
MasqHdr            input: craig < @ *LOCAL* >
MasqHdr            returns: craig < @ parrot . foobirds . org . >
HdrFromSMTP        returns: craig < @ parrot . foobirds . org . >
final              input: craig < @ parrot . foobirds . org . >
final              returns: craig @ parrot . foobirds . org
Rcode = 0, addr = craig@parrot.foobirds.org
> ^D
```

**NOTE** These tests were run with Sendmail 8.11. The output from older versions of Sendmail, which used ruleset numbers instead of names, will look slightly different.

The address returned by ruleset final, which is always the last ruleset to process an address, shows us the address that will be used on outbound mail after all of the rulesets have processed the address. With the default configuration, the input address craig is converted to craig@parrot.foobirds.org.

**NOTE** Ruleset final is also known as ruleset 4.

**Advanced Configuration**

**PART 3**

Next, run the `sendmail` command with the -C option to use the newly created `test.cf` configuration file. The –C option permits you to specify the Sendmail configuration file on the command line.

```
# sendmail -bt -Ctest.cf
ADDRESS TEST MODE (ruleset 3 NOT automatically invoked)
Enter <ruleset> <address>
> /tryflags HS
> /try smtp craig
Trying header sender address craig for mailer smtp
canonify          input: craig
Canonify2         input: craig
Canonify2        returns: craig
canonify         returns: craig
1                 input: craig
1                returns: craig
HdrFromSMTP       input: craig
PseudoToReal      input: craig
PseudoToReal     returns: craig
MasqSMTP          input: craig
MasqSMTP         returns: craig < @ *LOCAL* >
MasqHdr           input: craig < @ *LOCAL* >
MasqHdr          returns: craig < @ foobirds . org . >
HdrFromSMTP      returns: craig < @ foobirds . org . >
final             input: craig < @ foobirds . org . >
final            returns: craig @ foobirds . org
Rcode = 0, addr = craig@foobirds.org
> ^D
```

This test tells you that the value entered in the M macro is used to rewrite the sender address in the message header. You know this because the only change made to the `sendmail.cf` file was to set a value for M, and now the address returned from ruleset `final` is `craig@foobirds.org`. This is just what you wanted.

Don't make changes directly to the `sendmail.cf` file if you can avoid it. If you're called upon to help someone configure Sendmail on a system that doesn't already have the m4 source file installed, it may be easier to directly edit the `sendmail.cf` file, but only if the change is very small. If you really want to make major Sendmail configuration changes, use m4 to build your configuration.

# A Command Summary

Sendmail reads the sendmail.cf file every time it starts up. For that reason, the syntax of the commands in the sendmail.cf file is designed to be easily parsed by a machine, but not necessarily easy for a human to read. Table 7.4 summarizes all of the sendmail.cf commands.

**Table 7.4** The sendmail.cf Commands

| Command | Syntax | Meaning |
|---------|--------|---------|
| Version Level | V*level*[/*vendor*] | Specify the version level. |
| Define Macro | D*xvalue* | Set macro *x* to *value*. |
| Define Class | C*cword1*[ *word2*]... | Set class *c* to *word1 word2*... |
| Load Class | F*cfile* | Load class *c* from *file*. |
| Set Option | O *option*=*value* | Set *option* to *value*. |
| Trusted Users | T*user* | Add *user* to the trusted users. |
| Set Precedence | P*name*=*number* | Set *name* to precedence *number*. |
| Define Mailer | M*name*, *field*=*value*, ... | Define mailer *name* with the parameters set by *field* and *value*. |
| Define Header | H[?*mflag*?]*name*:*format* | Define a header format. |
| Set Ruleset | S*name*=*number* | Start a ruleset assigning it a *name* and *number*. |
| Define Rule | R*pattern template* | Rewrite addresses that match *pattern* to *template* format. |
| Key File | K*name type* [*argument*] | Define database *name*. |

**Advanced Configuration**

**PART 3**

This table, and this chapter, can help you read and understand the `sendmail.cf` file. But when it comes to creating that file, you'll build it with the m4 macro commands covered earlier in this book.

---

**Tell Me Again Why I Use *m4* Macros**

A persistent question raised by most Sendmail administrators is, "Why not just edit `sendmail.cf` directly?" After all, is

```
define(`ALIAS_FILE', `/etc/aliases')
```

really any simpler than

```
O AliasFile=/etc/aliases
```

The answer is no, individual m4 Sendmail macros are not any simpler to read or write than individual `sendmail.cf` commands once you understand the meaning and syntax of the `sendmail.cf` commands. However, m4 macro configuration files are certainly much shorter and easier to read than the `sendmail.cf` file, and individual m4 commands often do much more than individual `sendmail.cf` commands. m4 makes it possible to actual write a configuration from scratch. But you might not need to. Perhaps a sample `sendmail.cf` configuration provided by the Sendmail developers or your Linux vendor would work for you with only a few small changes. In that case, why do I repeatedly insist that you build your configuration with m4?

The reason is "because that's the way it's done." Everyone expects the Sendmail configuration to be defined in the m4 macro configuration file. That is where your colleagues will look for changes when they debug your system. Putting the configuration directly in the `sendmail.cf` file just makes a confusing system more confusing to those who must debug it. Worse yet is putting some changes in the macro configuration and some in `sendmail.cf`. That approach is doomed to failure. Stick with m4. It might not be simple, but it is better than the alternative and it is the way Sendmail configuration is done.

---

# In Sum

The `sendmail.cf` file is read by Sendmail every time it starts. `sendmail.cf` is the configuration file that provides Sendmail with:

- information about the local system
- options that define the Sendmail environment
- the format of standard mail headers
- definitions of the available mailers
- instructions on how to prepare a message for a specific mailer

The `sendmail.cf` file is large and complex. But it is always divided into the same seven parts. Understanding the role of each part of the file can help you locate a problem when you are forced to analyze a `sendmail.cf` file.

The commands that make up the `sendmail.cf` file have a terse and arcane syntax. However, there are only 12 different commands and the purpose of most commands is easy to grasp. Additionally, the fixed structure of every command means that the first character on the command line is always the command. This makes it easy to use a tool like `grep` to examine all of the C commands or D commands in a `sendmail.cf` file if you suspect that a variable is improperly set.

Obsessing over the meaning of every option, variable, and flag is a waste of time. Reduce the complexity of the `sendmail.cf` file by focusing on it at a global level. Use your knowledge of the meaning of the different sections of the `sendmail.cf` file and of the purpose of the different commands to focus down on a problem area. Then use the appendixes of this book as a reference for the specific options, flags, and variables. Attempting to learn all of the details ahead of time wastes time developing a skill you may never need.

The bulk of the `sendmail.cf` file is composed of R commands. R commands are the topic of our next chapter.

**Advanced Configuration**

**PART 3**

# 8

# Understanding
# Rewrite Rules

**S**endmail is essentially a mail router. It receives mail, analyzes the delivery address of that mail to determine how the mail should be delivered, formats the mail for delivery by the selected mailer, and hands the mail off to the delivery system, which in some cases is Sendmail itself. At the heart of most of these functions are rewrite rules. *Rewrite rules* analyze the delivery address, select the correct mailer, and format mail for delivery. About the only things they don't do is collect inbound mail or transport outbound mail. Mastering Sendmail requires mastering rewrite rules. This chapter will give you all the information you need to read, understand, and—when absolutely necessary—write rewrite rules.

The rules are organized into groups of related rules called *rulesets* that can be called like subroutines by sendmail.cf commands. Certain rulesets are used by Sendmail to process specific types of addresses. Before getting into the details of rewrite rule syntax, let's look at rulesets to gain a global view of how rewrite rules are organized and used.

## Basic Rulesets

Grouping rewrite rules into rulesets allows related rules to be referenced by a single name or a number. The S command marks the beginning of a ruleset and identifies it with a name, a number, or both. Every rewrite rule following an S command is part of that ruleset until another S command is encountered that marks the start of another ruleset.

Rulesets can be thought of as subroutines, or functions, designed to process e-mail addresses. They are called from mailer definitions, from individual rewrite rules, from header definitions, or directly by the Sendmail process. Six rulesets are called directly by Sendmail for normal address processing:

- Ruleset canonify, also known as ruleset 3, is called first to prepare all addresses for processing by the other rulesets.

- Ruleset parse, also known as ruleset 0, is applied to the mail delivery address to convert it to the (mailer, host, user) triple, which contains the name of the mailer that will deliver the mail, the recipient hostname, and the recipient username. Ruleset parse contains the rewrite rules that select which mailer will deliver the message.

- Ruleset sender, also known as ruleset 1, is applied to all sender addresses.

- Ruleset recipient, also known as ruleset 2, is applied to all recipient addresses.

- Ruleset final, also known as ruleset 4, is called last to convert all addresses from internal address formats into external address formats.

- Ruleset localaddr, also known as ruleset 5, is applied to local addresses after alias processing is completed.

---

**NOTE** Most sendmail.cf files do not contain all of these rulesets.

---

There are three basic types of addresses: delivery addresses, sender addresses, and recipient addresses. A recipient address and a delivery address sound like the same thing, but there is a difference. Think of a mailing list. There can be many recipients for a piece of mail, but mail is delivered to only one person at a time. The recipient address of the one person to which the current piece of mail is being delivered is the delivery address. Different rulesets are used to process the different types of addresses.

Figure 8.1 shows the rulesets that handle each address type. The S and R symbols in Figure 8.1 represent rulesets that have names, just like all normal rulesets, but the S and R ruleset names are defined in the S and R fields of the mailer definition, as described in Chapter 7, "The sendmail.cf File." Each mailer specifies its own S and R rulesets to process sender and recipient addresses just before the message is delivered.

**Figure 8.1** Addresses processed by Sendmail rulesets

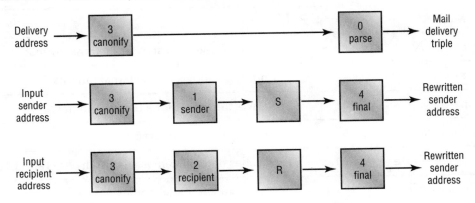

The rulesets shown in Figure 8.1 and described in the list above are automatically called by Sendmail, but that doesn't mean they necessarily exist in your configuration. Two good examples of this are ruleset 1 (sender) and ruleset 2 (recipient). By default, these rulesets are empty and thus are not even defined in the sendmail.cf file for Sendmail 8.11. (We'll see in Chapter 9, "Special m4 Configurations," that you can define your own rewrite rules for rulesets 1 and 2, if needed.) The fact that these rulesets are not defined in the sendmail.cf file does not cause Sendmail any problems. It simply calls them and goes on to the next ruleset when they are not found.

## More Rulesets

The six rulesets described so far are only those called directly by Sendmail. There are many more rulesets defined in the sendmail.cf file. For example, the sendmail.cf file created by the redhat.mc macro configuration has 47 named rulesets. Those other rulesets provide additional address processing. They include those rulesets identified as S and R in Figure 8.1 and those called from inside the sendmail.cf file by individual rewrite rules or H commands. Rulesets are called using the $>*name* syntax, where *name* is the name or number that identifies the called ruleset. We'll see more of the $>*name* syntax later when we discuss rewrite rules.

Table 8.1 lists many of the rulesets you'll find in the Rewriting Rules section of your sendmail.cf file. It identifies each ruleset by name, and when applicable by number, and provides a short description of the purpose of the ruleset. The rulesets are listed in the order in which they occur in the Rewriting Rules section.

**Table 8.1** Rulesets from the Rewriting Rules Section

| Name | Number | Purpose |
| --- | --- | --- |
| canonify | 3 | Puts addresses in a standard internal format. |
| final | 4 | Converts addresses to external formats. |
| parse | 0 | Selects the mailer for a delivery address. |
| localaddr | 5 | Processes local addresses. |
| Mailertable | 90 | Matches domain names against the mailertable. |
| MasqHdr | 93 | Masquerades header names. |
| MasqEnv | 94 | Masquerades envelope names. |
| LookUpDomain | | Finds domain names in the access database. |
| LookUpAddress | | Finds hostnames in the access database. |
| ParseRecipient | | Converts recipient addresses to the proper address format for relaying. |
| check_relay | | Checks relaying for the anti-spam features. |
| check_mail | | Checks sender addresses for the anti-spam features. |
| check_rcpt | | Checks recipient addresses for the anti-spam features. |
| trust_auth | | Tests whether or not the AUTH parameter should be trusted. |
| tls_client | | Verifies the TLS connection to a client. |
| tls_server | | Verifies the TLS connection to a server. |

Table 8.1 shows only part of the rulesets found in the Rewriting Rules section. There are several other rulesets that are subroutines of these rulesets or are called by these rulesets to complete their tasks.

- canonify has a subsection named Canonify2, also known as ruleset 96, that is used to obtain canonical hostnames from DNS.

- parse has two subsections named Parse0 and Parse1, and a subroutine named ParseLocal (or ruleset 98) that it calls to handle local addresses.

- Mailertable calls MailerToTriple, which is also known as ruleset 95, to help convert mailertable entries to mail delivery triples, and it uses CanonLocal to put local names from the mailertable into a standard format.

- ParseRecipient uses CanonAddr to put addresses into the standard format, which CanonAddr does by simply calling Parse0 and canonify.

- The bulk of the work of check_relay, check_mail, and check_rcpt is handled by subsections respectively named Basic_check_relay, Basic_check_mail, and Basic_check_rcpt. In turn, Basic_check_rcpt calls RelayAuth to check client authentication when that is required. SearchList is another routine called by check_mail and check_rcpt to process an internal syntax used by these anti-spam features. Recall the {src} class mentioned in Chapter 7; SearchList is where it is used.

- tls_client and tls_server call tls_connection to get the connection verified. tls_connection in turn uses max to determine if the appropriate number of cipher bits were used. Transport layer security is discussed in Chapter 12, "Sendmail Security."

Rulesets within rulesets and rulesets calling rulesets segment the complex task of processing e-mail. This makes the task of processing mail manageable for Sendmail, but it creates a large number of rulesets that in turn create confusion for the system administrator trying to understand what these rulesets do. My advice is: "Don't worry about it." A general idea of what these rulesets do is all that is required for Sendmail mastery. You don't modify the basic rulesets of Sendmail, even to create an advanced custom configuration. Instead, Sendmail provides several empty rulesets as hooks for your modifications:

- sender (ruleset 1) is available for custom processing of sender addresses. See the LOCAL_RULE discussion in Chapter 9.

- recipient (ruleset 2) is available for custom processing of recipient addresses. See the LOCAL_RULE discussion in Chapter 9.

- Local_localaddr is available for custom processing of local addresses before they are processed by localaddr (ruleset 5).

- Local_check_relay is available to customize anti-spam relaying rules. It is called before check_relay. See the discussion of anti-spam rules in Chapter 11, "Stopping Spam."

Advanced
Configuraton

PART 3

- `Local_check_mail` is available for custom anti-spam processing of the MAIL FROM: address. It is called before `check_mail`. See the discussion of anti-spam rules in Chapter 11.

- `Local_check_rcpt` is available for custom anti-spam processing of the RCPT TO: address. It is called before `check_rcpt`. See the discussion of anti-spam rules in Chapter 11.

- `Local_trust_auth` is available to customize the `trust_auth` ruleset. See the AUTH material in Chapter 12.

These rulesets provide more avenues for customizing Sendmail than you will ever use for any one configuration, even for the most advanced custom configuration. All of these hooks can be accessed through the m4 macro configuration, so even when custom rewrite rules are required, there is no need to directly edit the `sendmail.cf` file.

## Mailer Rulesets

Despite the large number of rulesets found in the Rewriting Rules section, it is not the only place in the `sendmail.cf` file where rulesets are found. The Mailer Definitions section includes the rulesets that are added by the various mailers. The macro configuration that built our sample `sendmail.cf` file had three sets of mailers:

```
MAILER(local)
MAILER(smtp)
MAILER(procmail)
```

These MAILER commands added the rulesets listed in Table 8.2 to the Mailer Declarations section of the `sendmail.cf` file. The rulesets are listed in Table 8.2 in the order in which they occur in the Mailer Declarations section. Each ruleset is identified by name and number. The table provides a short description of each ruleset.

**Table 8.2**  Rulesets Found in the Mailer Declarations Section

| Name | Number | Description |
|------|--------|-------------|
| MasqSMTP | 61 | Handles rewriting tasks common to sender and envelope masquerading. |
| PseudoToReal | 51 | Converts pseudo-domains to real domains. |
| EnvFromSMTP | 11 | Rewrites the envelope sender address. |
| EnvToSMTP | 21 | Rewrites the envelope recipient address. |

**Table 8.2**   Rulesets Found in the Mailer Declarations Section *(continued)*

| Name | Number | Description |
| --- | --- | --- |
| HdrFromSMTP | 31 | Rewrites the header sender address. |
| MasqRelay | 71 | Handles masquerading for the relay mailer. |
| EnvFromL | 10 | Rewrites the envelope sender for the local mailer. |
| EnvToL | 20 | Rewrites the envelope recipient for the local mailer. |
| HdrFromL | 30 | Rewrites the header sender for the local mailer. |
| HdrToL | 40 | Rewrites the header recipient for the local mailer. |
| AddDomain | 50 | Adds the local domain for the always_add_domain feature. |

Most of these rulesets deal with rewriting sender and recipient addresses in the envelope and the header. That's to be expected. After all, the S and R parameters of the mailer command (M) identify the rulesets used to rewrite sender addresses and recipient addresses for a specific mailer. It is only natural that these rulesets are included in the Mailer Definitions section of the sendmail.cf file.

Listing 8.1 shows two of these rulesets: EnvToL and HdrFromL. Each ruleset starts with an S command, and ends when the next S command is encountered. Therefore, the EnvToL ruleset contains only one rewrite rule, while the HdrFromL ruleset contains four rules.

**Listing 8.1**   Two Simple Rulesets

```
#
#  Envelope recipient rewriting
#
SEnvToL=20
R$+ < @ $* >        $: $1                  strip host part


#
#  Header sender rewriting
#
SHdrFromL=30
R<@>               $n                 errors to mailer-daemon
R@ <@ $*>          $n                 temporarily bypass Sun bogosity
R$+                $: $>AddDomain $1   add local domain if needed
R$*                $: $>MasqHdr $1     do masquerading
```

Advanced
Configuraton

PART 3

Every active line in a ruleset is an R command. The syntax of R commands is complex and difficult to read. Explaining the function and syntax of R commands consumes the rest of this chapter.

# Rewrite Rules

Rulesets are composed of individual rewrite rules that parse e-mail addresses from user mail programs and rewrite them into the form required by the mail delivery programs. Each rewrite rule is defined by an R command. The syntax of the R command that was introduced in Chapter 7 is:

```
Rpattern     template     comment
```

The fields in an R command are separated by tab characters. The *comment* field is ignored by the system, but good comments are vital to understanding what's going on. The *pattern* and *template* fields are the heart of this command.

## Pattern Matching

Rewrite rules match the input address against the pattern, and if a match is found, rewrite the address in a new format using the rules defined in the template. A rewrite rule may process the same address several times because, after being rewritten, the address is again compared against the pattern. If it still matches, it is rewritten again. The cycle of pattern matching and rewriting continues until the address no longer matches the pattern.

The pattern is defined using variables, classes, literals, and special symbols. The variables, classes, and literals provide the values against which the input is compared, and the symbols define the rules used in matching the pattern. Table 8.3 shows the symbols used for pattern matching.

**Table 8.3**  Pattern-Matching Symbols

| Symbol | Meaning |
| --- | --- |
| $@ | Match exactly zero tokens. |
| $* | Match zero or more tokens. |
| $- | Match exactly one token. |
| $+ | Match one or more tokens. |
| $x | Match all tokens in macro variable x. |

**Table 8.3**   Pattern-Matching Symbols *(continued)*

| Symbol | Meaning |
| --- | --- |
| $=x | Match any token in class variable *x*. |
| $~x | Match any token not in class variable *x*. |

All of the symbols match some number of tokens. A token is a string of characters delimited by an operator. The operators are the right (() and left ()) parentheses, right (<) and left (>) angle brackets, comma (,), semicolon (;), backslash (\), quotation mark ("), carriage return (**CR**), and line feed (**LF**), plus any characters defined by the OperatorChars option. A grep of the sendmail.cf file for OperatorChars shows the additional operator characters are ., :, %, @, !, ^, /, [, ], and +.

```
[craig]$ grep 'OperatorChars' /etc/sendmail.cf
O OperatorChars=.:%@!^/[]+
```

Operators also count as tokens when an address is parsed. Assume the following address:

```
sara@hawk.foobirds.org
```

This e-mail address contains seven tokens: sara, @, hawk, ., foobirds, ., and org. Three of these tokens, two . (dots) and an @, are operators. The other four tokens are strings. This address would match the symbol $+ because it contains more than one token, but it would not match the symbol $- because it does not contain *exactly* one token.

The symbols in Table 8.3 are particularly useful when paired with literal values and variables to create more complex patterns—for example:

```
$- @ $- .foobirds.org
```

The sample address sara@hawk.foobirds.org matches the pattern because:

- It has exactly one token before the literal @ that matches the requirement of the $- symbol.
- It has an @ that matches the pattern's literal @.
- It has exactly one token after the literal @ and before the literal .foobirds.org that matches the requirement of the second $- symbol.
- It has the string .foobirds.org that matches the pattern's literal .foobirds.org.

sara@hawk.foobirds.org matches this pattern, but many other addresses do not. For example, sara.henson@hawk.foobirds.org does not match because it has three tokens, sara, ., and henson, before the literal @. Therefore, it fails to meet the requirement of exactly one token specified by the first $- symbol. mandy@sooty.terns.foobirds.org fails to match the pattern because it has three tokens (sooty, ., and terns) after the literal @ and before the literal .foobirds.org.

Literals are such an important part of pattern matching that Sendmail inserts literal values, such as the angle brackets < and >, into addresses to make them easier to parse. Listing 8.2 shows this.

**Listing 8.2** Internal Use of Literal Values

```
[root]# sendmail -bt
ADDRESS TEST MODE (ruleset 3 NOT automatically invoked)
Enter <ruleset> <address>
> 3 craig.hunt@ibis.foobirds.org
canonify            input: craig . hunt @ ibis . foobirds . org
Canonify2           input: craig . hunt < @ ibis . foobirds . org >
Canonify2         returns: craig . hunt < @ ibis . foobirds . org . >
canonify          returns: craig . hunt < @ ibis . foobirds . org . >
> ^D
```

Listing 8.2 shows that Sendmail adds literal values to an address when the address is converted to the working format that Sendmail uses internally. The canonify ruleset adds angle brackets surrounding the domain name portion of the address. canonify calls Canonify2 to request the canonical form of the hostname from DNS. In this case, ibis.foobirds.org is the canonical name of the host, so all Canonify2 does is return the same name fully qualified to the root. (That's why the hostname has a dot appended.) The three tokens, <, >, and ., added by Sendmail are used internally to simplify address parsing. Before the mail is sent, these three tokens will be removed by the final ruleset.

---

**NOTE** In DNS, the dot at the end of a name is the root domain. Sendmail uses it internally to indicate that a name has been successfully processed by DNS.

---

About 75 percent of the rewrite rules in the sendmail.cf file make use of the inserted tokens by using angle brackets as part of the pattern field. The single rule from ruleset EnvToL in Listing 8.1 demonstrate this. That rule contains this pattern:

$+ < @ $* >

This pattern says to match any address that has one or more tokens ($+) before the literal value < @ and zero or more tokens after that literal value and before the literal value >. The craig.hunt<@ibis.foobirds.org.> address matches this pattern. It has three tokens (craig, ., and hunt) before the literal <@ and six tokens (ibis, ., foobirds, ., org, and .) between the literals <@ and >.

Literals are an important part of patterns but they lack the flexibility needed to create a general purpose configuration that can work on any system. That's where variables come in. In our first example we used the pattern:

```
$- @ $- .foobirds.org
```

The problem with this pattern is that it only works with addresses that have the domain name foobirds.org. The literal .foobirds.org works fine at our site, but isn't much help if we send this configuration to our friends at mammals.org. What we actually wanted to check was whether or not the address had the local domain name. The local domain name is stored by Sendmail in the m variable, so we can use $m in the pattern to match the local domain name. The following pattern is equivalent to the pattern above except that it works on any system:

```
$- @ $- .$m
```

Here we look for addresses that have exactly one token ($-), a literal @, exactly one token ($-), a literal ., and the value return from variable m.

Class variables can also be used in pattern matching. In fact, pattern matching is the only place where class values are useful. The symbols $= and $~ are designed to test whether or not a value from the input address is a member of the class. We can demonstrate this with the simple, although contrived, ruleset. Add the ruleset shown below to the test.cf file we created in Chapter 4:

```
SClassTest
R$+ @ $=w              $@ Found it
R$+ @ $~w              $@ Not in class w
R$*                    $: Wrong format
```

The S command starts the ruleset and names it ClassTest. It contains three R commands. ClassTest expects addresses in the format *user@host*. The pattern in the first rule matches one or more tokens ($+) before a literal @ and any value in class w ($=w). The pattern in the second rule matches one or more tokens ($+) before a literal @ and any value that is *not* in class w ($~w). The pattern in the last line catches everything that falls through to complain that the address didn't contain a literal @. The templates on these rules are contrived examples that will display a message when Sendmail is run in test mode, as it is in Listing 8.3.

**Listing 8.3**   Testing for Class Values

```
[root]# cat >> test.cf
SClassTest
R$+ @ $=w          $@ Found it
R$+ @ $~w          $@ Not in class w
R$*       $: Wrong format
[root]# sendmail -bt -Ctest.cf
ADDRESS TEST MODE (ruleset 3 NOT automatically invoked)
Enter <ruleset> <address>
> $=w
robin.foobirds.org
other.org
wren.foobirds.org
[172.16.12.3]
patient-rights.org
outofbusiness.com
wren
localhost
weRbroke.com
robin
thatplace.com
imaginary.com
> ClassTest christopher@robin
ClassTest          input: christopher @ robin
ClassTest          returns: Found it
> ClassTest sara@hawk
ClassTest          input: sara @ hawk
ClassTest          returns: Not in class w
> ClassTest craig
ClassTest          input: craig
ClassTest          returns: Wrong format
> ^D
```

In Listing 8.3, a cat command is used to append the ClassTest ruleset to the test.cf configuration file. Then the sendmail command is run with the –bt option and the modified test.cf configuration. The contents of class w are displayed. The values displayed for class w vary from system to system. If you run this test on your own system, use values from your system's class w.

In Listing 8.3, three tests of the ClassTest ruleset are run. First, we send ClassTest the address christopher@robin. The ruleset returns the value "Found it." A quick glance at the contents of class w shows that robin is indeed in the list. Next we send ClassTest the address sara@hawk, which returns "Not in class w." Again, a glance at the content of class w shows that hawk is not in the class. Finally, testing the address craig returns "Wrong format" because the address is not in the format *user@host*. Using symbols, variables, classes, and literals, patterns can be constructed to match any type of e-mail address.

The patterns used in the ClassTest ruleset are realistic, but the templates are contrived. An address goes into a rule and an address comes out. Clearly, the strings Found it, Not in class w, and Wrong format are not legitimate addresses. In the next section we look at how real templates are constructed and how they operate.

---

### Conditional Syntax

Before we leave the topic of pattern matching, the use of conditional syntax in rewrite rules deserves a mention. The "if" ($?) "else" ($|) syntax can legally be used in rewrite rules. In reality the $? symbol is never used in a rewrite rule. The pattern matching of a rewrite rule, by its very nature, is already a conditional. Adding an "if" to an existing conditional test would just increase the complexity of an already complex syntax. The "else" symbol ($|) is sometimes used, but it is used as more of an "or" symbol—e.g., this $| that could be read as "this or that."

Avoid using the conditional syntax in rewrite rules. Every rule starts with a conditional test. It is better to use two rules, each of which does one thing, than to try to combine multiple tests in a single rule.

---

## Transforming the Address

The template field, from the right-hand side of the rewrite rule, defines the format used for rewriting the address. It is defined with the same things used to define the pattern: literals, variables, and special symbols. Literals in the transformation are written into the new address exactly as shown. Variables are expanded and then written. The symbols perform special functions. Each symbol that can be used in a template and its purpose are shown in Table 8.4.

**Table 8.4** Template Symbols

| Symbol | Purpose |
|---|---|
| $n | Insert the value from indefinite token *n*. |
| $: | Terminate this rewrite rule. |
| $@ | Terminate the entire ruleset. |
| $>*name* | Call the ruleset identified as *name*. |
| $[*hostname*$] | Convert *hostname* to DNS canonical form. |
| $(*database-spec*$) | Get the value from a database. |

## Indefinite Tokens

When an address matches a pattern, the strings from the address that match the symbols are assigned to *indefinite tokens*. The matching strings are called indefinite tokens because they may contain more than one token value. The indefinite tokens are identified numerically according to the relative position in the pattern of the symbol that the string matched. In other words, the indefinite token produced by the match of the first symbol is called $1, the match of the second symbol is called $2, the third is $3, and so on. The $*n* symbol in Table 8.4 represents the use of an indefinite token in the template and the *n* stands for the number of the indefinite token. An indefinite token is expanded and then written to the new address. Indefinite token substitution is essential for flexible address rewriting. Without it, values could not be easily moved from the input address to the rewritten address. The example in Listing 8.4 demonstrates this.

**Listing 8.4** Testing Indefinite Token Substitution

```
[root]# cat >> test.cf
STokenTest
R$+ ! $+     $2 @ $1 . $m     convert host!user to user@host.domain
[root]# sendmail -bt -Ctest.cf
ADDRESS TEST MODE (ruleset 3 NOT automatically invoked)
Enter <ruleset> <address>
> $m
```

```
foobirds.org
> TokenTest plover!karen.ramsey
TokenTest          input: plover ! karen . ramsey
TokenTest          returns: karen . ramsey @ plover . foobirds . org
> ^D
```

Again we start with the `test.cf` file created in Chapter 4. To that we add a new ruleset we call TokenTest, which contains only one rewrite rule. Then we run the `sendmail` command with –bt and –Ctest.cf to test the new configuration.

When the address `plover!karen.ramsey` matched the pattern $+!$+, two indefinite tokens were created. The first is identified as $1 and contains the single token `plover` that matched the first $+ symbol. The second indefinite token is $2 and contains the three tokens, `karen`, `.`, and `ramsey`, that matched the second $+ symbol. The indefinite tokens created by the pattern matching are then referenced by name ($1 and $2) in the template portion of the R command to rewrite the address.

The template contains the indefinite token $2, a literal @, indefinite token $1, a literal dot (`.`), and the variable value $m. After the pattern matching, $2 contains `karen.ramsey` and $1 contains `plover`. From an earlier discussion of the m variable, you known that it contains the name of the domain of which the local system is part. Listing 8.4 shows that $m returns `foobirds.org` on the sample system. In Listing 8.4, the input address `plover!karen.ramsey` is rewritten as `karen.ramsey@plover.foobirds.org`.

Figure 8.2 illustrates this specific address rewrite. It shows the tokens derived from the input address, and how those tokens are matched against the pattern. It also shows the indefinite tokens produced by the pattern matching, and how the indefinite tokens, and other values from the transformation, are used to produce the rewritten address.

**Figure 8.2**    Rewriting an address

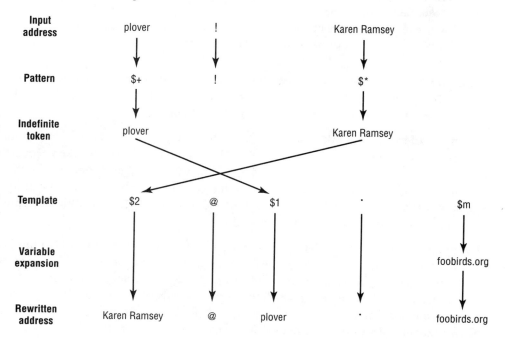

## Recursion and Flow Control

After rewriting, the address is again compared to the pattern. The address in Figure 8.2 fails to match the pattern the second time through because it no longer contains the literal !. Sometimes, however, the recursive nature of rewrite rules is used to create iterative processing. Listing 8.5 shows this with a simple ruleset designed to remove nested angle brackets.

**Listing 8.5**    The Recursive Nature of Rewrite Rules

```
[root]# cat >> test.cf
SRemoveAngles
R$* < $* >        $1 $2
[root]# sendmail -bt -Ctest.cf
ADDRESS TEST MODE (ruleset 3 NOT automatically invoked)
Enter <ruleset> <address>
> RemoveAngles craig<<<@wren>>>
RemoveAngles        input: craig < < < @ wren > > >
RemoveAngles        returns: craig @ wren
> ^D
```

In Listing 8.5, we create a ruleset named `RemoveAngles` that contains only one rule. The pattern in the rule matches any number of tokens (`$*`) before a literal < and any number of tokens (`$*`) between the literals < and >. The template in the rule rewrites the indefinite tokens without the literal angle brackets.

The `sendmail -bt` test in Listing 8.5 shows that the rule works; it removes all of the angle brackets from the address `craig<<<@wren>>>`. Don't assume, however, that it removes all of the angle brackets in one pass. The first time the address matches the pattern it is rewritten as `craig<<@wren>>`. The rewritten address is again compared to the pattern and it again matches. This time it is rewritten as `craig<@wren>`, which again matches the pattern. Finally, it is rewritten as `craig@wren`, which doesn't have the angle brackets required to match the pattern.

Once the pattern no longer matches, no further processing is done by this rewrite rule and the address is passed to the next rule in line. The `RemoveAngles` ruleset from Listing 8.5 contains no other rules so processing stops, but most rulesets have more than one rule. Rules in a ruleset are processed sequentially, although a few symbols can be used to modify this flow.

The recursion built into rewrite rules creates the possibility for infinite loops. The `$@` and the `$:` template symbols are used to control processing and to prevent loops. If the template begins with the `$@` symbol, the entire ruleset is terminated and the remainder of the template is the value returned by the ruleset. Use `$@` to exit a ruleset at a specific rule.

In Listing 8.3, the `$@` symbol was used to control the flow inside the `ClassTest` ruleset. The template in each rule in that ruleset starts with the `$@` symbol, so if a pattern match is found, the template is applied and the ruleset exits. Suppose the `$@` was not used on the first rule in that ruleset. In that case, the test of the address `christopher@robin` would have produced the response "Wrong format" instead of the response "Found it" that we expected. Here's why. The address `christopher@robin` matches the pattern of the first rule, which is `$*@$=w`. Therefore, the address is rewritten to `Found it`. If the `$@` symbol is not used, the address `Found it` is again compared to the pattern `$*@$=w` in the first rule. It doesn't match. The address is then processed by the next rules in line. `Found it` does not match the pattern of the second rule, which is `$*@$~w`. The address `Found it` is therefore passed on to the third rule in line. This time it does match the pattern `$*`, which essentially matches anything that hasn't been caught by the first two rules. The third rule rewrites the address `Found it` into the address `Wrong format`—not, of course, what we wanted. To get the result we want, every rule in ruleset `ClassTest` requires a flow control symbol, even the third rule.

When a template begins with the `$:` symbol, the individual rule is executed only once. In the `ClassTest` ruleset from Listing 8.3, that is exactly what we want to do with the third rule. At first glance, one might think that flow control is not required for that rule because it is the last rule in the ruleset and thus the ruleset will end after that rule executes. On closer examination the problem is clear: the third rule will never finish executing because it is an infinite loop. The $* pattern matches zero or more tokens, meaning it will match anything, even the string Wrong format. Thus, the pattern will match the output of the rule. Because the rule recursively processes its own output against the pattern $*, which matches anything, a loop will ensue. Sendmail detects loops and complains when one is found, as shown in Listing 8.6.

**Listing 8.6**   Results of a Tight Loop in the Sendmail Configuration

```
[root]# sendmail -bt -Ctest.cf
ADDRESS TEST MODE (ruleset 3 NOT automatically invoked)
Enter <ruleset> <address>
> =SClassTest
R$* @ $=w                $@ Found it
R$* @ $~w                $@ Not in class w
R$*             Wrong format
> ClassTest craig
ClassTest            input: craig
Infinite loop in ruleset ClassTest, rule 3
ClassTest            returns: Wrong format
> ^D
```

In Listing 8.6, sendmail is again run with the –bt argument. The =S command, described in Chapter 10 with other test commands, is used to display the contents of the ruleset ClassTest. In this example, the template in the third rule of the ruleset does not start with $:. In this case, when ClassTest is run with an input address of craig, an infinite loop ensues. Sendmail displays an error message stating that an infinite loop was encountered and exactly where the loop occurred.

Loops do not need to be as tight as the one shown in Listing 8.6. A loop can involve multiple rulesets because a ruleset can be called by a rule using the $>*name* syntax. When the called ruleset finishes processing, it returns a rewritten address to the calling rule. The returned e-mail address is then compared again to the pattern in the calling rule. If it still matches, the ruleset is called again. Use $: and $@ to prevent loops whenever they can occur.

The $>*name* symbol calls ruleset *name* and passes the address defined by the remainder of the template to that ruleset for processing. For example, both rules in the ruleset named CallRulesets, shown below, call other rulesets:

```
SCallRulesets
R$* @ $-                 $: $> canonify $1 @ $2
R$*             $: $> final $1
```

The template in the first rule calls ruleset canonify ($>canonify), and passes it the contents of $1, a literal @, and the contents of $2. The template starts with the $: symbol, so the first rule executes only once when the pattern matches. The template in the second rule calls ruleset final ($>final) and passes it the contents of $1. (Because the pattern in the second ruleset includes only one symbol, $1 contains the entire input address.) The second rule will also only execute once because its template starts with $:. Listing 8.7 shows the CallRulesets ruleset in action.

**Listing 8.7**   Calling Another Ruleset from a Rule

```
[root]# sendmail -bt -Ctest.cf
ADDRESS TEST MODE (ruleset 3 NOT automatically invoked)
Enter <ruleset> <address>
> CallRulesets julie@redbreast
CallRulesets     input: julie @ redbreast
canonify         input: julie @ redbreast
Canonify2        input: julie < @ redbreast >
Canonify2        returns: julie < @ robin . foobirds . org . >
canonify         returns: julie < @ robin . foobirds . org . >
final            input: julie < @ robin . foobirds . org . >
final            returns: julie @ robin . foobirds . org
CallRulesets     returns: julie @ robin . foobirds . org
> ^D
```

In Listing 8.7, CallRulesets is passed the address julie@redbreast, which matches the $*@$- pattern of the first rule in the ruleset. That rule calls ruleset canonify and passes it the three tokens julie, @, and redbreast. canonify "focuses" the address by placing angle brackets around the host portion and, in turn, it calls ruleset Canonify2. Canonify2 converts the address to julie<@robin.foobirds.org.>, which is the value that canonify returns to CallRulesets. The second rule in CallRulesets is then executed. The value julie<@robin.foobirds.org.> matches the $* pattern in the rule, so ruleset final is called and passed the address value. final "defocuses" the address and returns the value julie@robin.foobirds.org, which becomes the value returned by CallRuleset.

---

> **NOTE**   The words "focus" and "defocus" are used to describe the internal Sendmail processes that mark portions of the address for processing. Generally, this involves enclosing address components in angle brackets.

### Transforming Addresses with External Information

In Listing 8.7, CallRuleset simply matches the patterns and calls other rulesets to do all of the rewriting. It is also possible to use an external server, such as DNS, or an external database to convert an input address. The Canonify2 ruleset converts a hostname to the canonical DNS format for that hostname. It does this by querying DNS and using the information it gets in response to that query.

The $[*hostname*$] syntax converts a host's nickname or its IP address to its canonical name by passing the value *hostname* to the name server for resolution. Listing 8.8 shows the $[*hostname*$] symbol in action.

**Listing 8.8**   Retrieving a Canonical Name from DNS

```
[root]# sendmail -bt -Ctest.cf
ADDRESS TEST MODE (ruleset 3 NOT automatically invoked)
Enter <ruleset> <address>
> =SDNSTest
R$* @ $+                $: $1 @ $[ $2 $]
> DNSTest julie@redbreast
DNSTest            input: julie @ redbreast
DNSTest            returns: julie @ robin . foobirds . org .
> DNSTest julie@[172.16.5.2]
DNSTest            input: julie @ [ 172 . 16 . 5 . 2 ]
DNSTest            returns: julie @ robin . foobirds . org .
> ^D
```

The test.cf configuration file in Listing 8.8 contains a very simple ruleset named DNSTest, which is displayed by the =SDNSTest command. The ruleset has only one rewrite rule. The rule matches any address that contains zero or more tokens, a literal @, and one or more tokens. The template in the rule is:

```
$: $1 @ $[ $2 $]
```

The $: symbol ensures that the rule runs only once. The $1 symbol and the literal @ guarantee that any tokens occurring before the @ in the input address and the @ itself are replicated in the output address. The symbols $[ and $] enclose the value passed to DNS, which is the second indefinite token created by the pattern match. $2 includes all of the tokens after the literal @ in the input address.

In Listing 8.8, the first value passed to the rule is julie@redbreast. After the pattern match, $1 contains julie and $2 contains redbreast. The DNS query for redbreast returns robin.foobirds.org because the name server has a CNAME record for redbreast that indicates that robin is its canonical name.

The second test is even more interesting because it demonstrates that e-mail can be addressed with an IP address instead of a hostname. That test passes the address julie@[172.16.5.2] to the DNSTest ruleset. Clearly 172.16.5.2 is not a hostname; it is an IP address. In this case DNS is asked to return the canonical name for the address. If DNS has a PTR record for the address, the address can be mapped back to a name. In this case, it does have the PTR record, so the query for 172.16.5.2 returns the canonical name robin.foobirds.org.

---

**TIP**  Not sure about DNS CNAME records and PTR records? See *Linux DNS Server Administration* by Craig Hunt (Sybex, 2000), which is also part of the Craig Hunt Linux Library.

---

In the same way that a host name or address is used to look up a canonical name in the name server database, the $(*database-spec*$) syntax uses a key to retrieve information from a database. This is a more generalized database retrieval syntax than the one that returns canonical hostnames, and it is more complex to use. To use an external database to transform an address in a rewrite rule, include the database in the template part of a rule with the following syntax:

> $(*map key* [$@*argument*...] [$:*default*] $)

*map* is the name assigned to the database by a K command. Like mailer names, map names are arbitrary names only used inside of the sendmail.cf file. The map name used in the rewrite rule template must match the name assigned to the database by the K command. Because most K commands are the result of the m4 FEATURE commands used to create the configuration, the map names are the same on most Linux systems. (See Chapter 7 for a description of the K command syntax.)

*key* is the value used to index into the database. The value returned from the database for this key is used to rewrite the input address. If no value is returned, the input address is changed to the key unless a default value is provided using the $:*default* syntax.

An *argument* is a value passed to the database program along with the key. Multiple arguments can be used, but each argument must start with $@. The *argument* modifies the value returned to Sendmail. Arguments are referenced inside the database as %n, where *n* is a digit that indicates the order in which the argument appears in the string of arguments, when multiple arguments are used. Argument %0 is the key, %1 is the first argument, %2

Advanced Configuraton

PART 3

is the second argument, and so on. An example will make the use of arguments clear. Assume the following input address:

```
rebafro@eagle
```

Further, assume the following database with the internal Sendmail name of "hubs":

```
hawk      %1<@mailhub.aol.com>
eagle     %1<@mailhub.yahoo.com>
dove      %1<@mailhub.excite.com>
```

Finally, assume the following rewrite rule:

```
R$+@$-      $(hubs $2 $@ $1 $)
```

The input address `rebafro@eagle` matches the pattern because it has one or more tokens (`rebafro`) before the literal @ and exactly one token (`eagle`) after it. The pattern match creates two indefinite tokens. The template calls the database `hubs` and passes it token $2 as the key. The template also contains $@ $1 that says that token $1, which contains `rebafro`, is passed to the database as an argument. The database program uses the key `eagle` to retrieve `%1@mailhub.yahoo.com`, then uses the argument `rebafro` to replace %1, and returns `rebafro@mailhub.yahoo.com` to Sendmail.

Before a database can be used, it must be defined in the configuration. This is done with the K command. To define the `hubs` database file used in the example above, we might enter the following command in the `sendmail.cf` file:

```
Khubs hash /etc/mail/hubs
```

The sample `hubs` database is shown only to illustrate the syntax used to access a database from a rewrite rule's template. In reality, there are already more databases available for Sendmail than you will ever use without creating any of your own. (See Chapter 6, "Using Sendmail Databases.") It is far more likely that you will use one of the databases that come with Sendmail than that you will create one of your own. Listing 8.9 demonstrates the database syntax using the standard `virtusertable` database we created in Chapter 6.

**Listing 8.9**   Accessing a Database from a Rewrite Rule

```
[root]# cat /etc/mail/virtusertable
info@patient-rights.org   sara@hawk.foobirds.org
@imaginary.com            david@lion.mammals.org
sales@outofbusiness.com   error:nouser User address is not valid
sales@weRbroke.com        error:5.1.5 Destination address invalid
@other.org                %1@local.org
+*@thatplace.com          %2@newplace.com
```

```
[root]# sendmail -bt -Ctest.cf
ADDRESS TEST MODE (ruleset 3 NOT automatically invoked)
Enter <ruleset> <address>
> =SDBTest
R$* @ $+                    $: $( virtuser @ $2 $@ $1 $: $1 @ $2 $)
> DBTest fred@imaginary.com
DBTest            input: fred @ imaginary . com
DBTest            returns: david @ lion . mammals . org
> DBTest jim@other.org
DBTest            input: jim @ other . org
DBTest            returns: jim @ local . org
> DBTest info@patient-rights.org
DBTest            input: info @ patient-rights . org
DBTest            returns: info @ patient-rights . org
> ^D
```

Listing 8.9 opens with a cat command to show the contents of the virtusertable on this
sample system. Then sendmail -bt is run and the =SDBTest command is used to show
that the ruleset named DBTest contains only one rule. The pattern in the rule matches any
address that contains zero or more tokens ($*), a literal @, and one or more tokens ($+).
The pattern is simple; the template is the interesting part. It contains the following
components:

**$:**  Ensures that the rule executes only once.

**$(**  Marks the start of the database specification.

**virtuser**  Is the standard map name for the virtusertable inside the
sendmail.cf file.

**@ $2**  Is the key used to look up a value in the virtusertable. It is a literal @ fol-
lowed by the value obtained from indefinite token $2. Thus, this template will match
only keys that start with an @ in the database.

**$@ $1**  Is the %1 argument passed to the database. The value obtained from indefinite token $1 is the value of the argument.

**$: $1 @ $2**  Is the default value used if no match is found in the database. In this
case, the rule will return $1@$2 if no match is found. If a default was not specified,
the key, which in this case is @$2, would be returned if no match is found in the
database.

**$)**  Marks the end of the database specification.

The tests in Listing 8.9 show the effect the database has on different addresses. The first
test passes DBTest the address fred@imaginary.com, which matches the $*@$+ pattern.
The pattern puts fred in indefinite token $1 and imaginary.com in indefinite token $2.

The template uses a literal @ plus the values from $2 (@imaginary.com) as the key. The database returns david@lion.mammals.org as the value for that key—just what you would expect from looking at the cat of virtusertable.

The second test demonstrates the use of arguments. It passes the address jim@other.org to DBTest and gets jim@local.org in response. The key @other.org matches the value %1@local.org. The $1 token is the argument, so %1 is rewritten to jim, and the final value returned by the ruleset is jim@local.org.

The final test illustrates the use of the default value. The third test passes DBTest the address info@patient-rights.org. A quick look at the cat of virtusertable shows that info@patient-rights.org is a valid key and that sara@hawk.foobirds.org is the value assigned to that key. But DBTest does not return the value sara@hawk.foobirds.org. Here's why. info@patient-rights.org matches the pattern $*@$+. The template then uses @$2, which in this case is @patient-rights.org, as the key. @patient-rights.org, which is missing the string info before the @, is not a key found in this database. When a key is not found in a database, the template returns either the value defined as the default or, if no default is defined, the key. In this case, if no default were defined the value returned would be @patient-rights.org. However, a default was defined as $: $1@$2, so the value returned is info@patient-rights.org—the original address. Using a default is particularly important in a database like virtusertable, which uses different key formats. By returning the original address when a match is not found, the address can be passed on to the next rule in line for more processing. A database like virtusertable, which uses multiple key formats, is normally searched by a series of related rules that try all of the key formats. If DBTest contained another rule that used the entire input address as the key, info@patient-rights.org would return sara@hawk.foobirds.org.

The virtusertable used in the examples takes an input address as a key and returns a different address as the value, in most cases. However, two of the values in the virtusertable start with the word error and do not appear to be e-mail addresses. They aren't. They are values that can be used in a mailer triple, which is a special type of rewrite rule template used in ruleset 0 (ruleset parse).

# Special Ruleset 0 Rewrite Rules

There is a special rewrite rule syntax that is only used in ruleset 0. Ruleset 0 defines the triple (mailer, host, user) that specifies the mail delivery program, the recipient host, and the recipient user. The special template syntax used to do this is:

```
$# mailer $@ host $: user
```

*mailer* is a valid mailer name defined by an M command. *host* is the hostname of the system that will handle this mail, and *user* is the address of the e-mail recipient. An example of this syntax taken from the sample `sendmail.cf` file is:

```
R$* < @$* > $*      $#esmtp $@ $2 $: $1 < @ $2 > $3    user@host.domain
```

The comment `user@host.domain` at the end of this rule implies that the pattern will match addresses of that format. That's almost true. The addresses have already been through the `canonify` ruleset before they reach ruleset 0, so the input address will be "focused" with angle brackets. For example, the e-mail address `kathy<@wren.foobirds.org>` would match the pattern and be processed by this rule. The address matches the pattern `$*<@$*>$*` because:

- The address has zero or more tokens (the token `kathy`) that match the first `$*` symbol.
- The address has a literal `<@`.
- The address has one or more tokens (the five tokens `wren.foobirds.org`) that match the requirement of the second `$*` symbol.
- The address has a literal `>`.
- The address has zero or more—in this case, zero—tokens that match the requirement of the last `$*` symbol.

This pattern match produces two indefinite tokens. Indefinite token $1 contains `kathy` and $2 contains `wren.foobirds.org`. No other matches occurred, so $3 is empty. These indefinite tokens are used to rewrite the address into the following triple:

```
$#esmtp $@ wren.foobirds.org $: kathy<@wren.foobirds.org>
```

The components of this triple are:

**$#esmtp**  esmtp is the internal name of the mailer that delivers the message.

**$@ wren.foobirds.org**  wren.foobirds.org is the recipient host.

**$: kathy<@wren.foobirds.org>**  kathy<@wren.foobirds.org> is the recipient user.

The mail delivery triple is just that—three pieces of information needed to deliver the mail, including the mailer name, the host, and the e-mail address. The mail delivery triple is created in ruleset 0. Sometimes, however, a template that looks like a mail delivery triple is used for another purpose. These variations on the mail delivery triple can appear in any ruleset.

## Mailer Triple Variations

There are a few variations on the mailer triple syntax that are also used in the templates of some rules. Two of these variations use only the "mailer" component.

**$#OK** Indicates that the input address passed a security test. For example, the address is permitted to relay mail.

**$#discard** Indicates that the input address failed some security test and that the e-mail message should be discarded.

---

> **NOTE** Neither OK, discard, nor error, which is discussed in a second, are declared in M commands like real mailers. But the Sendmail documentation refers to them as "mailers" and so do we.

---

The $#OK and $#discard mailers are used in spam control and security. You will see more of them in later chapters. The $#discard mailer silently discards the mail and does not return an error message to the sender. The $#error mailer is another mailer that handles undeliverable mail, but unlike $#discard, it does return an error message to the sender. The template syntax used with the $#error mailer is more complex than the syntax of either $#OK or $#discard. That syntax is shown below:

**$#error** $@*dsn-code* $:*message*

To properly process an error message, the mailer must be $#error. The $:*message* field contains the text of the error message that you wish to send. The $@*dsn-code* field is optional. If it is provided, it appears before the *message* and must contain a valid DSN error code as defined by RFC 1893 ("Mail System Status Codes") or a valid Sendmail keyword. Table 8.5 lists the valid Sendmail error code keywords and their meanings.

**Table 8.5** Sendmail Error Code Keywords

| Keyword | Meaning |
| --- | --- |
| config | An internal configuration error or routing loop was detected. |
| nohost | The host portion of the sender or recipient address is invalid. |
| nouser | The user portion of the sender or recipient address is invalid. |
| protocol | Network delivery failed. |

**Table 8.5**　Sendmail Error Code Keywords *(continued)*

| Keyword | Meaning |
|---|---|
| tempfail | A temporary failure was detected. |
| unavailable | A delivery resource is not available. |
| usage | The syntax of the delivery address is bad. |

An error message using an error keyword would look something like the following:

```
R<@$+>      $#error $@nouser $:"user address required"
```

This works, but it is not the recommended format. In fact, not a single error message in the sendmail.cf file delivered with Sendmail 8.11.0 uses the keyword format. The preferred format is to use a DSN code in place of the keyword. The codes are clearly defined in an Internet standard and are understood by all mailers. DSN codes are composed of three dot-separated components:

*class*　Provides a broad classification of the status. Three values are defined for *class* in the RFC: 2 means success, 4 means temporary failure, and 5 means permanent failure.

*subject*　Classifies the error messages as relating to one of eight categories:

0 (**Undefined**)　The specific category cannot be determined.

1 (**Addressing**)　A problem was encountered with the address.

2 (**Mailbox**)　A problem was encountered with the delivery mailbox.

3 (**Mail system**)　The destination mail delivery system is having a problem.

4 (**Network**)　The network infrastructure is having a problem.

5 (**Protocol**)　A protocol problem was encountered.

6 (**Content**)　The message content caused a translation error.

7 (**Security**)　A security problem was reported.

*detail*　Provides the details of the specific error. The *detail* value is only meaningful in context of the subject code. For example $x.1.1$ means a bad destination user address and $x.1.2$ means a bad destination host address, while $x.2.1$ means the mailbox is disabled and $x.2.2$ means the mailbox is full. There are far too many detail codes to list here. See RFC 1893 for a full list.

If the error message shown above were rewritten to use the preferred DSN format, it would be:

```
R<@$+>       $#error$@5.1.1$:"user address required"
```

This rule returns the DSN code 5.1.1 and the message "user address required" when the address matches the pattern. The DSN code has a 5 in the *class* field, meaning it is a permanent failure; a 1 in the *subject* field, meaning it is an addressing failure; and a 1 in the *detail* field, meaning that, given the subject value of 1, it is a bad user address.

Error codes and the error syntax can be confusing. We return to this subject again in later chapters when we look at advanced configuration options, spam control, and security.

# In Sum

The bulk of the work done by Sendmail is done by rewrite rules. Correspondingly, rewrite rules make up the bulk of the `sendmail.cf` file. The rewrite rules occur in both the Rewriting Rules section and the Mailer Definitions section of the `sendmail.cf` file.

A rewrite rule matches an input address against a pattern composed of literals, variables, and special symbols. If the address matches the pattern, it is rewritten by the rule using a template that is also composed of literals, variables, and special symbols.

The syntax and usage of rewrite rules are complex, and very little can be done to filter out this complexity when rewrite rules are examined in detail. However, it is not always necessary to understand all of the details of an individual rule to know what the rules are doing.

Related rewrite rules are grouped together into rulesets. The purpose of each ruleset is described in this chapter. It is not necessary to know the function of every rule in the Canonify2 ruleset to know that it asks DNS for canonical hostnames. When it is necessary to understand the function of a single rule, the comment provided with the rule may provide all the understanding you need. Finally, if detailed understanding of a specific rule is necessary, the description of rewrite rule syntax in this chapter will provide all of the information you need to decipher the command.

Generally, there is no need to read the individual rules that already exist in the `sendmail.cf` file. Understanding the purpose of the rulesets is all you need to understand the functioning of the configuration. The real purpose of understanding the details of rewrite rule syntax is to write your own rules. It is rarely necessary for you to do so, but it is part of advanced configuration, as we will see in Chapter 9 and in some of the later chapters.

# 9

# Special *m4* Configurations

**T**en percent of the `sendmail.cf` options handles ninety percent of the configurations. The average Sendmail server can operate with the configuration provided by the Linux vendor, with little or no change. But not every server is average. Some systems require special options to handle special configuration requirements. m4 provides a plethora of configuration options to satisfy any need. Appendix A, "m4 Macro Command Reference," lists them all. This chapter helps you make sense of these options by organizing them into topics.

This chapter is something of a laundry list because it contains a few largely unrelated topics. I originally planned to title this chapter "Advanced m4 Configurations," but the truth is that there is nothing more advanced about these configuration options than there is about any others. The options used later in this book for spam control and security are at least as complex as any options discussed in this chapter. The real relationship among the topics in this chapter is that they are configuration options that are needed only in special circumstances. You'll probably discover that you don't need to use most of them, but you'll want to know something about all of them. In this chapter, you'll learn the advantages and the disadvantages of these options to better decide which ones are right for you.

One common thread that links many of the topics in this chapter is that they relate to the special needs of your enterprise. m4 configuration commands that are specific to your network or domain logically are placed in the DOMAIN file. This chapter makes extensive use of the DOMAIN file.

# Using the *DOMAIN* File

At the conclusion of Chapter 5, "Understanding a Vendor's Configuration," the redhat.mc file was rewritten to take advantage of the structure inherent in the Sendmail m4 configuration directory. In Listing 5.6, the large redhat.mc file was divided into three files: a macro control file named redhat811.mc, an OSTYPE file named redhat7.0.m4, and a DOMAIN file named foobirds.m4. Traditionally, the macro control file selects configuration components, the OSTYPE file configures operating system–specific values, and the DOMAIN file holds all configuration options that are specific to your network or domain. In the first few sections of this chapter, we stick to the traditional use of these files by making our changes to the foobirds.m4 file, which is shown in Listing 9.1.

**Listing 9.1**   A Sample DOMAIN File

```
[root]# cat ../domain/foobirds.m4
VERSIONID(`Settings for the foobirds.org domain')dnl
define(`confFORWARD_PATH',
    `$z/.forward.$w+$h:$z/.forward+$h:$z/.forward.$w:$z/.
forward')dnl
define(`confUSERDB_SPEC', `/etc/mail/userdb.db')dnl
FEATURE(always_add_domain)dnl
FEATURE(`access_db')dnl
FEATURE(`blacklist_recipients')dnl
FEATURE(`redirect')dnl
FEATURE(`use_cw_file')dnl
EXPOSED_USER(`root')
[root]# m4 ../m4/cf.m4 redhat811.mc > plain.cf
[root]# cp ../domain/foobirds.m4 ../domain/old-foobirds.m4
```

All of the commands in this file are explained in Chapter 5, and for the most part these existing commands don't have anything to do with the topics covered in this chapter. We process redhat811.mc, which is the macro control file that uses this DOMAIN file, through m4 to create plain.cf. That will be the baseline sendmail.cf file against which we can compare our changes. At the end of Listing 9.1, the original DOMAIN file is copied to old-foobirds.m4. That provides a backup file in case we don't like the changes we make in the next few sections, and an original against which we can compare the changes. These originals will be an important part of the test that helps us determine the impact of each additional configuration command.

> **NOTE**   Most system administrators follow the lead of the vendors and put the
> entire Sendmail configuration in the macro control file. This has the advantages
> and disadvantages inherent in having all of the configuration commands in one
> file. We use the DOMAIN file in this chapter primarily to illustrate its traditional role
> and to show that the vendor's way of doing things is not the only way. Choose the
> configuration format that you like best. They both work.

The laundry list of topics covered in this chapter needs to start somewhere. Let's start
with address masquerading. Of all the special configuration options discussed in this
chapter, it is the one I use most often.

# Address Masquerading

We played with address masquerading in Chapter 7, "The sendmail.cf File," by storing
a value in the sendmail.cf variable M. The value in M replaced the hostname portion of the
sender address in all outbound mail. In Sendmail parlance, the address is "masqueraded."

Addresses are masqueraded to hide the real name of the host that was the source of the
mail. This is done when the real hostname should not be advertised to the outside world.
The reasons you might not want to advertise real hostnames vary:

- Perhaps the source host does not collect its own inbound mail.
- Perhaps the firewall does not permit inbound mail to the source host.
- Perhaps your organization uses a standard address format across all hosts.
- Perhaps your security group does not want the names of internal hosts advertised to
  the outside world.

All of these are legitimate reasons for masquerading addresses. Of course, when you
decide to use masquerading, you don't configure it by editing the sendmail.cf file to set
the M variable. Instead, use the m4 configuration commands designed for masquerading.

## Enabling Masquerading

Use the MASQUERADE_AS macro to enable masquerading. For example, to enable masquerading as foobirds.org, put the following command in the macro configuration:

    MASQUERADE_AS(`foobirds.org')

The name provided in the MASQUERADE_AS command should be a valid, canonical DNS
name. Often, it is a domain name, instead of a hostname, when masquerading is being
used to create a simplified, standard addressing format for the entire enterprise.

The effect of the MASQUERADE_AS command shown above is the same as setting the sendmail.cf M variable to foobirds.org. In fact, the only thing that MASQUERADE_AS does is set a value for M. Listing 9.2 demonstrates this fact.

**Listing 9.2**    The Impact of MASQUERADE_AS on sendmail.cf

```
[root]# diff ../domain/old-foobirds.m4 ../domain/foobirds.m4
8a9
> MASQUERADE_AS(`foobirds.org')dnl
[root]# m4 ../m4/cf.m4 redhat811.mc > masquerade.cf
[root]# diff plain.cf masquerade.cf
128c128
< DM
---
> DMfoobirds.org
```

In Listing 9.2, the first diff command shows that the only difference between the two DOMAIN files is that the new file has a MASQUERADE_AS command that is not found in old-foobirds.m4. The new file is processed through m4 to build Sendmail configurations. The plain.cf configuration file was created in Listing 9.1. Listing 9.2 creates the configuration file named masquerade.cf. The second diff compares the contents of these two files. Where the plain.cf file stores no value in M, the masquerade.cf file stores foobirds.org in M. This is the only difference between these configurations and is the only change that the MASQUERADE_AS command makes.

From the testing we did in Chapter 7, we know that storing a value in M causes Sendmail to rewrite the host portion of header sender addresses to the value found in M. There are some limitations. The value in M is used to rewrite the address only if the input address has no host part or the host part from the input address is found in class w. Additionally, masquerading is only applied to the header sender address. The sendmail -bt tests in Listing 9.3 demonstrates these effects.

**Listing 9.3**    Testing the Default MASQUERADE_AS Settings

```
[root]# sendmail -bt -Cmasquerade.cf
ADDRESS TEST MODE (ruleset 3 NOT automatically invoked)
Enter <ruleset> <address>
> $=w
wren.foobirds.org
[172.16.12.3]
wren
localhost
> /tryflags HS
```

```
> /try esmtp craig@wren.foobirds.org
Trying header sender address craig@wren.foobirds.org for mailer esmtp
canonify            input: craig @ wren . foobirds . org
... Many lines deleted ...
final              returns: craig @ foobirds . org
Rcode = 0, addr = craig@foobirds.org
> /try esmtp craig@hawk.foobirds.org
Trying header sender address craig@hawk.foobirds.org for mailer esmtp
canonify            input: craig @ hawk . foobirds . org
... Many lines deleted ...
final              returns: craig @ hawk . foobirds . org
Rcode = 0, addr = craig@hawk.foobirds.org
> /tryflags ES
> /try esmtp craig@wren.foobirds.org
Trying envelope sender address craig@wren.foobirds.org for mailer esmtp
canonify            input: craig @ wren . foobirds . org
... Many lines deleted ...
final              returns: craig @ wren . foobirds . org
Rcode = 0, addr = craig@wren.foobirds.org
> ^D
```

Listing 9.3 is heavily edited to keep it to a reasonable length, but the key elements that
show the default masquerade settings are there. First, we display the contents of class w
to show that it contains only four values; these are the only four names that will be masqueraded. Then we use the /tryflags command to request processing for the header
sender (HS) address. The first test uses the /try command to process the address
craig@wren.foobirds.org for the esmtp mailer. The address is rewritten to
craig@foobirds.org, showing that this configuration masquerades wren.foobirds.org
as foobirds.org in the header sender address. Next, we process
craig@hawk.foobirds.org as the header sender address for the esmtp mail. This time the
address is not masqueraded. The reason is that hawk.foobirds.org is not a value in class
w. Finally, the address craig@wren.foobirds.org is processed again. But this time, the
/tryflags are set to request envelope sender (ES) processing. Even though the address is
in class w, it is not masqueraded because it is an envelope address.

## Masquerade Options

The default settings of masquerading only header sender addresses and only for hostnames identified in class w are usually adequate. In general, the purpose of masquerading
addresses is to provide the correct reply address to the remote user. The user normally sees
only the header addresses; the envelope addresses are used in the SMTP protocol
exchanges. Thus, header sender masquerading is usually sufficient.

If header sender address masquerading isn't sufficient for your configuration, there are two features available to extend masquerading to other types of addresses. These are:

**FEATURE(`masquerade-envelope`)** This feature causes Sendmail to masquerade envelope sender addresses. If this feature had been set, the third test in Listing 9.2 would have resulted in `wren.foobirds.org` being masqueraded as `foobirds.org` in the envelope sender address. This feature is useful if masquerading is being done to satisfy the security people. They like to be thorough!

**FEATURE(`allmasquerade`)** This feature causes Sendmail to masquerade recipient addresses. Generally, this is not a good idea. Masquerading is intended for hiding source addresses on outbound mail. Changing the address on inbound mail does not make much sense, as the user of a local system already knows the real name of that system. Additionally, adding a masqueraded hostname to an inbound address can cause the mail to bypass the alias process. Don't use the `allmasquerade` feature.

As mentioned above, the second limitation of the default masquerade settings is that only hosts identified in class w are masqueraded. This default makes sense, because the server masquerading the mail is often the server that will accept inbound mail. A server accepts mail for local delivery only for hosts in class w. Limiting masquerading to systems in class w creates a balance between how inbound mail and outbound mail are handled. But this only makes sense when the system masquerading the mail also collects the mail for every system that it masquerades. That is not always the case. A mail relay server may relay outbound mail and yet have no role in collecting inbound mail. There are some m4 macros and features that allow you to create a more flexible configuration.

Class M holds a list of hostnames that should be masqueraded. The values stored in class M are added to those in class w for masquerading. Values in class M are not, however, equivalent to values in class w because hostnames listed in class M are not aliases for the local host. Class M is used only for masquerading. The local system will not accept mail addressed to hosts in class M as local mail. Class M provides a finer level of control by permitting masquerading without granting any other type of access.

The `limited_masquerade` feature further refines your control over masquerading. By default, values in both class w and class M are masqueraded. To limit masquerading to *only* those values defined in class M, use the `limited_masquerade` feature. When masquerading is enabled, masquerading local host aliases is the logical thing to do, but class w can hold more than just local host aliases. In Chapter 6, "Using Sendmail Databases," we added virtual domain names to class w. You may not want to masquerade virtual domain names in outbound mail because you want external customers to believe that the virtual domains are real domains. In Listing 6.11, we created a virtual domain named `bridal-gowns.com` and stored it in class w. Outbound mail from `bridal-gowns.com` is masqueraded as mail from `foobirds.org` if `MASQUERADE_AS(`foobirds.org')` is used with the default settings. But if `FEATURE(`limited_masquerade')` is also used, the mail goes out as mail from `bridal-gowns.com`, unless you explicitly add `bridal-gowns.com` to class M.

Use `MASQUERADE_DOMAIN` to add individual values to class M. For example, to add `hawk.foobirds.org` to class M, add the following m4 macro to the macro configuration file:

> `MASQUERADE_DOMAIN(`hawk.foobirds.org')`

The `MASQUERADE_DOMAIN` macro is most useful when only a few values need to be added to class M and when those few values change very infrequently. Use the `MASQUERADE_ DOMAIN_FILE` macro to load class M from a file when you have more than a few domain names that you wish to masquerade. Assume that you wanted to load class M from a file named `/etc/mail/masquerade-domain-names`. You could add the following m4 macro to the macro configuration file:

> `MASQUERADE_DOMAIN_FILE(`/etc/mail/masquerade-domain-names')`

As the macro name `MASQUERADE_DOMAIN` implies, the values stored in class M do not have to be hostnames; they can be full domain names. But by default, the hostname portion of the input address must exactly match a value in class w or class M to be rewritten to the masquerade value. Thus, if class M contains `terns.foobirds.org`, the input address `kirstan@terns.foobirds.org` is rewritten but the address `kirstan@sooty.terns.foobirds.org` is *not* rewritten. This means that hosts in a domain are not masqueraded even if the name of the domain is found in class w or class M. Use `FEATURE(`masquerade_entire_domain')` to change this default behavior so that every component of a domain defined in class w or class M is masqueraded. If `masquerade_ entire_domain` is specified and class M contains `terns.foobirds.org`, the input address `kirstan@terns.foobirds.org` is rewritten and so is the address `kirstan@sooty.terns.foobirds.org`. Listing 9.4 illustrates the effect that these various options have on masquerading.

**Listing 9.4**  Testing Special Masquerade Options

```
[root]# diff ../domain/old-foobirds.m4 ../domain/foobirds.m4
8a9,12
> MASQUERADE_AS(`foobirds.org')dnl
> MASQUERADE_DOMAIN(`foobirds.org')dnl
> FEATURE(`limited_masquerade')dnl
> FEATURE(`masquerade_entire_domain')dnl
[root]# m4 ../m4/cf.m4 redhat811.mc > masquerade.cf
[root]# sendmail -bt -Cmasquerade.cf
```

```
ADDRESS TEST MODE (ruleset 3 NOT automatically invoked)
Enter <ruleset> <address>
> $=w
wren.foobirds.org
[172.16.12.3]
patient-rights.org
outofbusiness.com
wren
localhost
imaginary.com
> /tryflags HS
> /try esmtp fred@imaginary.com
canonify          input: fred @ imaginary . com
... Many lines deleted ...
final             returns: fred @ imaginary . com
Rcode = 75, addr = fred@imaginary.com
> $=M
foobirds.org
> /try esmtp sara@hawk.foobirds.org
Trying header sender address sara@hawk.foobirds.org for mailer esmtp
canonify          input: sara @ hawk . foobirds . org
... Many lines deleted ...
final             returns: sara @ foobirds . org
Rcode = 0, addr = sara@foobirds.org
> ^D
```

Listing 9.4 opens with a `diff` command that shows the four `m4` macros added to the
`foobirds.m4` configuration file. The four macros tell Sendmail to:

- Masquerade the host portion of outgoing addresses as `foobirds.org`.
- Store the value `foobirds.org` in class M.
- Only masquerade addresses if the host portion of the address matches the value in
  class M.
- Treat the value in class M as a domain and masquerade any hostname within that
  domain.

The new `test.mc` file is processed through `m4` to create a Sendmail configuration file
named `masquerade.cf`. The `sendmail` command is run with the `–bt` option to enter test
mode and with the `–C` option to load the new `masquerade.cf` configuration file. In test
mode, the contents of class w is displayed, the `/tryflags` are set to HS to request header
sender address processing, and the address `fred@imaginary.com` is processed for the
`esmtp` mailer. (`imaginary.com` is one of the virtual domains we created in Chapter 6.) The

address is not masqueraded, even though the host portion of the address is contained in class w and masquerading is enabled. This test shows the effect of the limited_ masquerade feature, which limits masquerading to values stored in class M and ignores values defined in class w.

Next, the contents of class M are displayed. It contains foobirds.org, which is the value we stored in class M with the MASQUERADE_DOMAIN macro. The address sara@hawk.foobirds.org is processed as a header sender address for the esmtp mailer. This time the address is masqueraded as sara@foobirds.org. We know that this is not because hawk.foobirds.org is in class w—it's not, and even if it was, class w is not being masqueraded. Additionally, hawk.foobirds.org is not in class M. The only value in class M is foobirds.org. The reason that hawk.foobirds.org is masqueraded is that this host is part of the foobirds.org domain and the masquerade_entire_domain option has been selected. Masquerading all of the hosts within a domain is very useful, particularly when a single mail server handles the mail for an entire domain.

Sometimes, of course, you want to masquerade most of the hosts in a domain, but not every host. In those cases, it is often simplest to use the masquerade_entire_domain feature to include the bulk of the domain's systems and then use the MASQUERADE_EXCEPTION macro to exclude the individual hosts that you don't want to masquerade. The configuration shown in Listing 9.4 masquerades every host in the foobirds.org domain. Assume that you wanted to masquerade every host except www.foobirds.org. You could add the following macro to the configuration shown in Listing 9.4 to accomplish this:

```
MASQUERADE_EXCEPTION(`www.foobirds.org')
```

Another exception to masquerading is created for special usernames. Class E contains the list of usernames that override masquerading. When the user portion of the input address contains a value found in class E, the host portion of the address is not masqueraded— even if the host portion of the address is listed in class w or class M. The usernames in class E are those names that are not unique among the systems being masqueraded. For example, every system has a root user and many have a postmaster account. If mail from root@wren.foobirds.org is masqueraded as mail from root@foobirds.org and mail from root@ibis.foobirds.org is also masqueraded as root@foobirds.org, there is no way for the mail server to determine the correct host when the recipient replies to root@foobirds.org. Placing the username root in class E prevents this problem. Use the EXPOSED_USER macro to add values to class E. The original old-foobirds.m4 file already had an EXPOSED_USER macro for root because it was derived from the redhat.mc file, which had this macro. The following two lines add both root and postmaster to class E:

```
EXPOSED_USER(root)
EXPOSED_USER(postmaster)
```

The EXPOSED_USER macro is not the only way to handle duplicate usernames. The macro works well for names like root, which have a special meaning and are found on all Linux systems, but it may not be the solution you want when the duplicated names are the logon names of real users. Instead of skipping masquerading for every user who has a duplicated name, you may want to replace the username portion of the outbound address. Rewriting usernames is our next topic.

## Masquerading Usernames

Transforming the user portion of an outbound address requires a database. Unlike hosts that can be masqueraded as a single value, each username requires a unique value. The user database and the genericstable, both described in Chapter 6, can be used to rewrite usernames. The user database, usually named **/etc/mail/userdb.db**, handles both inbound and outbound addresses—duplicating functions performed by the aliases database and the genericstable. The user database does not work very well with masquerading. For that reason, it is not covered here. See Chapter 6 for details of the user database. The genericstable, on the other hand, is an excellent corollary to masquerading. The genericstable handles the user portion of the outbound address while masquerading handles the host portion.

The input address passed to the genericstable for processing must either have no host portion or a host portion that matches a value in class G. Use the GENERICS_DOMAIN macro to add individual values in class G. Class G performs the same function for the genericstable as class M does for masquerading. To configure the genericstable to be compatible with masquerading, class G should contain the same values as class M.

If you plan to add more than a few values to class G, load class G from a file using the GENERICS_DOMAIN_FILE macro. Use the same file for class G that you use for class M if you want to make the genericstable compatible with masquerading. For example, you might have the following two macros in your configuration if you wanted to masquerade usernames on exactly the same systems that you masquerade hostnames:

```
MASQUERADE_DOMAIN_FILE(`/etc/mail/masquerade-domain-names')
GENERICS_DOMAIN_FILE(`/etc/mail/masquerade-domain-names')
```

Also like values in class M, values in class G require an exact match. Use the generics_entire_domain feature to override this default behavior. The generics_entire domain feature acts exactly like the masquerade_entire_domain feature described in the previous section. When generics_entire_domain is used, the values in class G are treated as domain names and any host within those domains is considered a match for class G. Listing 9.5 shows the effect of the genericstable on output addresses.

**Listing 9.5**   Using generic stable to Masquerade Usernames

```
[root]# cat /etc/mail/generic-names
craig    craig.hunt
kathy    kathy.mccafferty
sara     sara.henson
david    david.craig
becky    rebecca.fro
[root]# makemap hash genericstable < generic-names
[root]# diff ../domain/old-foobirds.m4 ../domain/foobirds.m4
8a9,12
> MASQUERADE_AS(`foobirds.org')dnl
> MASQUERADE_DOMAIN(`foobirds.org')dnl
> FEATURE(`limited_masquerade')dnl
> FEATURE(`masquerade_entire_domain')dnl
9a14,16
> FEATURE(`genericstable')dnl
> GENERICS_DOMAIN(`foobirds.org')dnl
> FEATURE(`generics_entire_domain')dnl
[root]# m4 ../m4/cf.m4 redhat811.mc > generics.cf
[root]# sendmail -bt -Cgenerics.cf
ADDRESS TEST MODE (ruleset 3 NOT automatically invoked)
Enter <ruleset> <address>
> /tryflags HS
> /try esmtp kathy@hawk.foobirds.org
Trying header sender address kathy@hawk.foobirds.org for mailer esmtp
canonify           input: kathy @ hawk . foobirds . org
... Many lines deleted ...
final              returns: kathy . mccafferty @ foobirds . org
Rcode = 0, addr = kathy.mccafferty@foobirds.org
> /try esmtp sara@patient-rights.org
Trying header sender address sara@patient-rights.org for mailer esmtp
canonify           input: sara @ patient-rights . org
... Many lines deleted ...
final              returns: sara @ patient-rights . org
Rcode = 75, addr = sara@patient-rights.org
> ^D
```

Listing 9.5 shows the contents of the genericstable. It also shows the m4 macros added
to the configuration for masquerading and for the genericstable. The genericstable
feature adds support for the genericstable to the Sendmail configuration. The
GENERICS_DOMAIN macro and the generics_entire_domain feature parallel the

MASQUERADE_DOMAIN macro and the masquerade_entire_domain feature, allowing the genericstable to work with masquerading.

The two sendmail -bt tests show the impact that these configuration choices have on output addresses. In both tests, we are processing header sender addresses for the esmtp mailer. The first input address is kathy@hawk.foobirds.org. It is rewritten to kathy.mccafferty@foobirds.org. Masquerading rewrote the host portion of the address and the genericstable rewrote the user portion. The address was rewritten because hawk.foobirds.org is a host in the domain foobirds.org, which is identified in both class M and class G.

The second address is sara@patient-rights.org. sara is a valid key in the genericstable, and patient-rights.org is a value found in class w. However, in this case the address is not rewritten because the configuration tells Sendmail to rewrite only addresses that are part of the domain identified in class M and class G.

The example in Listing 9.5 is very realistic. Many sites rewrite usernames to full names, and they usually do it while masquerading the hostname of the address. This provides the simple *first.last@domain* addressing that many organizations prefer. And it does it without interfering with virtual domains.

Masquerading hostnames and usernames both involve rewriting input addresses. An even more direct, though much more rarely used, method for rewriting addresses is to create your own rewrite rules. That is our next topic.

# Writing Local Rules

It is not necessary to directly edit the sendmail.cf file to add "raw" sendmail.cf configuration commands to the file. Sendmail provides several m4 macros for inserting text directly into sendmail.cf.

The LOCAL_CONFIG macro marks the beginning of text inserted into sendmail.cf at the end of the Local Info section. LOCAL_CONFIG allows you to define variables, classes, or databases. Because all of the standard variables, classes, and databases are created or modified by m4 commands, the LOCAL_CONFIG command is needed only to create private variables, classes, or databases. Listing 9.5 shows a comment, a D command, a second comment, and a K command that are to be added to the end of the Local Info section of the sendmail.cf file.

**Listing 9.6**   A LOCAL_CONFIG Example

```
LOCAL_CONFIG
### Store a host name in variable A
DAns.foobirds.org
### Define a special NIS database
Knishosts nis -m hosts.byname
```

Listing 9.6 assumes that A is a private variable and that nishosts is a private database. The LOCAL_CONFIG example in Listing 9.6 is contrived, but it shows the format used by all of the macros covered in this section. Each macro is a keyword that marks the start of a variable-length block of text. The block of text ends when the next m4 macro is encountered. The variation between the macros covered in this section is that each one inserts the text into a different part of the sendmail.cf file.

The MAILER_DEFINITIONS macro is used to define a mailer and add it to the Mailer Definitions section of the sendmail.cf file. The mailer is defined using the M command described in Chapter 7. If any special rulesets are required by the new mailer, they are also defined in the text that follows the MAILER_DEFINITIONS macro.

Rewrite rules, and even entire rulesets, can be added to the Rewriting Rules section of the sendmail.cf file. Use the LOCAL_RULESETS macro to add an entire ruleset. The first line following the LOCAL_RULESETS macro is a sendmail.cf S command that defines the name of the new ruleset. This is followed by the rewrite rules that make up the ruleset. Most often LOCAL_RULESETS are used for spam filtering or security. We cover the LOCAL_RULESETS macro in Chapter 11, "Stopping Spam."

To add individual rules to rulesets 0, 1, 2, or 3, use the LOCAL_RULE_*n* macro. The *n* in the name of this macro is the number of the ruleset to which the rules should be added. Listing 9.7 shows rules being added to ruleset 1, which is also called the sender ruleset.

**Listing 9.7**   Creating and Testing Additions to Ruleset 1

```
[root]# diff ../domain/old-foobirds.m4 ../domain/foobirds.m4
8a9
> MASQUERADE_AS(`foobirds.org')dnl
9a11,13
> FEATURE(`genericstable')dnl
> LOCAL_RULE_1
> R$- < @ $=w . >        $: $( generics $1 $: $1 $) < @ $2 .>
[root]# m4 ../m4/cf.m4 redhat811.mc > local-rule1.cf
[root]# sendmail -bt -C local-rule1.cf
ADDRESS TEST MODE (ruleset 3 NOT automatically invoked)
```

Advanced
Configuration

PART 3

```
Enter <ruleset> <address>
> =S1
R$- < @ $=w . >          $: $( genericstable $1 $: $1 $) < @ $2 . >
> $=G
> $=w
wren.foobirds.org
[172.16.12.3]
wren
localhost
[127.0.0.1]
> /tryflags HS
> /try esmtp craig@wren
Trying header sender address craig@wren for mailer esmtp
canonify          input: craig @ wren
Canonify2         input: craig < @ wren >
Canonify2         returns: craig < @ wren . foobirds . org . >
canonify          returns: craig < @ wren . foobirds . org . >
sender            input: craig < @ wren . foobirds . org . >
sender            returns: craig . hunt < @ wren . foobirds . org . >
... Many lines deleted ...
final             returns: craig . hunt @ foobirds . org
Rcode = 0, addr = craig.hunt@foobirds.org
> ^D
```

---

**NOTE**   As noted in Chapter 8, "Understanding Rewrite Rules," ruleset 1 is applied to all sender addresses after ruleset 3 (canonify). Yet ruleset 1 is, by default, empty. It is only used if you add rules to the ruleset using the LOCAL_ RULE_1 macro.

---

In Listing 9.7, the diff command shows that this version of the foobirds.m4 file has both masquerading and the genericstable enabled with default values, meaning that addresses matching class w and class M will be masqueraded and addresses matching class G will be processed by the genericstable. By default, the values in class w are not processed by the genericstable. Assume that you *want* to process addresses that match class w through the genericstable using your own rewrite rules. We accomplish this in Listing 9.7 by adding a single rule to ruleset 1.

The sendmail –bt test first shows that ruleset 1 contains only the rule that we added. The $=G command shows that class G is empty, and the $=w command shows the five values in class w. The address craig@wren is then processed as a header sender address for the esmtp mail. Despite the fact that wren is not in class G, the user portion of the address is rewritten using the genericstable because craig@wren matches the pattern in our new rewrite rule.

LOCAL_RULE_*n* allows you to specify whether the rules you enter are added to ruleset 0, 1, 2, or 3. The LOCAL_NET_CONFIG macro adds your rewrite rules to ruleset 0, specifically to the Parse1 ruleset used by ruleset 0. Rules added by the LOCAL_NET_CONFIG macro have a very specific purpose—they are used to select mail for delivery through local network services before the mail is sent to a relay server. For example, assume that you want to send all of your mail through a relay server except for mail to your local domain. You could add the following to your configuration:

```
LOCAL_NET_CONFIG
R$+ < @ $* $m . >            $#esmtp $@ $2.$m. $: $1 < @ $2.$m. >
```

The template of this rule is a standard mailer triple that takes addresses that match the pattern, formats them, and hands them to the esmtp mailer for delivery. The pattern matches addresses that have one or more tokens ($+), a literal <@, zero or more tokens ($*), the value found in variable m, and a literal .>. The m variable holds the local domain name. If m equals foobirds.org, the address craig<@foobirds.org.> matches the pattern and is sent to esmtp for delivery, but the address marylee<@library.org.> does not match and falls through to the next rule. If the SMART_HOST relay is defined, the next rule sends this mail to that relay for delivery. Thus, the LOCAL_NET_CONFIG macro gives you a means of short-circuiting SMART_HOST relay processing for some addresses.

The LOCAL_NET_CONFIG macro is used only when your local system is a client of a mail relay server. The m4 macros that you use to configure your system as a relay client are our next topic.

# Configuring a Relay Client

Linux systems support all of the features of Sendmail. Even a desktop Linux system is usually configured as a Sendmail server that directly collects and directly delivers mail for the system's users. In special cases, this standard configuration might not be what you want; you may want to route all mail through an external server. For example, if the desktop system is behind a firewall that blocks all incoming and outgoing mail except through an approved server, you may need to configure your Linux system to use that server for all mail. The nullclient feature creates this type of configuration. Listing 9.8 shows a complete nullclient configuration and the effect this configuration has on the sendmail.cf file.

**Listing 9.8** A Sample `nullclient` Configuration

```
[root]$ cat client-only.mc
OSTYPE(linux)
FEATURE(`nullclient', `wren.foobirds.org')
[root]# m4 ../m4/cf.m4 client-only.mc > client-only.cf
[root]# grep 'wren' client-only.cf
DSwren.foobirds.org
DHwren.foobirds.org
DMwren.foobirds.org
```

In this case, we don't use a DOMAIN file. Instead, we replace the entire configuration with the `client-only.mc` macro configuration file that contains only two lines. Unlike all of the other macro control files we have created in this book, `client-only.mc` does not even contain a MAILER command. The two lines in the file are a required OSTYPE command to specify that we're running Linux and the FEATURE command that creates the `nullclient` configuration. The `nullclient` feature requires an argument to identify the external server. In Listing 9.8, the remote server is identified as `wren.foobirds.org`.

When the small `client-only.mc` file is processed through m4 to produce the `client-only.cf` file, you might be surprised to find that this configuration file is no smaller than any other `sendmail.cf` file. The `nullclient` feature does not produce a radically different configuration. What it does is store the value from the argument field in the S, H, and M variables. S, H, and M direct how mail is processed in the `nullclient` configuration.

You're familiar with the M variable from the discussion of masquerading. The argument associated with the `nullclient` feature is used as the masquerade value so that all mail sent from the client is masqueraded as if it came from the external server.

The S variable holds the name of the SMART_HOST relay. The SMART_HOST is the server used for all outbound mail. The H variable holds the name of the MAIL_HUB server that collects all inbound mail, even mail addressed from one local user to another local user. The role of the MAIL_HUB is particularly surprising because local mail is not actually handled locally: the mail is sent to the MAIL_HUB. If H is set to a value, ruleset `localaddr` (ruleset 5) sends the mail to the host identified by variable H even if the mail is addressed to a local user.

> **WARNING** The `nullclient` configuration creates the possibility of mail routing loops. If an alias or `.forward` file on the MAIL_HUB forwards mail back to the client, the client might send the mail right back to the MAIL_HUB, kicking off a mail loop. Don't forward mail from a MAIL_HUB to its clients. It is safest for the clients to download mail using a separate tool, such as IMAP.

The `nullclient` feature is a simple way to create a client-only Sendmail configuration. But like many simple solutions, it lacks flexibility. With `nullclient`, SMART_HOST and MAIL_HUB are set to the same value. That might not be what you want. You may not even want to use both a SMART_HOST and a MAIL_HUB. Two `define` commands can be used to build the client configuration the way you want it.

**`define(SMART_HOST, mailer:server)`**   The SMART_HOST option allows you to identify the external server that should be used for outbound mail from the client. The optional *mailer* value can be used to specify the mailer used to relay mail to the external server. Sensibly enough, the `relay` mailer is used to relay mail to the external server if no *mailer* value is provided with the SMART_HOST option. The value provided to the SMART_HOST option is stored in variable S exactly as it is entered—i.e., *mailer:server* or just *server*.

**`define(MAIL_HUB, mailer:server)`**   The MAIL_HUB option identifies the external server that the client uses for inbound mail. Again, an optional *mailer* can be specified, and if it isn't, the `relay` mailer is used to relay the mail to the server. The value specified for MAIL_HUB is written to variable H exactly as entered.

---

**NOTE**   In addition to added flexibility, an advantage of using SMART_HOST and MAIL_HUB as opposed to `nullclient` is that you can select the mailer you want to use. If you use the *mailer:server* format with `nullclient`, the *mailer:server* value is written to S, H, and M, creating an invalid masquerade value.

---

When MAIL_HUB is used, mail for all local users is sent to the MAIL_HUB. This might not be what you want. For example, you might not want to send mail addressed to root to the MAIL_HUB for delivery. Use the LOCAL_USER macro to identify local users whose mail should be delivered locally even when a MAIL_HUB is defined. As an example, the following command prevents mail addressed to root from being sent to the MAIL_HUB for delivery:

    LOCAL_USER(root)

The LOCAL_USER macro adds values to class L. There is no macro that loads class L from a file. If you want to load class L from a file, you must use a `sendmail.cf` F command to do so. Assume that you have a file named `/etc/mail/local-user` that contains a list of users whose mail should not be sent to the MAIL_HUB. You could add the following to your macro configuration to load the file into class L:

    LOCAL_CONFIG

    FL/etc/mail/local-users

Conversely, there may be users whose mail should be sent to the MAIL_HUB even though those users are not really local users. The idea of "apparently local" users requires some explanation. When Sendmail is asked to deliver mail to an address that contains a user part but no host part, it assumes the address is the name of a local user. It verifies this through the aliasing process by checking whether or not the name is a local login name or a valid alias. If it is not either one of these things, the name is not considered local and is rejected. The name appeared to be local but it wasn't—it was an apparently local name. It is possible to configure Sendmail to send mail addressed to apparently local users to a relay server. Use the LUSER_RELAY macro to define the server if you want to do this. The following command would forward all apparently local users to the server wren.foobirds.org for processing:

```
LUSER_RELAY(wren.foobirds.org)
```

An LUSER_RELAY is most useful in an organization where every user has a unique username. When that is the case, mail can be addressed to the unique username of any user in the entire organization without adding the host part of the address. The Sendmail client detects that the address is apparently local, and sends the mail to the LUSER_RELAY. The relay server must then know how to deliver the mail to the correct user.

One other macro that you will occasionally see discussed for local mail relay is the LOCAL_RELAY macro. You should ignore it. This is a deprecated macro that has been superseded by the MAIL_HUB macro. LOCAL_RELAY should not be used in your configuration.

Finally, there are special relay servers for non-SMTP mail. These are:

**define(UUCP_RELAY, *mailer:server*)** The *server* is the name of the system that handles UUCP mail for all UUCP sites that are not directly connected to the local host. The *mailer* defaults to relay. It is very common to send UUCP mail from the client to the server using SMTP, which is the protocol used by the relay mailer. The server then forwards the mail on through UUCP. The argument provided to the UUCP_RELAY option is stored in the sendmail.cf variable Y.

**define(FAX_RELAY, *mailer:server*)** The FAX_RELAY option identifies the server used to deliver mail addressed to the pseudo-domain .FAX, which is obviously an external fax server. With this option set, users can address mail to a fax machine by using the syntax expected by the external fax server and the .FAX domain. *server* is the name of the external fax server and *mailer* is the mailer used to reach that server. *mailer* defaults to relay. The argument of the FAX_RELAY option is stored in the sendmail.cf variable F.

**define(DECNET_RELAY, *mailer:server*)** The DECNET_RELAY option identifies the mail gateway to a DECNET network. DECNET is an outdated network that was used by Digital Equipment corporation mini-computers. The argument of the DECNET_RELAY option is stored in the sendmail.cf variable C.

define(BITNET_RELAY, *mailer:server*)    The BITNET_RELAY option identifies a mail gateway to the BITNET network. BITNET is an outdated network that connected IBM mainframes in the days before IBM provided TCP/IP software. The argument of the BITNET_RELAY option is stored in the sendmail.cf variable B.

The three options LOCAL_RELAY, DECNET_RELAY, and BITNET_RELAY are never used because the commands or the networks they apply to are outdated. The UUCP_RELAY and the FAX_RELAY options are rarely used, because it is difficult to find anyone today who has only a fax machine or a UUCP connection and cannot receive SMTP mail from the Internet. The LUSER_RELAY is rarely used. There is little demand for it because users expect to add the @*host* part to e-mail addresses, and thus do not demand anything else. The configuration of a relay client comes down to just the SMART_HOST and MAIL_HUB options. Despite all of the possible options, client-side relay configuration is fairly simple. At most, one value is set for an outbound server and one is set for an inbound server.

The server side of relaying is much more complex than the client side. The client simply points to the server that will handle the mail. The server must decide if it wants to handle the mail and how to deliver the mail once it accepts it. Configuring a system as a relay server has become an issue of security and spam control. We will cover the server side of relaying in Chapter 11.

# In Sum

This chapter concludes Part 3, "Advanced Configuration," with a look at some of the special m4 configurations that can be used to customize Sendmail for your environment. Most of the configurations we looked at in this chapter fit well as part of the DOMAIN file because they relate to something that is special about your domain or your network.

We started by taking a look at address masquerading, which is the Sendmail feature that rewrites the host part of the sender address to a standard value for all outbound mail. Masquerading is simple to enable with the MASQUERADE_AS macro, but then there are eight different masquerading options available for your configuration. As you have seen before, Sendmail takes a simple idea and makes it complex by providing an array of choices. Don't get me wrong. Choice is great. It is what makes Sendmail so powerful and flexible, but it does add complexity. Attack the complexity by starting with the simple MASQUERADE_AS configuration. Run a series of tests to see if it gives you what you need. Then, using this book as a reference, add the features you think you want, testing as you go, until you get what you really need.

Masquerading the username portion of an e-mail address is generally related to host address masquerading. There are a couple of different ways this can be done, but the genericstable is a good choice. The genericstable also has a range of configuration options, but selecting the correct options is easy once the masquerade configuration has been finalized. You want to masquerade the user portion of the address when you masquerade the host portion. Once you have created the masquerading configuration, simply replicate that configuration for the genericstable.

Masquerading and databases are one way to rewrite addresses, but they are not the only way. Addresses can also be directly rewritten using custom rewrite rules. m4 provides several macros for inserting rewrite rules and their supporting configuration variables into the sendmail.cf file. There is no way to really reduce the complexity of rewrite rules. Do not attempt to write your own rules unless you understand what you are doing.

In addition to the various techniques for rewriting addresses, which usually apply to servers that are handling their own mail, we looked at the m4 configuration options that are used to create a mail relay client. m4 provides ten different relay options. Of these, only two are commonly used. SMART_HOST identifies the server that handles the client's outbound mail, and MAIL_HUB identifies the server that handles the client's inbound mail. Understand this, and you have mastered 99 percent of relay client configuration.

In this section, we have examined the inner workings of the sendmail.cf file, the details of rewrite rule syntax, and special m4 options that rewrite addresses and create relay clients. To help us understand these complex topics and to help us select the correct options, we tested the configurations and observed the effects of the configuration commands. In the next chapter, we will look in detail at the Sendmail test features to better understand what we have been doing during these tests and to better understand how to apply these test tools to other problems. Chapter 10, "Testing Sendmail," opens Part 4, "Maintaining a Healthy Server," which covers the ongoing tasks of troubleshooting, spam control, and security.

# Part 4

## Maintaining a Healthy Server

**Featuring:**

- Verifying e-mail addresses
- Maintaining and displaying persistent host status
- Displaying and processing the mail queue
- Using address test mode
- The need for an acceptable use policy
- The importance of the `identd` daemon
- Configuring a Sendmail server to properly relay mail
- Blocking spam with Sendmail and with the user's mailer
- Basic Linux server security
- Sendmail configuration security
- Sendmail authentication using the AUTH parameter
- The role of transport layer security for Sendmail

# 10

# Testing Sendmail

**S**endmail is complex; there is no avoiding the truth. Even the developers of Sendmail understand that it is complex and they have provided excellent built-in test features to help you master the complexity. We have used these features throughout this book to observe Sendmail in action. Unlike most testing tools, the Sendmail tools are not just used to fix things when they go wrong. More importantly, they are used to get things right from the start. We saw this in Chapter 9, "Special m4 Configurations," when we used Sendmail testing to select the correct masquerade options for a configuration. The ability to observe the impact that configuration changes have on Sendmail before the new configuration is fielded is of paramount importance for a system that has such a complex configuration. There is no need to guess whether or not the new configuration will work. Test it and you'll know.

In this chapter, you'll learn all the Sendmail testing tricks of the trade. The command-line options, test-mode commands, and debug options used earlier are clearly explained, along with several other test features that might be new to you. Let's start by looking at some interesting command-line options.

## Simple Command-Line Options

The sendmail command has many command-line options. Appendix B, "The sendmail Command," lists them all. Some of these options display useful information about Sendmail, others run the sendmail command in a special test mode. One of these options, which we have seen before, is –bv.

## Using the *-bv* Option

The -bv option processes a delivery address through Sendmail to determine whether or not the address is deliverable. If it is deliverable, the mail delivery triple for the address is displayed. If it is not deliverable, the specific problem with the address is printed as an error message. Listing 10.1 shows a few different -bv tests.

**Listing 10.1**   The -bv Option in Action

```
[root]# sendmail -bv sara@hawk.foobirds.org
sara@hawk.foobirds.org... deliverable: mailer esmtp,
    host hawk.foobirds.org., user sara@hawk.foobirds.org
[root]# sendmail -bv craig
craig... deliverable: mailer local, user craig
[root]# sendmail -bv joe
joe... User unknown
[root]# sendmail -bv MAILER-DAEMON
craig... deliverable: mailer local, user craig
[root]# sendmail -bv -Cclient-only.cf craig
craig... deliverable: mailer relay, host wren.foobirds.org,
    user craig@wren.foobirds.org
[root]# sendmail -bv -Cclient-only.cf joe
joe... deliverable: mailer relay, host wren.foobirds.org,
    user joe@wren.foobirds.org
```

The first example in Listing 10.1 shows -bv being used to process the external address sara@hawk.foobirds.org. Sendmail responds by echoing back the address and displaying the mailer/host/user delivery triple that will be used to deliver mail to that address. External addresses are not really verified, beyond determining that they are in the correct format. The primary thing of interest when processing a remote address with -bv is to find out what mailer is being used to deliver the mail. Knowing the mailer can be useful information for later debugging, as you'll see when we cover the -bt option. The mailer should be the mailer you expect based on your configuration.

The next three examples all process local addresses. For a couple of reasons, the output that -bv produces for local addresses is more interesting than the output for remote addresses. First, Sendmail can really verify local addresses. The successful test of sara@hawk.foobirds.org does not mean that there really is a sara account on hawk. It just means that the local system will send the mail to hawk for delivery using the esmtp mailer. But the test of craig literally means that the local system has an account named craig to which it will deliver mail. Likewise, the error message returned for the test of joe tells us that there is no joe account or alias on the local system.

One of the most useful things that the -bv option does is process the input address through the aliases database. The test of MAILER-DAEMON shows this. On this sample system MAILER-DAEMON is aliased to postmaster, which in turn is aliased to root. root is then aliased to craig. The address echoed back for the MAILER-DAEMON test is craig—the address after all aliasing has been performed.

The last two tests are interesting because they show how -bv can be used to test a new configuration. In this example, the client-only.cf configuration file created in Chapter 9 using the nullclient feature is tested. The nullclient feature sends local mail to the MAIL_HUB server. The second test of craig and joe clearly shows this. In the first test, with the default configuration, those addresses were delivered on the local host by the local mailer. In the last two tests, those addresses are sent via the relay mailer to wren .foobirds.org, which in this example is the MAIL_HUB server. The -bv test is a simple and useful tool for testing a relay client configuration.

The -C option is used in the last two -bv tests to test a new configuration. If -C is not used, Sendmail uses the default sendmail.cf file. On Linux systems, the default sendmail.cf is found in either /etc or /etc/mail, depending on your configuration. Use -C to test a new configuration file before you make it your default sendmail.cf configuration.

Another command-line option that, like -bv, was used earlier in this book is -v. The -v option runs the sendmail command in verbose mode.

## Running in Verbose Mode

Verbose mode was used in Chapter 1, "Internet Mail Protocols," to display the SMTP protocol interactions between two systems exchanging e-mail. In Chapter 1, we ran the sendmail command with the -v option for verbose output and the -t option so that we could type in the mail message from the terminal. It is not necessary to send a real message when all you want to do is observe the protocol interactions. For that, an empty message works as well as a real message. Listing 10.2 shows the output of the sendmail command when it is run in verbose mode with an empty message.

**Listing 10.2**   Using Sendmail Verbose Mode

```
[root]# sendmail -v craig@wren.foobirds.org < /dev/null
craig@wren.foobirds.org... Connecting to wren.foobirds.org.
    via esmtp...
220 wren.foobirds.org ESMTP Sendmail 8.11.0/8.11.0; Tue,
    31 Oct 2000 15:49:19 -0500
>>> EHLO ibis.foobirds.org
250-wren.foobirds.org Hello root@almond.nuts.com [172.16.12.1],
    pleased to meet you
```

```
250-ENHANCEDSTATUSCODES
250-EXPN
250-VERB
250-8BITMIME
250-SIZE
250-DSN
250-ONEX
250-ETRN
250-XUSR
250-AUTH DIGEST-MD5
250 HELP
>>> MAIL From:<root@ibis.foobirds.org>
250 2.1.0 <root@ibis.foobirds.org>... Sender ok
>>> RCPT To:<craig@wren.foobirds.org>
250 2.1.5 <craig@wren.foobirds.org>... Recipient ok
>>> DATA
354 Enter mail, end with "." on a line by itself
>>> .
250 2.0.0 e9VKnJp00881 Message accepted for delivery
craig@wren.foobirds.org... Sent (e9VKnJp00881
   Message accepted for delivery)
Closing connection to wren.foobirds.org.
>>> QUIT
221 2.0.0 wren.foobirds.org closing connection
```

Unlike in Chapter 1, this time the sendmail command is not run with the -t option.
Instead, the address of the remote recipient is typed in on the command line, and the contents of a file are provided to Sendmail to be used as the mail message. The recipient is
craig@wren.foobirds.org and the file is the null device, /dev/null. Clearly, the null
device will not provide any real content, so we are in fact sending an empty message. The
sole purpose of this test is to observe the protocol interactions.

---

***TIP***  Don't send empty messages to other users just to test e-mail. To test your
system, get a free e-mail account explicitly for this purpose and send the tests to
yourself at that account. To test a specific remote system, make arrangements
with the administrator of that system before you start sending test mail.

---

Listing 10.2, of course, begs the question "Why do you want to look at the protocol interactions?" SMTP has been around for a very long time. It is a simple protocol. Everybody
does it correctly. You're not looking for errors in the SMTP protocol. What you're really

looking for in a test like this is an unexpected result, either from changes to your own configuration or from problems at the remote end. You want to make sure that:

- The remote end answers.
- The remote server supports the extended SMTP protocol features that your system needs.
- Your system sends the remote server a valid address, and the remote server accepts it.
- The delivery address your system sends is a valid address for the remote system.

Sendmail is run in verbose mode primarily when you have a problem and you are trying to gather clues to help you analyze the problem. But the -v option is not just used to run Sendmail in verbose mode. It is also used to increase the level of detail displayed when the sendmail command is run with one of the command line options that request information—not mail delivery. One of these options is -bh, which is also known as the hoststat command.

## The *hoststat* Command

The -bh command-line option asks Sendmail to display the host status. On most systems the host status request produces no response, because the default Sendmail configuration does not maintain persistent host status. Normally, Sendmail internally tracks the status of its outbound network connections only for as long as needed. Before the -bh option can be used to any effect, the configuration must be changed so that Sendmail will write a permanent log of these connections that can be used to create a host status report.

Define confHOST_STATUS_DIRECTORY in your m4 configuration to enable persistent host status logging and to identify the directory where the status will be stored. The argument provided to confHOST_STATUS_DIRECTORY is the pathname of the directory where the status is logged. Listing 10.3 shows a configuration that will log host status in /var/state/sendmail.

**Listing 10.3**    Using the Host Status Directory

```
[root]# diff sendmail.mc host-status.mc
23a24
> define(`confHOST_STATUS_DIRECTORY', `/var/state/sendmail')dnl
[root]# m4 host-status.mc > host-status.cf
[root]# diff /etc/sendmail.cf host-status.cf
228c228
< #O HostStatusDirectory=.hoststat
---
```

```
> O HostStatusDirectory=/var/state/sendmail
[root]# mkdir /var/state/sendmail
[root]# cp /etc/sendmail.cf /etc/sendmail.cf.bak
[root]# cp host-status.cf /etc/sendmail.cf
cp: overwrite `/etc/sendmail.cf'? y
[root]# ../rc.d/init.d/sendmail restart
Shutting down sendmail:                                    [  OK  ]
Starting sendmail:                                         [  OK  ]
```

Listing 10.3 opens with a diff command that shows that the only difference between the sendmail.mc macro configuration file used to build sendmail.cf and the new host-status.mc file is a single define command. The command defines confHOST_STATUS_DIRECTORY and gives it the value /var/state/sendmail. The new macro configuration file is processed through m4 to create host-status.cf. A diff comparing that file to the current sendmail.cf file shows that the only difference is a single option (O) command. The option command sets the HostStatusDirectory option to /var/state/sendmail. Setting this option is the only effect that confHOST_STATUS_DIRECTORY has on the Sendmail configuration.

Notice that in the original sendmail.cf file the HostStatusDirectory option is commented out; notice also that it has a default value that would be used if the # was removed from the beginning of the line. The default path is .hoststat, which is a relative path. If a relative path is used, the host status directory is a subdirectory in the mail queue directory. The mail queue directory is defined in the m4 configuration with QUEUE_DIR and set in the sendmail.cf file as the QueueDirectory option. On our sample Linux system, it is /var/spool/mqueue. For our configuration, we decide not to use a relative path. Instead we put the host status log in /var/state/sendmail.

Before the directory can be used to log status, it must be created, which we do in Listing 10.3 with a mkdir command. We then move the new configuration to /etc/sendmail.cf, which is where this Red Hat system looks for the Sendmail configuration, and then we restart Sendmail. Now Sendmail is logging the host connection status. A few minutes later, running the sendmail command with the -bh and -v options produces the output shown in Listing 10.4.

**Listing 10.4**  A Sample Host Status Report

```
[root]# sendmail -bh -v
---- Hostname ----- How long ago -----------Results---------
ibis.foobirds.org   00:02:30        250 2.0.0 eA1BCqE01031
                                    Message accepted for delivery
goat.mammals.org    00:01:50        Deferred: Network is unreachable
```

> **NOTE** The -bh command-line option can be invoked with the hoststat command. Like the -bd option covered in Chapter 3 ("Running Sendmail") that can be run using the smtpd command, and the -bi option covered in Chapter 6 ("Using Sendmail Databases") that could be invoked with the command newaliases, the -bh option has a synonym. In this chapter, we will also see that -bH can be invoked with the purgestat command and -bp can be invoked with the mailq command. The command in Listing 10.4 could have been written hoststat -v.

Listing 10.4 was reformatted slightly to better fit a book page, but basically it is the type of host status report that would be seen soon after host status logging was enabled. Inbound connections are not logged. The log shows two outbound connections. Each log entry has three fields:

**Hostname**   The first field provides the complete domain name of the remote host.

**How long ago**   The second field indicates how long ago the status was updated. The format of this field is *dd+hh:mm:ss*, where *dd* is days, *hh* is hours, *mm* is minutes, and *ss* is seconds. Both of these entries were made in the last few minutes because this report was printed out shortly after host status logging was enabled. However, this is a *persistent* status report. Over time, these status entries will grow older, unless the status of one of the remote hosts changes. For example, the network connection to goat could be restored.

**Results**   The third field displays the result of the last attempt to deliver mail to the host identified by the hostname field. Unless the -v option is used with -bh, the results field may be truncated.

The first entry in Listing 10.4 shows that a successful delivery to ibis.foobirds.org took place two and a half minutes ago. That entry's results field contains the full response received from the remote system, including SMTP response code, DSN code, message ID, and text. Results fields are not always so complete; a successful connection might just generate a result of OK.

The second example shows an attempt to deliver mail to goat.mammals.org just under two minutes ago. The locally generated results field says the network that goat is connected to is unreachable. Further, it says that the mail was deferred, which means the message has been placed in the mail queue. The system will try to deliver the deferred mail during the next queue process. When it does, it will update the host status for goat.mammals.org.

The status entries in the host status directory are persistent. They will be automatically updated over time, but they will not be removed. This means that the directory can grow very large, and that the information in the directory can be very old. Use the -bH command-line option to periodically clean out the status directory. A periodic `cron` job that runs `hoststat` to print out the report and then cleans out the host status directory with a `purgestat` command is not a bad idea. The `purgestat` command is a synonym for `sendmail -bH`.

As the second host status entry in Listing 10.4 showed, mail that cannot be delivered is often deferred. When `hoststat` says that mail is deferred, it means that the mail has been added to the mail queue. Use the `sendmail` command's -bp option to examine the contents of the mail queue. The -bp option is our next topic.

## The *mailq* Command

The -bp option, which is also known as the `mailq` command, displays the contents of the mail queue. If no mail is queued, it simply prints out the pathname of the queue directory and declares it empty, as shown below:

```
[root]# mailq
/var/spool/mqueue is empty
```

An empty queue is a good thing. Everything is running smoothly and all of the mail sent by your users has been delivered. But things do not always run smoothly. As we saw in Listing 10.4, a remote host might be down or unreachable and the mail must be queued for later delivery. Listing 10.5 shows a `mailq` run that reports a piece of mail in the queue.

**Listing 10.5**  A Sample `mailq` Report

```
[root]# mailq
                /var/spool/mqueue (1 request)
----Q-ID---- --Size-- -----Q-Time----- -----Sender/Recipient--------
eA1Cej500742  1190   Wed Nov  1 07:40  craig
                (Deferred: goat.mammals.org.: Network is unreachable)
                        sara@goat.mammals.org
```

The first line of output from the `mailq` command prints the pathname of the queue and the number of items found in the queue. In this case, one item is found in the queue, therefore `mailq` displays the message "1 request." This is followed by a header line that defines the four fields found in a standard `mailq` report:

**Q-ID**    The first field is the unique queue identifier assigned to this piece of mail. The identifier is composed of a character string followed by the process ID (PID) of the process that originally attempted to deliver this mail. In Listing 10.5, the string eA1Cej5 is combined with the PID 00742 to create a unique identifier.

Optionally, a single character that indicates a special status for this piece of mail can follow the queue identifier. There are three possible single character values:

\*    indicates that the queue file containing the mail message is locked by a valid file-locking mechanism.

–    indicates that the `MinQueueAge` option has been set in the Sendmail configuration, and that this piece of mail has not been queued long enough to meet the `MinQueueAge` requirement. The `MinQueueAge` option sets the minimum amount of time a message must remain in the queue. It tells Sendmail not to deliver messages that fall below this minimum when Sendmail processes the queue. By default, this option is commented out of the `sendmail.cf` file and Sendmail delivers all of the messages from the queue that it can.

**X**    indicates that the load average of the server is currently too high to deliver this piece of mail.

**Size**    The second field contains the size of the mail message in bytes. In Listing 10.5, the message is 1190 bytes long.

**Q-Time**    The third field contains the date and the time that the message first entered the queue, displayed in a simple, straightforward manner.

**Sender/Recipient**    At a minimum, the fourth field contains the address of the sender and the address of the recipient of this piece of mail. Usually, this field has more information than just the addresses. The field begins with the sender address. In Listing 10.5, the sender address is `craig`. This is followed by the MIME message body type, if the message contains special MIME data. In Listing 10.5, no message body type is listed, so it is a traditional text message in an RFC 822 message format. After the message body type is listed, `mailq` displays the error message associated with the last delivery attempt enclosed in parentheses, if the queue file has kept a copy of the error message. In Listing 10.5, the error message is `Deferred: goat.mammals.org.: Network is unreachable`. Finally, the fourth field ends with the recipient address, which in Listing 10.5 is `sara@goat.mammals.org`.

The amount of information displayed by `mailq` is increased slightly if the `-v` option is added to the command line. When `mailq` is run in verbose mode, it adds a Priority field between the Size and Q-Time fields. The Priority field lists the queue priority of the message as calculated by Sendmail. The numeric priority value may end with an optional +. The + indicates that a warning message about the delivery failure has been sent to the originator of the message. Listing 10.6 shows verbose `mailq` output.

**Listing 10.6** Running `mailq` in Verbose Mode

```
[root]# mailq -v
                /var/spool/mqueue (4 requests)
----Q-ID---- --Size-- -Priority- ---Q-Time--- ---Sender/Recipient---
eA1FNdp00879    10    480000+   Nov  1 10:23 jill
            (Warning: could not send message for past 4 hours)
                                        craig@ani.foobirds.org
eA1FDvQ00821   108    570026+   Nov  1 10:13 kathy
            (Deferred: goat.mammals.org.: Network is unreachable)
                                        jay@goat.mammals.org
eA1EC3P00796   112    660032+   Nov  1 09:12 kathy
            (Deferred: goat.mammals.org.: Network is unreachable)
                                        jay@goat.mammals.org
eA1Cej500742   190    750033+   Nov  1 07:40 craig
            (Deferred: goat.mammals.org.: Network is unreachable)
                                        sara@goat.mammals.org
```

Beyond knowing that the users who sent these messages have received warning messages, the verbose output adds little of interest for a system administrator. The numeric priority that Sendmail has assigned to each message is essentially meaningless. Sendmail has calculated the value correctly, and if it hadn't you wouldn't know. Furthermore, you have no reason to fiddle with these priorities. If you want to move something out of the queue, you don't do it by messing with the priorities; you do it by manually running a queue process and selecting the message to be delivered.

### Manually Running the Queue

As we saw in Chapter 3, the queue is normally processed periodically, and the interval between queue process runs is configured as part of the basic Sendmail start-up, using the -q command line option. In Chapter 3, we saw configurations with -q set to 1h and 15m for a 1-hour queue run interval or a 15-minute queue run interval, respectively. Setting a queue interval at boot time and letting Sendmail handle it automatically is how it is normally done. But using the information you learn about the queue from the `mailq` command, you can manually, and selectively, process the queue if necessary.

Manually processing the queue is as simple as entering the command `sendmail -q`. This causes Sendmail to immediately process everything in the queue. To watch the progress of the queue process, add -v to the `sendmail` command line. Of course, you may not want to process everything in the queue. Using the information gained from the `mailq` report, you can select individual messages or groups of messages using the queue ID, the sender address, or the recipient address as arguments to the -q option on the `sendmail` command line. Listing 10.7 is an example of using `mailq` to validate arguments for the `sendmail` command, and then using the `sendmail` command with those arguments to actually process the queue.

**Listing 10.7**    Selectively Processing the Mail Queue

```
[root]# mailq -qScraig -qR@goat.mammals.org
                /var/spool/mqueue (1 request)
----Q-ID---- --Size-- -----Q-Time----- ------Sender/Recipient------
eA1Cej500742   1190   Wed Nov  1 07:40   craig
              (Deferred: goat.mammals.org.: Network is unreachable)
                            sara@goat.mammals.org
[root]# sendmail -v -qScraig -qR@goat.mammals.org
Running /var/spool/mqueue/eA1Cej500742 (sequence 1 of 1)
sara@goat.mammals.org... Connecting to goat.mammals.org. via esmtp...
220 goat.mammals.org ESMTP Sendmail 8.11.0/8.11.0; Sat, 4 Nov 2000
   12:49:56 -05
00
>>> EHLO wren.foobirds.org
250-goat.mammals.org Hello wren [172.16.12.3], pleased to meet you
... Several lines deleted ...
>>> MAIL From:<craig@wren.foobirds.org> SIZE=31
250 2.1.0 <craig@wren.foobirds.org>... Sender ok
>>> RCPT To:<sara@goat.mammals.org>
250 2.1.5 <sara@goat.mammals.org>... Recipient ok
>>> DATA
354 Enter mail, end with "." on a line by itself
>>> .
250 2.0.0 eA4Hnu301239 Message accepted for delivery
sara@goat.mammals.org... Sent (eA4Hnu301239
    Message accepted for delivery)
Closing connection to goat.mammals.org.
>>> QUIT
221 2.0.0 goat.mammals.org closing connection
```

The `mailq` command that starts Listing 10.7 has two command-line arguments: `-qScraig` and `-qR@goat.mammals.org`. These arguments select all queued mail that is from the sender address `craig` (`-qScraig`) and addressed to anyone on the host (`-qR@goat.mammals.org`). In this example, a partial recipient address is specified. A full address or any part of the address can be used to match sender or recipient addresses. If the messages displayed by the `mailq` command are the messages that you want to process through Sendmail, use the same `-q` arguments on the `sendmail` command as you used on the mailq command. In Listing 10.7, that is just what we did. Using verbose mode shows the mail being successfully delivered.

In addition to the -qSsender and -qRrecipient formats used in Listing 10.7, messages can be selected by queue ID using the -qIqid argument format. For example, sendmail -qIeA1FNdp00879 would process the first message from the queue shown in Listing 10.6. Use selective queue processing to move items out of the queue quickly after you fix the problem that caused the mail to be queued.

# Running Sendmail in Test Mode

The Sendmail option that has been used most extensively throughout this book is the -bt option, which is the option that puts Sendmail into address test mode. When Sendmail is in test mode, you can examine the content of sendmail.cf variables and classes, list the rules in rulesets, and examine the flow of addresses through the rewrite rules. The -bt option is the single most important tool you have for refining and debugging your Sendmail configuration.

In this book, you have seen many examples of running the sendmail command with the -bt option. But the emphasis in those examples was on the results of the tests; you haven't gotten much of an explanation of the magic commands used to create those tests. In this section, we take a close look at each command, its syntax, and its purpose.

When sendmail -bt is run, you see the following:

```
[rootl]# sendmail -bt
ADDRESS TEST MODE (ruleset 3 NOT automatically invoked)
Enter <ruleset> <address>
>
```

The first line displayed by Sendmail says that we have entered address test mode and that ruleset 3 is not automatically run. Ruleset 3 is the canonify ruleset. All addresses processed by Sendmail during a normal run are first processed through canonify and then through other rulesets depending on the address type. (If you're not sure what I'm talking about, you may want to refer to the ruleset material in Chapter 8, "Understanding Rewrite Rules.") At one time, address test mode processed every address through ruleset 3 whether you wanted it to or not. Now it doesn't, but it prints out this message to let old-timers know that addresses are processed through ruleset 3 only if you specifically request a test that sends the address through ruleset 3. The second line displayed tells you to enter a ruleset and an address at the > prompt. A ruleset followed by an address is one type of test that can be entered at the > prompt, but there are many others. Table 10.1 lists the commands that you can enter at the address test mode prompt.

**Table 10.1**    Address Test Mode Commands

| Command | Usage |
| --- | --- |
| *rulesets address* | Process the address through the comma-separated list of rulesets. |
| =S*ruleset* | Display the contents of the ruleset. |
| =M | Display all of the mailer definitions. |
| $*v* | Display the value of variable *v*. |
| $=*c* | Display the values in class *c*. |
| .D*vvalue* | Set the variable *v* to *value*. |
| .C*cvalue* | Add *value* to class *c*. |
| -d*value* | Set the debug level to *value*. |
| /tryflags *flags* | Set the flags used for address processing by /parse and /try. |
| /try *mailer address* | Process the *address* for the *mailer*. |
| /parse *address* | Return the mailer/host/user delivery triple for the *address*. |
| /canon *hostname* | Canonify *hostname*. |
| /mx *hostname* | Look up the MX records for *hostname*. |
| /map *mapname key* | Look up *key* in the database identified by *mapname*. |
| /quit | Exit address test mode. |

The first entry in Table 10.1 represents the traditional syntax of entering a list of rulesets and the address to be processed by those rulesets. Thus, entering canonify craig would process the address craig through the ruleset canonify and entering canonify,parse kathy@grebe.foobirds.org would process the address through canonify and parse. Listing 10.8 shows an example of using canonify and parse to process an address.

**Listing 10.8** Processing an Address through a Ruleset

```
[root]# sendmail -bt
ADDRESS TEST MODE (ruleset 3 NOT automatically invoked)
Enter <ruleset> <address>
> 3,parse al@bird.org
canonify          input: al @ bird . org
Canonify2         input: al < @ bird . org >
Canonify2       returns: al < @ bird . org . >
canonify        returns: al < @ bird . org . >
parse             input: al < @ bird . org . >
Parse0            input: al < @ bird . org . >
Parse0          returns: al < @ bird . org . >
ParseLocal        input: al < @ bird . org . >
ParseLocal      returns: al < @ bird . org . >
Parse1            input: al < @ bird . org . >
Mailertable       input: < bird . org > al < @ bird . org . >
Mailertable       input: bird . < org > al < @ bird . org . >
Mailertable     returns: al < @ bird . org . >
Mailertable     returns: al < @ bird . org . >
MailerToTriple    input: < > al < @ bird . org . >
MailerToTriple  returns: al < @ bird . org . >
Parse1          returns: $# esmtp $@ bird . org .
                         $: al < @ bird . org . >
parse           returns: $# esmtp $@ bird . org .
                         $: al < @ bird . org . >
> /quit
```

Listing 10.8 processes the address al@bird.org through ruleset 3, the canonify ruleset, and ruleset parse. This example shows that a ruleset can be identified by its name or its number, if it has a number. All of the other rulesets, Canonify2, Parse1, etc., that are shown in the example are called from either ruleset 3 or ruleset parse. (To find out more about what these individual rulesets do, see the description of the rulesets in Chapter 8.)

This type of test is generally used to observe the impact of a single ruleset on an address. A realistic example would be to process various local addresses through ruleset localaddr (ruleset 5) to observe the effect that defining MAIL_HUB has on the configuration. Multi-step tests that mimic basic Sendmail processing can often be more easily accomplished with some other test command.

## Testing with the */parse* Command

The /parse command canonifies and parses an address, creating the mail delivery triple. It then prepares the address for delivery based on the mailer selected for the mail delivery triple. Listing 10.9 shows the /parse command in action.

**Listing 10.9**  Processing an Address with the /parse Command

```
[root]# sendmail -bt
ADDRESS TEST MODE (ruleset 3 NOT automatically invoked)
Enter <ruleset> <address>
> /parse al@bird.org
Cracked address = $g
Parsing envelope recipient address
canonify       input: al @ bird . org
Canonify2      input: al < @ bird . org >
Canonify2      returns: al < @ bird . org . >
canonify       returns: al < @ bird . org . >
parse          input: al < @ bird . org . >
Parse0         input: al < @ bird . org . >
Parse0         returns: al < @ bird . org . >
ParseLocal     input: al < @ bird . org . >
ParseLocal     returns: al < @ bird . org . >
Parse1         input: al < @ bird . org . >
Mailertable    input: < bird . org > al < @ bird . org . >
Mailertable    input: bird . < org > al < @ bird . org . >
Mailertable    returns: al < @ bird . org . >
Mailertable    returns: al < @ bird . org . >
MailerToTriple input: < > al < @ bird . org . >
MailerToTriple returns: al < @ bird . org . >
Parse1         returns: $# esmtp $@ bird . org .
                        $: al < @ bird . org . >
parse          returns: $# esmtp $@ bird . org .
                        $: al < @ bird . org . >
2              input: al < @ bird . org . >
2              returns: al < @ bird . org . >
EnvToSMTP      input: al < @ bird . org . >
PseudoToReal   input: al < @ bird . org . >
PseudoToReal   returns: al < @ bird . org . >
MasqSMTP       input: al < @ bird . org . >
MasqSMTP       returns: al < @ bird . org . >
EnvToSMTP      returns: al < @ bird . org . >
```

```
final              input: al < @ bird . org . >
final              returns: al @ bird . org
mailer esmtp, host bird.org., user al@bird.org
> /quit
```

The /parse command starts by printing out two informational messages. The first one says that the input address is stored in the variable g for the duration of the process. The comment calls the input address the "cracked address." All that means is that any standard RFC 822 comment field that accompanied the address was removed before the addressed was stored in variable g. The second message tells us that the address is being processed as an envelope recipient address.

First the /parse command processes the address as a delivery address, passing it through ruleset 3 (canonify) and ruleset 0 (parse). Once the esmtp mailer is selected for the address, the canonical address is passed through ruleset 2, the envelope ruleset defined by the R parameter of the esmtp mailer (EnvToSMTP), and finally through ruleset 4 (final). This extensive processing is exactly the ruleset flow that was shown in Figure 8.1 in Chapter 8. The /parse command makes it possible for you to send an address through this complete process without even remembering the order in which the rulesets execute.

The last line displayed by the /parse command is the mail delivery triple that will be used for this address. If /parse believes there will be an error delivering the mail to the selected address, it will also display an error message, as shown below:

```
final              returns: al @ bird . org
al@bird.org... Transient parse error -- message queued
               for future delivery
mailer esmtp, host bird.org, user al@bird.org
```

## Processing a Specific Address Type

By default, the /parse command, and the /try command, process addresses as envelope recipient addresses. As you'll recall from Figure 8.1, different types of addresses are processed by different rulesets. Use the /tryflags command to select a different type of address processing. The /tryflags command accepts four possible values:

H   This flag requests header address processing.

E   This flag requests envelope address processing.

S   This flag requests sender address processing.

R   This flag requests recipient address processing.

The values are generally used in pairs to create the following four settings:

HS   This flag pair requests header sender address processing.

HR   This flag pair requests header recipient address processing.

ES   This flag pair requests envelope sender address processing.

ER   This flag pair requests envelope recipient address processing.

I recommend that you follow the standard practice and always set flags in pairs. There are two reasons I recommend this. First, Sendmail uses flags in pairs. If you don't explicitly set a value for one of the flags, Sendmail will use the value it already has for that flag. Second, flags are "sticky"—when a flag is set, it stays set until explicitly reset. This means you would have to keep track of the flag values if you have been fiddling with the flags. Thus, it is much simpler to be explicit, and set the values you want before you run the test.

The /tryflags settings affect both /parse and /try, but they don't all make sense for the /parse command. The first thing that /parse does is process the address as a delivery address. It then processes the address for the specific mailer. Only recipient addresses can be delivery addresses. Using the sender address to select the mailer that will be used doesn't make sense, because in any real situation the sender and the recipient will not be the same address. For this reason, while all /tryflags values affect /parse only ER and HR are truly useful.

## Testing with the */try* Command

The /try command, on the other hand, makes effective use of all /tryflags values. The /try command essentially performs the same processing as the second half of the /parse command. The /try command takes an address and processes it for a mailer. But unlike the /parse command that selects the mailer based on the address provided, you tell the /try command which mailer it should use. Listing 10.10 shows the /try command and the impact /tryflags has on it.

**Listing 10.10**   Using /try to Process an Address for a Mailer

```
[root]# sendmail -bt
ADDRESS TEST MODE (ruleset 3 NOT automatically invoked)
Enter <ruleset> <address>
> /tryflags HR
> /try esmtp al@bird.org
Trying header recipient address al@bird.org for mailer esmtp
canonify          input: al @ bird . org
Canonify2         input: al < @ bird . org >
Canonify2         returns: al < @ bird . org . >
```

Maintaining a
Healthy Server

PART 4

```
canonify         returns: al < @ bird . org . >
2                  input: al < @ bird . org . >
2                returns: al < @ bird . org . >
EnvToSMTP          input: al < @ bird . org . >
PseudoToReal       input: al < @ bird . org . >
PseudoToReal     returns: al < @ bird . org . >
MasqSMTP           input: al < @ bird . org . >
MasqSMTP         returns: al < @ bird . org . >
EnvToSMTP        returns: al < @ bird . org . >
final              input: al < @ bird . org . >
final            returns: al @ bird . org
Rcode = 0, addr = al@bird.org
> /tryflags HS
> /try esmtp craig
Trying header sender address craig for mailer esmtp
canonify           input: craig
Canonify2          input: craig
Canonify2        returns: craig
canonify         returns: craig
1                  input: craig
1                returns: craig
HdrFromSMTP        input: craig
PseudoToReal       input: craig
PseudoToReal     returns: craig
MasqSMTP           input: craig
MasqSMTP         returns: craig < @ *LOCAL* >
MasqHdr            input: craig < @ *LOCAL* >
MasqHdr          returns: craig < @ wren . foobirds . org . >
HdrFromSMTP      returns: craig < @ wren . foobirds . org . >
final              input: craig < @ wren . foobirds . org . >
final            returns: craig @ wren . foobirds . org
Rcode = 0, addr = craig@wren.foobirds.org
> /quit
```

In Listing 10.10, two different addresses are processed. First, we set /tryflags to HR to process the header recipient address, and use /try to process the address al@bird.org for the esmtp mailer. You'll notice that the results are very similar to those we saw in the /parse test in Listing 10.9. Next, we set the /tryflags to HS and use /try to process craig as a header sender address for the esmtp mailer. This is a realistic test that shows the processing that would happen to the sender address and the recipient address for the headers on a specific piece of mail. The sender and recipient address on a single piece of mail always go through the same mailer, because only the recipient address is used to select the mailer.

The /try command ends by displaying a return code (Rcode) and the final address after processing is complete. A return code of zero means that everything went okay. A non-zero return code means that a potential delivery problem was encountered. Running an address that produces a non-zero return code through /parse will produce an error message describing the return code, as we saw earlier.

I find that I use /try much more often than I use /parse. Most of the configurations I work with use a limited number of mailers, usually just esmtp for all external mail and local for all internal mail. I usually know what mailer will handle the mail without asking Sendmail. The /parse command is most useful when you have several different mailers. A great time to use /parse is when you have a mailertable. For a complex configuration, the /parse command tells you the mailer that Sendmail will use and then processes the recipient address for that mailer. You can then process the sender address with /try.

## Displaying and Setting Internal Values

The tests in listings 10.8, 10.9, and 10.10 all show address test mode being used to process an address through some rulesets. Address test mode can also be used to examine the contents of sendmail.cf variables and classes, to query for other types of runtime information, and even to set values to see how they affect the operation of the system, which is exactly what is done in Listing 10.11.

**Listing 10.11**    Setting and Viewing Variables and Classes

```
> $m
> /try esmtp craig@wren.foobirds.org
Trying header sender address craig@wren.foobirds.org for mailer esmtp
canonify           input: craig @ wren . foobirds . org
... Many lines deleted ...
final             returns: craig @ wren . foobirds . org
Rcode = 0, addr = craig@wren.foobirds.org
> .Dmfoobirds.org
> $m
foobirds.org
> /try esmtp craig@wren.foobirds.org
Trying header sender address craig@wren.foobirds.org for mailer esmtp
canonify           input: craig @ wren . foobirds . org
... Many lines deleted ...
```

Maintaining a Healthy Server

PART 4

```
final              returns: craig @ wren . foobirds . org
Rcode = 0, addr = craig@wren.foobirds.org
> /try esmtp sara@hawk.foobirds.org
Trying header sender address sara@hawk.foobirds.org for mailer esmtp
canonify           input: sara @ hawk . foobirds . org
... Many lines deleted ...
final              returns: sara @ hawk . foobirds . org
Rcode = 0, addr = sara@hawk.foobirds.org
> $=w
wren.foobirds.org
[172.16.12.3]
wren
localhost
[127.0.0.1]
> $=M
> .CMhawk.foobirds.org
> .CMibis.foobirds.org
> .CMowl.foobirds.org
> $=M
ibis.foobirds.org
owl.foobirds.org
hawk.foobirds.org
> /try esmtp sara@hawk.foobirds.org
Trying header sender address sara@hawk.foobirds.org for mailer esmtp
canonify           input: sara @ hawk . foobirds . org
... Many lines deleted ...
final              returns: sara @ hawk . foobirds . org
Rcode = 0, addr = sara@hawk.foobirds.org
```

Listing 10.11 is an excerpt from the middle of a long sendmail -bt run. The first line shows us querying the contents of a variable. $m asks for the values stored in the variable m. It is empty. From Chapter 9 we know that m contains the masquerade value. When it is empty, masquerading is turned off. The first /try test processes the address craig@wren.foobirds.org as a header sender address. The output of the final ruleset shows that the address is not being masqueraded. We then store the value foobirds.org in variable m using the command .Dmfoobirds.org, where .D is the command, m is the variable name, and foobirds.org is the value. A second /try test with the address craig@wren.foobirds.org returns the masqueraded address craig@foobirds.org. We changed the Sendmail configuration and observed the impact of the change in real time.

Next, we run another /try test to see if the address sara@hawk.foobirds.org is masqueraded. It isn't, because it is not defined in class w or class M. We use $=w to display all of the values in class w. wren.foobirds.org is there, so that's why it is masqueraded. But hawk.foobirds.org isn't in class w. We also check class M with the $=M command. That class is empty. We then use three .C commands to add values to class M. The first of these, .CMhawk.foobirds.org, where .C is the command, M is the class, and hawk.foobirds .org is the value, adds hawk to class M. After the three commands are entered, $=M displays three values for class M. A second /try test with the address sara@hawk.foobirds.org shows that hawk is now masqueraded.

The changes we made to the Sendmail configuration using .D and .C commands only last as long as the sendmail -bt run. Once we terminate the run, these temporary changes vanish. Setting values in address test mode allows you to observe the effect of potential configuration changes before you actually make the changes.

In Listing 10.12, we don't actually change configuration values. In this example, we ask Sendmail to display the values it obtains from external information sources.

**Listing 10.12**   Requesting Outside Information from Sendmail

```
> /mx foobirds.org
getmxrr(foobirds.org) returns 2 value(s):
        wren.foobirds.org.
        parrot.foobirds.org.
> /canon redbreast
getcanonname(redbreast) returns robin.foobirds.org
> /map generics kathy
map_lookup: generics (kathy) returns kathy.mccafferty (0)
```

Listing 10.12 is an excerpt from the middle of a sendmail -bt session. The first two commands in Listing 10.12 request information from the Domain Name System. The /mx command asks for the MX records assigned to the hostname foobirds.org. In this case, DNS returns two MX records: wren.foobirds.org and parrot.foobirds.org. The records are listed in priority sequence. Thus, wren.foobirds.org is the primary MX server for foobirds.org, and parrot.foobirds.org is the backup MX server. If the hostname provided to the /mx command does not have a true MX record in the DNS system, the value returned by the /mx command will be the hostname itself. For example, ibis does not have an MX record:

```
> /mx ibis.foobirds.org
getmxrr(ibis.foobirds.org) returns 1 value(s):
        ibis.foobirds.org.
```

The /mx command shows you the MX values that Sendmail will use to deliver mail to the specified host. In the case of foobirds.org, Sendmail will first try to deliver the mail to

wren.foobirds.org. If that system is unavailable, it will try parrot.foobirds.org. In
the case of ibis, Sendmail will deliver the mail directly to ibis.foobirds.org. The /mx
command lets you anticipate the delivery process.

The second command in Listing 10.12, /canon, asks DNS for a canonical name. In the
example, the /canon command is given the hostname redbreast, which it passes to DNS.
DNS returns the canonical name robin.foobirds.org for the hostname redbreast.

The last command in Listing 10.12 looks up a value in a database. In the example the
database is generics, which is the standard internal name for the genericstable. The
key used for the lookup is kathy. In Listing 10.12, the key kathy returns the value
kathy.mccafferty from the genericstable. Any database configured on the system can
be searched with the /map command.

The commands that query DNS or search databases were not used in any of the many
tests run earlier in this text. Generally, you are not interested in the value returned by
DNS or from the database; you're interested in the effect these values have on the
addresses that Sendmail is rewriting. About the only time you will directly query DNS or
a database is when you want to determine what values those systems are providing to
Sendmail. Because address test mode is generally used to debug or refine the Sendmail
configuration, it is more likely that you will use one of the address test mode commands
that let you examine the contents of the sendmail.cf file. Listing 10.13 shows these two
commands in action.

**Listing 10.13**   Looking at the Configuration File in Address Test Mode

```
> =M
mailer 0 (prog): P=/usr/sbin/smrsh S=EnvFromL/HdrFromL
   R=EnvToL/HdrToL M=0 U=0:0 F=9DFMeloqsu L=0 E=\n
   T=X-Unix/X-Unix/X-Unix A=smrsh -c $u
mailer 1 (*file*): P=[FILE] S=parse/parse R=parse/parse M=0 U=0:0
   F=9DEFMPloqsu L=0 E=\n T=X-Unix/X-Unix/X-Unix A=FILE $u
mailer 2 (*include*): P=/dev/null S=parse/parse R=parse/parse
   M=0 U=0:0 F=su L=0 E=\n T=<undefined>/<undefined>/<undefined>
   A=INCLUDE $u
mailer 3 (smtp): P=[IPC] S=EnvFromSMTP/HdrFromSMTP
   R=EnvToSMTP/EnvToSMTP M=0 U=0:0 F=DFMXmu L=990 E=\r\n
   T=DNS/RFC822/SMTP A=TCP $h
mailer 4 (esmtp): P=[IPC] S=EnvFromSMTP/HdrFromSMTP
   R=EnvToSMTP/EnvToSMTP M=0 U=0:0 F=DFMXamu L=990 E=\r\n
   T=DNS/RFC822/SMTP A=TCP $h
```

```
mailer 5 (smtp8): P=[IPC] S=EnvFromSMTP/HdrFromSMTP
    R=EnvToSMTP/EnvToSMTP M=0 U=0:0 F=8DFMXmu L=990 E=\r\n
    T=DNS/RFC822/SMTP A=TCP $h
mailer 6 (dsmtp): P=[IPC] S=EnvFromSMTP/HdrFromSMTP
    R=EnvToSMTP/EnvToSMTP M=0 U=0:0 F=%DFMXamu L=990 E=\r\n
    T=DNS/RFC822/SMTP A=TCP $h
mailer 7 (relay): P=[IPC] S=EnvFromSMTP/HdrFromSMTP
    R=MasqSMTP/MasqSMTP M=0 U=0:0 F=8DFMXamu L=2040 E=\r\n
    T=DNS/RFC822/SMTP A=TCP $h
mailer 8 (procmail): P=/usr/bin/procmail S=EnvFromSMTP/HdrFromSMTP
    R=EnvToSMTP/HdrFromSMTP M=0 U=0:0 F=9DFMPShnu L=0 E=\n
    T=DNS/RFC822/X-Unix A=procmail -Y -m $h $f $u
mailer 9 (local): P=/usr/bin/procmail S=EnvFromL/HdrFromL
    R=EnvToL/HdrToL M=0 U=0:0 F=/59:@ADFMPSfhlnqsw| L=0 E=\n
    T=DNS/RFC822/X-Unix A=procmail -Y -a $h -d $u
> =Sfinal
R$* < @ >                        $@
R$* < @ $+ . > $*                $1 < @ $2 > $3
R$* < @ *LOCAL* > $*             $1 < @ wren . foobirds . org > $2
R$* < $+ > $*                    $1 $2 $3
R@ $+ : @ $+ : $+                @ $1 , @ $2 : $3
R@ $*                            $@ @ $1
R$+ @ $- . UUCP                  $2 ! $1
R$+ % $=w @ $=w                  $1 @ $2
```

The =M command prints out all of the mailer definitions in the current Sendmail configuration. All of the fields displayed by =M are the fields discussed in the "Mailer Definitions" section of Chapter 7, "The sendmail.cf File." But there are a couple of interesting things displayed by the =M command that cannot be found simply by perusing the sendmail.cf file. First, you'll notice that each mailer has an identifying number as well as a name. Second, and more important, there are two mailers that do not appear in the sendmail.cf file:

*file*   The *file* mailer is an internal mailer used to send the contents of a mail message directly to a file.

*include*   The *include* mailer is an internal mailer that attaches the mail message to a :include: list.

The =S command displays all of the rewrite rules in a given ruleset. In Listing 10.13, we ask Sendmail to display the contents of the final ruleset. When a ruleset is displayed by the =S command, any variables contained in the ruleset are replaced by the values stored in the variables. In Listing 10.13, the third rule after the =S command appears to contain the literal string wren.foobirds.org. In reality the rule contains $j, so the string wren.foobirds.org must be the value stored in the variable j on our sample system. Generally, the =S command is used to examine a ruleset to see if the changes you made to the ruleset appear as you expect, or because you're trying to figure out why a ruleset does what it does.

To really examine the details of a ruleset in action, you can use a debug mode. Use the -d command to select a debug level inside of address test mode. Listing 10.14 shows a test with and without debug mode 21.12 set.

**Listing 10.14**  Using a Debug Setting during Address Test Mode

```
[root]# sendmail -bt
ADDRESS TEST MODE (ruleset 3 NOT automatically invoked)
Enter <ruleset> <address>
> final sara < @ foobirds . org . >
final                 input: sara < @ foobirds . org . >
final               returns: sara @ foobirds . org
> -d21.12
> final sara < @ foobirds . org . >
final                 input: sara < @ foobirds . org . >
-----trying rule: $* < @ >
----- rule fails
-----trying rule: $* < @ $+ . > $*
-----rule matches: $1 < @ $2 > $3
rewritten as: sara < @ foobirds . org >
-----trying rule: $* < @ $+ . > $*
----- rule fails
-----trying rule: $* < @ *LOCAL* > $*
----- rule fails
-----trying rule: $* < $+ > $*
-----rule matches: $1 $2 $3
rewritten as: sara @ foobirds . org
-----trying rule: $* < $+ > $*
----- rule fails
-----trying rule: @ $+ : @ $+ : $+
----- rule fails
-----trying rule: @ $*
----- rule fails
-----trying rule: $+ @ $- . UUCP
----- rule fails
```

```
-----trying rule: $+ % $=w @ $=w
----- rule fails
final            returns: sara @ foobirds . org
> /quit
```

In Listing 10.14, the address sara<@foobirds.org.> is run through ruleset final, producing the output address sara@foobirds.org. That is exactly what we expected, but address test mode just shows the value that went into the ruleset and the value that comes out; it does not show any of the intervening details. From the =S command in Listing 10.13, we know that the final ruleset contains eight individual rules. With the default settings, we can't see the individual rules in action. Therefore, we use the -d21.12 command to set the debug level to 21.12.

A second test is made where the address sara<@foobirds.org.> is run through ruleset final. This time the action of each rewrite rule is displayed. Sendmail displays the string trying rule: followed by the pattern field of the rule. If the address does not match the pattern, Sendmail displays the string rule fails and moves on to the next rule. If the address does match the pattern, Sendmail prints the string rule matches: followed by the template field from the rule, and then prints out the rewritten address. It keeps on in this manner until the entire ruleset has been run or a rule has been encountered that causes Sendmail to exit the ruleset. This level of detail is probably needed only when you're debugging a ruleset that you have written that does not perform as you expected.

The 21.12 debug level is useful inside address test mode because it affects the level of detail displayed during the test. However, most debug levels used with address test mode are invoked on the sendmail command line, not inside address test mode. The next section covers some useful debug levels.

# Using Debug Levels

The sendmail command accepts hundreds of different debug values. All of the debug levels that I know about are listed in Appendix B for those of you who are curious to see them. The vast majority of these debug levels are there to help the Sendmail developers debug source code. Only a few of these debug levels are actually useful for a system administrator who is testing and debugging a new configuration. We saw one of these helpful debug levels in Listing 10.14. This section covers the few other useful debug levels.

As you no doubt noticed in the discussion of Listing 10.14, a debug level is made up of two numbers separated by a dot. The first number in the pair is the category number, and the second number is the level. Listing 10.14 used category 21 and level 12, thus 21.12. Category 21 is the category of debugging that traces rewrite rules. In fact, the level of detail seen when the sendmail command is run with the -bt option is equivalent to debug level 21.1. However, from the point of view of the system administrator, the category and level numbers are insignificant. In reality, debug levels are simply arbitrary numbers, a few of which produce useful information.

A few debug levels in category 0, the category that prints information about the Sendmail version, are useful. We saw an example of debug level 0.1 in Chapter 6. Two other category 0 debug levels that I sometimes use are 0.4 and 0.10. Listing 10.15 shows the information printed by debug level 0.10.

**Listing 10.15**    The Output of Debug Level 0.10

```
[root]# sendmail -bt -d0.10
Version 8.11.0
 Compiled with: MAP_REGEX LOG MATCHGECOS MIME7TO8 MIME8TO7 NAMED_BIND
                NETINET NETUNIX NEWDB NIS QUEUE SASL SCANF SFIO
                SMTP STARTTLS USERDB
    OS Defines: HASFCHOWN HASFLOCK HASGETDTABLESIZE HASINITGROUPS
                HASLSTAT HASRANDOM HASSETREUID HASSETRLIMIT HASSETSID
                HASSETVBUF HASSNPRINTF HASURANDOMDEV HASUNAME
                HASUNSETENV HASWAITPID IDENTPROTO USE_SIGLONGJMP
 Def Conf file: /etc/sendmail.cf
  Def Pid file: /var/run/sendmail.pid
canonical name: wren.foobirds.org
        a.k.a.: wren
 UUCP nodename: wren.foobirds.org
        a.k.a.: wren
        a.k.a.: [172.16.12.3]
============ SYSTEM IDENTITY (after readcf) ============
    (short domain name) $w = wren
 (canonical domain name) $j = wren.foobirds.org
        (subdomain name) $m = foobirds.org
             (node name) $k = wren.foobirds.org
========================================================
```

Debug level 0.10 was used in Listing 10.15 because debug levels are cumulative within a category. Thus the display generated by 0.10 contains the information that 0.1 and 0.4 would show and makes it possible for us to display all three debug levels with one listing. Level 0.1 displays the version number, the Sendmail compiler options, and the system identity. Debug level 0.4 displays the same three fields plus the names and addresses derived from the network interfaces. The names and addresses are listed under the headings "canonical name" and "UUCP nodename." Level 0.10 prints all of the information included in the other two levels plus the operating system definitions that were used during the compile, and the default pathnames for the configuration file and the PID file. For me, debug level 0.1 is the most useful because it provides the Sendmail compiler options and the system identity, which are the pieces of information from this display that I find most helpful.

Debug level 35.9 is interesting because it shows you all of the sendmail.cf variables and the values they have been assigned. Listing 10.16 shows the information displayed by debug level 35.9.

**Listing 10.16**   The Output of Debug Level 35.9

```
[root]# sendmail -bt -d35.9
define(deliveryMode as b)
define(* as $*)
define(+ as $+)
... Many lines deleted ...
define(8 as $8)
define(9 as $9)
define(n as MAILER-DAEMON)
define(v as 8.11.0)
define(w as wren.foobirds.org)
define(j as wren.foobirds.org)
define(m as foobirds.org)
define(k as wren.foobirds.org)
define(b as Sat, 4 Nov 2000 09:33:49 -0500)
define(load_avg as 0)
define(opMode as t)
redefine(w as wren)
define(S as )
define(R as )
define(H as )
define(M as )
redefine(n as MAILER-DAEMON)
define(Z as 8.11.0)
redefine(deliveryMode as b)
define(_ as root@localhost)
redefine(deliveryMode as i)
redefine(deliveryMode as i)
define(i as eA4EXni00755)
```

---

**NOTE**   Many lines were deleted from Listing 10.16 to make it a more reasonable length for a book. To see the full listing, simply run `sendmail -bt -d35.9` on your own system.

---

Frankly, I prefer to look at variables one at a time with the $v command syntax. I find the full list overwhelming. I prefer to work methodically, with one variable at a time, using a reference to remind me of what the variable does. (The `sendmail.cf` variables are listed and described in Appendix C, "Sendmail Variables, Options, and Flags.") But debug level 35.9 is useful for people who can sort out the wheat from the chaff, and it has the advantage of showing the variables as they are being set and reset. Notice that this instantiation of Sendmail is identified as eA4EXni00755. Clearly that is a real-time variable because it contains the PID of this specific Sendmail process. (The i variable is the unique identifier that will be used to create queue files.) Also notice the redefines of `DeliveryMode` as Sendmail changes from background mode, which address test mode uses during initialization, to interactive mode. `DeliveryMode` is not specifically a variable. It can also be treated as an option.

Debug level 37.1 is similar to 35.9 except that it shows the values for options instead of variables. Listing 10.17 shows the options list from our sample Red Hat system.

**Listing 10.17**   Output from Debug Level 37.1

```
[root]# sendmail -bt -d37.1
setoption SevenBitInput (7)=False
setoption EightBitMode (8)=pass8
setoption AliasWait (a)=10
setoption AliasFile (A)=/etc/aliases
setoption MinFreeBlocks (b)=100
setoption BlankSub (B)=.
setoption HoldExpensive (c)=False
setoption DeliveryMode (d)=background
setoption AutoRebuildAliases (D)=
setoption TempFileMode (F)=0600
setoption HelpFile (H)=/etc/mail/helpfile
setoption SendMimeErrors (j)=True
setoption ForwardPath (J)=$z/.forward.$w:$z/.forward
setoption ConnectionCacheSize (k)=2
setoption ConnectionCacheTimeout (K)=5m
setoption HostStatusDirectory (0x9b)=/var/state/sendmail
setoption UseErrorsTo (l)=False
```

```
setoption LogLevel (L)=9
setoption CheckAliases (n)=False
setoption OldStyleHeaders (o)=True
setoption DaemonPortOptions (O)=Name=MTA
Daemon MTA flags:
setoption DaemonPortOptions (O)=Port=587, Name=MSA, M=E
Daemon MSA flags: NOETRN
setoption PrivacyOptions (p)=authwarnings
setoption QueueDirectory (Q)=/var/spool/mqueue
setoption Timeout (r).connect=1m
setoption Timeout (r).queuereturn=5d
setoption Timeout (r).queuewarn=4h
setoption SuperSafe (s)=True
setoption StatusFile (S)=/var/log/sendmail.st
setoption DefaultUser (u)=8:12
setoption UserDatabaseSpec (U)=/etc/mail/userdb.db
setoption TryNullMXList (w)=true
setoption SmtpGreetingMessage (0x90)=$j Sendmail $v/$Z; $b
setoption UnixFromLine (0x91)=From $g $d
setoption OperatorChars (0x92)=.:%@!^/[]+
setoption DontProbeInterfaces (0xa1)=true
setoption HoldExpensive (c)=F
setoption DeliveryMode (d)=
```

Debug level 35.9 is perhaps more *interesting* than 37.1 because it shows variables changing. But I find debug level 37.1 more *useful* than 35.9. While variables can be individually checked with the $v command syntax, there is no address test mode command for examining an individual option. To see the options that are set and the values that they are set to, you need to run address test mode with the debug level set to 37.1. If the problem you're having with your configuration is related to an option setting, this is a good way to check on it. For a complex test, I sometimes print out a hard copy of the 37.1 output and keep it on hand as a reference while I run through the tests that I have planned for the configuration.

The six debug levels mentioned in this chapter are the only ones I use and are the only ones I find useful in address test mode. There are a huge number of debug options, as Appendix B makes clear. Few are of interest to a system administrator and even fewer have any impact on address test mode. Most debug levels log the debug information through the `syslogd` daemon process. Setting debugging can cause your log files to grow at an enormous rate. Use caution when playing with debug modes.

# In Sum

Sendmail is an enormously complex system that is difficult to configure, but thanks to its array of fine tools, it is not difficult to test. Sendmail comes with several command-line options that can be used to query Sendmail, watch it in action, or run it in test mode.

**–C**   This option specifies the Sendmail configuration file that will be used during the test.

**–bv**   This option asks Sendmail for the mail delivery triple for an e-mail address.

**–v**   This option causes Sendmail to print out additional information. When used during a normal delivery, the SMTP protocol interactions are displayed.

**–bh**   This option prints out the host status report. It can also be invoked by the hoststat command.

**–bH**   This option clears the host status directory to force the system to collect all fresh data. It is equivalent to the purgestat command.

**–bp**   This option displays the contents of the mail queue. The command mailq is the same as this option.

**–bt**   This option causes Sendmail to enter address test mode, which is an interactive test mode. In address test mode, you can check the setting of variables and classes, and watch rewrite rules in action. This mode takes you inside the sendmail.cf file.

Address test mode is a particularly powerful tool for observing the results of configuration choices and for fine tuning those selections. Combining -bt with -C on the sendmail command line allows you to test and analyze a new configuration before you deploy it.

Address test mode is an implement that cuts through complexity to help you understand your Sendmail configuration. Don't turn address test mode into something complex. Find the subset of address test mode commands that you feel comfortable with, and stick with them. Keep it simple, and in the long run you will be more productive.

Avoid using optional debug levels that add a lot more detail to the display. Generally, detail confuses more than it enlightens. Turn to debug levels only when you must.

Testing is an ongoing process. You will use it over time to learn more about Sendmail and to improve your configuration. All of the tasks required to maintain a healthy server are ongoing tasks. The battle against spam, which is the topic of our next chapter, is also an ongoing, and it seems never-ending, process.

# 11

# Stopping Spam

SPAM® is a world-famous canned luncheon meat from Hormel Foods. In a classic Monty Python comedy skit, John Cleese plays a waiter reciting a menu. In the first recitation the menu has one SPAM® selection but with each iteration of reciting the menu more and more of the items become SPAM® until he finally describes the menu as "Spam, spam, spam, spam, and spam." Similarly, e-mail spam replicates itself through every possible mailing list until you find yourself with a mailbox full of exactly the same message repeated over and over again. It is this mindless repetition that gives spam e-mail its name.

Spam e-mails are the unsolicited advertisements you receive trying to sell you a college diploma, pheromones that women can't resist, or pornography if those pheromones don't work. I'm sure you know what I mean because everyone attached to the Internet gets tons of this stuff. One of your tasks as the administrator of a mail server is to reduce the amount of junk mail moving through the network. The techniques used for that task are the topic of this chapter.

## Don't Be a Spam Source

To paraphrase Polonius' famous injunction against money lending, "Neither a spammer nor a victim be." While it is clear that you don't want to be a victim of spam, you may bristle at the suggestion that you might be a spammer. Yet your server may unwittingly contribute to the spam problem, either from a bad user who is an intentional spammer, or from configuration problems that allow your server to be exploited by remote spammers.

Your first duty in the spam war is to make sure that your system is not a source of spam. A Sendmail system can be a source of locally generated spam or it can be a relay for spam generated elsewhere. You need to respond to both possibilities.

## Define an Acceptable Use Policy

To prevent locally generated spam, you need to make sure that everyone using your server knows that sending unsolicited advertisements from your server is not permitted. Write an acceptable use policy (AUP) that tells people what type of use is allowed and what is not allowed. If you're not sure what an acceptable use policy should look like, ask your ISP for a copy of their policy or check a national ISP. A copy of the UUNET acceptable use policy is available at www.us.uu.net/support/usepolicy/, or check out the Sprint-link acceptable use policy at www.sprint.net/acceptableuse.htm.

Technical people are not interested in policy matters, so the idea of writing a policy may not appeal to you. You may not even have the authority to write a policy. Nevertheless, someone has to do it. If you're working in a small organization, you're probably the person responsible for this type of thing. Write the policy and get the backing from management that you need to enforce it. If you are part of a large organization, you may already have a policy. The government agencies and large businesses that I work with always have an acceptable use policy. These organizations consider an acceptable use policy an important part of overall system security, and many lawyers think it is a necessary component of limiting an organization's liability. If your organization has an acceptable use policy, make sure that it includes language that clearly condemns spam. Without a written policy that all users must agree to, you may not have the authority to stop spammers from using your system.

## Run the Identification Daemon

Running the auth server (identd) also helps to discourage home-grown spammers. The identification daemon monitors port 113. If it gets a request from a remote system, it tells that system the name of the user running the current connection process to that system. This allows remote mail servers to put a real username on the Received: header in incoming e-mail. Many Linux systems provide this service by default, as the grep of /etc/services and inetd.conf in Listing 11.1 shows.

**Listing 11.1** Checking that identd Is Configured

```
[craig]$ grep ^auth /etc/services
auth    113/tcp    ident    # User Verification
[craig]$ grep ^auth /etc/inetd.conf
auth stream tcp nowait nobody /usr/sbin/in.identd in.identd -t120
```

Listing 11.1 shows that `identd` is preconfigured to run from `inetd` on a Caldera 2.3 server system. Many Linux systems run `identd` on demand from `inetd` or `xinetd`. A few others run `identd` as part of the boot; for example, Red Hat changed to running `identd` at boot time as part of release 6.2. A quick `ps` command can check to see if the `identd` daemon is running on your Linux system. If your system doesn't run `identd` by default, either at boot time or on demand, add it to your configuration.

When `identd` is running, the remote server can query about any TCP connections from your server to the remote server by sending the source and destination port pair to the identification server. Your system then responds by sending either the username associated with the connection or an error. Spammers do not like to have their real usernames known. Providing their names to their victims makes it hard for spammers to stay in business.

> **NOTE** If you masquerade usernames for security reasons, your security people may not want you to run `identd` because it will expose the real usernames. However, masquerading should be used to create consistent, readable addresses, not for security reasons. I recommend running `identd` even if you masquerade user names.

## Properly Configure Mail Relaying

In addition to discouraging local users from generating spam, you need to discourage remote users from using your server as a tool for distributing spam. Nobody likes spammers and the spammers know it. They do their best to hide the true source of the spam by relaying their junk mail through other people's servers. If your mail server allows relaying, spammers will make use of it.

To discourage spam, the default configuration of Sendmail from version 8.9 on properly handles local mail but does not relay messages for any outside sources. Blocking all relaying works in most cases because most systems that run Sendmail are not mail servers—they're desktop Linux or Unix systems dedicated to a single user. Because the user's mail originates on the system that is running Sendmail, the mail is handled as local mail and relaying for outside systems is not required. Also, the definition of local mail is fairly broad. As we saw in Chapter 6, "Using Sendmail Databases," every host listed in class `w` is considered to be the local host. Therefore, the default configuration works in many cases.

### Relaxing Relay Restrictions

However, blocking all relaying doesn't work in every case, particularly if the system is a mail server. Most of the mail a server delivers originates on its clients—these might be

Windows clients that can't run their own Sendmail program. Blocking relaying at the server causes the client to get an error. For example, a client running Netscape Messenger would get a pop-up box saying "An error occurred while sending mail. The mail server responded: Relaying denied. Please check the message recipients and try again." There is nothing wrong with the recipients. What's wrong is that the user configured the "Outgoing mail SMTP server" box with the name of your server, and your server is running the default Sendmail configuration, which denies all relaying.

To create a mail server, you must allow some level of relaying. Use the Sendmail feature that relaxes the relay restrictions just enough to get the job done. Don't overdo it, or you will open the door to spammers. There are several relay features from which you can choose.

Class R can be used to extend relaying services to specific clients. As described in Chapter 6, there are three ways to store hostnames in class R. Individual values can be stored in class R using the RELAY_DOMAIN macro. A file can be loaded into class R using either the confCR_ FILE option or the RELAY_DOMAIN_FILE macro. See "The relay-domains File" section of Chapter 6 for more information about these commands.

Listing 11.2 shows a simple relay-domains file and the effect it has on mail delivery. Listing 11.2 contains output from two different systems. The prompt [ed@ox]$ shows the mail delivery attempts from the user ed logged on the system ox.mammals.org both before and after changes were made to the configuration of the mail server wren.foobirds.org. The changes made to wren are indicated by the [root@wren]# prompt. The "Relaying denied" error in the first test is highlighted in bold italic. Many lines were deleted to keep the listing to a reasonable length, but everything important is still there.

**Listing 11.2** Enabling Relaying with Class R

```
[ed@ox]$ sendmail -v jill@robin.foobirds.org < /dev/null
jill@robin.foobirds.org... Connecting to wren.foobirds.org.
    via esmtp...
... Lines deleted ...
>>> MAIL From:<ed@ox.mammals.org>
250 2.1.0 <ed@ox.mammals.org>... Sender ok
>>> RCPT To:<jill@robin.foobirds.org>
550 5.7.1 <jill@robin.foobirds.org>... Relaying denied
... Lines deleted
>>> QUIT
221 2.0.0 wren.foobirds.org closing connection
```

```
[root@wren]# grep '^FR' /etc/sendmail.cf
FR-o /etc/mail/relay-domains
[root@wren]# cat > relay-domains
ibis.foobirds.org
192.168.30.20
mammals.org
172.30
^D
[root@wren]# ps -ax | grep sendmail
 1439 ?        S       0:00 sendmail: accepting connections
[root]# kill -HUP 1439

[ed@ox]# sendmail -v jill@robin.foobirds.org < /dev/null
jill@robin.foobirds.org... Connecting to wren.foobirds.org.
     via esmtp...
... Lines deleted ...
>>> MAIL From:<ed@ox.mammals.org>
250 2.1.0 <ed@ox.mammals.org>... Sender ok
>>> RCPT To:<jill@robin.foobirds.org>
250 2.1.5 <jill@robin.foobirds.org>... Recipient ok
>>> DATA
354 Enter mail, end with "." on a line by itself
>>> .
250 2.0.0 eA8MABw01422 Message accepted for delivery
jill@robin.foobirds.org... Sent (eA8MABw01422
     Message accepted for delivery)
Closing connection to wren.foobirds.org.
>>> QUIT
221 2.0.0 wren.foobirds.org closing connection
```

In Listing 11.2, the administrator of wren uses grep to check that the sendmail.cf file is already configured to read the relay-domains file into class R. It is. If it wasn't, a configuration file change, using either the confCR_FILE option or the RELAY_DOMAIN_FILE macro, would be needed before the relay-domains file would be effective. After creating the relay-domains file, the administrator passes Sendmail a SIGHUP signal to make sure it reads the new configuration. After the reload, wren relays mail for any system in the mammals.org domain, including ox.mammals.org, as the final test clearly shows.

In Listing 11.2, class R contains four values. The first two values illustrate that individual hosts can be granted relay privileges either by specifying the host's fully qualified name or by specifying the host's IP address. Both the hostname ibis.foobirds.org and the host whose address is 192.168.30.20 are granted relay access in Listing 11.2. The third value in the example is a domain name. It grants relaying to every host in the mammals.org domain. The last value in class R is a network address that grants relaying privileges to every host on the network 172.30.

The access database can also be used to relax relay restrictions for hosts, domains, and networks. The same four items in the relay-domains file shown in Listing 11.2 could be granted relay privileges with the following access database entries:

```
ibis.foobirds.org      RELAY
192.168.30.20          RELAY
mammals.org            RELAY
172.30                 RELAY
```

Again, the systems granted access are identified by name or address. But this time the specific action to be taken is explicitly spelled out by the RELAY keyword. The other keywords and values that can be used in the action field of an access database entry mean that the database can be used for much more than just enabling relaying. As you'll see later in this chapter, the access database is also a powerful anti-spam tool. Because it holds everything in one file—both the entries that enable relaying and the entries that block spam—I prefer to use the access database over the relay-domains file. I like to have access controls in one place where they can be evaluated together as a whole. By their nature, access controls are most effective if they are coordinated, and a single file makes that coordination easier. (The details of the syntax and structure of the access database are covered in Chapter 6.)

The systems granted relaying through class R or the access database are identified as individual hosts, entire domains, or entire networks. Generally, the hosts, domains, and networks identified in class R or the access database are remote hosts, domains, and networks. If you want to relay mail for the hosts in your own domain, Sendmail provides a simpler way to handle your local domain.

The relay_entire_domain feature grants relaying to every host in the domains listed in class m. Because class m is used for more than just relaying, only local domains should be listed in this class. Adding the following command to the sample server configurations shown throughout this book would enable relaying for every host in the foobirds.org domain:

```
FEATURE(relay_entire_domain)
```

At first glance, the relay_local_from feature appears to do the same thing as the relay_entire_domain feature—they both relay mail from every host in the local domain. The difference is that they do this in different ways. The relay_entire_domain feature checks the source of the mail connection against the values in class m to see if the connection came from a local host. `relay_local_from` relays mail that contains the local domain name in the MAIL From: header. Because the MAIL From: header can be written to contain anything the source system wants, `relay_local_from` is not as secure as `relay_entire_domain`.

The `relay_based_on_MX` feature is another feature that grants relaying to a group of hosts. This feature will relay mail for any host for which the local host is an MX server. This is a useful feature if the server that handles inbound mail for your clients is also the system that handles their outbound mail. The MX record that routes mail through the server to its clients can also be the signal to relay outbound mail from those same clients. The weakness of this approach is that the Sendmail administrator cannot control all of the MX records in the domain name system. A remote site could relay mail through your server by simply adding an MX record to their domain. Despite this weakness, this feature is still an effective defense against spammers. Because they want to hide the true source of spam mail, spammers don't send mail that can be tracked back to their own domain names, and thus they cannot write MX records for the domain names they do use.

The last feature that relaxes relaying restrictions is probably the most dangerous. It is the `FEATURE('promiscuous_relay')` command. Current versions of Sendmail block all relaying. This is just the opposite of earlier versions of Sendmail that relayed all mail by default. The `promiscuous_relay` feature returns to the past by telling Sendmail to relay all mail from any source. This is exactly the configuration spammers hope to find and is the configuration they love to exploit. This feature can only be used if your server is completely cut off from the Internet, either because you have no connection or because your connection is through a firewall that does not allow any external mail delivery to the server. Regardless of your network connection, I recommend against using this feature because it exposes your system to exploitation.

All of the features listed in this section weaken the barrier to mail relaying, although some are worse than others. `promiscuous_relay` should not be used because it returns to the past and makes your system a potential spam relay. Avoid the `relay_local_from` feature because it is very easy for spammers to write anything they want in the MAIL From: header, including your local domain name. Be careful when using any of the features described in this section that you don't weaken the Sendmail configuration so much you become a spam source.

# Use Sendmail to Block Spam

The world will be grateful that your server is not a source for junk mail, but your users will only be happy if they are not the targets for spam. Sendmail provides a few different techniques for blocking incoming spam. One thing the default Sendmail configuration does is block mail delivery from all remote systems that do not have a valid hostname. Thus mail from hosts that do not exist in the domain name system is rejected. Spammers love to use fake hostnames that cannot be traced back to them, so rejecting mail from invalid sources is a useful first step to blocking spam. Unfortunately, you may find that the Sendmail configuration delivered with your system weakens this first line of defense. The `accept_unresolvable_domains` feature tells Sendmail to accept mail from a host even if the host cannot be found in DNS or the host table. This feature is intended for those times when Sendmail can't resolve domain names reliably because of intermittent connectivity or a restrictive firewall. A laptop Linux system that does not always have access to a DNS server may need this feature, but otherwise I wouldn't use it.

The `accept_unresolvable_domains` feature is used in the default configuration of some Linux systems. Red Hat is a notable example, because the Linux vendors want Sendmail to work even if the DNS server is unreliable. Of course, the proper approach to this problem is to get DNS running reliably. However, the Linux vendor has no control over your DNS server configuration, so they opt for creating a Sendmail configuration that will work even if the DNS server is unreliable. If you're responsible for the DNS server, see *Linux DNS Server Administration* (Sybex, 2000), which is also part of the Craig Hunt Linux Library, for advice on configuring and maintaining a reliable DNS server.

The first step toward blocking spam is to remove the feature `accept_unresolvable_domains` from the configuration of your system. Of course, this is just a first step that returns your system to a nominal level of spam control. Sendmail provides other features that increase spam controls. One uses a DNS-based service to block spam sources, another uses a local database that you create, and still others use custom rewrite rules. The first is easy and convenient; the second gives you greater control; the third gives you complete control. Not surprisingly, the more control and flexibility provided by an anti-spam technique, the more complex the technique becomes. This section examines all of these techniques to help you decide which are right for you.

## Using the Realtime Blackhole List

The simplest way to block spam is to let someone else do it. Sendmail allows you to use the Realtime Blackhole List (RBL) that comes from the Mail Abuse Prevention System (MAPS). The RBL is a DNS database that contains the IP addresses of spam sources. The sources can be the original source of the spam, or a mail server that permits spammers to relay mail.

Using the RBL is very easy because the system is implemented through DNS. Every Linux system can issue DNS queries, so this is a very effective way to distribute information. Of course, a program can only make use of the information if it understands it. Sendmail does. If you want to use the MAPS RBL to block spam, add the following feature to your Sendmail configuration:

```
FEATURE('dnsbl')
```

With this feature enabled, mail from every site listed in the MAPS RBL is rejected.

There are many systems listed in the MAPS RBL. MAPS enforces a very stern policy. Any site that relays spam—which could be your site if you don't properly configure Sendmail—is listed in the RBL. The RBL is one of the reasons that it is essential to configure relaying properly. A mistake in configuring relaying could get your site added to the blackhole list. If a site stops relaying spam, it is removed from the list after about a month. If your site gets added to the RBL, apply to have it removed from the list by following the instructions on the MAPS Web site. Visit the Web site at maps.vix.com to find out more about the MAPS system.

While enabling dnsbl is simple, it isn't a perfect solution because you can't choose which sites listed in the RBL are rejected. It is an all-or-nothing proposition. In fact, that's what makes it as easy as turning a light switch on or off. This means that you might be blocked from receiving e-mail from a friendly site just because the administrator at that site forgot to turn off relaying. For this reason, some organizations decide to build their own DNS-based blackhole list.

The dnsbl feature accepts two arguments. The first of these is the name of the domain that contains the blackhole list. This defaults to rbl.maps.vix.com, which is the home of the MAPS RBL. Point this argument to the domain in which you build your own blackhole list. If the DNS administrator created such a list in the dnsbl.foobirds.org domain, the following command would configure Sendmail to make use of it:

```
FEATURE(`dnsbl', `dnsbl.foobirds.org')
```

For this to work, the DNS administrator needs to place the proper entries in the DNS server. Blackhole entries are simply DNS address records. The records are constructed by reversing the IP address of the blacklisted system to create a DNS name field for the record and using the address 127.0.0.2 as the data field of the address record. This format means that hosts are blacklisted by IP address instead of by name. For example, if you wanted to blacklist clueless.nexploited.com, whose IP address is 192.168.72.37, you would need to place an address record for the hostname 37.72.168.192 within your blackhole domain. Some sample blackhole entries from the dnsbl.foobirds.org zone file might look like the following:

```
18.12.20.172.dnsbl.foobirds.org.      IN A 127.0.0.2
16.16.31.172.dnsbl.foobirds.org.      IN A 127.0.0.2
```

```
37.72.168.192.dnsbl.foobirds.org.    IN A 127.0.0.2
9.200.168.192.dnsbl.foobirds.org.    IN A 127.0.0.2
```

> **NOTE** To find out more about building a DNS zone file, see *Linux DNS Server Administration* by Craig Hunt (Sybex, 2000).

Once the DNS zone has been created and a Sendmail configuration has been built using the correct dnsbl feature, the new configuration can be tested by running the sendmail command with the -bt option. Listing 11.3 shows a test of the dnsbl.foobirds.org domain.

**Listing 11.3**   Testing the dnsbl Feature

```
$ sendmail -bt -Ctest-dnsbl.cf
ADDRESS TEST MODE (ruleset 3 NOT automatically invoked)
Enter <ruleset> <address>
> .D{client_addr}172.16.12.1
> Basic_check_relay <>
rewrite: ruleset 192 input: < >
rewrite: ruleset 192 returns: OK
> .D{client_addr}192.168.72.37
> Basic_check_relay <>
rewrite: ruleset 192 input: < >
rewrite: ruleset 192 returns: $# error $@ 5 . 7 . 1
        $: "550 Mail from " 192 . 168 . 72 . 37
        " refused by blackhole site dnsbl.foobirds.org"
> ^D
```

The client_addr variable normally contains the IP address of the remote system that initiated the mail connection. Because this is a -bt test, there is no mail connection involved, so we use the .D command to place a test value in the client_addr variable. Next, the ruleset Basic_check_relay is run without any input address, which is why the address focus characters < and > are used but do not enclose any address value. The Basic_check_relay ruleset does not process the input address; it processes the address found in client_addr. The first test returns OK, which shows that the local address 172.16.12.1 is an acceptable source for e-mail. Next, the address 192.168.72.37 is stored in client_addr and ruleset Basic_check_relay is run again. This time the address is found in the dnsbl.foobirds.org domain, and the Basic_check_relay ruleset returns the error message "550 Mail from 192.168.72.37 refused by blackhole site dnsbl.foobirds.org."

The second argument available for the dnsbl feature is the error message that should be displayed when mail is rejected because of the blackhole server. The default message is the one displayed at the end of Listing 11.3. Its format is "550 Mail from " $&{client_addr} " refused by blackhole site *dnsbl-domain*," where $&{client_addr} is the IP address that was rejected and *dnsbl-domain* is the value from the first argument provided to the dnsbl feature. Although I see no advantage to changing the standard error message, you could change it to "Mail rejected. " $&{client_addr} " is a suspected spam relay." with the following command:

```
FEATURE(`dnsbl', `dnsbl.foobirds.org', `"Mail rejected. "$&{client_
addr}" is a suspected spam relay."')dnl
```

As usual, the choice between using the MAPS RBL or building your own blackhole server is a choice between simplicity and flexibility. Most small sites choose simplicity. If your site is small, you probably have a small set of other sites with which you exchange mail. The likelihood of any of those sites appearing in the RBL is very slim. Additionally, you probably don't have the available staff necessary to build and maintain your own blackhole site. If you run the mail server for a large site, you may want to define your own e-mail access list to ensure that continued connectivity to all of the sites you want to reach is under your direct control. Creating your own blackhole server is one technique that Sendmail provides for you to do that. Another is to define access controls in the access database.

## Using the *access* Database

The Sendmail access database defines e-mail sources using e-mail addresses, domain names, and IP network numbers along with the action that Sendmail should take when it receives mail from the specified source. Earlier we saw it used to enable relaying. An even more powerful use for the access database is as a tool to block mail from or to known spammers. For example:

```
spammer@bigisp.com        REJECT

wespamu.com               REJECT

172.18                    REJECT
```

These access database entries tell Sendmail to reject any mail from the e-mail address spammer@bigisp.com, from any host in the domain wespamu.com, and from any computer whose IP address begins with network number 172.18. Each entry in the database begins with the source of the mail followed by a keyword that tells Sendmail what action to take. Chapter 6 describes all of the valid keywords and the actions they cause. Only three values can be used in the action field to block spam:

**DISCARD**  The DISCARD keyword causes Sendmail to silently drop any message received from the specified source. In the fight against spam, DISCARD is generally considered the least useful of the three actions listed here because it does not return an error message to the source of the e-mail. Without the feedback of an error message, there is nothing to discourage the spammer or inform the administrator of the remote system that might be an unwitting spam relay. On the other hand, some system administrators prefer the DISCARD action. They suggest that sending back an error tells spammers where there are functioning mail servers, which may prompt more and different attacks. Also, without an error spammers are not alerted that they were unsuccessful, so they continue to waste time sending mail into oblivion. I'm not personally a fan of DISCARD, but I understand why some administrators use it.

**REJECT**   The REJECT keyword causes Sendmail to issue an error message and drop any mail from the specified address. This is a very good selection for an anti-spam rule. The error message provides all the feedback needed to discourage spammers and inform system administrators, and it is just as easy as creating a DISCARD entry.

*error message*   If the action field contains an error message, Sendmail drops the mail and returns the specified error message to the source address. This provides the flexibility you need to deal with a variety of error situations. It is probably unnecessary to design your own error message for spammers. But if you want to, you can.

In addition to a variety of actions, the access database allows you to specify a variety of sources: full e-mail addresses, usernames, domains, networks, and IP addresses. Listing 6.7 in Chapter 6 shows the address field syntax for all possible address values.

By default, the address in the access database is considered to be the source of the e-mail. Use the blacklist_recipients feature to apply the access database to both the source and the destination address. You might use this to prevent users from responding to a spammer, or you might use it to prevent mail from going to a site that has complained that a bad guy on your system is spamming them. Generally, the access database is used to block inbound mail from a bad source. But if you need to, you can use it to block outbound mail with the blacklist_recipients feature.

Even more address flexibility is provided by the tag keyword. (See Chapter 6 for the syntax of the tag keywords.) The tag keyword lets you specify how an individual address should be interpreted. Instead of saying that every database entry applies to source addresses, or source and destination addresses, the tag field tells Sendmail exactly to which type of address an individual access database entry applies. A tag field of:

- From: tells Sendmail this is the source address
- To: tells Sendmail this is the destination address
- Connect: tells Sendmail this is either the {client_addr} or {client_name} address derived from the mail connection

### Creating an Anti-Spam *access* Database

The format of the entries in the `access` database is the easy part. Deciding exactly what to put in the database is harder. There are organizations on the Internet that collect information about spammers that might help you build an anti-spam `access` database. A few sites to start with are `maps.vix.com`, `spam.abuse.net/spam/`, and `www.mids.org/nospam`. These sites are a starting point for locating information about known spammers.

Of course, in addition to extracting data from online lists of spammers, you can enter your own entries directly into the `access` database using your favorite editor. I find this the simplest method, and the most flexible for responding to the spam problems of my individual users.

If you just love X Windows tools, you can even use `linuxconf` to build the `access` database. Figure 11.1 shows an anti-spam filter being created with `linuxconf`.

**Figure 11.1**    Using `linuxconf` to create the access database

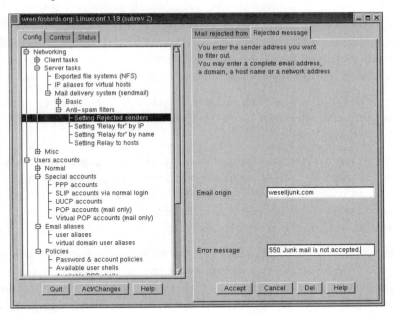

Maintaining a Healthy Server

PART 4

On the left-hand side of the window, select one of the items from the `linuxconf` **Anti-Spam Filters** menu. There are four possible selections:

**Setting Rejected Senders**  The Setting Rejected Senders selection creates a spam filter. The selection opens the Mail Rejected From tab. Click Add to open the tab shown in Figure 11.1. The Rejected Message tab is the place you define the anti-spam rule, including both the source of the e-mail and the error message that will be sent to that source. Figure 11.1 shows that mail from `wesbelljunk.com` will be rejected with the error message "550 Junk mail is not accepted." This is the only `linuxconf` menu selection that blocks e-mail. The other three mail filtering selections are used to loosen the mail-relaying restrictions so that you can create a mail server.

**Setting 'Relay for' by IP**  Use this selection to define a host or network for which the server should relay mail. Identify the host or network by IP number. This enables mail relaying for the specified host.

**Setting 'Relay for' by Name**  Use this selection to define a host or domain for which the server should relay mail. Identify the host or network by name.

**Setting Relay to Hosts**  This selection identifies remote hosts to which the server should relay mail. A possible use is to identify an external mail server that your system relays mail through—for example, your corporate mail server.

The `linuxconf` tool will build the `access` database file for you when you click the Act/Changes button, which stands for activate changes. `linuxconf` creates both the text file and the actual database.

If, like me, you build your access list manually with a text editor, you must also manually build the database. Use the `makemap` command that comes with Sendmail to convert the text file into a database. You also need to let Sendmail know that you have an `access` database and that you want to use it. Use the `access_db` feature to do that. See Chapter 6 for details on building the `access` database and configuring Sendmail to use it.

The fine level of control that the `access` database gives you over selecting addresses and the various actions you can choose from when you get an address match means that the `access` database is the right tool for most sites to use to block spammers. But if you need even more control over the process, you can define your own Sendmail rewrite rules to process the e-mail addresses.

## Using Anti-Spam Rewrite Rules

Most administrators think of Sendmail rewrite rules as a way to modify addresses on outbound e-mail that originates on the local system in the user's mailer. The anti-spam rulesets allow you to process the addresses and headers from incoming mail. Sendmail provides three anti-spam rulesets for your personal rules. These are:

**Local_check_relay**    This is a ruleset where you can define rules for handling mail that is being relayed.

**Local_check_rcpt**    This is a ruleset where you can define rules to process mail based on the recipient address.

**Local_check_mail**    This is a ruleset where you can define rules to process mail based on the sender address.

Assume that you have been receiving junk mail that is trying to masquerade as local mail by using a From: address that contains only a username. Further, assume that you have configured your mail server so that the From: address of local mail always includes the hostname. You could use `Local_check_mail` to check the sender address as shown in Listing 11.4.

**Listing 11.4**    A Simple Anti-Spam Ruleset

```
SLocal_check_mail
# Check for user@host
R$+ @ $+        $@ $#OK
R$*             $#error $: 550 Invalid From address
```

The first line in Listing 11.4 is an S command that defines the ruleset with the name of the ruleset `Local_check_mail`. The first R command matches the incoming address against the pattern $+ @ $+, which looks for one or more tokens ($+), a literal at-sign (@), and one or more tokens. Any address in the form of *user@host* matches this pattern. The transformation says that if the address matches the pattern, exit the ruleset ($@) and return the mailer name $#OK to the calling ruleset. The mailer name $#OK is a phony mailer used to indicate that the address is valid.

The second R command matches every address that failed to match the first rule. For all of these addresses, the rule returns the mailer name $#error and the text of an error message. The $#error mailer is a special mailer that returns the mail to the sender along with an error message. An alternative to this would have been the $#discard mailer that silently discards the mail. Most administrators prefer to return an error message.

---

**NOTE**    The ruleset in Listing 11.4 is just a teaching example, which was designed to be easily explained and reasonably short. It is too simple to effectively handle focus addresses and the various valid local address formats.

---

**Maintaining a Healthy Server**

**PART 4**

### Processing Input Mail Headers

In addition to defining your own rulesets, you can call a ruleset from a header definition to check the format of the headers your system receives. Sometimes spammers use malformed headers that indicate the mail is spam. Assume you're getting spammed by someone who forgets to create a valid-looking Message-Id: header. You could use code like that shown in Listing 11.5.

**Listing 11.5**  Checking Header Contents

```
LOCAL_RULESETS
HMessage-Id: $>check_MID_header

Scheck_MID_header
R$+ @ $+          $@ $#OK
R$*               $#error $: 550 Invalid Header
```

The LOCAL_RULESETS section contains an H command for the sendmail.cf file. Unlike the H commands we saw in Chapter 7, "The sendmail.cf File," this one doesn't contain a header format. Instead, it uses the $> syntax to call a ruleset to process the header. This example calls ruleset check_MID_header because that is the name of the new ruleset defined in Listing 11.5.

The Scheck_MID_header command is the first line of ruleset check_MID_header. This ruleset is essentially identical to the one described in the previous example. It checks to make sure that the Message-Id: header contains both a unique message identifier and a hostname in the form *identifier@host*. All other formats are rejected as errors.

I don't recommend that you use either of these rewrite rule examples because I don't use them. I simply created them to illustrate how these rulesets are used. Frankly, I don't develop rewrite rules to fight spam. First, rewrite rules can be complex and difficult to develop. I don't want the cure to be worse than the disease. Second, the format of spam mail is constantly changing. The rule I write today may be useless tomorrow. I think it is better to rely on the MAPS RBL, the access database, and the ability of the user's mailer to filter mail.

# Filtering Out Spam at the Mailer

Despite your best efforts, spam and other unwanted mail will get to your users. In part this is because you can't block all of the spam and in part this is because not all unwanted e-mail is spam. Sometime a user just doesn't want to look at some legitimate e-mail simply because of personal preference. In this case, the mail needs to be filtered at the user's mail reader. Most mail readers provide this capability. For example, the `elm` mailer provides a tool named `filter` for this purpose and Netscape Messenger provides a graphic interface for creating mail filtering rules.

In general, filtering at the mail reader is the user's responsibility. After all, some of the mail that the user wants to filter is not really spam. There is no way that the administrator can know the user's preferences or can be responsible for implementing them.

However, placing responsibility for spam filtering on the end user is a mistake, because users will not do a consistently good job of blocking spam. This is one of the reasons that Sendmail makes it possible for you to integrate `procmail` into the Sendmail configuration. `procmail` has advanced mail-filtering capabilities, and unlike most mailers that do filtering, the filtering abilities of `procmail` are available to both the administrator and the end user. The power of filtering with `procmail` is a useful tool that the Sendmail administrator can use in the fight against spam.

## Managing Mail with *procmail*

As mentioned in Chapter 5, "Understanding a Vendor's Configuration," `procmail` is the default local mail delivery program for Linux systems. `procmail` provides the most powerful and complex e-mail filtering system available for Linux. `procmail` filters are defined by the user in the `.procmailrc` file. Additionally, the system administrator can define systemwide filters in the `/etc/procmailrc` file. The format of both files is the same. The system administrator uses the `/etc/procmailrc` file for general anti-spam filtering. The end user can then use `.procmailrc` to add filtering for personal preferences.

> **NOTE** The examples in this section show both anti-spam filters and personal preference filters for the sake of completeness.

The `procmailrc` file contains two type of entries: environment variable assignments and mail filtering rules, which `procmail` calls "recipes." Environment variable assignments are straightforward and look just like these assignments would in a shell initialization script like `.bashrc`. For example, `HOME=/home/craig` is a valid environment variable assignment. Assignment statements are rarely needed because the variables usually have the correct values for your system. See the `procmailrc` manual page for the full listing of the more than 30 environment variables.

The real substance of a `procmailrc` file are the recipes. The syntax of each recipe is:

`:0 [flags] [:[lockfile]]`

`[* condition]`

`action`

Every recipe begins with :0, which differentiates it from an assignment statement. The :0 is optionally followed by flags that change how the filter is processed. Table 11.1 lists all of the flags and their use.

**Table 11.1**    procmail Recipe Flags

| Flag | Meaning |
|------|---------|
| A | Execute this recipe if the preceding recipe evaluates to true. |
| a | This has the same meaning as the A flag, except that the preceding recipe must also have successfully completed execution. |
| b | Pass the body of the message on to the destination. This is the default. |
| B | Filter the message body. |
| c | Create a carbon copy of this mail. |
| D | Tests are case sensitive. By default case is ignored. |
| e | Execute this recipe if the execution of the preceding recipe returned an error. |
| E | Execute this recipe if the preceding recipe was not executed. |
| f | Pass the data through an external filter program. |
| H | Filter the message headers. This is the default. |
| h | Pass the message header on to the destination. This is the default. |
| I | Ignore write errors for this recipe. |
| r | Write the mail out "as is" without ensuring it is properly formatted. |
| w | Check the exit code of the external filter program. |
| W | This is the same meaning as the w flag, except no error message is printed. |

An optional *lockfile* can be identified to prevent multiple copies of procmail from writing to the same mailbox at the same time. This can happen on a busy system, causing some pretty strange-looking mail. The *lockfile* name is preceded by a colon. If the colon is used and no name is specified, a default name created from the mailbox name and the extension .lock is used.

The conditional test is optional. If no *condition* is provided, the recipe acts as if the *condition* is true, which means that the *action* is taken. If a condition is specified it must begin with an asterisk (*). The condition is written as a regular expression. If the value defined by the regular expression is found in the mail, the condition evaluates to true and the action is taken. To take an action when mail does NOT contain the specified value, put an exclamation in front of the regular expression. Here are some examples of valid conditional tests:

```
* ^From.*neil@sybex.com
* !^Subject: Chapter
```

The first conditional checks to see if the mail contains a line that begins with (^) the literal string From followed by any number of characters (.*) and the literal string neil@sybex.com. The second conditional matches all mail that does not (!) contain a line that begins with the string Subject: Chapter. If multiple conditions are defined for one recipe, each condition appears on a separate line.

While there may be multiple conditions in a recipe, there can be only one action. The action can direct the mail to a file, forward it to another e-mail address, or send it to a program, or the action can define additional recipes to process the message. If the action is an additional recipe, it begins with :0. If the action directs the mail to an e-mail address, it begins with an exclamation (!), and if it directs it to a program it begins with a vertical bar (|). If the action directs the mail to a file, just the name of the file is specified.

### Reading a *procmailrc* File

Using the syntax described above, you might create a procmailrc file such as the one shown in Listing 11.6.

**Listing 11.6**   A Sample procmailrc File

```
MAILDIR=$HOME/mail
:0 c
backup
:0:
* ^From.*@sybex.com
editors
:0 c
* ^From.*mike1
* ^Subject:.*TCP/IP
```

```
!robert@bobsnet.org
   :0 A
   crabbook
:0
* ^From.*@wespamu.com
/dev/null
:0 B
* .*pheromones
| awk -f spamscript > spam-suspects
```

The sample procmailrc file begins with an environment variable assignments statement. This statement assigns a value to the variable MAILDIR and it uses the value of the HOME variable. Thus it illustrates both assigning a variable and using a variable. Frankly, the statement is just there to illustrate how variables are used. It was not really needed for this file.

The first recipe in Listing 11.6 is:

```
:0 c

backup
```

This recipe makes a carbon copy of the mail and stores it in a mailbox named backup. The recipe came straight from the procmailrc documentation where it is suggested as a way to ensure that no mail is lost when you're first debugging the procmailrc file. After all of the recipes work as you want, remove this recipe from the file so that you don't continue to keep two copies of every piece of mail.

The second recipe in Listing 11.6 is:

```
:0:

* ^From.*@sybex.com

editors
```

This recipe puts all the mail that contains a line that begins with (^) the literal From, any number of characters (.*), and the literal @sybex.com into the mailbox named editors. The most interesting thing in this recipe is the first line. Notice the :0: value. From the syntax, you know that the second colon precedes the name of the lock file. In this case, no lock file name is provided so the name defaults to editors.lock.

The third recipe in Listing 11.6 is:

```
:0 c

* ^From.*mikel

* ^Subject:.*TCP/IP
```

```
!robert@bobsnet.org
 :0 A
 crabbook
```

This recipe searches for mail that is from someone named `mikel` and that has a subject of `TCP/IP`. A carbon copy is made of the mail and is mailed to `robert@bobsnet.org`. The other copy of the mail is stored in the `crabbook` mailbox.

The fourth recipe is:

```
:0
* ^From.*@wespamu.com
/dev/null
```

This recipe shows how spam mail is deleted using `procmail`. All mail from `wespamu.com` is deleted by sending it to /dev/null—the null device.

The final recipe is:

```
:0 B
* .*pheromones
| gawk -f spamscript > spam-suspects
```

This recipe illustrates how mail is passed to an external program for processing. All messages that contain the word "pheromones" anywhere in the message body are passed to `gawk` for processing. In this example, `gawk` runs a program file named `spamscript` that extracts information from the mail and stores it in a file named `spam-suspects`. You can imagine that the administrator of this system created an awk program named `spamscript` to extract all of the e-mail addresses from suspected spam.

This range of recipes illustrates the power and flexibility of `procmail`. Despite the obscure syntax of a `procmailrc` file, it may be the best tool for filtering e-mail.

The Sendmail feature `local_procmail` makes it easy to pass all inbound mail through `procmail` for filtering. Some Linux vendors—Red Hat is an example—make the `local_procmail` feature a part of their default Sendmail configuration. In the fight against spam, you'll need all the help you can get. Don't overlook `procmail` as an effective tool for mail filtering.

# In Sum

Spam e-mail is an annoyance to your users that clogs their mailboxes with trash that must be waded through and discarded. As a Sendmail administrator, you must do your part to reduce the burden that spam places on the network and its users. Begin by ensuring that your system is not a source of spam:

- Create a policy that makes it clear to your users that they are not allowed to generate spam.
- Run the identd daemon to help remote administrators trace connections from your system in case you do have a spammer on your system.
- Limit relaying through your server to just those clients who should be allowed to relay mail.

By default, Sendmail blocks all relaying except for local mail—i.e., mail from a source listed in class w. Sendmail provides half a dozen features that can be used to relax this relaying restriction so that a server can provide relaying for its clients. In most cases, the complexity of choosing between so many options can be avoiding by placing the entire relay and spam control configuration in the access database.

The access database is a list of addresses and the action that Sendmail should take when dealing with mail to or from that address. It consolidates both relay and spam control in a single file. Yet even the access database can become complex if you try to put in an entry for every known spammer. To avoid this complexity, use the MAPS RBL.

The advantage of the MAPS RBL is that it is very simple. The disadvantage is that you give up all control. It reduces complexity, but for many sites it reduces it too much. Sometimes you just can't filter out all of the complexity and get what you really want.

To use all of your weapons against spam, you should call on your users for help. When a user complains about a spammer, help the user create a filter for their mail reader that reduces spam and in the long run reduces your workload.

Fighting spam is a never-ending struggle. Closely related to the fight against the people who exploit systems by making them into unwitting spam relays is the fight against the people who exploit system security holes. In the next chapter, we conclude this book with a look at security and the techniques that you can use to create a more secure Sendmail server.

# 12

# Sendmail Security

The system administrator is responsible for the security of the Sendmail server. This is not an easy task. Sendmail is one of the prime targets for network intruders. The SANS Institute lists Sendmail as one of the top ten targets for security exploits. As a Sendmail system administrator, you need to be keenly aware of security techniques and of security threats. There are two basic types of threats:

**Unauthorized access**  Any time that someone who should not be allowed to access your system gains access, you've had an *unauthorized access*. Unauthorized access threatens the secrecy and integrity of data. An intruder can examine files you don't want disclosed to the general public and can modify the files on your system.

**Denial of service**  When a security problem prevents you from using your server to its full capacity, you've suffered a *denial of service* attack. Denial of service (DoS) is a threat to the availability of data.

These security problems are the same ones that threaten all computer systems. To counter these threats, you need to follow the same basic security procedures for your Sendmail server that you would follow for any computer system. These basic security procedures, customized for the special needs of a Linux Sendmail server, are the first topic of this chapter.

In addition to the basic security problems that all systems face, a Sendmail server has a unique set of challenges that spring from the fact that Sendmail is a prime security target and yet a Sendmail server can only do its job by communicating with systems all over the world. These special security issues for Sendmail servers are also discussed in this chapter.

The final topics of this chapter are the new Sendmail security protocols. The lifting of U.S. export restrictions and the end of certain security patents mean that Linux systems now include advanced encryption tools. These tools make it practical for Sendmail to implement cryptographic security techniques. These new techniques are described. Before getting into such advanced topics, let's begin by looking at the basic steps for securing your server.

# Basic Security

A Sendmail server runs on top of computer hardware and the Linux operating system just like any other server and therefore has the same basic security requirements. Don't let the hype over sophisticated network attacks obscure the importance of basic security. Good fundamental system administration is still the best defense against security problems.

Also, don't assume a firewall or fancy security tool will really make your site secure. Even if your server is protected by a firewall, you must take full responsibility for securing your server. Firewalls secure networks, but good system administration is needed to secure servers and clients. The network and every system on the network need to be secured to provide a *defense in depth*, which is the best way to defend against security attacks.

Despite the best firewall and the best system administration, your system will always be vulnerable to security problems. You should assume that you will have problems and that you will need to quickly recover from those problems. Prepare a disaster recovery plan and follow it. Make sure you have the backup hardware, software, and data you need to quickly restore service when things go wrong.

Good security preparation will lessen the number of problems you have to recover from. Begin your security preparations by securing your hardware.

## Secure the Hardware

The best security firewall in the world won't protect your server from a real fire. Floods, fires, earthquakes, storms, and other natural disasters are a real threat to your server. More server time is lost to power outages, disasters, hardware failures, and disgruntled employees than is lost because of a network-based security attack. Don't overlook obvious physical security issues. Your server can't run without hardware, so you need to protect it.

First, the Sendmail server hardware must be in a locked and secured location. If you have a computer room with controlled access that is staffed 24x7, that's ideal. At the very least, the server must be in a locked room. You don't want a disgruntled employee taking an axe to the server. (Think that's farfetched? At the very first place I worked, a berserk contractor used metal cutters on the back plane of an IBM mainframe!) A more common threat is that a disgruntled employee will gain access to the console and use that access to attack the server.

Even placing the Sendmail server in a locked room may not be enough. Many computer rooms run unattended, and they grant room access to several employees. These people can then gain access to the console of the Sendmail server at odd hours. There are some things you can do to increase the physical security of the server and the console in an unattended computer room.

To prevent unwanted reboots, the server box must be secured. If people have access to the power buttons or power cords of the server, they can force the server to reboot. The only way to completely prevent this is to lock the server and its uninterruptible power supply (UPS) in a cabinet that itself has a secured power connection. Make sure the cabinet has adequate ventilation to support both the server and the UPS to prevent overheating.

The keyboard must also be secured to prevent keyboard reboots with the "three-finger salute" (Ctrl+Alt+Del). This can be done by placing the keyboard in a locked cabinet, if one is used, or by disabling the function of the Ctrl+Alt+Del keyboard interrupt in the /etc/inittab file.

The local power company is generally a bigger threat to uptime than disgruntled employees or intruders. Make sure you provide a UPS for the server. Given the fact that Linux runs on standard PC hardware, it is very simple to provide UPS backup for your server. A small UPS that provides an hour of runtime for a PC may be adequate for your site, depending on the frequency and duration of power outages in your area. If critical systems in your organization have diesel generator backup power, you may be able to tie into that system. Evaluate your needs and your options and then make sure you have an adequate level of backup power.

The low cost of the PC hardware makes it possible to afford a complete set of backup hardware for your Linux Sendmail server. A disk crash denies service to your users just as effectively as the malicious actions of a network intruder. Having hardware on hand will shorten the amount of time before service is restored.

Securing the hardware is only the first step in securing your Sendmail server. Power outages may be a big source of downtime and insiders may pose a big security threat, but they are only part of the story. Software holes can be as easily exploited as unattended hardware.

## Secure the Software

Failure to keep software updated and to fix well-known bugs is the leading cause of network-based break-ins. Most break-ins are not the work of sophisticated security crackers. Experts may be the first to discover a vulnerability, but they rarely waste their time exploiting the vulnerability to break into every small business connected to the Internet. Most break-ins are the work of unsophisticated computer users called "script kiddies." They run attack scripts available from places like `rootshell.com` and `insecure.org`, and let the scripts do the work. The scripts look for and exploit well-known vulnerabilities to give the script kiddy unauthorized access to the target systems. The scripts can be configured to scan thousands of systems for vulnerabilities. Tracking the vulnerabilities exploited by the scripts and closing those holes as they appear are important components of improving the security of your server.

### Tracking Vulnerabilities

To secure a system, you need to know its vulnerabilities. Your goal should be to stay as well informed about Linux and Sendmail vulnerabilities as the vandals are. Frankly, you won't be able to. *You* have a life and responsibilities, so the vandals who have nothing better to do will get ahead of you and may compromise your system. Despite the difficulty, you should do your best to keep up to date about security problems.

There are several good sources of information about known security vulnerabilities.

- General information about security vulnerabilities is available from the `bugtraq` list at `http://geek-girl.com/bugtraq`.

- Good sites for security advisories are `www.10pht.com` and `www.cert.org`.

- A good site for Linux software updates and security hole announcements is `www.freshmeat.com`.

- The `www.sendmail.org` Web site provides information on Sendmail vulnerabilities.

You should also check the Web site maintained by your Linux distribution vendor for security announcements. Additionally, I recommend going to the SANS Institute Web site, `www.sans.org`, and signing up for the Security Alert Consensus, which is listed under the Security Digests. It is easy to pick the Linux-specific items out of the report, and the report keeps you updated on current vulnerabilities.

In addition to visiting the sites that report bug and security problems, visit the Web sites that provide attack scripts. Two such sites are `www.rootshell.com` and `www.insecure.org`. Make sure that your system is not vulnerable to the old attacks and evaluate the new scripts as they are released to understand the vulnerabilities they exploit. In addition to providing scripts, these sites provide information about what is currently going on in the network security world.

## Closing the Holes

The most important thing you can do to improve the security of your system against network-based attacks is to install security updates as soon as they become available. To update the software, you must know what software needs to be updated and where to find it. Security advisories and vulnerability reports sometimes include fixes.

Unfortunately, the fix is not always included in a vulnerability report, and you may need to look for Sendmail and Linux fixes yourself. The Linux vendor's Web site and `www.sendmail.org` are good place to look for fixes. Many Linux vendors provide security fixes for their distributions online.

---

***TIP***   The Linux vendor is a good place to get fixes because you can have confidence that the fixes do not contain malicious code. It is important to know where your patches come from. Get your fixes from a reliable source. Otherwise you risk opening up another security hole.

---

Figure 12.1 shows a security report on the Red Hat Web site. The report describes the problem and provides a link to the software update. Clicking a link leads to a fix that can be downloaded and installed using the `rpm` command.

**Figure  12.1**    The Red Hat Security Advisory site

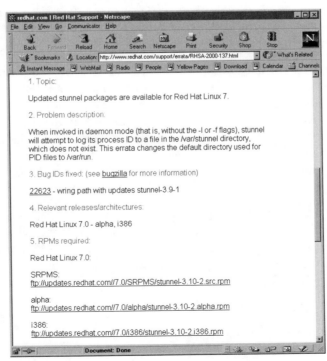

Maintaining a Healthy Server

PART 4

If you're looking for a specific fix, you can search through the security advisories on the vendor's Web page. The big advantage of this is that you will often find fixes for bugs that you have never heard of. On the downside, sometimes you find out that a bug you have heard of has not yet been fixed. Nevertheless, you should take all of the bug fixes that are offered and periodically check back to see if the bug you're concerned about does get fixed.

> **TIP**   Frequently, administrators complain that the authors of software don't fix bugs, but I find a much more common problem is that system administrators don't use the bug fixes that are out there. Set aside a time each month to download and install the fixes provided by your software vendor. Make it part of your routine.

Vulnerabilities are not limited to Sendmail. Most of the network software that runs on your Linux system has vulnerabilities that have been exploited at one time or another. It is not enough to keep the Linux operating system and the Sendmail software up to date. You must keep all software packages updated to keep your server secure.

### Removing Unneeded Software

Reduce the burden of keeping software updated by removing all of the software you don't really need. If you have a dedicated Sendmail server, it doesn't need to run `httpd`, `ftpd`, or any of a host of other network daemons. Unneeded software on a server can open a hole for an attacker. Everything you have on your server is a potential tool for an intruder. Think hard about what is really needed for the server to do its job.

Security is one of the reasons I'm a big fan of dedicated servers. A dedicated server is a system that provides only one network service. For example, a mail relay server that provides only SMTP is a dedicated server. Most e-mail servers cannot be dedicated servers because e-mail is a user service. Every general-purpose Linux system that permits users to log on runs Sendmail. However, when mail hubs and mail relay servers are used, they should be dedicated to e-mail service and not cluttered with unrelated services. Using dedicated servers for mail hubs and mail relays makes it much easier to limit the software installed on those servers.

There are two ways to limit the software installed on a server. First, don't install what you don't need when you do the initial Linux installation. During the initial installation, you select the software packages that are installed and the daemons that are loaded. Choose carefully based on your plan for the system that you're installing.

The other way to limit the software on a system is to remove it after it is installed. For example, to remove FTP from a system with rpm you could enter:

```
rpm -e ftp-0.17-6
```

Package managers such as RPM and dpkg are very effective and easy to use. Removing software without a package manager can be difficult, particularly if unanticipated software dependencies arise. From a system security perspective, the role that package managers play in removing software is just as important as the role they play in installing software.

### Disabling Unneeded Software

It is not necessary to remove software in order to prevent it from running. Sometimes you want to keep software so that it can be enabled for special occasions. Other times you want to evaluate the impact before removing software. If you're not sure you want to remove a network daemon, start by disabling it until you are sure that doing so has no negative impact on your users or your server. There are two simple ways to prevent daemons from running.

**Remove unneeded daemons from the** inetd **or** xinetd **configuration**    Most network services are started by inetd. The services it starts are listed in the inetd.conf file. Removing a service from the file prevents outsiders from using the specified network service but does not block you from using the service on outbound connections. Thus, if ftp is deleted from inetd.conf, you can still ftp to remote sites but no one from a remote site can use ftp to connect into your server.

xinetd is an alternative to inetd that is used on some Linux distributions, most notably Red Hat 7. xinetd starts the services listed in the /etc/xinetd.conf file. In the Red Hat 7 configuration, xinetd.conf includes by reference all of the scripts defined in the directory /etc/xinetd.d. To disable an unneeded daemon in Red Hat 7, use the same chkconfig command that is used to control boot scripts. For example, to disable rlogind, enter chkconfig rlogin off at the command prompt.

**Remove start-up scripts that launch unneeded daemons**    Some network services—Sendmail is a good example—are started at boot time. Use chkconfig, tksysv, or a similar tool to remove unneeded daemons from the start-up. For example, your Sendmail server may not need to run the httpd start-up script because it is not a Web server. You're still able to use a Web browser even if the httpd script is not run at start-up.

In addition to installing the latest software updates and removing unneeded software, limit access to the software and services running on your server to just those systems that you actually want to serve. Linux distributions use two different access control mechanisms: `tcpd` and `xinetd`. Both of these access control mechanisms are covered in the following sections.

## Limit Login Access

For security reasons, you want to limit remote login access to the server. Deleting `telnetd` and `rlogind` from the `inetd.conf` file as described in the previous section eliminates the basic remote login services. Eliminating all remote logins would provide an ideal level of security, but it is usually impractical. Many users want to read e-mail directly on the server, which requires a logins account. Other users want POP or IMAP access, which also requires a user account and password on the server. As the system administrator, you need to provide secure remote login and controlled access.

If a user requires only POP or IMAP access, create the user's account without a valid `login` shell. The username and password from the account will provide IMAP or POP access, yet the user will not be granted login access without a valid shell. `/bin/false` is commonly used as the shell for this type of account. This works for users that require only POP or IMAP, but it does not work if the user also requires login access. In those cases, you may need to provide secure login software.

The secure shell (`ssh2`) program is probably the most secure remote login software available. It supports secure login and even secure X Windows access. Some Linux systems include `openssh`, a version of `ssh` that does not use any patented cryptographic techniques. If secure shell is not provided with your Linux distribution, it is available on the network. Go to `www.ssh.org` for more information about secure shell and to download the latest source code.

POP and IMAP services can be run inside a secure connection using `stunnel`. `stunnel` is a program that uses Secure Sockets Layer (SSL) to encrypt traffic for daemons that do not encrypt their own traffic. When run over `stunnel`, POP is called `pops` and assigned TCP port 995, and IMAP is called `imaps` and assigned TCP port 993. For example, the following command added to the start-up of a Caldera system would run POP inside an SSL tunnel:

```
stunnel -d 995 -l /usr/sbin/ipop3d -- ipop3d
```

That same system could run `pops` inside `stunnel` from `inetd` using the following entry in the `inetd.conf` file:

```
pops stream tcp nowait root /usr/sbin/stunnel -l /usr/sbin/ipop3d --
    ipop3d
```

Listing 12.1 shows the `xinetd.conf` entry for `imaps` on a Red Hat 7 system.

**Listing 12.1** Running the imaps Service from xinetd

```
service imaps
{
        socket_type             = stream
        wait                    = no
        user                    = root
        server                  = /usr/sbin/stunnel
        server_args             = -l /usr/sbin/imapd -- imapd
        log_on_failure          += USERID
}
```

stunnel, however, has nothing specific to do with POP, IMAP, or e-mail. It can be used to secure a wide variety of daemons. See the stunnel man page for more details about stunnel. See *Linux Security* by Ramon Hontañón (Sybex, 2001) for more information about securing a variety of services.

The primary reason for running POP or IMAP through stunnel is to ensure that the user's password cannot be stolen from a POP or IMAP session and then used by the thief to log in to the server. stunnel encrypts everything: the login and the download of mail. This guarantees that the contents of the mail cannot be surreptitiously read by a snooper during the download, but from the point of view of the system administrator securing the content of the mail is usually unimportant. In all likelihood the mail moved through the Internet to the server unencrypted. Encrypting it while it moves from the server to the reader is a little silly after the worldwide exposure the mail has already received. The password is really the only piece of information you want to protect. Using a stronger form of authentication than simple clear text passwords can protect it. POP provides strong authentication through the optional APOP command of the POP3 protocol.

To offer the APOP command to your POP3 clients, you must install a daemon, such as Qualcomm's Qpopper, that implements the command. Qpopper is available as an RPM from many Linux vendors and can be located through rpmfind.net. Once you install it, make sure that the entry for POP in inetd.conf or xientd.conf points to the new in.qpopper program. The Qpopper package adds a program named popauth that is used to create passwords for the APOP command. Listing 12.2 shows an administrator adding an APOP password for the user craig.

**Listing 12.2** Using the popauth Command

```
[root]# popauth -user craig
Changing only APOP password for craig.
New password: SecretPassword
Retype new password: SecretPassword
```

Maintaining a
Healthy Server

PART 4

All of the things described above—removing `rlogind` and `telnetd`, limiting logins to secure shell, creating POP and IMAP users without login shells, protecting POP and IMAP passwords through encryption or strong authentication—are all done to prevent unauthorized login access. Of course, login access may not be the only network service that you want to protect on your Sendmail server. To control access to all services started by `inetd`, use the wrapper.

### Controlling Network Access with Wrapper

The wrapper daemon, named `tcpd`, is executed by `inetd`. It is an integral part of most Linux distributions. Using the wrapper on a Linux system is easier than it is on many other systems because the entries in the `inetd.conf` file already point to the `tcpd` program. Listing 12.3 is a few lines from the `inetd.conf` file on a Caldera Linux system.

**Listing 12.3**  Linux Is Pre-configured for Wrapper

```
ftp     stream tcp  nowait root /usr/sbin/tcpd in.ftpd -l -a
telnet  stream tcp  nowait root /usr/sbin/tcpd in.telnetd
shell   stream tcp  nowait root /usr/sbin/tcpd in.rshd
login   stream tcp  nowait root /usr/sbin/tcpd in.rlogind
imap    stream tcp  nowait root /usr/sbin/tcpd imapd
```

In Listing 12.3, bold text is used to highlight the reference to `tcpd` in each line of the `inetd.conf` file. The path to `tcpd` is used in place of the path of each network service daemon. Therefore, when `inetd` receives a request for a service, it starts `tcpd`. `tcpd` then logs the service request, checks the access control information, and, if permitted, starts the real daemon to handle the request.

The wrapper package performs two basic functions: it logs requests for Internet services and provides an access control mechanism for those services. If the `tcpd` access control files are not found, `tcpd` allows every host to have access and simply logs the access request. The wrapper uses the `authpriv` facility of `syslogd` to log its messages. Look in the `/etc/syslog.conf` file to find out where your system logs `authpriv` messages. (On a Caldera system, these messages are logged to `/var/log/secure`.) Logging requests for specific network services is a useful monitoring function, especially if you are looking for possible intruders. If logging were all it did, wrapper would be a useful package. But the real power of wrapper is its ability to control access to network services.

***tcpd* Access Control Files**    Two files define access controls for `tcpd`. The `hosts.allow` file lists the hosts that are allowed to access the system's services and the `hosts.deny` file lists the hosts that are denied service. The format of entries in both files is the same:

```
services : clients [: shell-command]
```

*services* is a comma-separated list of network services or the keyword ALL. ALL is used to indicate all network services. Otherwise, each individual service is identified by its process name, which is the name that immediately follows the path to `tcpd` in the `inetd.conf` file. For example, the process name in the following `inetd.conf` entry is `imapd`:

```
imap stream tcp  nowait root /usr/sbin/tcpd imapd
```

*clients* is a comma-separated list of hostnames, domain names, Internet addresses, network numbers, and the keyword LOCAL. Alternately it can be the keyword ALL. ALL matches all hostnames and addresses. LOCAL matches all hostnames that do not include a domain name part. A hostname matches an individual host. An IP address can be defined by itself to match a specific host or with an address mask to match a range of addresses. A domain name starts with a dot (.) and matches every host within that domain. A network number ends with a dot (.) and matches every IP address within the network address space.

*shell-command* is an optional shell command that `tcpd` executes when a match occurs. If a match occurs, `tcpd` logs the access, grants or denies access to the service, and then passes the shell command to the shell for execution. The shell command allows you to define additional processing that is triggered by a match in the access control list. In all practical examples, this feature is used in the `hosts.deny` file to gather more information about the intruder or to provide immediate notification to the system administrator about a potential security attack.

`tcpd` reads the `hosts.allow` file first and then reads the `hosts.deny` file. It stops as soon as it finds a match for the host and the service in question. Therefore, access granted by `hosts.allow` cannot be overridden by `hosts.deny`. For this reason, I usually start by inserting an entry in `hosts.deny` that denies all access to all systems. The rule in the `hosts.deny` file that blocks access from all other computers is:

```
ALL : ALL
```

Next, I put entries in the `hosts.allow` file that permit access to just those systems that I really want to provide services to. Here is something from an imaginary `hosts.allow` file:

```
ALL : LOCAL, .foobirds.org
```

The keyword ALL in the *services* field indicates that the first rule applies to all network services. In the *clients* field, the keyword LOCAL indicates that all hostnames without a domain part are acceptable, and the `.foobirds.org` matches all hostnames in that domain. By itself, LOCAL would match wren but not wren.foobirds.org. Combining these two tests in a single rule allows every system in our local domain to use all of the network services.

Use hosts.deny to block login access from all remote systems and then use hosts.allow to permit only those computers that you truly want to give login access through the blockade.

### Controlling Network Access with *xinetd*

An alternative to inetd is xinetd. xinetd is configured in the /etc/xinetd.conf file, which provides the same information to xinetd as inetd.conf provides to inetd. But instead of using positional parameters with meanings determined by location on a configuration line, xinetd.conf uses attribute names that identify the purpose of each parameter. Listing 12.4 shows a sample xientd.conf entry.

**Listing 12.4** An xinetd.conf Entry from Red Hat 7

```
# default: on
# description: rlogin is the server for the rlogin(1) program. \
#       The server provides a remote login facility with \
#       authentication based on privileged port numbers from \
#       trusted hosts.
service login
{
        socket_type          = stream
        wait                 = no
        user                 = root
        log_on_success       += USERID
        log_on_failure       += USERID
        server               = /usr/sbin/in.rlogind
}
```

The service, socket_type, wait, user, and server values all parallel values shown in the inetd.conf file, except that the path provided for the server does not invoke the tcpd wrapper program. The wrapper is not used because xinetd provides capabilities similar to those of wrapper on its own. xinetd provides its own logging and its own access controls.

---

**NOTE** The xinetd daemon on Red Hat 7 Linux systems consults the /etc/ hosts.allow and /etc/hosts.deny files in addition to the access controls defined in the xinetd.conf file.

The `log_on_success` and `log_on_failure` lines in Listing 12.4 add the user ID of the remote user to the standard log entry when a successful connection is made or a connection attempt fails. The += syntax means that this value is added to the other values already being logged. In addition to logging the user ID of the remote user, `log_on_success` and `log_on_failure` allow you to log:

**HOST**    The address of the remote host. Like USERID, this value can be used for both success and failure.

**PID**    The process ID of the server started to handle the connection. PID applies only to `log_on_success`.

**DURATION**    Logs the length of time that the server handling this connection ran. DURATION applies only to `log_on_success`.

**EXIT**    Logs the exit status of the server when the connection terminates. EXIT applies only to `log_on_success`.

**ATTEMPT**    Logs unsuccessful connection attempts. ATTEMPT applies only to `log_on_failure`.

**RECORD**    Logs the connection information received from the remote server. This parameter applies only to `log_on_failure`.

In addition to logging, `xinetd` provides access control. `xinetd` provides three different attributes for access control. It can be configured to accept connections from certain hosts, paralleling the `host.allow` file, to reject connections from certain hosts, paralleling the `host.deny` file, and to accept connections only at certain times of the day. These attributes are described below.

**only_from**    This attribute identifies the hosts that are allowed to connect to the service. Hosts can be defined using:

- a numeric address. For example, 172.16.12.5 defines a specific host and 129.6.0.0 defines all hosts with an address that begins with 129.6. The address 0.0.0.0 matches all addresses.
- an address scope. For example, 172.16.12.{3,6,8,23} defines four different hosts: 172.16.12.3, 172.16.12.6, 172.16.12.8, and 172.16.12.23.
- a network name. The network name must be defined in the `/etc/networks` file.
- a canonical hostname. The IP address provided by the remote system must reverse-map to this hostname.
- a domain name. The hostname returned by the reverse lookup must be in the specified domain. For example, the value `.foobirds.org` requires a host in the `foobirds.org` domain. Note that when a domain name is used it starts with a dot.

- an IP address with an associated address mask. For example, 172.16.12.128/25 would match every address from 172.16.12.128 to 172.16.12.255.

**no_access**    This attribute defines the hosts that are denied access to the service. Hosts are defined using exactly the same methods as those described above for the only_from attribute.

**access_times**    This attribute defines the time of day a service is available, in the form *hour*:*min*-*hour*:*min*. A 24-hour clock is used. Hours are 0 to 23 and minutes are 0 to 59. Time restrictions have limited utility on an e-mail server. Users read e-mail 24 hours a day.

If neither only_from nor no_access is specified, access is granted to everyone. If both are specified, the most exact match applies—for example:

```
no_access          = 172.16.12.250
only_from          = 172.16.12.0
```

The only_from command in this example permits every system on network 172.16.12.0 to have access to the service. The no_access command takes away that access for one system. It doesn't matter whether the no_access attribute comes before or after the only_from attribute. It always works the same way because the more exact match takes precedence.

Listing 12.5 shows the sample rlogin entry from Red Hat 7 with some access controls added.

**Listing 12.5**   xinetd.conf Access Controls

```
# default: on
# description: rlogind is the server for the rlogin(1) program. \
#        The server provides a remote login facility with \
#        authentication based on privileged port numbers from \
#        trusted hosts.
service login
{
        socket_type           = stream
        wait                  = no
        user                  = root
        log_on_success        += USERID
        log_on_failure        += USERID
        only_from             = 172.16.12.0
        no_access             = 172.16.12.231
        server                = /usr/sbin/in.rlogind
```

In Listing 12.5 the `only_from` attribute permits access from every system on network 172.16.12.0, which is the local network for this sample system. At the same time, it blocks access from every other system. In Listing 12.5, that is not exactly what we want. There is one system, 172.16.12.231, that is not trusted to have login access. The `no_access` attribute is added to deny access to anyone on the system 172.16.12.231.

Listing 12.5 shows that the `only_from` command both grants access and denies access— at the same time that the sample `only_from` command is granting the local network access, it is blocking access from the outside world. Additionally, Listing 12.5 illustrates that the more exact match, in this case the `no_access` command, takes precedence. Both the `only_from` command and the `no_access` commands match the host 172.16.12.231. However, the `only_from` command matches it as part of a network while the `no_access` command matches it exactly.

This section introduced the role that `tcpd` and `xinetd` can play in limiting network access to your server. Neither of these tools is specific to Sendmail, so the complete details of the complex syntax of both are beyond the scope of this book. If you want to learn more about them, and more about general Linux security, see Ramon Hontañón's *Linux Security*.

Sendmail, like all other servers, runs on an operating system and hardware. Securing the underlying operating system and hardware is the most important part of securing your server. However, it is not the complete story. Once you have made sure that the system your mail server runs on is secure, you need to make sure that Sendmail is as secure as you can make it. The next section leaves the topic of general system security and focuses directly on Sendmail security.

# Securing a Sendmail Server

Many discussions of Sendmail security focus on spam controls and relay configuration. In those discussions, spam is viewed as a form of denial of service called *theft of service*. I find that view of spam much too extreme: spam is an annoyance; it isn't a security threat. Real DoS attacks overwhelm the server and effectively block useful inbound and outbound mail. (For example, a mail-bombing attack delivers so much mail so rapidly to a single target that the target system is unable to keep up with the workload.) Sendmail provides a few configuration parameters that can be used to deal with real denial of service attacks.

> **confMAX_DAEMON_CHILDREN** This parameter defines the maximum number of Sendmail processes that can be running simultaneously. Every system has an upper limit on the number of processes it can effectively handle. A variety of DoS attacks are designed to overwhelm a system by launching so many mail processes that the system is no longer able to do any productive work. The `confMAX_DAEMON_CHILDREN` parameter protects the operating system from this type of attack.

Maintaining a
Healthy Server

PART 4

By default, Sendmail sets no upper limit on the number of child processes that can be launched to process mail. To limit Sendmail to two hundred children, put the following command in the m4 macro configuration file:

```
define(`confMAX_DAEMON_CHILDREN', `200')dnl
```

With this setting, Sendmail accepts mail only when fewer than two hundred children are running. This is not a recommended value; it is just an example. Study the actual usage patterns of your system before you select a value, and then set the value at least 50 percent above the observed maximum value to allow for usage spikes.

confMAX_DAEMON_CHILDREN is most useful for systems that do more than just provide Sendmail service. A great place to use this parameter is on a Linux desktop system that runs its own Sendmail server. A desktop system has a relatively light e-mail workload and it provides many other important services to the user of the desktop. The confMAX_DAEMON_CHILDREN parameter protects the other services from runaway Sendmail daemons. It makes sure that the user can still open an X window or start an editor even if the Sendmail server is under attack. confMAX_DAEMON_CHILDREN provides this protection for the other services at the cost of making it simple for the attacker to shut down mail service. Simply sending enough mail to exceed the maximum number of children shuts down the SMTP port. Use this parameter carefully.

**confCONNECTION_RATE_THROTTLE**    This parameter defines the maximum number of SMTP connections that are permitted for any one-second period. Like the confMAX_DAEMON_CHILDREN parameter, the confCONNECTION_RATE_THROTTLE parameter protects the server from being overwhelmed by e-mail. Neither of these parameters protects Sendmail from attack; they both protect the system when Sendmail is under attack.

By default, Sendmail sets no limit on the rate at which new SMTP connections can be made. It is designed to handle connections as fast as they arrive. To limit Sendmail to ten new connections per second, put the following command in the m4 macro configuration file:

```
define(`confCONNECTION_RATE_THROTTLE', `10')dnl
```

With this setting, Sendmail rejects any network connections after the first ten in any one-second period. As before, this is not a recommended value; it is just an example.

Study the actual usage patterns of your system before you select a value, and then set the value at least 50 percent above the observed maximum value to allow for usage spikes.

confCONNECTION_RATE_THROTTLE is useful on exactly the same systems as confMAX_ DAEMON_CHILDREN. In fact, the two parameters are often used together. confMAX_DAEMON_CHILDREN sets the absolute upper limit on the number of simultaneous e-mail connections and confCONNECTION_RATE_THROTTLE sets the rate at which you will climb to that maximum. An attacker can easily overrun the connection rate you set in order to deny you mail access. However, setting the rate can protect the other services on your system so that you have an operational system to help you deal with the attack.

**confMAX_MESSAGE_SIZE**    This parameter defines the maximum size of messages that the mail server will accept. Any messages larger than this size are rejected. By default, Sendmail accepts messages of any size. The following command overrides that default and sets the maximum message size to 2,000,000 bytes.

```
define(`confMAX_MESSAGE_SIZE', `2000000')dnl
```

Some DoS attacks are designed to overwhelm the file systems by writing enough large e-mail messages to completely fill the disk containing the spool directory. This parameter is intended to protect against these attacks, but it is largely ineffective because the attacker can just send a larger number of smaller messages for the same effect.

It is impossible to completely protect Sendmail from denial of service attacks. Limiting the amount of damage done by the attack is the real purpose of the parameters described above. Similarly, the techniques used to protect Sendmail from unauthorized access are really meant to protect the system as a whole.

## Securing Sendmail against Unauthorized Access

The most dangerous security exploits are those attacks that use unauthorized access to grab root permission. Once an intruder has gained root access, nothing can be done to protect anything on the system, including Sendmail. The purpose of most Sendmail security is to make sure that Sendmail is not used as the means for an intruder to gain unauthorized access or root permission. To that end, the user IDs and files that Sendmail depends on must be secured.

Sendmail uses three different user IDs depending on the action it is taking. The three user IDs are:

**DefaultUser**   This is an option in the sendmail.cf file that identifies the user ID and group ID used to run mailers and other external commands. There are three possible default values for the DefaultUser option:

1. If the user mailnull is defined in the /etc/passwd file, the user ID and group ID assigned to mailnull are used.

2. If mailnull is not defined and the user daemon is defined in the /etc/passwd file, the user ID and group ID assigned to daemon are used.

3. If neither mailnull nor daemon is defined in the /etc/passwd file, 1 is used as the user ID and 1 is used as the group ID.

The default value for the DefaultUser option can be overridden by defining a specific value for the option in the m4 macro configuration file with the confDEF_USER_ID parameter. The macro configuration file delivered with Red Hat 7 contains the following confDEF_USER_ID command:

```
define(`confDEF_USER_ID', `8:12')dnl
```

This define command sets the user ID to 8 and the group ID to 12. These are the values associated with the username mail in the /etc/passwd file delivered with the Red Hat 7 system. It is interesting to note that the Red Hat 7 /etc/passwd file also has an entry for the user mailnull and one for the user daemon. daemon is no surprise because it is used by several different daemon processes. On the other hand, the user mailnull must have been specifically added to act as a default value for the DefaultUser option because it serves no other purpose. Given that, it is not clear why Red Hat also defined a value for the confDEF_USER_ID parameter. Here are the mail and mailnull entries from the Red Hat 7 /etc/passwd file and the /etc/shadow file:

```
[craig]$ grep mail /etc/passwd
mail:x:8:12:mail:/var/spool/mail:
mailnull:x:47:47::/var/spool/mqueue:/dev/null
[root]# grep mail /etc/shadow
mail:*:11267:0:99999:7:::
mailnull:!!:11267:0:99999:7:::
```

While Red Hat provides two /etc/passwd entries that are specifically defined to be used by the DefaultUser option, many Linux systems don't provide any such entries. Both of the Red Hat entries show two of the characteristics you need to be aware of if you add a `mailnull` user account. `mailnull` cannot have an associated password and it cannot have a valid `login` shell. In the example, `mailnull` has `/dev/null` as the `login` shell defined for it in the `/etc/passwd` file. Additionally, the `mailnull` user does not have a valid password in either the `/etc/passwd` file or the `/etc/shadow` file. Therefore, the `mailnull` user account meets the first two requirements. The third requirement for the `mailnull` user account is that it cannot own any files. These three requirements prevent the account from being exploited to gain unauthorized access.

**TrustedUser**  This option defines the user that owns Sendmail's files, such as the database files. The `TrustedUser` option defaults to `root`. The default value can be overridden by defining a value for `confTRUSTED_USER` in the `m4` macro configuration file—for example:

```
define(`confTRUSTED_USER', `mailuser')dnl
```

This example assumes there is a user account named `mailuser` defined in the `/etc/passwd` file. The user account does not have a password or a valid `login` shell. But unlike the `DefaultUser`, the `TrustedUser` does own files. The `/etc/mail` directory is owned by the `TrustedUser` and the permissions for that directory are set to 755. The individual files inside the `/etc/mail` directory belong to the `TrustedUser` and have their permissions set to 644—execute permissions are not granted to anyone. If Sendmail files fall outside of the `/etc/mail` directory—for example, `/etc/sendmail.cf` and `/etc/aliases`—they are also owned by the `TrustedUser` and assigned 644 as their permissions. The `TrustedUser` does not own the mail queue or the mail spool directories.

The `DefaultUser` is allowed to execute commands, such as mailers, but is not allowed to own files. The `TrustedUser` is allowed to own files but is not allowed to execute commands. This division of labor is intended to improve security. However, it is the division that improves security, not the specific user ID selected to be the `TrustedUser`. The `root` user, which is the default value for `TrustedUser`, should be just as secure as any other user ID. Sendmail administrators who change `TrustedUser` to another user ID do so because they fear that a file owned by root will be left with an execute bit on and that an intruder will find a way to exploit that fact to run a script from the file that grants `root` access. Most administrators, however, don't bother to change the default value of the `TrustedUser` option.

**RunAsUser**  This option defines the user ID under which Sendmail runs. By default, this option is not defined and Sendmail runs as `root`. If this option is defined, Sendmail relinquishes root privilege as soon as it binds to the SMTP port and switches to the user ID defined by the `RunAsUser` option. After that, everything is run under the

RunAsUser user ID—that includes Sendmail itself and all of the mailers and commands executed by Sendmail. All of the files read by Sendmail must be readable by this user and all of the files written by Sendmail must be writeable by this user.

The RunAsUser option is intended for use only on firewall mail servers. On a firewall mail server, the mail is received, processed, and then forwarded on to the internal mail server where users read their mail. The firewall mail server does not have any user accounts, so there is no need for the Sendmail program to assume the identity of a specific user or of root in order to deliver mail or write a file into a user's mailbox. The RunAsUser option is not used on a regular mail server.

For most configurations, all you need to do is define the user mailnull in the /etc/passwd directory. The mailnull user becomes the DefaultUser, which gives you the separation between file creation and command execution that is the key benefit of having different user IDs for Sendmail. Once mailnull is defined for the DefaultUser option, there is very little reason to define a value for TrustedUser. For most systems, root is a fine TrustedUser. Additionally, root is the correct RunAsUser for the vast majority of Sendmail servers.

## Securing Files and File Access

Using the correct user IDs is only part of the story. Sendmail also needs to be careful about the files it reads and what is in them. Maintaining the following standards will help avoid problems:

- Files that Sendmail reads should not grant group or world write permission. For example, if the relay-domains file is world writeable, anyone on the system can grant relay permission to their favorite spammer. The recommended permission for files read by Sendmail is 644.

- Files read by Sendmail should not be in group- or world-writeable directories. Again, anyone in a given group, or perhaps anyone on the system, could create a file giving Sendmail bad instructions. The recommended directory permissions for directories used by Sendmail is 755.

- Files read or written by Sendmail should not be symbolic links.

In some conditions—for example, reading a .forward file—Sendmail checks that these standards are being maintained. You can disable the file access checks that Sendmail performs by setting the DontBlameSendmail option using the confDONT_BLAME_SENDMAIL parameter in the m4 configuration file. All of the DontBlameSendmail settings reduce security, so they are not covered here. For more information about this option, see Appendix C, "Sendmail Variables, Options, and Flags."

Sendmail takes special care with the .forward file because that file can contain an e-mail address that forwards the mail to a program using the | *program* syntax, where *program* is the name of the program to be executed. The aliases database can also use this syntax in a recipient address to forward mail to a program. You do not define the .forward file for every user, but as the Sendmail administrator you are responsible for the contents of the aliases database.

Make sure that no one else can modify the aliases database. The aliases file and the directory that contains the aliases file should only be writeable by the owner, which is the TrustedUser (usually root). If you put an alias in the database that sends mail to a program, you must be absolutely sure that the program you send the mail to handles the data properly. Buffer overflows and other data-handling problems are a big security hole commonly exploited by intruders. Personally, I never alias mail to a program.

You might not be able to create the .forward file for every user, but you can control the programs that are available to the user through the | *program* syntax. Controlling those programs is the primary function of smrsh.

### Using the *smrsh* Feature

The smrsh feature was introduced during the discussion of the Red Hat configuration in Chapter 5, "Understanding a Vendor's Configuration." smrsh is the Sendmail Restricted Shell. It replaces /bin/sh as the program used for the prog mailer. The prog mailer is the mail delivery agent used when Sendmail processes an address that uses the | *program* syntax. On most Linux systems /bin/sh is the Bourne Again Shell (bash), which means that any command that can be processed by bash can be processed by the prog mailer. This is a very flexible configuration but a potentially dangerous one. Anyone who can get a command to the prog mailer has essentially the same access to the system as a user logged on to a terminal. smrsh limits the flexibility and reduces the danger.

smrsh is a restricted shell. Some built-in shell commands—exec, exit, and echo—work, but most do not. smrsh does not allow standard I/O redirection. Most of the special characters used by the shell—carriage return, newline, <, >, ;, $, (, and )—are not allowed; only || and && are accepted. Most importantly, only those commands that can be run by exec or those that you choose to make available to smrsh through a special execution directory are available to the user.

smrsh forwards only to programs found in the /usr/adm/sm.bin directory. The Sendmail administrator creates the /usr/adm/sm.bin directory and then populates it with the programs that are trusted to be accessible through the prog mailer. smrsh strips the initial pathname off of the program to which mail is being forwarded. Thus, if the user enters /usr/local/vacation as the program name, smrsh strips the program name down to vacation and looks for a file of that name in the /usr/adm/sm.bin directory.

/usr/adm/sm.bin is the default execution directory used by smrsh. Compile smrsh with either the –DPATH or –DCMDBIN compile options to specify a different execution path. The execution path is often changed on Linux systems. For example, Red Hat defines the path as /etc/smrsh. On a Red Hat system, programs trusted to receive forwarded mail are stored in the /etc/smrsh directory.

Take care when adding programs to the smrsh execution directory. Poorly written programs are popular targets for attackers. Every program is a potential hole for an intruder to exploit. Choose them carefully.

# Sendmail Security Protocols

The first two sections of this chapter cover techniques for securing a Sendmail server. None of the things you do to make your server more secure can ensure the security of mail as it moves through the network. Mail can be corrupted or read at any point as it travels through the network. No one can have a reasonable expectation of privacy with e-mail. It is cleartext data moving through a shared network. Everyone knows that their e-mail is an open communication shouted to the world.

Sometimes, however, you want to keep your mail private. This can be done using add-on tools, such as Pretty Good Privacy (PGP) or Gnu Privacy Guard (GnuPG), to secure messages. These tools, however, are not integrated into Sendmail. Starting with Sendmail 8.11, some standard Internet security protocols have been added to Sendmail to authenticate clients and secure connections. Four basic protocols have been added to Sendmail to support secure mail messages:

**STARTTLS**   RFC 2487 ("SMTP Service Extension for Secure SMTP over TLS") defines the STARTTLS protocol that standardizes the transmission of encrypted e-mail. STARTTLS depends on transport layer security (TLS).

**TLS**   RFC 2246 ("The TLS Protocol Version 1.0") defines a protocol that provides encrypted communications between two applications, such as two message transfer agent (MTA) programs. TLS is based on Secure Sockets Layer (SSL). SSL is the security mechanism used for e-commerce on the Web. TLS and SSL have slight differences, but the TLS RFC allows for compatibility with SSL. Sendmail takes advantage of this and uses SSL for its transport layer security.

**AUTH**   RFC 2554 ("SMTP Service Extension for Authentication") defines the AUTH protocol that is used to authenticate the end points in an e-mail exchange. AUTH depends on the Simple Authentication and Security Layer (SASL).

**SASL**   RFC 2222 ("Simple Authentication and Security Layer (SASL)") defines a generalized method for adding authentication to connection-oriented protocols, such as SMTP.

Sendmail implements the AUTH protocol and the STARTTLS protocol, but it depends on Linux for TLS and SASL. We saw this dependency in Chapter 3, "Running Sendmail," when we attempted to install the RPM version of Sendmail 8.11 on a Linux system that did not have SSL or SASL installed. RPM complained that Sendmail 8.11 depended on openssl and libsasl and that neither was provided. It is the convergence of cryptographic support in the operating system and in Sendmail that makes it possible for your server to support secure e-mail.

The Sendmail security protocols ensure the authenticity of MTAs and the integrity of e-mail in the network. To accomplish these tasks, the protocols use cryptography to authenticate and secure SMTP communications. This isn't a book about cryptography; however, some cryptographic concepts are essential for understanding the Sendmail security protocols.

## Encryption and Cryptography

There are two basic types of cryptography: *secret key*, which is also called symmetric cryptography, and *public key*, which is sometimes called asymmetric cryptography. Symmetric cryptography is easy to understand. Cooperating systems use the same key and the same algorithm to encrypt and decrypt data. The problem with symmetric cryptography is that a prior agreement must be reached among all participating systems about the key and the algorithm to be used. The secret key in a secret key system is far from being a secret because every system must have a copy of the key. The more systems sharing the secret, the greater the possibility that the secret will be compromised.

Public key cryptography is a much more interesting system. It uses two keys—a public key that can be openly available to everyone and a private key that does not need to be shared with anyone. When the public key is used to encrypt a message, the message can be decrypted only with the private key. Thus, anyone can encrypt a message bound for the target system by using the public key, but only the target system can decrypt and read the message using its private key. Equally important, only messages encrypted with the private key can be decrypted with the public key. This elegant system is not without complexity. Two things are required to make it work:

**Authentication**   In a secret key cryptography system, the mere fact that a message is properly encrypted means that it must have come from a trusted system that has the secret key. A public key system is different. Because the public key is available to everyone, a method for authenticating the source of an encrypted message is needed. Messages are authenticated by a digital signature. A digital signature is produced by running a cryptographic checksum using the content of the message as the data for the checksum and the private key of the source of the message for the encryption. Since the digital signature was produced with the source's private key, it can only be decrypted with the source's public key, proving the message came from the source. Additionally, the fact that the checksum was produced using the original content of the message means that the recipient can detect corrupted data by rerunning the checksum. This provides authentication for both the source and the content.

**Secure key distribution**    A weakness of public key cryptography is that you must trust the source of the public key. Everything—authentication, encryption, and decryption—depends on the public key. A key obtained from a corrupted server undermines the security of everything. Some commercial outfits offer public key servers on a fee basis. Most organizations use these services. Other organizations create bilateral agreements establishing trust between the organizations for the purpose of distributing keys. In effect, an organization tells its partners to trust a specific server as the source of its public keys.

The Sendmail security protocols do not define a mechanism for distributing public keys. These protocols assume that the keys have been obtained from a trusted public key server or distributed by some other secure mechanism.

## Sendmail Authentication

The AUTH extension to SMTP is used to authenticate the SMTP client and individual messages transmitted by the client. This extension does not encrypt messages. Instead it provides some assurance that the source of the message is who it claims to be. AUTH is used to validate the client system when the system cannot be validated by its IP address—for example, when the client is a mobile system or when the client connects to the server through a third party that dynamically assigns the client an IP address. The keyword AUTH is used in three distinct ways.

AUTH appears in the list of keywords displayed in response to the EHLO command. When used in this way, AUTH advertises the fact that the server supports the AUTH extension to SMTP and advertises the authentication methods supported by the server. We first saw this in Listing 1.2 of Chapter 1, "Internet Mail Protocols," when the server displayed the following informational message:

```
250-AUTH DIGEST-MD5
```

This message tells the client that the server supports the AUTH SMTP extension and that it uses DIGEST-MD5 for authentication. Message Digest 5 (MD5) is an encryption system that is generally used for authentication.

The list of authentication techniques advertised by the server is determined by the intersection of the techniques supported by the SASL library (libsasl) and the techniques requested by the administrator in the Sendmail configuration using the AuthMechanisms option. The `AuthMechanisms` option is defined using the `confAUTH_MECHANISMS` parameter in the `m4` macro configuration file—for example:

```
define(`confAUTH_MECHANISMS', `DIGEST-MD5 CRAM-MD5')dnl
```

This `define` command tells the system to use either `DIGEST-MD5` or `CRAM-MD5` (Challenge/Response Authentication Mode) for client authentication. If the SASL library on the server is configured for one or both of those authentication techniques, that is what will be advertised in response to the `EHLO` command.

The client then picks an authentication technique from those that are advertised and uses the `AUTH` command to start the authentication process. This is the second use for the `AUTH` keyword. The client simply sends the command `AUTH` followed by the authentication techniques selected from the list of advertised techniques—for example:

```
AUTH CRAM-MD5
```

Listing 12.6 shows a more complete example of the authentication exchange between a client and a server. In Listing 12.6, the server advertises DIGEST-MD5 as the only authentication technique. The client decides to use it and responds with the necessary AUTH command. The server then sends a challenge string written in BASE64 encoding. The client encrypts the challenge string and its own authentication data, converts the encrypted response to a BASE64 string, and sends that back to the server. In Listing 12.6, the server accepts the reply and the authenticated session is off and running.

**Listing 12.6**   An Authenticated SMTP Session

```
220 wren.foobirds.org ESMTP Sendmail 8.11.0/8.11.0; Mon, 18 Oct 2000
    11:42:34 -0400
>>> EHLO ani.foobirds.org
250-wren.foobirds.org Hello root@ani.foobirds.org [172.16.12.1], pleased to
meet you
250-ENHANCEDSTATUSCODES
250-EXPN
250-VERB
250-8BITMIME
250-SIZE
250-DSN
250-ONEX
250-ETRN
250-XUSR
250-AUTH DIGEST-MD5
250 HELP
>>> AUTH DIGEST-MD5
```

```
334 INNTEDTNeUxFREJoUondurnbmhNWitOMjNGNb29kLmlubm9zb2ZOLmNvbT4=
>>> MIjgetFnd5ZTk1YW41miebtVlMDljNDBhZkjfyHHVSWEMGMyYjNNzg2ZQ==
235 Authentication successful.
>>> MAIL From:<craig@ani.foobirds.org> AUTH=craig@ani.foobirds.org
250 <craig@ani.foobirds.org>... Sender ok
>>> RCPT To:<craig@wren.foobirds.org>
250 <craig@wren.foobirds.org>... Recipient ok
>>> DATA
354 Enter mail, end with "." on a line by itself
>>> .
250 NAA01047 Message accepted for delivery
>>> QUIT
221 wren.foobirds.org closing connection
```

---

**NOTE** The session in Listing 12.6 appears as it would in a verbose Sendmail session. The >>> prompt that flags client input would not appear in a real SMTP protocol exchange. Additionally, the challenge string and response have been cut down to one line to save the trees. In reality they can be much longer.

---

Listing 12.6 shows the third use for the AUTH keyword. Look at the MAIL From: envelope header. The keyword AUTH appears after the sender address. The authenticated client system uses the AUTH keyword in this way to authenticate the user that sent this individual piece of mail. In effect, the source of the mail is "vouched for" by a client that the server now trusts. If the server relays this mail to another server, it will make sure to forward this validated address on with the mail.

For the DIGEST-MD5 authentication shown in Listing 12.6 to work, the client and server must agree on a shared secret password. The password is configured on the server using the saslpasswd command as shown below:

```
[root]# saslpasswd craig
Password: Let'skeepthissecret!
Again (for verification): Let'skeepthissecret!
```

The administrators of the server and the client must manually coordinate the password. The same password that is defined on the server using the saslpasswd command must be defined on the client when the client is configured.

### Configuring an Authentication Client

There are two ways that the AUTH client can communicate with your server:

- The client may run an MUA that uses your server as an MSA. Some MUAs, such as pine and Eudora, support the AUTH extension. Using this approach, the client's MUA talks directly to your server's Sendmail.

- The client may run Sendmail and act as an MTA treating your server as an MTA. The advantage of running Sendmail on the AUTH client is that every MUA running on the client has access to the AUTH extension through the client's copy of Sendmail. Sendmail provides a couple of parameters to configure a system as an AUTH protocol client.

The DefaultAuthInfo option points to the file that contains the information used to authenticate the system when it acts as an AUTH client. By default, this option is undefined and the system does not attempt to use AUTH when acting as a client. Use confDEF_AUTH_ INFO in the m4 macro configuration file to define a file for the AUTH authentication data—for example:

```
define(`confDEF_AUTH_INFO', `/etc/mail/default-auth-info')dnl
```

The file can be given any name you wish, but the name /etc/mail/default-auth-info is the name recommended by the Sendmail developers. The file must be in a directory that can only be written by root or the TrustedUser. The file itself must be owned by root or the TrustedUser and must be readable only by its owner.

The file, default-auth-info in our example, contains four pieces of information used to authenticate the AUTH client. Explained in SASL terms, the four pieces of information are:

**Authorization identity**    This is the identity under which action will be taken on the remote system. This is the username that grants privileges on the remote system. For example, craig is a user ID that grants ownership write privileges for every file owned by craig. The authorization identity determines the privileges.

**Authentication identity**    This is the username that is being authenticated by the challenge/response protocol. It does not need to be the same username as the authorization identity. However, once the authentication identity (authid) is authenticated, the authid is accepted as a proxy for the authorization identity and is granted the same privileges as those granted to the authorization identity. For example, assume that craig is the authorization identity and that kathy is the authentication identity. After authenticating, kathy is given ownership privileges to the files owned by craig. In terms of the DIGEST-MD5 example given above, the authentication identity should match a user name for which saslpasswd was used to create a password.

**Shared secret**   The shared secret is the key used by shared secret security mechanisms, such as DIGEST-MD5. The key is stored as plain text, making it critically important that the `default-auth-info` file be kept secure. In terms of the DIGEST-MD5 example given above, the shared secret should match the password defined with the `saslpasswd` command for the authentication identity.

**SASL realm**   The realm is an arbitrary name for a set that encompasses a group of users, systems, and services that share a common authentication environment. Every item in the set uses the same realm value during authentication. The concept of a realm is intended to make it possible to create authentication groups within larger groups. In practice, most SASL systems use the DNS domain name as the SASL realm. Sendmail defaults to using the fully qualified hostname of the client as the realm, if no realm is defined in the `default-auth-info` file.

> **NOTE**   The fact that the authorization identity and the authentication identity appear to be user names can cause some confusion when examined from the point of view of the AUTH extension. The AUTH extension validates a client computer, not an individual user. The confusion arises from the fact that SASL is a general-purpose system that can be used to authenticate a wide range of things, including users. The SASL names for the fields can lead you to believe that every user on a client would requires a separate entry. That is not the case because AUTH authenticates entire systems.

The values required for authentication are defined by SASL. How they are used on a Sendmail system acting as an AUTH client is defined by AUTH and Sendmail. A realistic `default-auth-info` file might contain the following:

```
craig

craig

Let'skeepthissecret!

ibis.foobirds.org
```

The first two lines are the authorization identity and the authentication identity. They both have the same value—in this case `craig`. Sendmail expects these to be the same value. If they aren't, Sendmail will not relay mail for the client. (Of course, you can change this behavior by writing your own rewrite rules; but the default configuration expects these values to match.) The third line is the secret key used to encrypt the client's response to the server. The last line is the hostname of the client, which is the default realm value used by Sendmail.

The preceding paragraph points out that the Sendmail server checks the values provided by the client to determine if it should relay the client's mail. The examples of relay configuration in Chapter 11 all relied on IP addresses or domain names. The mobility and dynamic address assignment in today's network means, however, that clients do not always have fixed addresses or names that can be resolved back to fixed addresses. The sole reason that Sendmail has for authenticating clients with the AUTH extension is to decide whether or not the mail from that client should be relayed without regard to the domain name or address of the client.

### The Role of Authentication in Relaying

The server in Listing 12.6 offers the client only one type of authentication. If the client cannot perform DIGEST-MD5 authentication, the client can proceed to send the mail without initiating authentication. All servers accept unauthenticated mail—they just might not relay it.

If the client is authenticated by a trusted authentication method, the client is allowed to relay mail. Use the TRUST_AUTH_MECH macro to list the trusted authentication methods. For example, to trust DIGEST-MD5, place the following macro in the m4 macro configuration file:

```
TRUST_AUTH_MECH(`DIGEST-MD5')dnl
```

Even a client authenticated by a trusted mechanism is not allowed to relay mail for everyone. The authorization identity and the authentication identity must agree for mail to be relayed. To change that behavior, you need to create your own rewrite rules. Custom rewrite rules can be defined in the Local_check_rcpt ruleset or the Local_trust_auth ruleset. The Local_check_rcpt ruleset is used to verify whether the client is authenticated and what authentication method was used to do the job. The Local_trust_auth ruleset is used to modify the fact that Sendmail trusts the AUTH keyword on the MAIL From: header only if the user it identifies is the same as the user that was authenticated by the challenge/response. Three variables contain authentication information that can be used in these rulesets. The variables are:

{**auth_type**}   This variable contains the name of the authentication technique that was used to authenticate the client—for example, DIGEST-MD5.

{**auth_authen**}   This variable contains the name that was authenticated by the original challenge/response exchange of the client and the server.

{**auth_author**}   This variable initially contains the value from the authorization identity. If a value is defined by the AUTH keyword on the MAIL From: header, that becomes the value for the {auth_author} variable.

The fact that authentication is used only for relaying reduces the overall security importance of the AUTH protocol. Readers familiar with encryption may have been hoping that AUTH was used to provide cryptographic authentication of both the source and the content of e-mail messages. That is not really the case. AUTH is most effective as another tool in the fight against spam and unauthorized relaying.

RFC 2554 does state that the AUTH extension can be optionally used to negotiate a security layer for subsequent protocol interaction, meaning message encryption. However, it is not really used in this way. STARTTLS is the protocol used to encrypt message transfers.

## Transport Layer Security

The AUTH extension uses a shared secret key. The authentication data is encrypted and decrypted with the same key, making AUTH a symmetric encryption system. TLS, on the other hand, is a public key encryption system. In fact, TLS is SSL, the public key encryption system used to secure Web communications. Securing e-mail with SSL requires the same information that is used to secure Web communications with SSL.

---

**NOTE**  To find out more about using SSL for a Linux Web server, see *Linux Apache Web Server Administration* by Charles Aulds (Sybex, 2000).

---

SSL public key cryptography requires three things:

**A certificate authority**  Public key cryptography requires a trusted third party called a certificate authority (CA). The CA is a server from which public keys are obtained. You cannot trust a public key that is obtained directly from the end system, because until you have the key you cannot authenticate that the system is the host it claims to be. On the other hand, the CA is a well-known server. Some tools, such as the Netscape browser, come preconfigured to recognize many certificate authorities.

**A certificate**  This is your public key. It is written in the form of an X.509 certificate, which contains your public key, the identity of your system, and dates that verify that the key is currently valid. The X.509 certificate is signed by a CA. Thus, when you send your certificate to a remote server, the server can decrypt your certificate using the well-known public key of your CA to determine your identity and your public key.

**A private key**  This is the key you use to encrypt your communications, which are then decrypted by the public key, or to decrypt communications that have been encrypted by the public key. The private key must be kept secure, but it cannot be stored in an encrypted format.

These essential pieces of information must be identified to Sendmail in the configuration. The path to the directory where certificates are stored is defined by the confCACERT_PATH parameter, and the certificate for a single CA is defined using the confCACERT parameter. Both can be used in the m4 configuration file—for example:

```
define(`confCACERT_PATH', `/etc/httpd/conf/ssl.crt')
define(`confCACERT', `/etc/httpd/conf/ssl.crt/verisign.crt')
```

In this example, we use the same certificate directory that was already set up for the Apache server on our system. This is, however, completely arbitrary. Certificates can be stored anywhere as long as the directory and the certificates in the directory can be written only by root.

In addition to information about CA certificates, Sendmail needs to know about the public and private keys it should use to identify itself and encrypt its own communication. Sendmail uses a different set of public and private keys depending on whether it is acting as a server or a client. These values are defined by four m4 parameters:

**confSERVER_CERT**   This parameter sets a value for the ServerCertFile option. The ServerCertFile option identifies the file that contains the X.509 certificate used when Sendmail acts as a server. In effect, this is the server's public key. For example:

```
define(`confSERVER_CERT', `/etc/httpd/conf/ssl.crt/server.crt')
```

**confSERVER_KEY**   This parameter sets a value for the ServerKeyFile option. The ServerKeyFile option identifies the file that contains the private key used when Sendmail acts as a server. The confSERVER_KEY parameter could be defined as follows:

```
define(`confSERVER_KEY', `/etc/httpd/conf/ssl.crt/server.key')
```

**confCLIENT_CERT**   This parameter sets a value for the ClientCertFile option. The ClientCertFile option identifies the file that contains the X.509 certificate used when Sendmail acts as a client. In effect, this is the client's public key. The following example points to a certificate in the Apache SSL directory:

```
define(`confCLIENT_CERT', `/etc/httpd/conf/ssl.crt/client.crt')
```

**confCLIENT_KEY**   This parameter sets a value for the ClientKeyFile option. The ClientKeyFile option identifies the file that contains the private key used when Sendmail acts as a client. The following command tells Sendmail where the client's private key is stored:

```
define(`confCLIENT_KEY', `/etc/httpd/conf/ssl.crt/client.key')
```

In the examples above, we used the same certificates and keys for Sendmail that we used for Apache. This is possible, but only if you run Sendmail and Apache on the same server.

**Maintaining a Healthy Server**

**PART 4**

If you don't, you need to obtain certificates and keys for the Sendmail server. There are two ways to do this:

- Obtain your certificate and keys from a certificate authority.
- Create a self-signed certificate.

There are about 50 commercial firms that act as CAs. A quick search for "certificate authority" at Excite produced many valid hits. To obtain a certificate and key from a commercial CA, all you need to do is follow their instructions and pay the necessary fees. If the Web administrator has already dealt with a CA, you probably want to work with the same one. Some large firms act as their own CA. They make their public key available from a well-known and trusted server, and their customers download the CA certificate from that server. If you work for a large company, check to see if your company acts as its own CA.

The advantage of working with a well-known CA is that many applications worldwide are already configured to recognize these CAs. Systems from around the world can obtain your certificate from the CA without any direct involvement on your part.

Despite the advantages of using a well-known CA, some Sendmail systems use self-signed certificates. They can use a self-signed certificate because they only use STARTTLS with a small number of sites. Therefore it is possible for the Sendmail administrator to manually distribute the CA certificate to the few clients that will use the STARTTLS service.

To create a self-signed certificate, you must first make your Sendmail server a CA, which is a complex task. You need to understand the `openssl.cnf` file to define where the certificates are stored and you need to master the `openssl` command to build the certificates. The `openssl` command has more than 25 "sub-commands," each of which has many options. `openssl` is almost as complex as Sendmail, and is beyond the scope of this book. My advice is to use a commercial CA.

Once a Sendmail server is configured with the appropriate certificates and keys, it advertises the availability of TLS by displaying the keyword STARTTLS in response to the EHLO command. A client who wishes to use TLS for a session issues the STARTTLS command. If the server responds that it is ready for TLS, the keys are exchanged and a secure connection is opened.

### Sendmail's Uses for TLS

Sendmail is not normally used as a message user agent (MUA) and it is not the final recipient of e-mail. Whether or not the content of a message is authenticated or encrypted is of no interest to Sendmail. It uses the information provided by TLS to authenticate the remote server in order to decide whether the SMTP connection should be accepted and whether the mail should be relayed. Several variables and rulesets are involved in these decisions.

Table 12.1 lists the variables that hold STARTTLS values. The name of each variable is given along with the value it stores.

**Table 12.1**  STARTTLS Variables

| Variable | Stores |
| --- | --- |
| {cert_issuer} | The name of the CA. |
| {cert_subject} | The name of the remote Sendmail system. |
| {cipher} | The encryption technique used for the connection. |
| {cipher_bits} | The number of bits in the encryption key. |
| {server_addr} | The address of the server of the current outgoing SMTP connection. |
| {server_name} | The name of the server of the current outgoing SMTP connection. |
| {tls_version} | The TLS/SSL version used for the connection: TLSv1, SSLv3, or SSLv2. |
| {verify} | The result of the verification process. |

While all of these variables are available for use, the most important TLS variable for deciding whether or not an SMTP connection should be allowed or mail should be relayed is the {verify} variable. It stores the result of the TLS authentication process, and it is generally the first TLS value examined when making a connection or relaying decision. Table 12.2 shows the different values that can be returned by the {verify} variable.

**Table 12.2**  Possible Results of the Verification Process

| Response | Meaning |
| --- | --- |
| OK | The remote system was successfully authenticated. |
| NO | A certificate was not provided. |

Maintaining a Healthy Server

PART 4

**Table 12.2** Possible Results of the Verification Process *(continued)*

| Response | Meaning |
|----------|---------|
| FAIL | The provided certificate could not be verified. |
| NONE | STARTTLS was not run. |
| TEMP | A temporary error occurred. |
| PROTOCOL | An error in the TLS protocol occurred. |
| SOFTWARE | The STARTTLS handshake failed. |

Three rulesets are involved in deciding whether or not an SMTP connection should be created or mail forwarded when TLS is used. These rulesets process the variables listed in Table 12.1. The three rulesets are:

**RelayAuth** The RelayAuth ruleset determines whether or not mail received from a remote system over a TLS connection can be relayed. First RelayAuth checks the value stored in {verify}. If {verify} does not contain the value OK, the connection is assumed to be a regular connection. RelayAuth exits and the normal relay rules are applied to the mail. If {verify} contains the value OK, this is assumed to be a TLS connection and RelayAuth performs two additional checks: It looks up the value from {cert_issuer} in the access database, using the tag value CERTISSUER:. If the lookup returns nothing, the regular relay rules apply to the mail. If the lookup returns RELAY, the mail is relayed. If the lookup returns SUBJECT, the value from {cert_subject} is looked up in the access database, using the tag value CERTSUBJECT:. If this lookup returns RELAY, the mail is relayed. Otherwise the normal relay rules are applied to the mail.

**tls_server** The tls_server ruleset is called after Sendmail, acting as a client, sends the STARTTLS command to a remote server. The value in {verify} is checked to see if the TLS handshake completed. (A value of SOFTWARE means it failed to complete.) The ruleset also looks up {server_name} in the access database using the tag TLS_Srv:. If {server_name} is not found, {server_addr} is looked up using the tag TLS_Srv:. If these entries are not found in the access database, the {verify} variable determines whether or not the SMTP connection is allowed. If entries are found, the access database determines whether or not the connection is made.

**tls_client**   The tls_client ruleset is called after Sendmail, acting as a server, receives a STARTTLS command from a remote client. The value in {verify} is checked to see if the TLS handshake completed. The ruleset also looks up {client_name} in the access database using the tag TLS_Clt:. If {client_name} is not found, {client_addr} is looked up using the tag TLS_Clt:. If no entries for the client are found in the access database, the {verify} variable determines whether or not the SMTP connection is allowed. If entries are found, the access database determines whether or not the connection is made.

> **NOTE**   Don't remember {client_name} and {client_addr}? They are covered in Chapter 11, "Stopping Spam."

Chapter 6, "Using Sendmail Databases," describes the syntax of the access database including the use of tag fields. In Chapter 6, only three tag fields are described—To:, From:, and Connect:. TLS adds four additional tag fields to the access database syntax—CERTISSUER:, CERTSUBJECT:, TLS_Clt:, and TLS_Srv:. Only access database entries that start with these tags are used for TLS processing. In addition to four new tag values, TLS adds two new actions to the access database. These are:

**[PERM+|TEMP+]VERIFY[:*bits*]**   The VERIFY keyword requires that verification completed successfully—i.e., {verify} must be equal to OK. Optionally, a colon and a number may be added to the keyword. If *bits* is defined, the encryption key used for this connection must be at least the specified number of bits long. By default, the verification failure returns a temporary error code, meaning the remote system can retry the connection. Putting the string PERM+ in front of the keyword VERIFY causes Sendmail to send a permanent error code. The TEMP+ string causes Sendmail to send a temporary error code, which is the default unless TLS_PERM_ERR is used in the m4 macro configuration file.

**[PERM+|TEMP+]ENCR:*bits***   The ENCR keyword requires that the encryption key used for this connection must be at least *bits* number of bits long. Putting the string PERM+ in front of the keyword ENCR cause Sendmail to send a permanent error code. The TEMP+ string causes Sendmail to send a temporary error code, which is the default unless TLS_PERM_ERR is used in the m4 macro configuration file.

A few sample access database lines will clarify how these values are used.

```
TLS_Clt:ibis.foobirds.org          PERM+VERIFY:128

TLS_Srv:wolf.mammals.org           ENCR:128
```

The first line says reject the connection with a permanent error code if a client named ibis.foobirds.org fails verification or fails to use a 128-bit encryption key. The second line says reject the connection if the remote server `wolf.mammals.org` uses an encryption key less than 128 bits long.

Again, as was the case with AUTH, Sendmail uses TLS primarily to control relaying or manage connections. It does not use it to provide end-to-end encryption and authentication of mail messages, and there are some very good reasons for this.

### The Limits of TLS

Sendmail is not an MUA. It is an MTA. It transfers mail to a remote MTA, not to a remote user. Encrypting mail between two Sendmail systems protects the mail from snooping or corruption in the network, but it does not protect the mail from snooping or corruption on the end systems. With TLS, the mail is still queued as unencrypted text on the sending system and spooled as unencrypted text on the recipient system. The system administrators or any other highly privileged users on both systems can read the e-mail. TLS is more important in the fight against spam than it is for securing highly sensitive information.

Except for completely private mail servers, TLS must be an option. TLS cannot be required by any server that is identified by an MX record. A mail exchange server may offer TLS, but it cannot require it.

TLS is vulnerable to "man in the middle" attacks. It is very unlikely that anyone would mount such an attack, because e-mail has long been sent in the open and thus is rarely used for sensitive communications. But if someone wanted to, they could, because the offer of TLS is made in the clear with the STARTTLS response to the EHLO command. The "man in the middle" system could filter out the STARTTLS response to get the client to send the mail in the clear. You can fight this attack by putting an entry in the access database that requires successful TLS verification for the remote server before you will create the connection. But that requires that you know the server and you know it offers TLS.

When using systems like AUTH or TLS, understand their limitations so that you don't assume a higher level of security than is really offered. It is generally safest to assume that nothing is as secure as you would want it to be.

## In Sum

There are two main types of security problems threatening your system:

- Denial of service, which prevents you from using all of the capacity of your system
- Unauthorized access, which gives access to your system or data to people who should not have that access

There are three levels of security used to defend against these problems:

- Secure the system, which includes securing the hardware and the operating system software
- Secure the server, which in the context of this book means securing the Sendmail server
- Secure the communications, which includes securing the messages sent between systems

This chapter covered all three of the topics listed above. The topics become increasingly complex as you move down the list and through the chapter. The easiest way to attack this complexity is to realize that the more complex topics, such as STARTTLS, are not as important as the more basic topics. If you master the first topic and secure the system, you have completed 99 percent of the important security work for a Sendmail server. Most of the security vulnerabilities of your server lie in the system as a whole, not just in Sendmail. The single most important thing you can do to secure your server is to keep the software updated by applying security fixes when they become available.

The security problems in Sendmail do not tend to be configuration problems. Sendmail ships with security buttoned up pretty tight. Learning what the different security parameters do is helpful in understanding how the system works, but it is unlikely you can tighten the security of these parameters. Most changes to the default settings actually weaken security—for example, to better support relaying. Most Sendmail security problems tend to be bugs, and the best way to handle these bugs is to apply the fixes as soon as they become available.

Encryption sounds good. It sounds like it should fix all of your problems. In reality it doesn't. To be truly useful, mail needs to be able to come from anywhere and go to anywhere. You need to be able to talk to people and systems you can't really trust. Encrypted mail has its place, but it can never be the total solution and it can never take the place of good system security. A root compromise of your server gives the intruder access to your private keys, just like it gives the intruder access to everything else on the system. Nothing can replace good solid system administration.

This chapter completes a book that has attempted to balance the complex details of Sendmail with a realistic expectation of what it is you actually need to know. We started with the protocols and architecture used to build an e-mail system with Sendmail. We learned the m4 language, using it to build a simple configuration and, just as importantly, to read the configuration delivered with a Linux system. Finally, we refined our configuration with advanced features.

I believe that the time we have spent together will give you insights into Sendmail that will make you a better Sendmail administrator. I enjoyed writing this book for you. I hope that you enjoyed reading it, and that you will benefit from having done so.

Maintaining a Healthy Server

PART 4

# Appendices

- Appendix A: *m4* Macro Command Reference

- Appendix B: The *sendmail* Command

- Appendix C: Sendmail Variables, Options, and Flags

# *m4* Macro Command Reference

This appendix is a reference guide to the m4 macro commands used to construct a Sendmail configuration file. Most of this book is a tutorial on how m4 macros are used to configure Sendmail. This appendix is not a tutorial; it is a reference that describes the syntax and function of the macros. It lists every macro and all of the parameters that can be defined for Sendmail configuration. In one sense, this appendix completes the discussion begun in the body of the text because it includes all macros and parameters, even those that you will probably not use on a Linux system.

---

**TIP** The information provided in this appendix is accurate for Sendmail version 8.11.0. For the most current and accurate description of these macros, see the README file located in the cf directory that comes with the Sendmail distribution.

---

## A Quick Reference

m4 is a general-purpose macro language. It is not intended specifically for Sendmail configuration. The Sendmail developers use the basic m4 language to define macros for Sendmail configuration. You create a Sendmail configuration by using the macros that they developed. The macro configuration file you build can legally contain any valid m4 source code. However, you will use only a few of the built-in m4 language elements along with the Sendmail m4 macros. The macros built by the Sendmail developers handle most of the configuration.

Table A.1 lists the Sendmail m4 macros as well as the few built-in m4 commands that you might use to create a configuration. In this table, and by convention, commands that are part of the m4 language are shown in lowercase and macros developed specifically for Sendmail configuration are shown in uppercase.

**Table A.1**    Sendmail m4 Macros and Configuration Commands

| Command | Usage |
|---------|-------|
| CANONIFY_DOMAIN | Lists domains that should be converted to canonical name format even if the nocanonify feature is selected. |
| CANONIFY_DOMAIN_FILE | Identifies a file that lists domains that should be converted to canonical name format even if the nocanonify feature is selected. |
| DAEMON_OPTIONS | Defines runtime options for the Sendmail daemon. |
| define | Defines a value for a configuration variable. |
| divert | Directs the output of the m4 process. |
| dnl | Deletes all characters up to and including the next newline character. |
| DOMAIN | Selects a file containing attributes for your specific domain. |
| EXPOSED_USER | Lists usernames that should be exempted from masquerading. |
| FEATURE | Identifies an optional Sendmail feature to be included in the configuration. |
| GENERICS_DOMAIN | Defines fully qualified domains that should be converted by the genericstable database. |

**Table A.1**   Sendmail m4 Macros and Configuration Commands *(continued)*

| Command | Usage |
| --- | --- |
| GENERICS_DOMAIN_FILE | Identifies a file that lists fully qualified domains that should be converted by the genericstable database. |
| HACK | Selects a file containing a locally defined temporary fix. |
| INPUT_MAIL_FILTER | Defines a mail filter and the variables necessary to call the filter. |
| LDAPROUTE_DOMAIN | Defines a domain for which mail should be routed based on an LDAP directory entry. |
| LDAPROUTE_DOMAIN_FILE | Identifies a file that lists domains for which mail should be routed based on entries in an LDAP directory. |
| LOCAL_CONFIG | Marks the start of a section that contains raw sendmail.cf commands. |
| LOCAL_DOMAIN | Defines an alias hostname for the mail server. |
| LOCAL_NET_CONFIG | Marks the start of raw rewrite rules that define how mail destined for the local network is handled. |
| LOCAL_RULE_*n* | Marks the start of a section that contains raw rewrite rules. The *n*, which must be 0, 1, 2, or 3, identifies the ruleset to which the rewrite rules are added. |
| LOCAL_RULESETS | Marks the start of a ruleset to be added to the configuration. |
| LOCAL_USER | Lists usernames that should be exempted from relaying even when local mail is being relayed. |
| MAIL_FILTER | Defines a mail filter. |
| MAILER | Identifies a set of mailers to be included in the sendmail.cf file. |

**Appendices**

**Table A.1** Sendmail m4 Macros and Configuration Commands *(continued)*

| Command | Usage |
|---|---|
| MAILER_DEFINITIONS | Marks the start of a section containing raw sendmail.cf mailer commands. |
| MASQUERADE_AS | Defines the domain name used to masquerade outbound mail. |
| MASQUERADE_DOMAIN | Defines a domain that should be masqueraded. |
| MASQUERADE_DOMAIN_FILE | Identifies a file that lists domains that should be masqueraded. |
| MASQUERADE_EXCEPTION | Defines a host that should not be masqueraded. |
| MODIFY_MAILER_FLAGS | Overrides the flags defined for a mailer. |
| OSTYPE | Selects a file containing operating system–specific attributes. |
| RELAY_DOMAIN | Defines a domain for which mail should be relayed. |
| RELAY_DOMAIN_FILE | Identifies a file that lists domains for which mail should be relayed. |
| SITE | Identifies a locally connected UUCP host. |
| SITECONFIG | Identifies the file that lists all of the locally connected UUCP sites. |
| TRUST_AUTH_MECH | Defines a list of trusted authorization mechanisms. |
| undefine | Clears the value set for a configuration variable. |
| UUCPSMTP | Maps a UUCP hostname to an Internet hostname. |
| VERSIONID | Defines version control information for the configuration. |

**Table A.1**   Sendmail m4 Macros and Configuration Commands *(continued)*

| Command | Usage |
| --- | --- |
| VIRTUSER_DOMAIN | Defines a virtual domain that will be accepted for processing through the virtusertable. |
| VIRTUSER_DOMAIN_FILE | Identifies the file that lists virtual domains that will be accepted for processing through the virtusertable. |

The built-in m4 commands shown in Table A.1—those listed in lowercase characters—are divided between two commands used to control the flow of output and two commands used to set macro values. The two commands that control the flow of output are dnl and divert. The dnl command is used at the end of a line to clean blank lines from the output or at the beginning of a line to indicate that the line is a comment. The divert(-1) command marks the start of a block of comment text and the divert(0) command marks the end of the block of comments. In addition to -1 and 0, the divert command accepts nine other numeric arguments: the values 1 to 9. (See Table 4.2 in Chapter 4, "Creating a Basic Sendmail Configuration.") These other nine values are used in the Sendmail m4 macros to direct data to various parts of the sendmail.cf file. But you will not use these values directly in your own configuration.

A group of commands—examples of which are LOCAL_CONFIG, LOCAL_RULESET, and MAILER_DEFINITION—allows you to send data to various parts of the sendmail.cf file without using the various divert values directly. Commands such as LOCAL_CONFIG and MAILER_DEFINITION mark the start of raw sendmail.cf code that should be included in some part of the output file. These commands make it possible for you to customize the sendmail.cf file in any possible way. See the "Local Code" section later in this appendix for a full list of these macros.

The two built-in m4 commands that set macro values are define and undefine. define sets a variable to a value and undefine resets it to its default value. More configuration parameters can be controlled through the define command than through any other; correspondingly, more of this appendix is dedicated to define variables than to anything else.

Several of the macros—almost half—do essentially the same thing as the define command: they set a variable to a value. MASQUERADE_AS, MASQUERADE_DOMAIN, and VIRTUSER_DOMAIN_FILE are all examples of commands used to set variables. All of these commands are covered later in this appendix.

**Appendices**

The TRUST_AUTH_MECH macro is a good example of a macro that complements a define. As you'll see in the "define" section of this appendix, the parameter confAUTH_MECHANISMS can be used to define the trust mechanisms that your server will advertise to other servers. The TRUST_AUTH_MECH macro is the inverse of this. It identifies the mechanism that your server will accept from other servers. The same list of keywords used to configure the confAUTH_MECHANISMS parameter in the "define" section can be used to set TRUST_AUTH_MECHANISMS.

The macro names OSTYPE, DOMAIN, FEATURE, MAILER, HACK, and SITECONFIG are all names of subdirectories within the cf directory. The value passed to each of these macros is the name of a file within the specified directory. For example: the command OSTYPE(linux) tells m4 to load the file linux.m4 from the ostype directory and process the m4 source code found there. The .m4 source files pointed to by the OSTYPE, DOMAIN, FEATURE, and MAILER commands are built primarily from define and FEATURE commands.

Two of the macros that are also directory names, SITECONFIG and HACK, are rarely used. SITECONFIG points to a source file that contains SITE macros that define the UUCP sites connected to the local host. You create the file containing the SITE macros yourself and then invoke it with the SITECONFIG command. These commands, along with UUCPSMTP, are obsolete and only maintained for backward compatibility.

The HACK macro points to an m4 source file that contains a temporary site-specific fix to a Sendmail problem. You create the file in the hack directory and then use the HACK command to add that file to the configuration. The use of hacks is discouraged and is generally unnecessary.

# Complete Command Reference

Table A.1 contains approximately forty entries. If you have experience configuring Sendmail with m4, you might be surprised by the sheer number of these commands. Sendmail, like everything else, has been suffering from "feature creep." A few years ago, Sendmail configuration had reached its simplest point. Most of the old mailers were no longer in use. Everything was being sent by SMTP, and configurations were relatively simple. Then abuse of the system by spammers and security crackers caused new features and new commands to be added to the configuration. Some of these new features—for example, the new databases—have made older commands such as SITE, SITECONFIG, and UUCPSMTP obsolete. Still, there are lots of commands. And they can't really be described in a quick reference. Descriptions of these commands make up the rest of this appendix. Use the quick reference to help you read existing files and the more detailed information when you need to write your own configuration file.

## *define*

define sets a value for a sendmail.cf macro, option, or class. Most parameter values are defined in the m4 source files that are called by the .mc file, not in the .mc file itself. Because many define parameters are equivalent to options, macros, and classes, the command

    define(`confMAILER_NAME', `MAILER_DAEMON')

placed in an m4 source file has the same effect as

    DnMAILER_DAEMON

placed directly in the sendmail.cf file.

Most of the parameters default to a reasonable value and thus do not have to be explicitly set in the m4 source file. The undefine command sets a variable back to its default. For example:

    undefine(`confAUTO_REBUILD')

resets confAUTO_REBUILD to the default value false even if the configuration had previously set it to true.

The list of define parameters shown below is quite long. The default value of each parameter is shown in the listing—unless there is no default. In the parameter description list, the name of the corresponding sendmail.cf option, macro, or class is shown enclosed in square brackets ([]). Macro names begin with a dollar sign ($j), class names begin with a dollar sign and an equal sign ($=w), and options are shown with long option names (SingleThreadDelivery).

**confALIAS_WAIT**   Sets the amount of time to wait for the aliases database rebuild. Defaults to 10m. [AliasWait]

**confALLOW_BOGUS_HELO**   Defines normally illegal special characters that will be allowed in the DNS hostname on a HELO command line. [AllowBogusHELO]

**confAUTH_MECHANISMS**   Defines a space-separated list of authentication mechanisms that will be used for SMTP AUTH. [AuthMechanisms] The default is:

    define(`confAUTH_MECHANISMS', `GSSAPI KERBEROS_V4 DIGEST-MD5
      CRAM-MD5')

**confAUTH_OPTIONS**   The AUTH argument is added to the MAIL From header only when authentication succeeds if this is set to A. [AuthOptions]

**confAUTO_REBUILD**   Automatically rebuilds the aliases database if true. Defaults to false. [AutoRebuildAliases]

**confBIND_OPTS**   Sets DNS resolver options. None are defined by default. [ResolverOptions]

**confBLANK_SUB**   Defines the character used to replace unquoted blank characters in e-mail addresses. [BlankSub]

**confCACERT**   Identifies a file containing a cryptographic certificate from a certificate authority. [CACERTFile]

**confCACERT_PATH**   Defines the path to the directory that contains the cryptographic certificates. [CACERTPath]

**confCF_VERSION**   Sets the Sendmail version number. [$Z]

**confCHECKPOINT_INTERVAL**   Sets the maximum number of queued items processed before Sendmail checkpoints the queue. Default is 10. [CheckpointInterval]

**confCHECK_ALIASES**   Looks up every alias during the aliases database build. Default is false. [CheckAliases]

**confCLIENT_CERT**   Identifies the file containing the cryptographic certificate Sendmail uses when it acts as a client. [ClientCertFile]

**confCLIENT_KEY**   Identifies the file containing the private key associated with the certificate used when Sendmail acts as a client. [ClientKeyFile]

**confCLIENT_OPTIONS**   Defines the port options used for outbound SMTP client connections. [ClientPortOptions]

**confCOLON_OK_IN_ADDR**   Tells Sendmail to treat colons as regular characters in addresses. Default is false. [ColonOkInAddr]

**confCONNECTION_RATE_THROTTLE**   Sets the maximum number of connections permitted per second. [ConnectionRateThrottle]

**confCONNECT_ONLY_TO**   Defines limited connectivity. Only needed when Sendmail is tested by the developers. This is not used in production environments. [ConnectOnlyTo]

**confCONTROL_SOCKET_NAME**   Defines a socket used for managing the Sendmail daemon. [ControlSocketName]

**confCON_EXPENSIVE**   Tells Sendmail to hold mail bound for mailers that have the e flag set until the next queue run. Defaults to false. [HoldExpensive]

**confCOPY_ERRORS_TO**   Sets the e-mail address that receives copies of error messages. [PostmasterCopy]

**confCR_FILE**   Points to the file that lists the hosts for which this server will relay mail. Defaults to /etc/mail/relay-domains. [$=R]

**confCT_FILE**   Defines the file of trusted usernames. Defaults to /etc/mail/trusted-users. [$=t]

**confCW_FILE**   Points to the file of local host aliases. Defaults to /etc/mail/local-host-names. [$=w]

**confDEAD_LETTER_DROP** Defines the file where failed messages that could not be returned to the sender or sent to the postmaster are saved. [DeadLetterDrop]

**confDAEMON_OPTIONS** Sets options for the Sendmail daemon. [DaemonPortOptions]

**confDEF_AUTH_INFO** Identifies the file that contains the authentication information used for outbound connections. [DefaultAuthInfo]

**confDEF_CHAR_SET** Defines the default character set for unlabeled eight-bit MIME data. Defaults to unknown-8bit. [DefaultCharSet]

**confDEF_USER_ID** Defines the user ID and group ID used by Sendmail. Defaults to 1:1. [DefaultUser]

**confDELIVERY_MODE** Sets the default delivery mode. Defaults to background. [DeliveryMode]

**confDF_BUFFER_SIZE** Defines the maximum amount of buffer memory that will be used before a disk file is used. [DataFileBufferSize]

**confDH_PARAMETERS** Identifies the file that contains the DH parameters for the DSA/DH digital signature algorithm. [DHParameters]

**confDIAL_DELAY** Sets the time delay used before retrying a "dial on demand" connection. 0s means "don't retry." Defaults to 0s. [DialDelay]

**confDOMAIN_NAME** Defines the system's full hostname. [$j]

**confDONT_BLAME_SENDMAIL** Tells Sendmail not to perform file security checks if set. By default, the checks are performed. Don't use this option. It is a threat to the security of your server. [DontBlameSendmail]

**confDONT_EXPAND_CNAMES** Tells Sendmail not to convert nicknames to canonical names if true. Defaults to false. False means "do convert." [DontExpandCnames]

**confDONT_INIT_GROUPS** If true, disables the initgroups routine. Defaults to false. False means "use the initgroups routine." [DontInitGroups]

**confDONT_PROBE_INTERFACES** Tells Sendmail not to automatically accept the addresses of the server's network interfaces as valid addresses if set to true. Defaults to false. [DontProbeInterface]

**confDONT_PRUNE_ROUTES** True tells Sendmail not to prune route-addresses to the minimum possible. Defaults to false, meaning that Sendmail will prune routes. [DontPruneRoutes]

**confDOUBLE_BOUNCE_ADDRESS** When errors occur while sending an error message, this option tells Sendmail the address to which to send the second error message. The address defaults to postmaster. [DoubleBounceAddress]

**Appendices**

**confEBINDIR** Defines the directory where executables for FEATURE(`local_lmtp') and FEATURE(`smrsh') are stored. The default directory is /usr/libexec.

**confEIGHT_BIT_HANDLING** Defines how eight-bit data is handled. Defaults to pass8, which passes eight-bit data through the server. [EightBitMode]

**confERROR_MESSAGE** Points to a file containing a message that is prepended to error messages. [ErrorHeader]

**confERROR_MODE** Defines how errors are handled. Defaults to print. [ErrorMode]

**confFALLBACK_MX** Defines a backup MX host. [FallbackMXhost]

**confFORWARD_PATH** Defines places to search for .forward files. Defaults to $z/.forward.$w:$z/.forward. [ForwardPath]

**confFROM_HEADER** Defines the From: header format. Defaults to $?x$x <$g>$|$g$. .

**confFROM_LINE** Defines the format of the Unix From line. Defaults to From $g $d. [UnixFromLine]

**confHOSTS_FILE** Defines the path to the hostname file. Defaults to /etc/hosts. [HostsFile]

**confHOST_STATUS_DIRECTORY** Defines the directory in which host status is saved. [HostStatusDirectory]

**confIGNORE_DOTS** True tells Sendmail to ignore dots in incoming messages. This option defaults to false, meaning that a line containing only a dot signals the end of a message. [IgnoreDots]

**confLDAP_DEFAULT_SPEC** Defines the defaults used for LDAP databases unless specifically overridden by a K command for an individual map. [LDAPDefaultSpec]

**confLOCAL_MAILER** Defines the mailer used for local connections. Defaults to local.

**confLOG_LEVEL** Defines the level of detail for the log file. Defaults to 9. [LogLevel]

**confMAILER_NAME** Defines the sender name used on error messages. Defaults to MAILER-DAEMON. [$n]

**confMATCH_GECOS** If set to true, Sendmail matches the e-mail username to the GECOS field. This match is not done if this is not set. [MatchGECOS]

**confMAX_ALIAS_RECURSION** Aliases can refer to other aliases. This sets the maximum depth that alias references can be nested. The default is 10. [MaxAliasRecursion]

**confMAX_DAEMON_CHILDREN** Sendmail refuses connections when this number of children is reached. By default, connections are never refused. [MaxDaemonChildren]

**confMAX_HEADERS_LENGTH**    Defines the maximum length of the sum of all headers in bytes. [MaxHeadersLength]

**confMAX_HOP**    Defines the counter used to determine mail loops. Defaults to 25. [MaxHopCount]

**confMAX_MESSAGE_SIZE**    Sets the maximum size for a message the server will accept. By default, no limit is set. [MaxMessageSize]

**confMAX_MIME_HEADER_LENGTH**    Defines the maximum length of MIME headers. [MaxMimeHeaderLength]

**confMAX_QUEUE_RUN_SIZE**    Defines the maximum number of entries processed in a single queue run. Defaults to 0, which means process everything in the queue. [MaxQueueRunSize]

**confMAX_RCPTS_PER_MESSAGE**    Defines the maximum number of recipients allowed for a piece of mail. [MaxRecipientsPerMessage]

**confMCI_CACHE_SIZE**    Sets the number of open connections that can be cached. Defaults to 2. [ConnectionCacheSize]

**confMCI_CACHE_TIMEOUT**    Sets the amount of time inactive open connections are held in the cache. Defaults to 5m. [ConnectionCacheTimeout]

**confME_TOO**    True tells Sendmail to send a copy of the mail to the sender. The default is false. [MeToo]

**confMIME_FORMAT_ERRORS**    True tells Sendmail to send MIME-encapsulated error messages. The default is true. [SendMimeErrors]

**confMIN_FREE_BLOCKS**    Sets the minimum number of blocks that must be available on the disk to accept mail. Defaults to 100. [MinFreeBlocks]

**confMIN_QUEUE_AGE**    Sets the minimum time a job must be queued. Defaults to 0. [MinQueueAge]

**confMUST_QUOTE_CHARS**    Adds characters to the list of characters that must be quoted when they are included in the user's full name ($x). The characters @,;:\()[] are always quoted. By default . and ' are added to the list. [MustQuoteChars]

**confNO_RCPT_ACTION**    Defines handling for mail with no recipient headers. Possible values are:

    **none**    Do nothing

    **add-to**    Add a To: header

    **add-apparently-to**    Add an Apparently-To: header

    **add-bcc**    Add a Bcc: header

    **add-to-undisclosed**    Add a To: undisclosed-recipients header

**Appendices**

**confOLD_STYLE_HEADERS**   True tells Sendmail to treat headers without special characters as old style headers. This defaults to `true`. [OldStyleHeaders]

**confOPERATORS**   Defines the address operator characters. Defaults to `.:%@!^/[]+`. [OperatorChars]

**confPID_FILE**   Specifies the path of the PID file. [PidFile]

**confPRIVACY_FLAGS**   Sets flags that restrict the use of some mail commands. Defaults to `authwarnings`. [PrivacyOptions]

**confPROCESS_TITLE_PREFIX**   Identifies the string used on this system as the prefix for the process title in `ps` listings. [ProcessTitlePrefix]

**confQUEUE_FACTOR**   Defines a value used to calculate when a loaded system should queue mail instead of attempting delivery. Defaults to 600000. [QueueFactor]

**confQUEUE_LA**   Tells Sendmail to send mail directly to the queue when this load average is reached. Defaults to 8. [QueueLA]

**confQUEUE_SORT_ORDER**   Tells Sendmail to sort the queue in `Priority` or `Host` order. The default is `Priority` order. [QueueSortOrder]

**confRAND_FILE**   Identifies the file that contains random data needed by STARTTLS if Sendmail was not compiled with the HASURANDOM flag. [RandFile]

**confRECEIVED_HEADER**   Defines the `Received:` header format. Defaults to `$?sfrom $s $.$?_($?s$|from $.$_) $.by $j ($v/$Z)$?r with $r$. id $i$?u for $u$.; $b` .

**confREFUSE_LA**   Defines the load average at which incoming connections are refused. Defaults to 12. [RefuseLA]

**confREJECT_MSG**   Defines the message displayed when mail is rejected because of the access control database. Defaults to 550 `Access denied`.

**confRELAY_MAILER**   Defines the default mailer name for relaying. Defaults to `relay`.

**confRRT_IMPLIES_DSN**   True tells Sendmail to interpret a Return-Receipt-To: header as a request for delivery status notification (DSN). The default is `false`. [RrtImpliesDsn]

**confRUN_AS_USER**   Tells Sendmail to run as the specified user to read and deliver mail. Used only on firewall systems that have no normal user accounts. [RunAsUser]

**confSAFE_FILE_ENV**   Tells Sendmail to `chroot` to this directory before writing files. Normally Sendmail does not run `chroot`. [SafeFileEnvironment]

**confSAFE_QUEUE**   Tells Sendmail to create a queue file before attempting delivery. [SuperSafe]

**confSAVE_FROM_LINES**   Tells Sendmail not to discard Unix From lines, which is the normal practice. [SaveFromLine]

**confSEPARATE_PROC**   True tells Sendmail to deliver messages with separate processes. Defaults to false. [ForkEachJob]

**confSERVER_CERT**   Identifies the file that contains the cryptographic certificate used when this system acts as a server. [ServerCertFile]

**confSERVER_KEY**   Identifies the file that contains the private key associated with the cryptographic certificate used when this system acts as a server. [ServerKeyFile]

**confSERVICE_SWITCH_FILE**   Defines the path to the service switch file. Defaults to /etc/mail/service.switch. [ServiceSwitchFile]

**confSEVEN_BIT_INPUT**   True forces input to seven bits. The default is false. [SevenBitInput]

**confSINGLE_LINE_FROM_HEADER**   True forces a multiline From: line to a single line. The default is false. [SingleLineFromHeader]

**confSINGLE_THREAD_DELIVERY**   True forces single-threaded mail delivery if HostStatusDirectory is also defined. The default is false. [SingleThreadDelivery]

**confSMTP_LOGIN_MSG**   Defines the SMTP greeting message. Defaults to $j Sendmail $v/$Z; $b. [SmtpGreetingMessage]

**confSMTP_MAILER**   Defines the mailer used for SMTP connections; must be smtp, smtp8, or esmtp. Defaults to esmtp.

**confTEMP_FILE_MODE**   Sets the file mode used for temporary files. Defaults to 0600. [TempFileMode]

**confTIME_ZONE**   Sets the time zone from the system (USE_SYSTEM) or the TZ variable (USE_TZ). Defaults to USE_SYSTEM. [TimeZoneSpec]

**confTO_COMMAND**   Sets the maximum time to wait for a command. Defaults to 1h. [Timeout.command]

**confTO_CONNECT**   Sets the maximum time to wait for a connect. [Timeout.connect]

**confTO_CONTROL**   Sets the maximum amount of time allowed for a control socket transaction to complete. The default is two minutes (2m). [Timeout.control]

**confTO_DATABLOCK**   Sets the maximum time to wait for a block during DATA phase. Defaults to 1h. [Timeout.datablock]

**confTO_DATAFINAL**   Sets the maximum time to wait for a response to the terminating ".". Defaults to 1h. [Timeout.datafinal]

**confTO_DATAINIT**   Sets the maximum time to wait for a DATA command response. Defaults to 5m. [Timeout.datainit]

**Appendices**

**confTO_FILEOPEN**   Sets the maximum time to wait for a file to open. Defaults to 60s. [Timeout.fileopen]

**confTO_HELO**   Sets the maximum time to wait for a HELO or EHLO response. Defaults to 5m. [Timeout.helo]

**confTO_HOSTSTATUS**   Sets the timer for stale host status information. Defaults to 30m. [Timeout.hoststatus]

**confTO_ICONNECT**   Sets the maximum time to wait for the very first connect attempt to a host. [Timeout.iconnect]

**confTO_IDENT**   Sets the maximum time to wait for an ident query response. Defaults to 30s. [Timeout.ident]

**confTO_INITIAL**   Sets the maximum time to wait for the initial connect response. Defaults to 5m. [Timeout.initial]

**confTO_MAIL**   Sets the maximum time to wait for a MAIL command response. Defaults to 10m. [Timeout.mail]

**confTO_MISC**   Sets the maximum time to wait for other SMTP command responses. Defaults to 2m. [Timeout.misc]

**confTO_QUEUERETURN_NONURGENT**   Sets the "Undeliverable mail" timeout for low priority messages. [Timeout.queuereturn.non-urgent]

**confTO_QUEUERETURN_NORMAL**   Sets the "Undeliverable mail" timeout for normal priority messages. [Timeout.queuereturn.normal]

**confTO_QUEUERETURN_URGENT**   Sets the "Undeliverable mail" timeout for urgent priority messages. [Timeout.queuereturn.urgent]

**confTO_QUEUERETURN**   Sets the time until a message is returned from the queue as undeliverable. Defaults to 5d. [Timeout.queuereturn]

**confTO_QUEUEWARN_NONURGENT**   Sets the time until a "still queued" warning is sent for low priority messages. [Timeout.queuewarn.non-urgent]

**confTO_QUEUEWARN_NORMAL**   Sets the time until a "still queued" warning is sent for normal priority messages. [Timeout.queuewarn.normal]

**confTO_QUEUEWARN_URGENT**   Sets the time until a "still queued" warning is sent for urgent priority messages. [Timeout.queuewarn.urgent]

**confTO_QUEUEWARN**   Sets the time until a "still queued" warning is sent about a message. Defaults to 4h. [Timeout.queuewarn]

**confTO_QUIT**   Sets the maximum time to wait for a QUIT command response. Defaults to 2m. [Timeout.quit]

**confTO_RCPT**   Sets the maximum time to wait for a RCPT command response. Defaults to 1h. [Timeout.rcpt]

**confTO_RESOLVER_RETRANS**   Defines, in seconds, the retransmission timer for all resolver lookups. [Timeout.resolver.retrans]

**confTO_RESOLVER_RETRANS_FIRST**   Defines, in seconds, the retransmission timer for the resolver lookup for the first attempt to deliver a message. [Timeout.resolver.retrans.first]

**confTO_RESOLVER_RETRANS_NORMAL**   Defines, in seconds, the retransmission timer for all resolver lookups after the first attempt to deliver a message. [Timeout.resolver.retrans.normal]

**confTO_RESOLVER_RETRY**   Defines the total number of times to retry a resolver query. [Timeout.resolver.retry]

**confTO_RESOLVER_RETRY_FIRST**   Defines the number of times the resolver query for the first delivery attempt is retried. [Timeout.resolver.retry.first]

**confTO_RESOLVER_RETRY_NORMAL**   Defines the number of times to retry resolver queries after the first delivery attempt. [Timeout.resolver.retry.normal]

**confTO_RSET**   Sets the maximum time to wait for a RSET command response. Defaults to 5m. [Timeout.rset]

**confTRUSTED_USER**   Defines the user who controls the Sendmail daemon and owns the files created by Sendmail. Do not confuse this option with confTRUSTED_USERS. [TrustedUser]

**confTRUSTED_USERS**   Adds users to the list of those who can send mail under other usernames. This list always includes root, uucp, and daemon. [$=t]

**confTRY_NULL_MX_LIST**   True tells Sendmail to connect to the remote host directly if the MX record points to the local host. The default is false. [TryNullMXList]

**confUNSAFE_GROUP_WRITES**   True tells Sendmail not to reference programs or files from group-writable :include: and .forward files. Defaults to false. [UnsafeGroupWrites]

**confUSERDB_SPEC**   Defines the path of the user database file. [UserDatabaseSpec]

**confUSE_ERRORS_TO**   True tells Sendmail to deliver errors using the Errors-To: header. This defaults to false. [UserErrorsTo]

**confUUCP_MAILER**   Defines the default UUCP mailer. Defaults to uucp-old.

**confWORK_CLASS_FACTOR**   Defines the factor used to favor high-priority jobs. Defaults to 1800. [ClassFactor]

**confWORK_RECIPIENT_FACTOR**   Defines the factor used to lower the priority of a job for each additional recipient. Defaults to 30000. [RecipientFactor]

**confWORK_TIME_FACTOR**   Defines the factor used to lower the priority of a job for each delivery attempt. Defaults to 90000. [RetryFactor]

**Appendices**

**confXF_BUFFER_SIZE**    Defines the maximum amount of buffer memory that can be used for a transcript file before the file must be written to disk. The default is 4096 bytes. [XScriptFileBufferSize]

Despite the enormous length of this list, there are more define parameters. Additional lists of parameters are covered under the DOMAIN and the OSTYPE macros later in this appendix. define commands are the most common commands in the m4 source files. The next most commonly used is the FEATURE macro.

## FEATURE

The FEATURE macro processes m4 source code from the cf/feature directory. Source files in that directory define optional Sendmail features. The syntax of the FEATURE macro is:

FEATURE(*name*, [*argument*])

The *argument* field is optional. If an argument is passed to the source file, the argument is used by the source file to generate code for the sendmail.cf file. For example:

FEATURE(`mailertable', `dbm /etc/mail/mailertable')

generates the code for accessing the mailertable and defines that table as being a dbm database located in the file /etc/mail/mailertable.

The available features are listed in Table A.2. The table provides the name of each feature and its purpose.

**Table A.2**    Features

| Name | Purpose |
|---|---|
| accept_unqualified_senders | Allow network mail from addresses that do not include a valid hostname. |
| accept_unresolvable_domains | Accept mail from hosts that are unknown to DNS. |
| access_db | Use the access database to control relaying. |
| allmasquerade | Masquerade recipient addresses. |

**Table A.2**   Features  *(continued)*

| Name | Purpose |
| --- | --- |
| always_add_domain | Add the local hostname to all locally delivered mail. |
| bestmx_is_local | Accept as local, mail addressed to a host that lists us as its MX server. |
| bitdomain | Use a table to map BITNET hosts to Internet addresses. |
| blacklist_recipients | Filter incoming mail based on values set in the access database. |
| delay_checks | Delay the check_mail and check_relay rulesets until check_rcpt is called. |
| dnsbl | Reject mail from hosts listed in a DNS-based rejection list. Replaces rbl. |
| domaintable | Map domain names using a domain table. |
| generics_entire_domain | Map domain names identified in class G through the genericstable. |
| genericstable | Use a table to rewrite local addresses and addresses from class G. |
| ldap_routing | Enable LDAP-based e-mail routing. |
| limited_masquerade | Only masquerade hosts listed in $=M. |
| local_lmtp | Use mail.local with LMTP support. |
| local_procmail | Use procmail as the local mailer. |
| loose_relay_check | Disable validity checks for addresses that use the % hack. |
| mailertable | Route mail using a mailer table. |

**Appendices**

**Table A.2** Features *(continued)*

| Name | Purpose |
| --- | --- |
| masquerade_entire_domain | Masquerade all hosts within the masquerading domains. |
| masquerade_envelope | Masquerade the envelope sender address in addition to the header sender address. |
| no_default_msa | Allow the default configuration of the Message Submission Agent to be overridden by the DAEMON_OPTIONS macro. |
| nocanonify | Don't convert addresses and hostnames using DNS. |
| nodns | Don't include DNS support. |
| nouucp | Don't include UUCP address processing. |
| nullclient | Forward all mail to a central server. |
| promiscuous_relay | Relay mail from any site to any site. |
| rbl | The obsolete Realtime Blackhole List feature has been replaced by dnsbl. |
| redirect | Support the .REDIRECT pseudo-domain. |
| relay_based_on_MX | Relay mail for any site whose MX record points to this server. |
| relay_entire_domain | Relay mail for any host in your domain. |
| relay_hosts_only | Only relay mail for hosts listed in the access database. |
| relay_local_from | Relay mail if the source is a local host. |
| relay_mail_from | Relay mail if the sender is listed as RELAY in the access database. |
| smrsh | Use smrsh as the prog mailer. |

**Table A.2** Features *(continued)*

| Name | Purpose |
|------|---------|
| stickyhost | Treat "user" differently than "user@local.host." |
| use_ct_file | Load $=t from the file defined by confCT_FILE. |
| use_cw_file | Load $=w from the file defined by confCW_FILE. |
| uucpdomain | Use a table to map UUCP hosts to Internet addresses. |
| virtuser_entire_domain | Map entire domain names through the virtusertable. |
| virtusertable | Map virtual domain names to real mail addresses. |

Several FEATURE macros remove unneeded lines from the sendmail.cf file. nouucp removes the code to handle UUCP addresses for systems that do not have access to UUCP networks, and nodns removes the code for DNS lookups for systems that do not have access to DNS. nocanonify disables the code that converts nicknames and IP addresses into hostnames. Finally, the nullclient feature strips everything out of the configuration except for the ability to forward mail to a single mail server via a local SMTP link. The name of that mail server is provided as the argument on the nullclient command line— e.g., FEATURE(nullclient, big.isp.net) forwards all mail to big.isp.net without any local mail processing.

Many features relate to mail relaying and masquerading. Examples are: stickyhost, allmasquerade, relay_based_on_MX, relay_hosts_only, and masquerade_entire_domain. All of these features, and all of the others relating to relaying and masquerading, are covered in the "DOMAIN" section of this appendix.

Several features define databases that are used to perform special address processing. All of these features accept an optional argument that defines the database. (See the sample mailertable command at the beginning of this section for an example of defining the database with the optional argument.) If the optional argument is not provided, the database description always defaults to hash -o /etc/mail/*filename*, where *filename*

**Appendices**

matches the name of the feature. For example, `mailertable` defaults to the definition `hash -o /etc/mail/mailertable`. The database features are:

**`mailertable`**    This database maps host and domain names to specific `mailer:table` pairs. The mailer, host, user triple is returned by ruleset 0 based on the delivery address. The `mailertable` allows you to define the mailer and the host of the delivery triple based on the domain name in the delivery address.

If the host or domain name in the delivery addresses matches a key field in the `mailertable` database, it returns the mailer and host for that address. The format of a `mailertable` entry is:

>  *domain-name*         *mailer:host*

where *domain-name* is either a full hostname (host plus domain) or a domain name. If a domain name is used, it must start with a dot (.), and it will match every host in the specified domain.

**`domaintable`**    This database converts an old domain name to a new domain name. The old name is the key and the new name is the value returned for the key.

**`bitdomain`**    This database converts a BITNET hostname to an Internet hostname. The BITNET name is the key and the Internet hostname is the value returned. The `bitdomain` program that comes with the Sendmail distribution can be used to build this database. BITNET is obsolete.

**`uucpdomain`**    This database converts a UUCP name to an Internet hostname. The key is the UUCP hostname and the value returned is the Internet hostname. This is useful if you still have users who address e-mail using old UUCP addresses.

**`genericstable`**    This database converts a sender e-mail address. The key to the database is either a username or a full e-mail address (username and hostname). The value returned by the database is the new e-mail address. `genericstable` is often used to convert the same addresses as those processed for masquerading, so the features that affect masquerading and the `genericstable` conversion are set in exactly the same way. See Chapter 9, "Special *m4* Configurations," for an example of using the `genericstable`, and masquerading on the same addresses. If you use the `genericstable` and you use masquerading, set GENERICS_DOMAIN and GENERICS_DOMAIN_ FILE to the same values that you set for MASQUERADE_DOMAIN and MASQUERADE_ DOMAIN_FILE.

**`virtusertable`**    This database aliases incoming e-mail addresses. Essentially, this is an extended `aliases` database for aliasing addresses that are not local to this host. The key to the database is a full e-mail address or a domain name. The value returned by the database is the recipient address to which the mail is delivered. If a domain name is used as a key, it must begin with an at-sign (@). Mail addressed to any user in the specified domain is sent to the recipient defined by the virtusertable database. Any hostname used as a key in the virtusertable database must also be defined in class w or class {VirtHost}. A hostname can be added to class w with the LOCAL_DOMAIN macro. Hostnames can be added to the {VirtHost} class using the VIRTUSER_DOMAIN macro. The {VirtHost} class can be loaded from a file using the VIRTUSER_DOMAIN_FILE macro.

Some features are important in the fight against spam because they help you control what mail your server will deliver or forward on for delivery. These are accept_unqualified_senders, accept_unresolvable_domains, access_db, blacklist_recipients, and dnsbl. All of these are covered in Chapter11, "Stopping Spam," and in the "DOMAIN" section of this appendix.

The always_add_domain macro makes Sendmail add the local hostname to all locally delivered mail, even to those pieces of mail that would normally have just a username as an address. The bestmx_is_local feature accepts mail addressed to a host that lists the local host as its preferred MX server as if the mail was local mail. If this feature is not used, mail bound for a remote host is sent directly to the remote host even if its MX record lists the local host as its preferred MX server. The bestmx_is_local feature should not be used if you use a wildcard MX record for your domain.

The use_cw_file and the use_ct_file features illustrate how define commands affect features. Both of these features use a file. The file ame can be set by a define command. If a define is used to modify a value used by a FEATURE, the define should be included in the macro configuration file before the FEATURE.

The redirect feature handles mail for users who no longer read mail at your site. When properly configured, it returns an error to the sender providing them with the user's new e-mail address. Configuring the redirect feature is covered in Chapter 9.

There are three features that select optional programs for the local and the prog mailers. local_procmail selects procmail as the local mailer. Provide the path to procmail as the argument in the FEATURE command. The local_lmtp feature selects mail.local, a mailer provided with the Sendmail distribution, as the local mailer. The smrsh feature selects the SendMail Restricted SHell (smrsh) as the prog mailer. smrsh provides improved security over /bin/sh, which is normally used as the prog mailer. Provide the path to smrsh as the argument in the FEATURE command.

The FEATURE commands discussed in this section and the define macros discussed previously are used to build the m4 source files. The next few sections describe the purpose and structure of the OSTYPE, DOMAIN, and MAILER source files that are built with define and FEATURE commands.

## OSTYPE

The OSTYPE command points to the m4 source file that contains the operating system–specific information for this configuration. This required file is examined in detail in Chapter 5, "Understanding a Vendor's Configuration."

While all m4 macros can be used in OSTYPE source files, Table A.3 lists the **define** parameters most frequently associated with the OSTYPE file and the function of each parameter. If the parameter has a default value, it is shown enclosed in square brackets after the parameter's functional description.

**Table A.3**    OSTYPE Defines

| Parameter | Function |
| --- | --- |
| ALIAS_FILE | Name of the aliases database. [/etc/mail/aliases] |
| CYRUS_BB_MAILER_ARGS | cyrusbb mailer arguments. [deliver -e -m $u] |
| CYRUS_BB_MAILER_FLAGS | Flags added to lsDFMnP for the cyrusbb mailer. [u] |
| CYRUS_MAILER_ARGS | cyrus mailer arguments. [deliver -e -m $h -- $u] |
| CYRUS_MAILER_FLAGS | Flags added to lsDFMnPq for the cyrus mailer. [A5@/:\|] |
| CYRUS_MAILER_MAX | Maximum size message for the cyrus mailer. |
| CYRUS_MAILER_PATH | Path to the cyrus mailer. [/usr/cyrus/bin/deliver] |
| CYRUS_MAILER_USER | User and group used to run the cyrus mailer. [cyrus:mail] |
| DSMTP_MAILER_ARGS | dsmtp mailer arguments. [IPC $h] |
| ESMTP_MAILER_ARGS | esmtp mailer arguments. [IPC $h] |
| FAX_MAILER_ARGS | FAX mailer arguments. [mailfax $u $h $f] |
| FAX_MAILER_MAX | Maximum size of a FAX. [100000] |
| FAX_MAILER_PATH | Path to the FAX program. [/usr/local/lib/fax/mailfax] |
| HELP_FILE | Name of the help file. [/etc/mail/helpfile] |

**Table A.3**   OSTYPE Defines *(continued)*

| Parameter | Function |
|---|---|
| LOCAL_MAILER_ARGS | Arguments for local mail delivery. [mail -d $u] |
| LOCAL_MAILER_CHARSET | Character set for local 8-bit MIME mail. |
| LOCAL_MAILER_DSN_<br>DIAGNOSTIC_CODE | The delivery status notification code used for local mail. [X-Unix] |
| LOCAL_MAILER_EOL | The end-of-line character for local mail. |
| LOCAL_MAILER_FLAGS | local mailer flags added to lsDFMAw5:/|@q. [Prmn9] |
| LOCAL_MAILER_MAX | Maximum size of a local mail message. |
| LOCAL_MAILER_MAXMSG | The maximum number of messages delivered with a single connection. |
| LOCAL_MAILER_PATH | The local mail delivery program. [/bin/mail] |
| LOCAL_SHELL_ARGS | Arguments for prog mail. [sh -c $u] |
| LOCAL_SHELL_DIR | Directory in which the shell should run. [$z:/] |
| LOCAL_SHELL_FLAGS | Flags added to lsDFM for the shell mailer. [eu9] |
| LOCAL_SHELL_PATH | Shell used to deliver piped email. [/bin/sh] |
| MAIL11_MAILER_ARGS | mail11 mailer arguments. [mail11 $g $x $h $u] |
| MAIL11_MAILER_FLAGS | Flags for the mail11 mailer. [nsFx] |
| MAIL11_MAILER_PATH | Path to the mail11 mailer. [/usr/etc/mail11] |
| PH_MAILER_ARGS | phquery mailer arguments. [phquery -- $u] |
| PH_MAILER_FLAGS | Flags for the phquery mailer. [ehmu] |
| PH_MAILER_PATH | Path to the phquery program. [/usr/local/etc/phquery] |
| POP_MAILER_ARGS | POP mailer arguments. [pop $u] |
| POP_MAILER_FLAGS | Flags added to lsDFMq for the POP mailer. [Penu] |

**Table A.3**    OSTYPE Defines  *(continued)*

| Parameter | Function |
| --- | --- |
| POP_MAILER_PATH | Path of the POP mailer. [/usr/lib/mh/spop] |
| PROCMAIL_MAILER_ARGS | Procmail mailer arguments. [procmail -Y -m $h $f $u] |
| PROCMAIL_MAILER_FLAGS | Flags added to DFM for the Procmail mailer. [SPhnu9] |
| PROCMAIL_MAILER_MAX | Maximum size message for the Procmail mailer. |
| PROCMAIL_MAILER_PATH | Path to the procmail program. [/usr/local/bin/procmail] |
| QPAGE_MAILER_ARGS | qpage mailer arguments. [qpage -10 -m -P$u] |
| QPAGE_MAILER_FLAGS | Flags for the qpage mailer. [mDFMs] |
| QPAGE_MAILER_MAX | Maximum qpage mailer message size. [4096] |
| QPAGE_MAILER_PATH | Path of the qpage mailer. [/usr/local/bin/qpage] |
| QUEUE_DIR | Directory containing queue files. [/var/spool/mqueue] |
| RELAY_MAILER_ARGS | Relay mailer arguments. [IPC $h] |
| RELAY_MAILER_FLAGS | Flags added to mDFMuX for the relay mailer. |
| RELAY_MAIL_MAXMSG | The maximum number of messages for the relay mailer delivered by a single connection. |
| SMTP8_MAILER_ARGS | smtp8 mailer arguments. [IPC $h] |
| SMTP_MAILER_ARGS | smtp mailer arguments. [IPC $h] |
| SMTP_MAILER_CHARSET | Character set for SMTP 8-bit MIME mail. |
| SMTP_MAILER_FLAGS | Flags added to mDFMuX for all SMTP mailers. |
| SMTP_MAILER_MAX | Maximum size of messages for all SMTP mailers. |

**Table A.3**   OSTYPE Defines *(continued)*

| Parameter | Function |
|-----------|----------|
| SMTP_MAIL_MAXMSG | The maximum number of SMTP messages delivered by a single connection. |
| STATUS_FILE | Name of the status file. [/etc/mail/statistics] |
| USENET_MAILER_ARGS | Arguments for the Usenet mailer. [-m -h -n] |
| USENET_MAILER_FLAGS | Usenet mailer flags. [rsDFMmn] |
| USENET_MAILER_MAX | Maximum size of Usenet mail messages. [100000] |
| USENET_MAILER_PATH | Program used for news. [/usr/lib/news/inews] |
| UUCP_MAILER_ARGS | UUCP mailer arguments. [uux - -r -z -a$g -gC $h!rmail ($u)] |
| UUCP_MAILER_CHARSET | Character set for UUCP 8-bit MIME mail. |
| UUCP_MAILER_FLAGS | Flags added to DFMhuU for the UUCP mailer. |
| UUCP_MAILER_MAX | Maximum size for UUCP messages. [100000] |
| UUCP_MAILER_PATH | Path to the UUCP mail program. [/usr/bin/uux] |

The essential characteristic of the items in Table A.3 is that they all have something to do with the location of files on the system. Some of these, such as HELP_FILE, STATUS_FILE, ALIAS_FILE, and QUEUE_FILE, are obviously file locations. The other definitions, all of which relate to mailers, might not be so obviously linked to file locations until you realize that most of the mailers require a pathname. If some mailer options are going to be placed in the OSTYPE source file, it only makes sense to put all of them here. Because file locations vary from system to system, it is traditional to put file locations and mailer options in the OSTYPE source file.

The MODIFY_MAILER_FLAGS macro can be used to change the flags of a mailer. This is slightly different than the mailer flags definitions covered in Table A.3. All of those definitions can add flags, but none of them can remove a flag that is already defined. For example:

```
define(`LOCAL_MAILER_FLAGS', `9')
```

and

```
MODIFY_MAILER_FLAGS(`local', `+9')
```

do the same thing—they both add the 9 flag to the local mailer. But

```
MODIFY_MAILER_FLAGS(`local', `-w')
```

does something that the define cannot do. It removes the w flag from the local mailer definition.

## DOMAIN

The DOMAIN macro points to the m4 source file that contains configuration information specific to your domain. Because the DOMAIN file is specific to your domain, you are responsible for creating it. Chapter 5 provides an example of creating a domain source file and then calling that file with the DOMAIN macro.

Table A.4 lists the define macros that commonly appear in DOMAIN source files. All of these parameters define mail relay hosts. The value provided for each parameter is either a hostname—i.e., the name of a mail relay server—or a *mailer:hostname* pair where *mailer* is an internal mailer name and *hostname* is the name of the mail relay server. If only a hostname is used, the mailer defaults to relay, which is the name of the SMTP relay mailer.

**Table A.4**   Mail Relay Defines

| Parameter | Defines the: |
| --- | --- |
| UUCP_RELAY | Server for UUCP-addressed e-mail. |
| BITNET_RELAY | Server for BITNET-addressed e-mail. |
| DECNET_RELAY | Server for DECnet-addressed e-mail. |
| FAX_RELAY | Server for mail to the .FAX pseudo-domain. The fax mailer overrides this value. |
| LOCAL_RELAY | Server for unqualified names. This is obsolete. |
| LUSER_RELAY | Server for apparently local names that really aren't local. |
| MAIL_HUB | Server for all incoming mail. |
| SMART_HOST | Server for all outgoing mail. |

The precedence of the relays defined by these parameters is from the most specific to the least specific. If both the UUCP_RELAY and the SMART_HOST relay are defined, the UUCP_RELAY is used for outgoing UUCP mail even though the SMART_HOST relay is defined as handling "all" outgoing mail. If you define both LOCAL_RELAY and MAIL_HUB, use the FEATURE(stickyhost) command to have the LOCAL_RELAY handle all local addresses that do not have a host part, and MAIL_HUB handle all local addresses that do have a host part. If stickyhost is not specified and both relays are defined, the LOCAL_RELAY is ignored and MAIL_HUB handles all local addresses.

In addition to the defines shown in Table A.4, macros that relate to masquerading and relaying also appear in the DOMAIN source file. These macros are:

**LOCAL_USER(*usernames*)**    This macro defines local usernames that should not be relayed even if LOCAL_RELAY or MAIL_HUB are defined. This command is the same as adding usernames to class L in the sendmail.cf file.

**RELAY_DOMAIN(*otherhost.domain*)**    This macro identifies a host for which mail should be relayed. The host identified in this manner is added to class R.

**RELAY_DOMAIN_FILE(*filename*)**    This macro identifies a file that contains a list of hosts for which mail should be relayed. This macro loads class R from the specified file.

**MASQUERADE_AS(*host.domain*)**    This macro converts the host portion of the sender address on outgoing mail to the specified domain name. Sender addresses that have no hostname or that have a hostname found in the w class are converted. This has the same effect as the M macro in the sendmail.cf file. See examples of MASQUERADE_AS and variable M in Chapter 9.

**MASQUERADE_DOMAIN(*otherhost.domain*)**    This macro converts the host portion of the sender address on outgoing mail to the domain name defined by the MASQUERADE_AS command, if the host portion of the sender address matches the value defined here. This command must be used in conjunction with MASQUERADE_AS. Its effect is the same as adding hostnames to class M in the sendmail.cf file. See Chapter 9.

**MASQUERADE_DOMAIN_FILE(*filename*)**    This macro loads class M hostnames from the specified file. This can be used in place of multiple MASQUERADE_DOMAIN commands. Its effect is the same as using the FM*filename* command in the sendmail.cf file.

**MASQUERADE_EXCEPTION(*host.domain*)**    This macro defines a host that is not masqueraded, even if it belongs to a domain that is being masqueraded. This allows you to masquerade an entire domain with the MASQUERADE_DOMAIN macro and then exempt a few hosts that should be exposed to the outside world.

**Appendices**

**EXPOSED_USER(*username*)**   This macro disables masquerading when the user portion of the sender address matches *username*. Some usernames, such as root, occur on many systems and are therefore not unique across a domain. For those usernames, converting the host portion of the address makes it impossible to sort out where the message really came from and makes replies impossible. This command prevents the MASQUERADE_AS command from having an effect on the sender addresses for specific users. This is the same as setting the values in class E in the sendmail.cf file.

There are also several features that affect relaying and masquerading. We have already discussed FEATURE(stickyhost). Others that relate to masquerading are:

**FEATURE(masquerade_envelope)**   This feature causes envelope addresses to be masqueraded in the same way that sender addresses are masqueraded. See Chapter 9 for an example of this command.

**FEATURE(allmasquerade)**   This masquerades recipient addresses in the same way that sender addresses are masqueraded. Thus, if the host portion of the recipient address matches the requirements of the MASQUERADE_AS command, it is converted. Don't use this feature unless you are positive that every alias known to the local system is also known to the mail server that handles mail for the masquerade domain.

**FEATURE(limited_masquerade)**   This feature limits masquerading to those hosts defined in class M. The hosts defined in class w are not masqueraded.

**FEATURE(masquerade_entire_domain)**   This feature masquerades all hosts within the entire MASQUERADE_DOMAIN. If this feature is not used, only an address that exactly matches the value defined by MASQUERADE_DOMAIN is converted. If this feature is used, then all addresses that end with the value defined by MASQUERADE_DOMAIN are converted. For example, assume MASQUERADE_AS(foobirds.org) and MASQUERADE_DOMAIN(swans.foobirds.org) are defined. If FEATURE(masquerade_entire_domain) is set, every hostname in the swans.foobirds.org domain is converted to foobirds.org on outgoing e-mail. Otherwise, only a specific host named swans.foobirds.org would be converted.

Some features define how the server handles mail if it is the mail relay server. These features, which are described in Chapter 11, are:

**FEATURE(access_db)**   Maps a user, a domain name, or an IP address to a keyword that tells Sendmail how to handle relaying for the host, domain, or network. This database is used in Chapter 11.

**FEATURE(blacklist_recipient)**   Uses the access database to control delivery of mail based on the recipient address. The basic access_db feature controls relaying and delivery based on the source of the message. This feature adds to that the ability to control mail relaying and delivery based on the destination.

**FEATURE(dnsbl)**   Controls mail delivery based on a DNS blacklist. Source addresses and destination addresses listed in the DNS database may be denied mail delivery or relay services.

**FEATURE(promiscuous_relay)**   Relays mail from any site to any site. Normally, Sendmail does not relay mail. Using this feature is a bad idea because it makes you a possible relay server for spammers.

**FEATURE(relay_entire_domain)**   Relays mail from any domain defined in class M to any site.

**FEATURE(relay_hosts_only)**   Relays mail from any host defined in the access database or in class R.

**FEATURE(relay_based_on_MX)**   Relays mail from any site for which your system is the MX server.

**FEATURE(relay_local_from)**   Relays mail with a sender address that contains your local domain name.

---

***WARNING***   Mail relays can be abused by spammers and spoofers. Use them with caution.

Inbound mail can also be filtered to reduce the impact of spammers. Two macros are available for this purpose:

**MAIL_FILTER(`name`, `equates`)**   This macro defines a mail filter using the Sendmail Mail Filter API syntax.

**INPUT_MAIL_FILTER(`name`, `equates`)**   This macro defines a mail filter and sets up the call for that mail filter.

The DOMAIN source file is also used for features and macros that directly relate to DNS. These features are:

**FEATURE(accept_unqualified_senders)**   This feature accepts mail from the network even if the sender address does not include a hostname. Normally, only mail from a user directly logged on to the system is accepted without a hostname. This is a dangerous feature that should be used only on an isolated network.

**FEATURE(accept_unresolvable_domains)**   This feature accepts mail from hostnames that cannot be resolved by DNS. This is a dangerous feature that is used only on systems that lack full-time DNS service.

**Appendices**

**FEATURE(`always_add_domain`)**    This feature adds the hostname of the system to all local mail. With this feature enabled on a server named `ibis.foobirds.org`, mail from the local user `craig` to the local user `kathy` would be delivered as mail from `craig@ibis.foobirds.org` to `kathy@ibis.foobirds.org`.

**FEATURE(`bestmx_is_local`)**    With this feature, mail addressed to any host that lists the Sendmail server as its MX server is accepted by the Sendmail server as local mail.

The DNS macros are:

**CANONIFY_DOMAIN(*domain*)**    This macro defines a domain name that will be passed to DNS for conversion to its canonical form even if the `nocanonify` feature is in use. Computers can be known by aliases. The official domain name of a host stored in DNS is called its canonical name. This macro is generally used to enable canonification of the local domain when `nocanonify` is in use.

**CANONIFY_DOMAIN_FILE(*filename*)**    This macro identifies a file containing a list of domain names that should be converted to canonical form even if `nocanonify` has been selected.

**LOCAL_DOMAIN(*alias-hostname*)**    This macro defines an alias for the local host. Mail addressed to the alias will be accepted as if it were addressed directly to the local host.

The macros and features described in this section are not limited to the DOMAIN source file. They can appear in any m4 source file, and, in fact, are often found in the macro control file. I listed them here because they are most naturally associated with the DOMAIN file. I took my cue in this from the documentation in the `cf/cf/README` file.

## MAILER

The MAILER macro points to an m4 source file that contains the configuration commands that define a Sendmail mailer. A least one MAILER command must appear in the configuration file. Generally, more than one MAILER command is used.

It is possible that you will need to customize a file location in an OSTYPE file or that you will need to define domain-specific information in a DOMAIN file, but unless you develop your own mail delivery program you will not need to create a MAILER source file. Instead, you will need to invoke one or more existing files in your macro configuration file.

Table A.5 lists each MAILER value and its function. These are invoked using the MAILER(*value*) command in the macro configuration (`.mc`) file.

**Table A.5**  MAILER Values

| Name | Function |
|------|----------|
| local | The local and prog mailers. |
| smtp | All SMTP mailers: smtp, esmtp, smtp8, and relay. |
| uucp | All UUCP mailers: uucp-old (uucp) and uucp-new (suucp). |
| usenet | Usenet news support. |
| fax | Fax support using HylaFAX software. |
| pop | Post Office Protocol (POP) support. |
| procmail | An interface for procmail. |
| mail11 | The DECnet mail11 mailer. |
| phquery | The phquery program for CCSO phone book. |
| qpage | The QuickPage mailer used to send e-mail to a pager. |
| cyrus | The cyrus and cyrusbb mailers. |

Your macro configuration file should have a MAILER(local) and a MAILER(smtp) entry. Selecting local and smtp provides everything you need for a standard TCP/IP installation. The other mailers are:

**uucp**   This mailer provides UUCP mail support for systems directly connected to UUCP networks. The uucp-old mailer supports standard UUCP mail and the uucp-new mailer is used for remote sites that can handle multiple recipients in one transfer. Specify MAILER(uucp) after the MAILER(smtp) entry if your system has both TCP/IP and UUCP connections.

**usenet**   This mailer sends local mail that contains group.usenet in the recipient name to the program inews. Most current user mail agents support Usenet news directly and most users already have a favorite news tool. Posting news through Sendmail with the group.usenet syntax is not common.

**fax**   This is an experimental mailer that supports the HylaFAX software. The fact that this software has been described as experimental for a number of years makes me think that it is not widely used.

**Appendices**

**pop** This mailer supports the Post Office Protocol. On Linux systems, POP support is provided by a specialized POP mail daemon, so the MAILER(pop) command is not needed or used.

**procmail** This mailer provides a procmail interface for the mailertable. Even though procmail is used as the Linux local mailer, the MAILER(procmail) command is not required. See the discussion of procmail in Chapter 11.

**mail11** This is an obsolete mailer that was used only on DECnet mail networks that used the mail11 mailer.

**phquery** This mailer provides CCSO phone book (ph) directory service using the phquery program. User directory services are usually configured in the user mail agent, not in Sendmail.

**cyrus** This mailer provides a local mail delivery program that uses a mailbox architecture. This architecture permits the use of the *user+detail* address syntax where *detail* is interpreted as a mailbox name. Despite some advanced features, cyrus and cyrusbb mailers are not widely used.

**qpage** This mailer provides an interface from e-mail to pagers using the QuickPage program.

Not everything about mailers is defined in the source files loaded by the MAILER macros. We have already seen that many define commands relating to mailers are specified in the OSTYPE source file. Additionally, you can define your own mailers or override mailer parameters using macro commands that let you put raw sendmail.cf code directly into an m4 source file.

## Local Code

There are several m4 macros that allow you to directly modify the sendmail.cf file with unadulterated sendmail.cf configuration commands. These macros are placed at the beginning of a block of sendmail.cf code and they tell m4 where to put that code in the output file. These macros are:

**LOCAL_RULE** LOCAL_RULE_*n* heads a section of code to be added to ruleset *n*, where *n* is 0, 1, 2, or 3. The code that follows the LOCAL_RULE command is sendmail.cf rewrite rules.

**LOCAL_CONFIG** LOCAL_CONFIG heads a section of code to be added to the sendmail.cf file after the local information section and before the rewrite rules. The section of code contains standard sendmail.cf configuration commands.

**LOCAL_RULESETS** This macro heads a section of code that contains a complete ruleset that is to be added to the sendmail.cf file. Generally, these are named as opposed to numbered rulesets.

**LOCAL_NET_CONFIG**   This macro heads a section of sendmail.cf rewrite rules that defines how mail for the local network is handled.

**MAILER_DEFINITIONS**   This macro is placed before a sendmail.cf mailer definition.

## *DAEMON_OPTIONS*

The DAEMON_OPTIONS macro defines parameters for the Sendmail daemon when it is acting as an MTA and when it is acting as an MSA. (See Chapter 2, "Understanding E-Mail Architecture," for information about the purpose of an MTA and an MSA.) Two DAEMON_OPTIONS commands are needed to set the parameters for both the MTA and the MSA. The Sendmail configuration defaults to the following values:

```
DAEMON_OPTIONS(`Port=25, Name=MTA')

DAEMON_OPTIONS(`Port=587, Name=MSA, M=E')
```

These two lines assign the standard ports to the MTA and the MSA, and a modifier to the MSA. Use the no_default_msa feature to clear the MSA defaults before you set new MSA values with the DAEMON_OPTIONS macro. And then use two DAEMON_OPTIONS commands: the first one for the MTA and the second one for the MSA.

DAEMON_OPTIONS parameters are assigned using *keyword=value* pairs. The possible keywords and values are listed below:

**Port**   The Port keyword assigns a network port number to the daemon. The standard port for an MTA is 25 and the standard port for an MSA is 587. Changing these standard ports means that clients will have difficulty locating the service. The port numbers are therefore rarely changed.

**Name**   The Name identifies the aspect of the Sendmail daemon for which the parameters are being set. There are four documented values:

**MTA**   This identifies the traditional Mail Transport Agent interface of Sendmail that is used to deliver mail.

**MSA**   This identifies the Mail Submission Agent interface of Sendmail that can be used by external MUAs to submit mail. In practice, this function is identical to the MTA function, except for port number, because both aspects of Sendmail ensure that all mail, no matter how it arrives, is processed through all necessary rulesets, filters, and databases.

**MTA-v4**   This is the same as the MTA interface and is designed to handle e-mail delivery to hosts with standard 32-bit IPv4 addresses.

**MTA-v6**   MTA-v6 is an interface designed to handle delivery to hosts that use the 128-bit IPv6 addresses.

**Appendices**

**Family** The Family keyword defines the address family. By default this is inet, which means that standard IPv4 addresses should be used. An alternate value is inet6, which requests IPv6 addressing.

**M** The M keyword is a modifier that requests optional processing. M=E turns off the ESMTP ETRN command. This setting is the default for the MSA because it is required by the MSA standard. The M=a setting requires authentication by a trusted authentication method before the MSA will accept the mail message.

## LDAP Mail Routing

In addition to the various databases built into Sendmail, a Lightweight Directory Access Protocol (LDAP) server can be used with Sendmail. If your site uses LDAP for other purposes, you may find some benefit in using it with Sendmail. LDAP support is added to Sendmail using the following defines, features, and macros:

**define(`confLDAP_DEFAULT_SPEC', `*ldap-arguments*')** This define command sets arguments that are required for the LDAP map definition. At a minimum, the name of the LDAP server (**-h** *server*) and the base distinctive name (**-b** o=*org*,c=*country*) must be provided. For example:

```
define(`confLDAP_DEFAULT_SPEC', `-h egret.foobirds.org -b
   o=foobirds.org,c=us')
```

**FEATURE(`ldap_routing')** This feature adds the necessary support for LDAP routing to the configuration.

**LDAPROUTE_DOMAIN(*domainname*)** Adds a domain to the class {LDAPRoute}. Mail routing information for domains in that class is looked up via the LDAP server.

**LDAPROUTE_DOMAIN_FILE(*filename*)** This macro identifies the file from which the {LDAPRoute} class is loaded. The file contains a list of the domains for which mail routing information should be obtained from the LDAP server.

# B

# The *sendmail* Command

In the course of this book we have run the `sendmail` command to collect mail, to send mail, to verify delivery addresses, to test the configuration, to print the queue, to report on status, and more. All of these different Sendmail personalities emerge when you provide the right input on the `sendmail` command line. The syntax of the `sendmail` command is deceptively simple:

**sendmail** [*switch*] [*address*]

The optional *address*, if one is specified, is the address to which the mail is delivered. The *address* field is used only when the `sendmail` command is used to send mail. When the `sendmail` command is used to send mail, it reads the mail message from standard input. The complexity of the `sendmail` command does not come from e-mail addresses or message files; it comes from the large number of command-line switches that can be specified with the `sendmail` command. The *switch* field is the key to changing the personality of Sendmail. The switches and the values that can be provided to them are the subject of this appendix.

# Command-Line Switches

This appendix is a complete reference for the sendmail command. The sendmail command accepts a large number of switches, all of which are listed in Table B.1. The table lists each switch and provides a short description of its purpose.

**Table B.1** Command-Line Switches

| Switch | Purpose |
| --- | --- |
| -B*type* | Set message body *type* to 7bit or 8BITMIME. |
| -ba | Send mail using an outdated FTP-based protocol. |
| -bD | Run as a daemon in the foreground. |
| -bd | Run as a background daemon. |
| -bH | Clear the host status directory. Same as the purgestat command. |
| -bh | Display the host status report. Same as the hoststat command. |
| -bi | Build the aliases database. Same as the newaliases command. |
| -bm | Send mail. This is the default mode. |
| -bp | Display the mail queue. Same as the mailq command. |
| -bs | Makes Sendmail compatible with execution by inetd or xientd. |
| -bt | Run address test mode. |
| -bv | Display the mail delivery triple for the given address. |
| -bz | Create a "parsed" copy of the configuration file. |
| -C | Specify the configuration file pathname. |
| -c | Set the HoldExpensive option to true. |
| -d*level* | Specify the debug *level*. |
| -e | Set the ErrorMode option. |
| -F | Set the sender's full name. |

**Table B.1** Command-Line Switches *(continued)*

| Switch | Purpose |
|--------|---------|
| -f | Set the sender's address. |
| -h | Manually define the minimum hop count. |
| -I | An alternate way to specify -bi. |
| -i | Set the IgnoreDots option to true. |
| -M | Set a value for a variable. |
| -m | Set the MeToo option to true. |
| -N | Specify DSN NOTIFY information for the RCPT To: header. |
| -n | Disable aliasing. |
| -O | Set an option. |
| -o | Set an option using the old single character option name. |
| -p | Set the sending protocol and hostname for UUCP. |
| -q | Process the queue. Optionally sets conditions for processing. |
| -R | Set the DSN code for returned mail. |
| -r | An alternate way to specify -f. |
| -s | Set the SaveFromLine option to true. |
| -T | Set the QueueTimeout option to a specific value. |
| -t | Use the recipients from the To: header instead of the command line. |
| -U | Used by an MUA to indicate that the mail comes directly from the user interface. |
| -V | Set an envelope ID. |
| -v | Run Sendmail in verbose mode. |
| -X | Log all mail to the specified file. |

**Appendices**

Table B.1 lists over 30 command-line switches, most of which you will never use, although you never know when you will need a quick reference on one of them. Several are redundant forms of other switches, some of which are outdated. Perhaps the best known switch that is now outdated is the –bz switch. At one time it was used to pre-process the sendmail.cf file and store a copy of the processed file, which was called a "frozen" file in Sendmail lingo. The idea was that storing the processed configuration would enhance speed. This outdated switch no longer works. If you come to Linux from an older Unix system, you might mistakenly believe you need this switch. Attempting to run it on a current Linux system will just return an error.

While the function of the –bz switch is no longer needed, other outdated switches have useful functions, but those functions are now handled by other switches. For example, –c, –e, –I, –m, –r, –s, and –t are all deprecated switches that have been replaced by newer switches. All of the switches that set sendmail.cf options, even those that are not deprecated, such as –i and –o, can be replaced by the –O switch. For example, the command line

```
sendmail -m -s < mail.file
```

could be replaced by

```
sendmail –OMeToo=true –OSaveFromLine=true < mail.file
```

The new form may appear a little more long-winded, but the –O switch provides the distinct advantage of being able to set any sendmail.cf option. Switches such as –m and –s set only one option each. Additionally, most administrators find the new format easier to read and comprehend, particularly when the sendmail command is included inside a script.

Clearly, most of the switches in Table B.1 will not be useful for your configuration. The switches that you are most likely to use are:

**–bd**   Every time Sendmail is run from a start-up script, this switch is used. It starts Sendmail as a background daemon that listens for inbound mail on TCP port 25. This switch causes Sendmail to receive inbound mail. Without it, Sendmail only sends mail.

**–q[*argument*]**   This switch is also used every time Sendmail is run from a start-up script. The –q switch causes Sendmail to process the mail queue. If entered on the command line without an associated argument, the queue is processed immediately. The optional argument can schedule queue processing for a specific interval—for example, every 15 minutes (–q15m) or every hour (–q1h). When run from a start-up script, the –q switch always includes an argument to specify how often the queue is processed. The optional argument can also select individual items from the queue for processing based on sender, recipient, or queue identifier using the following syntax:

**–qS***sender*    Selects any item in the queue that contains the string *sender* in the sender address field. For example, –qSfoobirds.org would select every item that contained the string foobirds.org anywhere in the sender address.

**–qR***recipient*    Selects any item in the queue that contains the string *recipient* in the recipient address field. For example, –qSdavid would select every item that contained the string david anywhere in the recipient address.

**–qI***id*    Selects any item in the queue that contains the string *id* in its queue identifier. For example, –qI00796 would select the item that contained the string "00796" in its queue ID.

**–bi**    The –bi switch is used every time the aliases database is rebuilt. It is equivalent to the newaliases command.

**–bp**    This switch displays the current contents of the queue. It is equivalent to the mailq command.

**–bt**    The –bt switch causes Sendmail to run in address test mode. This switch is used extensively when testing a new configuration.

**–C***path*    The –C switch precedes the pathname of the Sendmail configuration file. If it is not used, the default configuration file is loaded. Use this switch to load a new configuration during testing.

**–bv**    This switch causes Sendmail to display the mail delivery triple for the e-mail address supplied on the command line.

**–d[***level***]**    This switch causes Sendmail to enter the specified debug level.

All of the switches in this list are covered in this book. Most are shown in several examples and some in several different chapters. Of these commonly used command-line switches, –d is the least commonly used and by far the most complex. Its complexity comes from the enormous number of debug level values that are available. The next section of this appendix lists those various debug levels.

# Debug Levels

Sendmail debug levels are specified as two numeric values separated by a dot, using the following format:

–d*category*.*level*

The first number is the category of information requested. Valid category numbers range from 0 to 99, although only about 60 of the category numbers are actually used. A range of categories can be specified using a dash between two numbers. For example, enter 1-60 in the *category* field to select all categories from 1 to 60. If *category* is not specified, Sendmail defaults to all categories—i.e., 0 to 99. Thus, the following debug argument would set all categories to level 4:

```
-d.4
```

The second number is the level of information within the category. Valid level numbers range from 0 to 255, although the highest level number that has any effect on Sendmail is 127. A level of 0 produces no output, effectively turning off debugging. Levels above 100 change the way that Sendmail itself operates. For this reason, the maximum recommended debug level is 99.

*level* defaults to 1, which provides the minimal debug output for the selected category. Add to this the fact that *category* defaults to all categories, and it is clear that specifying the debug switch (–d) without *category* or *level* turns on basic debugging for all categories. Even at level 1, enabling debugging for all categories produces an enormous amount of data.

Many debug levels are more useful for Sendmail code developers than they are for system administrators. Wading through a mountain of debug information often takes longer than resolving the problem through other means. For this reason, I use very few of the debug settings. See Chapter 10, "Testing Sendmail," for realistic examples of using debugging.

You might be more creative than I am when it comes to using Sendmail debugging. You may encounter a problem that debugging output really helps with. You might just be curious to know more about debugging. For whatever reason, if you want to see a full list of the valid debug levels, they are listed in Table B.2 along with a short description of the information each level provides.

---

**NOTE** Debug levels are cumulative within a category. Thus, if 0.1 displays the version, compiler options, and system identity, 0.4 displays all of that plus the hostname aliases.

**Table B.2**    Debugging Level Settings

| Setting | Information Displayed |
|---------|----------------------|
| 0.1 | Version, Sendmail compiler options, and system identity. |
| 0.4 | Hostname aliases. |
| 0.10 | Operating system compiler options. |
| 0.15 | Mailer information. |
| 0.20 | Network interface addresses. |
| 0.22 | The reason the local UUCP name was not found. |
| 0.40 | The start of interface scan. |
| 0.44 | The memory addresses at which strings are stored. |
| 0.90 | The contents of the first 10 rulesets. |
| 1.1 | The sender address. |
| 1.5 | Additional sender information. |
| 2.1 | The exit status. |
| 2.9 | The properties of any open file descriptors. |
| 3.1 | The current load average. |
| 3.5 | The load average for the last minute. |
| 3.15 | The load averages for the last 1, 5, and 15 minutes. |
| 3.20 | The memory offset for where the load average is stored. |
| 3.30 | Whether mail will be queued or delivered under the current load. |
| 4.80 | The disk space available to queue mail. |
| 5.4 | The time when the events queue will next be examined. |
| 5.5 | A message when events are queued and cleared. |

Appendices

**Table B.2** Debugging Level Settings *(continued)*

| Setting | Information Displayed |
|---------|----------------------|
| 5.6 | A message when an event is triggered. |
| 6.1 | The error mode used when a message fails to be delivered. |
| 6.5 | The current error state. |
| 6.20 | The sender address of returned mail. |
| 7.1 | The unique identifier used for the queue files. |
| 7.2 | The complete queue filename. |
| 7.9 | The file descriptor for the queue file. |
| 7.20 | The name of each queue file as it is being processed. |
| 8.1 | An error message if an MX lookup fails. |
| 8.2 | A trace of the hostname lookup process. |
| 8.3 | A message indicating the local system is the preferred MX server. |
| 8.5 | Each hostname being sent to DNS. |
| 8.7 | A yes or no indicating if the hostname lookup was successful. |
| 8.8 | Resolver debug output for failed MX lookups. |
| 8.20 | An error message when the resolver library fails. |
| 9.1 | Responses to identd queries. |
| 9.3 | The identd response in its raw format. |
| 9.10 | The identd query being sent. |
| 10.1 | The delivery triple for the current recipient. |
| 10.2 | The address of the controlling user for this recipient. |
| 10.5 | The MeToo address if MeToo is not true. |

**Table B.2**   Debugging Level Settings *(continued)*

| Setting | Information Displayed |
|---------|----------------------|
| 10.100 | A dump of all file descriptors before delivering the mail. |
| 11.1 | A trace of the mail delivery. |
| 11.2 | The real and effective user ID and group ID used for mail delivery. |
| 11.20 | The directories used by Sendmail during the mail delivery. |
| 12.1 | The recipient host address before being made RFC 822 compliant. |
| 13.1 | The delivery mode and recipient information for each piece of mail. |
| 13.5 | Recipient addresses to which mail should not be delivered. |
| 13.6 | A trace of the envelope processing. |
| 13.10 | The envelope identifier and flags. |
| 13.20 | The final delivery mode. |
| 13.21 | The final send queue. |
| 13.25 | A trace of the owner deliveries. |
| 13.29 | A status message after no recipients are left to process. |
| 13.30 | Messages relating to a scan of the send queue. |
| 14.2 | Each recipient header line that may need commas added. |
| 15.1 | Information about connecting a listener to port 25. |
| 15.2 | A message about forking a child to handle incoming mail. |
| 15.101 | Output from TCP kernel debugging for incoming connections. |
| 16.1 | Information about outbound TCP connections. |
| 16.101 | Output from TCP kernel debugging for outgoing connections. |
| 17.1 | A colon-separated list of MX records return by DNS. |

**Table B.2**   Debugging Level Settings *(continued)*

| Setting | Information Displayed |
| --- | --- |
| 17.9 | The hash used to randomize MX records that have equal preference. |
| 18.1 | All SMTP responses sent from this server. |
| 18.2 | The preparation of the MAIL From: header. |
| 18.100 | This halts Sendmail on an SMTP read error. |
| 19.1 | Optional ESMTP MAIL From: and RCPT To: parameters. |
| 20.1 | The delivery address before processing by rulesets 3 and 0. |
| 21.1 | A trace of address rewriting similar to –bt output. |
| 21.2 | The current value of runtime variables. |
| 21.3 | The output of each ruleset that is called. |
| 21.4 | The rewritten address produced by each rule. |
| 21.10 | A message when the address does not match the rule pattern. |
| 21.12 | A message when the address matches the rule pattern. |
| 21.15 | The replacements made by indefinite tokens. |
| 21.35 | Every token match in each rule. |
| 21.36 | Every class variable match in each rule. |
| 22.1 | A trace of the tokenizing process. |
| 22.11 | The address before it was tokenized. |
| 22.12 | The address after it was tokenized. |
| 22.36 | Each token taken from the address as it was tokenized. |
| 22.101 | A character-by-character trace of tokenizing the address. |
| 24.4 | A message showing internal address-processing flags. |

**Table B.2**     Debugging Level Settings *(continued)*

| Setting | Information Displayed |
| --- | --- |
| 24.5 | A trace of the flags and tokens used to build an address. |
| 24.6 | The result of building the address from tokens. |
| 25.1 | Each recipient as it is added to the send list. |
| 26.1 | Each recipient address as it is added to the send queue. |
| 26.8 | Addresses being tested for endless loops. |
| 26.10 | The contents of the entire send queue after loop checking. |
| 27.1 | A trace of the aliasing process. |
| 27.2 | The name of each file involved in aliasing. |
| 27.3 | The pathname of each forwarding directory. |
| 27.4 | The name of any forwarding file not owned by the user or by root. |
| 27.5 | A detailed dump of each address processed by aliasing. |
| 27.8 | The value set for the aliases database. |
| 27.9 | The changes to user ID and group ID that occur during aliasing. |
| 27.14 | The controlling user when a change in user ID or group ID occurred. |
| 27.20 | The alias query created by Sendmail. |
| 28.1 | A trace of user database lookups. |
| 28.2 | A message when a user database lookup fails. |
| 28.4 | A status message each time a database is opened. |
| 28.8 | A login status message when hesiod is used to process logins. |
| 28.16 | Any MX records for the host to which mail is being forwarded. |
| 28.20 | A message each time the user database lookup routine is called. |

**Table B.2** Debugging Level Settings *(continued)*

| Setting | Information Displayed |
|---------|---------------------|
| 28.80 | The query being sent to the user database. |
| 29.1 | The address being sent to ruleset 5. |
| 29.4 | A trace of any attempt to match the address to GECOS data. |
| 29.5 | The address being tested for ruleset 5 processing. |
| 29.7 | A message indicating that GECOS matching failed. |
| 30.1 | A message indicating that the end of the header section was found. |
| 30.2 | Messages indicating that the Unix From header has been processed. |
| 30.3 | The header added to a mail message lacking a recipient header. |
| 30.35 | The machine state as inbound mail is collected. |
| 30.94 | The machine state for each individual character in inbound mail. |
| 31.2 | A message when the From: and Resent From: headers are checked. |
| 31.6 | A status message as each header is processed. |
| 32.1 | The headers taken from inbound mail. |
| 32.2 | The processed header if the outdated –ba switch was set. |
| 33.1 | The full address line and the cleaned-up address. |
| 34.1 | A message when the routine that adds headers is entered. |
| 34.11 | A trace of the process of inserting headers. |
| 35.9 | The name and value of each variable as it is defined. |
| 35.14 | The internal identifier used for each variable. |
| 35.24 | Each variable before and after it has been expanded. |
| 36.5 | A trace of the symbol table processing. |

**Table B.2**    Debugging Level Settings *(continued)*

| Setting | Information Displayed |
| --- | --- |
| 36.9 | The hash value used for each symbol table entry. |
| 36.90 | The name and type of each symbol from the table as it is applied. |
| 37.1 | The name and value of each option as it is set. |
| 37.8 | The class name and value as each value is added to the class. |
| 38.2 | A message as each database is initialized and opened. |
| 38.3 | A message for each of three passes used to open each database. |
| 38.4 | The result of each map open. |
| 38.9 | A message as each database is closed. |
| 38.10 | A trace of the search for the end of the aliases database when NIS is used. |
| 38.12 | A trace of values being written to maps that allow updates. |
| 38.19 | A status message when the nsswitch.conf file is used. |
| 38.20 | A detailed trace of database lookups. |
| 38.44 | The results of NIS hostname lookups. |
| 39.1 | The results of database lookups after applying replacement values. |
| 40.1 | A trace of storing mail in and retrieving mail from the queue. |
| 40.3 | The envelope flags from the queue entry. |
| 40.4 | Each line from the queue file as it is read. |
| 40.8 | An error message if Sendmail was unable to process a queue file. |
| 40.9 | The queue file and lock file descriptors. |
| 40.32 | A list of the send queue recipients. |
| 41.1 | The queue as it is ordered for processing. |

**Table B.2** Debugging Level Settings *(continued)*

| Setting | Information Displayed |
| --- | --- |
| 41.2 | A message if Sendmail cannot open a queue file. |
| 41.49 | The queue files not included in the current run, and the reasons why. |
| 41.50 | Every file in the queue directory, even those that don't start with qf. |
| 42.2 | Status of the connection when ConnectionCacheSize is used. |
| 42.5 | A message each time a connection is cached or un-cached. |
| 43.1 | A message about 8-bit to 7-bit MIME data conversions. |
| 43.3 | The final MIME boundary name. |
| 43.5 | A trace of the search for MIME boundaries. |
| 43.8 | The result of Sendmail's attempt to determine MIME content type. |
| 43.35 | The boundary lines Sendmail inserts into outbound mail. |
| 43.36 | The Content-Transfer-Encoding headers that Sendmail inserts. |
| 43.40 | The contents of the Content-Type: header. |
| 43.99 | The comments that precede and follow the MIME boundaries. |
| 43.100 | A message when the collect and putheader routines are called. |
| 44.4 | A trace of file permission checking. |
| 44.5 | The filename and flags used to call the Sendmail write routine. |
| 45.1 | The envelope sender before it is rewritten. |
| 45.3 | The domain part of the address saved by Sendmail. |
| 45.5 | The sender address when mail is not being returned to the sender. |
| 46.9 | The file descriptor for the xf queue file. |
| 48.2 | The workspace passed to the anti-spam rulesets. |

**Table B.2**    Debugging Level Settings *(continued)*

| Setting | Information Displayed |
|---------|----------------------|
| 49.1 | The arguments passed to the checkcompat routine. |
| 50.1 | A message about de-allocating resources once the mail is delivered. |
| 50.2 | Four return values after delivery. |
| 50.10 | A list of the current send queue. |
| 51.4 | A message each time a queue entry is unlocked. |
| 51.104 | This value prevents Sendmail from removing xf files from the queue. |
| 52.1 | A message when Sendmail disconnects from the controlling terminal. |
| 52.100 | This value stops Sendmail from disconnecting from the controlling terminal. |
| 53.99 | A message each time a file is closed. |
| 54.1 | The exit value sent to an internal error routine. |
| 54.8 | The error message generated by the exit value. |
| 55.60 | A message each time a file is locked. |
| 56.1 | A trace of maintaining persistent host status. |
| 56.2 | Additional details about persistent host status. |
| 56.12 | A message when the host status file is successfully locked. |
| 56.80 | A message about creating the status file if it doesn't exist. |
| 56.93 | A dump of the persistent host status record. |
| 57.2 | A warning message if the vsnprintf routine has a buffer overflow. |
| 60.1 | Database status messages for lookups by rewrite rules. |
| 61.10 | Status messages from gethostbyname queries. |
| 62.1 | The state of all file descriptors before and after each delivery. |

**Appendices**

**Table B.2** Debugging Level Settings *(continued)*

| Setting | Information Displayed |
|---------|---------------------|
| 62.8 | The state of all file descriptors before each delivery. |
| 62.10 | The state of all file descriptors after each delivery. |
| 91.100 | Log via syslogd each time a connection is cached or un-cached. |
| 99.100 | Same as using the –bD switch. |

> **NOTE** The Table heading says "Information Displayed." However, three of the debug levels, 18.100, 51.104, and 52.100, do not just display information. Those three levels change how Sendmail operates.

This book has attempted to reduce the complexity of Sendmail by focusing on common Sendmail administration tasks and the tools you really need to use to get those tasks done. There is really no way to reduce the complexity of all these debug levels except to say that only the few levels covered in Chapter 10 are really useful. If you feel you must dig deeper into Sendmail debug levels, I recommend you get the book *sendmail* by Bryan Costales and Eric Allman (O'Reilly, 2nd ed.,1997).

# Sendmail Variables, Options, and Flags

**T**his appendix is a reference for the variables, classes, options, and flags that you may encounter inside the `sendmail.cf` file. While you will not directly edit the `sendmail.cf` file to manipulate these values, you may see these values when testing a configuration. This appendix is a reference for those times when you need just enough information to interpret the output of a test run. These values are affected by the m4 macros you select and the values you set for those macros.

As you'll see, there are hundreds of variables, classes, and options. Don't expect most of these to be set in your configuration. In general, the default values are the correct ones, so there is no need to explicitly set a different value.

You may never need to refer to this appendix. But it is here in case you need it as an aid for testing.

## Variables

The `sendmail.cf` file contains a large number of variables. Variables are useful because they can store values specific to your configuration and yet be referenced by a variable name that is independent of your configuration. This makes it possible to use a configuration file that is essentially the same on many different systems simply by changing the value stored in a variable. This appendix lists all of the variables in two tables. Table C.1 lists all of the variables that use single-character names.

> **NOTE** Throughout this text the term "variable" is used to refer to the indirect values used in the sendmail.cf file. Sendmail documentation calls these same variables "macros." We call them variables to avoid confusing them with the m4 macros. However, when you refer to the Sendmail documentation you should be aware of the fact that these same values will be called macros.

**Table C.1**   Reserved Variables with Single-Character Names

| Variable | What It Holds |
|----------|--------------|
| a | The date and time the mail was sent. |
| b | The current date in RFC 822 format. |
| B | The name of the BITNET relay. |
| c | The number of times the mail has been forwarded. |
| C | The name of the DECnet relay. |
| d | The current date and time in ctime format. |
| E | Sendmail reserves this for an X.400 relay. |
| f | The sender address. |
| F | The name of the FAX relay. |
| g | The sender address written as a full return address. |
| h | The recipient host. |
| H | The name of the mail hub. |
| i | The queue identifier. |
| j | The fully qualified domain name of the local computer. |
| k | The local system's UUCP node name. |
| L | The name of the LUSER_RELAY. |

**Table C.1**    Reserved Variables with Single-Character Names *(continued)*

| Variable | What It Holds |
| --- | --- |
| m | The name of the local domain. |
| M | The name used to masquerade outbound mail. |
| n | The sender name used for error messages. |
| p | The PID of the Sendmail process running as a mail delivery agent. |
| r | The protocol used when the message was first received. |
| R | The name of the LOCAL_RELAY. |
| s | The hostname of the sender's machine. |
| S | The name of the SMART_HOST relay. |
| t | A numeric representation of the current date and time. |
| u | The username of the recipient. |
| U | A local UUCP name that overrides the value of the k variable. |
| v | The version number of Sendmail that is running. |
| V | The name of the UUCP relay for class V hosts. |
| w | The hostname of the local system. |
| W | The name of the UUCP relay for class W hosts. |
| x | The full name of the sender. |
| X | The name of the UUCP relay for class X hosts. |
| Y | The name of the UUCP relay for all other hosts. |
| z | The home directory of the recipient. |
| Z | The version number. |
| _ | Sender address validated by identd. |

**Appendices**

The current version of Sendmail allows variables to have multi-character names. Table C.2 lists the variables that use long names.

**Table C.2** Reserved Variables with Long Names

| Variable | What It Holds |
|---|---|
| {auth_authen} | Identity of the authenticated user. |
| {auth_author} | Identity of the authorized user. |
| {auth_ssf} | The number of bits in the encryption key used by AUTH. |
| {auth_type} | The type of authentication mechanism used. |
| {bodytype} | The values from the ESMTP BODY parameter. |
| {cert_issuer} | The distinguished name of the certificate authority. |
| {cert_subject} | The distinguished name of the subject of the certificate. |
| {cipher_bits} | The length of the encryption key used for the connection. |
| {cipher} | The encryption technique used for the connection. |
| {client_addr} | The IP address of the remote client connected to TCP port 25. |
| {client_name} | The canonical name of the client connected to TCP port 25. |
| {client_port} | The source port number used by the remote client. |
| {client_resolve} | The keyword OK, FAIL, FORGED, or TEMP that indicates the result of a reverse DNS lookup using the client's IP address. |
| {currHeader} | The contents of the current header during header processing. |
| {daemon_addr} | The IP address of the network interface from which the daemon accepts mail. Normally 0.0.0.0 to indicate all interfaces. |
| {daemon_family} | The protocol family being used. Normally inet to indicate TCP/IP. Other values are inet6, iso, and ns. |
| {daemon_flags} | The flags set by the DaemonPortOption command, if any. |
| {daemon_info} | General information about the daemon. |

**Table C.2** Reserved Variables with Long Names *(continued)*

| Variable | What It Holds |
|---|---|
| {daemon_name} | The daemon name, which is usually Daemon1 unless a daemon name is defined by the DaemonPortOptions command. |
| {daemon_port} | The port that the daemon is listening on, usually 25. |
| {deliveryMode} | The current delivery mode. |
| {envid} | The DSN ENVID value from the Mail From: header. |
| {hdrlen} | The length of the string stored in {currHeader}. |
| {hdr_name} | The name of the current header during header processing. |
| {if_addr} | The IP address of the network interface used by the current incoming connection. |
| {if_name} | The hostname assigned to the network interface used by the current incoming connection. |
| {mail_addr} | The user's mail address from the mail delivery triple created from the MAIL From: envelope header. |
| {mail_host} | The hostname from the mail delivery triple created from the MAIL From: envelope header. |
| {mail_mailer} | The mailer name from the mail delivery triple created from the MAIL From: envelope header. |
| {MessageIdCheck} | The value from the incoming Message-Id: header. |
| {ntries} | The number of delivery attempts. |
| {opMode} | The operating mode from the sendmail command line. |
| {queue_interval} | The length of time between queue runs defined by the -q command-line option. |
| {rcpt_addr} | The user's mail address from the mail delivery triple created from the RCPT To: envelope header. |

**Table C.2**    Reserved Variables with Long Names *(continued)*

| Variable | What It Holds |
|---|---|
| {rcpt_host} | The hostname from the mail delivery triple created from the RCPT To: envelope header. |
| {rcpt_mailer} | The mailer name from the mail delivery triple created from the RCPT To: envelope header. |
| {server_addr} | The IP address of the remote server for the outgoing connection. |
| {server_name} | The name of the remote server for the outgoing connection. |
| {tls_version} | The TLS/SSL version used for the connection. |
| {verify} | The result of the verification process. |

# Class Variables

The variables covered in the previous section can hold only a single value. Variables that hold multiple values are called classes. Table C.3 lists all of the class variables.

**Table C.3**    Sendmail Class Variables

| Class | Values Stored |
|---|---|
| B | Domain names included in the bestmx-is-local process. |
| e | Supported MIME Content-Transfer-Encodings. Initialized to 7bit, 8bit, and binary. |
| E | Usernames that should not be masqueraded. |
| G | Domains that should be looked up in the genericstable. |
| k | The list of UUCP names for this system. |
| L | Local users that are not forwarded to MAIL_HUB or LOCAL_RELAY. |
| m | The local domain names for this host. |

**Table C.3**    Sendmail Class Variables *(continued)*

| Class | Values Stored |
|-------|---------------|
| M | Domains that should be masqueraded. |
| n | MIME body types that should never be 8bit to 7bit encoded. Initialized to `multipart/signed`. |
| N | Hosts and domains that should not be masqueraded. |
| O | Characters that cannot be used in local usernames. |
| P | Pseudo-domain names, such as REDIRECT. |
| R | Domains for which this system will relay mail. |
| s | MIME message subtypes that can be processed recursively. Initialized to `rfc822`. |
| t | The list of trusted users. |
| U | The UUCP hosts that are locally connected. |
| V | The UUCP hosts reached via the relay defined by $V. |
| w | The hostname aliases for this system. |
| W | The UUCP hosts reached via the relay defined by $W. |
| X | The UUCP hosts reached via the relay defined by $X. |
| Y | Directly connected "smart" UUCP hosts. |
| Z | Directly connected UUCP hosts that use domain names. |
| . | A literal dot (.). |
| [ | A literal left bracket ([). |
| {LDAPRoute} | A list of domains that can be routed based on LDAP lookups. |
| {VirtHost} | A list of hosts and domains that are valid virtual hostnames. |

**Appendices**

# Options

A large number of Sendmail options are set inside of the `sendmail.cf` file. Chapter 7 describes the Options section of the `sendmail.cf` file and provides several examples of options. The complete list of options is shown below.

**AliasFile=[*type*:]*path*, [*type*:]*path*...**    Specifies the location of the `aliases` file(s). *path* is the pathname of the `aliases` file. *type* is the `aliases` database type. Valid types are `implicit`, `hash`, `dbm`, `stab` (internal symbol table), or `nis`. The selected database type must be compiled into Sendmail on your system. *type* defaults to `implicit`.

**AliasWait=*timeout***    Defines the amount of time Sendmail waits for an `@:@` entry to appear in the `aliases` database during start-up. The `@:@` entry signals the end of the `aliases` database. If `@:@` is not found, it means the database is still being rebuilt. If the timeout expires without the `@:@` being detected, Sendmail automatically rebuilds the database if `AutoRebuildAliases` is set, otherwise it issues a warning message and continues on.

**AuthMechanisms=*list***    Lists the supported authentication mechanisms.

**AuthOptions**    Lists the options supported with the SMTP `AUTH` argument.

**AllowBogusHELO**    Tells Sendmail to accept illegal `HELO` SMTP commands that don't contain a hostname. Breaking the protocol rules is not a good idea.

**AutoRebuildAliases**    Causes Sendmail to automatically rebuild the `aliases` database when necessary. The preferred method is to rebuild the `aliases` database with an explicit `newaliases` command.

**BlankSub=*c***    Uses *c* as the blank substitution character to replace unquoted spaces in addresses. The default is to replace spaces with dots (.).

**CACERTFile=*filename***    Identifies the file that contains the certificate of a certificate authority.

**CACERTPath=*path***    Defines the path to the directory that contains the certificates of various certificate authorities.

**CheckAliases**    Tells Sendmail to check that the delivery address for each alias is valid when rebuilding the `aliases` database. Normally, this check is not done. Adding this check slows the database build substantially.

**CheckpointInterval=*n***    Causes Sendmail to checkpoint the queue after every *n* items are processed to simplify recovery if your system crashes during queue processing. The default is 10.

**ClassFactor=*factor***    *factor* is the multiplier used to favor messages with a higher value in the Priority: header. Defaults to 1800.

**ClientCertFile=*file*** Identifies the file that contains the certificate used by Sendmail when it acts as a client.

**ClientKeyFile=*file*** Identifies the file that contains the private key used by Sendmail when it acts as a client.

**ClientPortOptions=*options*** Defines non-standard settings that Sendmail use when acting as an SMTP client. *options* is a comma-separated list of *keyword=value* pairs. Valid *keyword=value* pairs are:

**Port=*port*** Defines the source port number the client uses for outbound connections. *port* can be specified by number or name. If a name is used, the name must be defined in /etc/services. By default, the source port for an outbound connection is generated by the system for the connection.

**Addr=*address*** Defines the address of the network interface the client uses for outbound connections. The value for *address* can be written in dotted decimal notation or as a name. By default, any available interface is used.

**Family=*protocol*** Defines the protocol family used for the connection. inet, which is the default, is the protocol family for TCP/IP.

**SndBufSize=*bytes*** Defines the size of the send buffer.

**RcvBufSize=*bytes*** Defines the size of the receive buffer.

**Modifier=*flags*** Defines the daemon flags for the client. Only one flag, h, is available. The h flag tells the client to use the name assigned to the interface on the SMTP HELO or EHLO command.

**ColonOkInAddr** Tells Sendmail to accept colons in e-mail addresses. Colons are always accepted in pairs in mail routing (*nodename::user*) or in RFC 822 group constructs (*groupname: member1, member2, ...;*). By default, this option is enabled.

**ConnectionCacheSize=*n*** *n* is the number of connections that can be cached by this instantiation of Sendmail. The default is two. Four is the maximum. Zero causes connections to close immediately after the data is sent, which is the traditional way that Sendmail operates.

**ConnectionCacheTimeout=*timeout*** *timeout* is the amount of time an inactive cached connection is held open. After *timeout* minutes of inactivity, it is closed. The default is five minutes.

**ConnectionRateThrottle=*n*** Limits the number of incoming connections accepted in any one-second period to *n*. The default is zero, which means no limit.

**ConnectOnlyTo=*address*** Is used only for testing, as it limits all SMTP connections to a single destination address.

**ControlSocketName=*path***   Defines the path of the Unix control socket used to manage daemon connections. By default, this is not defined.

**DaemonPortOptions=*options***   Sets SMTP server options. The *options* are keyword=value pairs. The options are:

**Name=*type***, where *type* is the type of daemon. *type* can be either MTA or MSA.

**Port=*portnumber***, where *portnumber* is any valid port number. It can be specified with the number or the name found in /etc/services. The default is port 25 for the MTA and 587 for the MSA.

**Addr=*mask***, where *mask* is an IP address mask specified either in dotted decimal notation or as a network name. The default is INADDR-ANY, which accepts all addresses.

**Family=*addressfamily***, where *addressfamily* is a valid address family. The default is INET, which allows IP addresses to be used.

**Listen=*n***, where *n* is the number of queued connections allowed. The default is 10.

**SndBufSize=*n***, where *n* is the send buffer size.

**RcvBufSize=*n***, where *n* is the receive buffer size.

**DataFileBufferSize=*bytes***   Defines the maximum amount of memory that can be used to buffer a data file.

**DeadLetterDrop=*file***   Defines the file where messages that cannot be returned to the sender or sent to the postmaster account are stored.

**DefaultAuthInfo=*file***   Defines the file that contains the authentication information needed for outbound connections.

**DefaultCharSet=*charset***   Defines the character set placed in the MIME Content-Type: header when eight-bit data is converted to seven-bit format. The default is unknown-8bit. This option is overridden by the Charset= field of the mailer descriptor.

**DefaultUser=*user*[:*group*]**   Sets the default user ID and group ID for mailers without the S flag in their definitions. If group is omitted, the group associated with the user in the /etc/passwd file is used. The default is 1:1.

**DeliveryMode=*mode***   Starts Sendmail in the specified *delivery mode*. The *mode* can be interactive, background, queue, or deferred. The default is background. Sendmail can change the mode during a run.

**DHParameters=*parameters***   Defines the DH parameters used when Sendmail uses DSA/DH encryption.

**DialDelay=*delaytime*** *delaytime* is the number of seconds Sendmail should delay before redialing a failed connection on dial-on-demand networks. The default is 0 (no redial).

**DontBlameSendmail=*options*** Disables Sendmail's security checks. Disabling security is generally a bad idea, so this option should be used only if absolutely necessary. *options* is a comma-separated list of keywords that disable specific security checks. Table C.4 lists the keywords and the effect each one has on security.

**Table C.4** Possible Settings for the DontBlameSendmail Option

| Keyword | What It Tells Sendmail |
|---|---|
| AssumeSafeChown | The chown command is safe because it is only available to the root user. |
| ClassFileInUnsafeDirPath | Accept any directory path in an F command. |
| DontWarnForwardFileInUnsafeDirPath | Don't issue warning about the path of the .forward file. |
| ErrorHeaderInUnsafeDirPath | Accept the error header file regardless of its directory path. |
| FileDeliveryToHardLink | Permit delivery to a file that is really a hard link. |
| FileDeliveryToSymLink | Permit delivery to a file that is really a symbolic link. |
| ForwardFileInUnsafeDirPath | Accept a .forward file even if it is in an unsafe directory. |
| ForwardFileInUnsafeDirPathSafe | Accept program and file references from a .forward file even if it is in an unsafe directory. |
| ForwardFileIngroupWritableDirPath | Accept a .forward file even if it is in a group-writeable directory. |

**Table C.4** Possible Settings for the DontBlameSendmail Option *(continued)*

| Keyword | What It Tells Sendmail |
|---------|------------------------|
| GroupWritableAliasFile | Accept the aliases file even if it is group-writeable. |
| GroupWritableDirPathSafe | Accept all group-writeable directories as "safe." |
| GroupWritableForwardFileSafe | Accept a .forward file even if it is group-writeable. |
| GroupWritableIncludeFileSafe | Accept :include: files even if they are group-writeable. |
| HelpFileinUnsafeDirPath | Accept the help file even if it is in an unsafe directory. |
| IncludeFileInUnsafeDirPath | Accept :include: files even if they are from unsafe directories. |
| IncludeFileInUnsafeDirPathSafe | Accept program and file references from an :include: file even if it is in an unsafe directory. |
| IncludeFileIngroupWritableDirPath | Accept an :include: file even if it is in a group-writeable directory. |
| InsufficientEntropy | Use STARTTLS even if the random seed generator for SSL is inadequate. |
| LinkedAliasFileInWritableDir | Accept an aliases file that is a link in a writeable directory. |
| LinkedClassFileInWritableDir | Load class values from files that are links in writeable directories. |
| LinkedForwardFileInWritableDir | Accept .forward files that are links in writeable directories. |

**Table C.4**    Possible Settings for the DontBlameSendmail Option *(continued)*

| Keyword | What It Tells Sendmail |
| --- | --- |
| LinkedIncludeFileInWritableDir | Accept :include: files that are links in writeable directories. |
| LinkedMapInWritableDir | Accept database files that are links in writeable directories. |
| LinkedServiceSwitchFileInWritableDir | Accept a service switch file that is a link in a writeable directory. |
| MapInUnsafeDirPath | Accept database files that are in unsafe directories. |
| NonRootSafeAddr | Don't flag file and program deliveries as unsafe when Sendmail is not running as root. |
| RunProgramInUnsafeDirPath | Run programs that are in writeable directories. |
| RunWritableProgram | Run programs that are group or world writeable. |
| Safe | Leave all of the safety checks on. This is the default. |
| TrustStickyBit | Trust group and world writeable directories if the sticky bit is set. |
| WorldWritableAliasFile | Accept the aliases file even if it is world writeable. |
| WriteMapToHardLink | Write to databases files even if they are really hard links. |
| WriteMapToSymLink | Write to databases files even if they are really symbolic links. |

Appendices

**Table C.4** Possible Settings for the DontBlameSendmail Option *(continued)*

| Keyword | What It Tells Sendmail |
|---|---|
| WriteStatsToHardLink | Write to the status file even if it is really a hard link. |
| WriteStatsToSymLink | Write to the status file even if it is really a symbolic link. |

**DontExpandCnames**    Disables the conversion of nicknames to canonical names.

**DontInitGroups**    Limits the mail delivery agent run for a user to the group associated with that user in the /etc/passwd file. It is used to reduce the load on NIS servers.

**DontProbeInterfaces**    If set to true, stops Sendmail from adding the names and addresses of the network interfaces to class w. The default is false, so interface names and addresses are stored in class w.

**DontPruneRoutes**    Prevents Sendmail from optimizing explicit mail routes. Normally, Sendmail makes a route as direct as possible. However, optimizing the route may not be appropriate for systems located behind a firewall.

**DoubleBounceAddress=*address***    Tells Sendmail where to send the report of an error that occurs when sending an error message. The default for *address* is postmaster.

**EightBitMode=*action***    Specifies how undeclared eight-bit data is handled. The possible *actions* are: s—strict, reject undeclared eight-bit data; m—mime, convert the data to MIME format; and p—pass, send the data through unaltered.

**ErrorHeader=*file-or-message***    Specifies the file or message that is prepended to outgoing error messages. If *file-or-message* is the path to a text file, it must begin with a slash. If this option is not defined, nothing is prepended to error messages.

**ErrorMode=*action***    *action* tells Sendmail how to handle error messages. If this option is not defined, error messages are printed. The valid actions are:

**p**    Print error messages.

**q**    Return an exit status but send no error message.

**m**    Mail the error message back to the sender.

**w**    Write the error messages to the user's terminal.

**e**    Mail the error message back, but always give zero exit status.

**FallbackMXhost=*fallbackhost*** *fallbackhost* is the host Sendmail should use as a backup MX server for every host.

**ForkEachJob** Runs a separate process for every item delivered from the queue, which reduces the amount of memory needed to process the queue at the cost of speed.

**ForwardPath=*path*** Defines the path searched for .forward files. Multiple paths can be defined by separating them with colons. The default is $z/.forward.$w:$z/ .forward.

**HelpFile=*path*** Defines the path to the help file.

**HoldExpensive** Tells Sendmail to queue mail for outgoing mailers that have the e (expensive) mailer flag set. Normally, mail is delivered immediately.

**HostsFile=*path*** Defines the path to the hosts file. The default is /etc/hosts.

**HostStatusDirectory=*path*** Defines the directory in which host status information is stored.

**IgnoreDots** Causes Sendmail to ignore dots in incoming messages. Dots cannot be ignored in SMTP mail because they are used to mark the end of a mail message.

**LDAPDefaultSpec=*specification*** Defines the default specification used for LDAP databases.

**LogLevel=*n*** *n* tells Sendmail how much detail to store in the log file. *n* defaults to 9, which is normally plenty of detail.

**MatchGECOS** Normally, the username from the e-mail address is checked against the aliases database and the username field of the passwd file to determine if the user is local. This option adds a check against the GECOS field of the passwd file.

**MaxAliasRecursion=*n*** Aliases can point to other aliases before finally resolving to the actual mail address. This option defines how deep aliases can be nested before resolving to a mail address. The default for *n* is 10.

**MaxDaemonChildren=*n*** Directs Sendmail to refuse connections when *n* children are processing incoming mail. Normally, Sendmail sets no arbitrary limit on child processes.

**MaxHeadersLength=*bytes*** Defines the maximum length allowed for all of the headers taken together.

**MaxHopCount=*n*** Tells Sendmail to assume a message is looping when it has been processed more than *n* times. The default is 25.

**MaxMessageSize=*n*** Sets the maximum message size advertised in response to the ESMTP EHLO command. Messages larger than this size are rejected.

**MaxMimeHeaderLength=*size*** Defines the maximum length of MIME header fields.

**Appendices**

**MaxQueueRunSize=***n*   Sets the maximum number of items that can be processed in a single queue run. The default is no limit.

**MaxRecipientsPerMessage=***n*   *n* limits the maximum number of recipients for a single message. If it is not specified, there is no limit.

**MeToo**   Tells Sendmail to send a copy of the message back to the sender.

**MinFreeBlocks=***n*   Tells Sendmail to reject incoming mail unless *n* disk blocks are free for the queue file.

**MinQueueAge=***n*   Tells Sendmail to skip processing of any jobs that have been in the queue for fewer than *n* minutes.

**MustQuoteChars=***characters*   Defines the list of characters added to the set @,;:\()[] that must be quoted when used in the username part of an address. If MustQuoteChars is specified without a value for *characters*, it adds . and ' to the standard set of quoted characters.

**NoRecipientAction=***action*   Tells Sendmail what to do when a message has no valid recipient headers. *action* can be:

> **none**   Passes the message on unmodified.
>
> **add-to**   Adds a To: header using the recipient addresses from the envelope.
>
> **add-apparently-to**   Adds an Apparently-To: header.
>
> **add-to-undisclosed**   Adds a To: undisclosed-recipients:; header.
>
> **add-bcc**   Adds an empty Bcc: header.

**OldStyleHeaders**   Allows spaces to delimit names. Normally, commas delimit names.

**OperatorChars=***charlist*   Lists the operator characters used to determine tokens within addresses for address rewriting.

**PidFile=***path*   Specifies the path to the Sendmail PID file.

**PostmasterCopy=***username*   Tells Sendmail to send a copy of error messages to *username*. The default is not to send copies of error messages to the postmaster account.

**PrivacyOptions=***options*   Sets the SMTP protocol options. The *options* value is a comma-separated list containing one or more of these keywords:

> **public**   Allows all commands to be used.
>
> **needmailhelo**   Requires a valid HELO or EHLO command before the MAIL From: envelope header will be accepted.
>
> **needexpnhelo**   Requires a valid HELO or EHLO command before the EXPN command will be accepted.
>
> **noexpn**   Disables the EXPN command.

**needvrfyhelo**    Requires a valid HELO or EHLO command before the VRFY command will be accepted.

**novrfy**    Disables the VRFY command.

**restrictmailq**    Restricts use of the mailq command to users with group access to the queue directory.

**restrictqrun**    Tells Sendmail that only the root user and the owner of the queue directory are allowed to run the queue.

**noreceipts**    Tells Sendmail not to return messages verifying successful delivery.

**goaway**    Disables all SMTP status queries.

**authwarnings**    Tells Sendmail to insert X-Authentication-Warning: headers in messages.

**ProcessTitlePrefix=*prefix***    Defines a string used on the heading of the process status reports.

**QueueDirectory=*path***    Defines the path to the queue directory.

**QueueFactor=*factor***    *factor* is a numeric value used with the difference between the current load and the load average limit and with the message priority to determine if a message should be queued or sent immediately. The idea is to queue low-priority messages if the system is currently heavily loaded. It defaults to 600,000.

**QueueLA=*n***    Directs Sendmail to queue messages when the system load average exceeds *n*. The default is 8.

**QueueSortOrder=*sequence***    Defines the sequence in which the queue is sorted. Priority ordering is the default. The valid *sequence* values are:

**h**    Sorts in hostname sequence.

**t**    Sorts in submission time sequence.

**p**    Sorts in message priority order.

**RandFile=*file***    Points to a file that provides pseudo-random data for certain encryption techniques. This is used only if the compile option HASURANDOM is not available.

**RecipientFactor=*factor***    Directs Sendmail to lower the priority of a job by this factor for each recipient, so that jobs with large numbers of recipients have lower priority. Defaults to 30,000.

**RefuseLA=*n***    Tells Sendmail to refuse incoming SMTP connections when the system load average exceeds *n*. The default is 12.

**Appendices**

**ResolverOptions=*options*** Sets resolver options. Available *options* values are: debug, aaonly, usevc, primary, igntc, recurse, defnames, stayopen, and dnsrch. The option can be preceded by a plus (+) to turn it on or a minus (–) to turn it off. One other option, HasWildcardMX, is specified without a + or –. Simply adding HasWildcardMX turns the option on. See *Linux DNS Server Administration* by Craig Hunt (Sybex, 2000), for more information about resolver options.

**RetryFactor=*factor*** *factor* is used to decrease the priority of a job every time it is processed, so that mail that cannot be delivered does not keep popping to the top of the queue. The default is 90,000.

**RrtImpliesDsn** If set to true, tells Sendmail to treat a Return-Receipt-To: header as a request for delivery service notification (DSN). The default is false.

**RunAsUser=*userid*[:*groupid*]** Defines the user ID and group ID that Sendmail will run under instead of under root. This may enhance security when Sendmail is running on a well-maintained firewall. On general purpose systems, this may decrease security because it requires that many files be readable or writeable by this user ID.

**SafeFileEnvironment=*directory*** Tells Sendmail to chroot to the specified directory before writing a file and to refuse to deliver to symbolic links.

**SaveFromLine** Tells Sendmail to save Unix-style From lines at the front of headers. Normally, they are discarded.

**SendMIMEErrors** Tells Sendmail to send error messages in MIME format.

**ServerCertFile=*file*** Identifies the file that contains the certificate Sendmail should use when this system acts as a mail server.

**ServerKeyFile=*file*** Identifies the file that contains the private key Sendmail should use when this system acts as a mail server.

**ServiceSwitchFile=*path*** Defines the path to a file that lists the methods used for various services. The ServiceSwitchFile contains entries that begin with the service name followed by the service method. Sendmail checks for services named aliases and hosts and supports dns, nis, nisplus, or files as possible service methods, assuming that support for all of these methods is compiled into this copy of Sendmail. ServiceSwitchFile defaults to /etc/mail/service.switch on Sendmail 8.11. If that file does not exist, Sendmail uses the following service methods: aliases are looked up in the aliases files, and hosts are looked up first using DNS, then NIS, and finally the hosts file. Most Linux systems have a built-in service switch feature configured by the nsswitch.conf file, so it is used and this option is ignored. See the *Linux DNS Server Administration* book for a description of the nsswitch.conf file.

**SevenBitInput** Causes Sendmail to strip input to seven bits for compatibility with old systems. This shouldn't be necessary.

**SingleLineFromHeader** For compatibility with some versions of Lotus Notes, causes Sendmail to unwrap From: lines that have embedded newlines into one long line.

**SingleThreadDelivery** Tells Sendmail not to open more than one SMTP connection to a remote host at the same time. This option works only if the option HostStatusDirectory is also specified.

**SmtpGreetingMessage=*message*** Defines the greeting sent to the remote host when it connects to the SMTP server port.

**StatusFile=*file*** Tells Sendmail to log summary statistics in the specified *file*. By default, summary statistics are not logged.

**SuperSafe** Tells Sendmail to create a queue file for every piece of mail, even when attempting immediate delivery.

**TempFileMode=*mode*** Sets the file access permissions for queue files. *mode* is an octal value. It defaults to 0600.

**Timeout.command=*timeout*** Defines how long Sendmail will wait when issuing a command.

**Timeout.connect=*timeout*** Defines how long Sendmail will wait for the connection to complete.

**Timeout.control=*timeout*** Defines how long Sendmail will wait for control socket transmission to complete.

**Timeout.datablock=*timeout*** Defines how long Sendmail will wait for a block of data during the DATA phase.

**Timeout.datafinal=*timeout*** Defines how long Sendmail will wait for a response to the dot (.) that terminates the DATA phase.

**Timeout.datainit=*timeout*** Defines how long Sendmail will wait for a response to a DATA command.

**Timeout.fileopen=*timeout*** Defines how long Sendmail will wait for a file to open.

**Timeout.helo=*timeout*** Defines how long Sendmail will wait for a response to a HELO or EHLO command.

**Timeout.hoststatus=*timeout*** Defines how long Sendmail will hold host status information before deciding the information is stale.

**Timeout.iconnect=*timeout*** Defines how long Sendmail will wait for the connection to the first host in a message to complete.

**Appendices**

**Timeout.ident=*timeout*** Defines how long Sendmail will wait for a response to an identd query.

**Timeout.initial=*timeout*** Defines how long Sendmail will wait for a response to the initial connection.

**Timeout.mail=*timeout*** Defines how long Sendmail will wait for a response to a MAIL command.

**Timeout.misc=*timeout*** Defines how long Sendmail will wait for a response to any SMTP command not covered by its own timer.

**Timeout.queuereturn=*timeout*** Defines how long Sendmail will hold a message in the queue before returning it to the sender.

**Timeout.queuereturn.non-urgent=*timeout*** Defines how long Sendmail will hold a non-urgent message in the queue before returning it to the sender.

**Timeout.queuereturn.normal=*timeout*** Defines how long Sendmail will hold a normal message in the queue before returning it to the sender.

**Timeout.queuereturn.urgent=*timeout*** Defines how long Sendmail will hold an urgent message in the queue before returning it to the sender.

**Timeout.queuewarn=*timeout*** Defines how long Sendmail will hold a message in the queue before warning the sender that the message is queued and has not yet been delivered.

**Timeout.queuewarn.non-urgent=*timeout*** Defines how long Sendmail will hold a non-urgent message in the queue before warning the sender that the message is queued and has not yet been delivered.

**Timeout.queuewarn.normal=*timeout*** Defines how long Sendmail will hold a normal message in the queue before warning the sender that the message is queued and has not yet been delivered.

**Timeout.queuewarn.urgent=*timeout*** Defines how long Sendmail will hold an urgent message in the queue before warning the sender that the message is queued and has not yet been delivered.

**Timeout.quit=*timeout*** Defines how long Sendmail will wait for a response to a QUIT command.

**Timeout.rcpt=*timeout*** Defines how long Sendmail will wait for a response to a RCPT command.

**Timeout.resolver.retrans=*timeout*** Sets the timeout interval for first and normal resolver queries.

**Timeout.resolver.retrans.first=*timeout*** Sets the timeout interval for the first resolver query for a given lookup.

`Timeout.resolver.retrans.normal=`*timeout* Sets the timeout interval for normal resolver queries.

`Timeout.resolver.retry=`*retries* Sets the number of times to retry a resolver query.

`Timeout.resolver.retry.first=`*retries* Sets the number of times to retry the first resolver query for a given lookup.

`Timeout.resolver.retry.normal=`*retries* Sets the number of times to retry a normal resolver query.

`Timeout.rset=`*timeout* Defines how long Sendmail will wait for a response to a RSET command.

`TimeZoneSpec=`*tzinfo* Sets the local time zone information to *tzinfo*. If `TimeZoneSpec` is not set, the system default is used; if set to null, the user's TZ environment variable is used.

`TrustedUser=`*users* Defines the list of users trusted to send mail using another user's name.

`TryNullMXList` Causes Sendmail to connect directly to any remote host that lists the local system as its most preferred MX server, as if the remote host had no MX records.

`UnixFromLine=`*fromline* Defines the format for Unix-style From lines.

`UnsafeGroupWrites` Prevents Sendmail from allowing group writeable `:include:` and `.forward` files from referencing programs or writing directly to files. World-writeable files always have these restrictions.

`UseErrorsTo` Tells Sendmail to return error messages to the addresses listed in the Errors-To: header. Normally, errors are sent to the sender address from the envelope.

`UserDatabaseSpec=`*udbspec* Defines the user database specification. See Chapter 6.

`XscriptFileBufferSize=`*bytes* Specifies the amount of buffer memory used for processing an `xf` queue file.

# Mailer Flags

Mailer flags are declared in the F field of the mailer definition. Each mailer flag is set by a single character that represents that flag. For example, `F=lsDFMe` sets six different flags. Table C.5 lists the single-character name and function of each flag.

**Table C.5** Mailer Flags

| Name | Function |
| --- | --- |
| C | Adds @*domain* to addresses that do not have an @. |
| D | Adds a Date: header line to outgoing mail. |
| E | Adds > to message lines that begin with From:. |
| e | Indicates that this is a resource-intensive mailer. |
| F | Adds a From: header line to outgoing mail. |
| f | Indicates that this mailer allows trusted users to send mail under other names. |
| h | Preserves uppercase in hostnames. |
| I | Indicates that this mailer uses SMTP. |
| L | Limits the line length as required by RFC 821. |
| l | Indicates that this is a local mailer. |
| M | Adds a Message-Id: header line to outgoing mail. |
| m | Indicates that the mailer can send to multiple users in one transaction. |
| n | Indicates that Unix-style From: lines should not be used. |
| P | Adds a Return-Path: header to outgoing mail. |
| R | Uses the MAIL From: return-path rather than the return address. |
| r | Indicates that this mailer allows trusted users to send mail under other names. |
| S | Prevents the user ID from being reset before calling the mailer. |
| s | Strips quotes off of the address before calling the mailer. |
| U | Indicates that the mailer requires Unix-style From: lines. |
| u | Preserves uppercase in usernames. |

**Table C.5**  Mailer Flags *(continued)*

| Name | Function |
|------|----------|
| X | Prepends a dot to lines beginning with a dot. |
| x | Indicates that the mailer wants a Full-Name: header line. |

# Index

**Note to the reader:** Throughout this index **boldfaced** page numbers indicate primary discussions of a topic. *Italicized* page numbers indicate illustrations.

Index

## O

O (set option) command, 215
OK keyword in access database, 159, 160
OldStyleHeaders option in sendmail.cf, 426
ONEX, 22
operating systems, configuration files for, 89
OperatorChars option in sendmail.cf, 426
Options section (sendmail.cf file), **199–201**
OSTYPE command (m4), 88–89, 92, 94, 96,
    262, 364, **382–386**
    in generic-linux.mc file, 98, **109–112**
outbound addresses
    converting, 156
    server for, 262
outbound mail, blocking with blacklist_
    recipients feature, 310
output stream, divert command to direct, 93
owner-staff alias, 152

## P

P class variable, 187–188
P command, 201
P (set precedence) command, 215
package management systems, 61
    dependencies, 66–67
/parse command, **283–284**
parse ruleset, 44, 220, 222, 223
ParseRecipient ruleset, 222, 223
PASS command (POP), 23
passwd man pages, 67
patches to software, security holes in, 325
Path (P) field in mailer definition, 208, 210
pattern matching in rewrite rules, **226–231**
PGP (Pretty Good Privacy), 342
phquery mailer, 392
physical security, **322–323**

PID (process ID), 51
    determining, 60–61
PidFile option in sendmail.cf, 426
plain.cf configuration file, 250
pop mailer, 392
POP (Post Office Protocol), **22–25**
    through stunnel, 329
popauth program, 329
port for Sendmail daemon, 393
Post Office Protocol (POP), **22–25**
    commands, 23
    through stunnel, 329
postmaster alias, 152
PostmasterCopy option in sendmail.cf, 426
presistent status report, 275
Pretty Good Privacy (PGP), 342
priority, assigning to messages, 201–202
PrivacyOptions option in sendmail.cf,
    426–427
private key, 350
process ID (PID), 51
    determining, 60–61
ProcessTitlePrefix option in sendmail.cf, 427
procmail mailer, 207, 392
    access to, 168–169
    filter, **315–319**
PROCMAIL_MAILER_PATH variable,
    110, 132
.procmailrc file, 315
    reading, 317–319
prog mailer, 207
promiscuous_relay feature, 305, 378, 389
protocol keyword for Sendmail error
    code, 244
protocols, 3
    IMAP (Internet Mail Access Protocol),
        **25–29**
    mailbox, **22–29**

Index

Index

Index